AutoCAD for Architecture®

for AutoCAD® Release 10, 11, and 12

James E. Fuller

GLENCOE

Macmillan/McGraw-Hill

New York, New York
Columbus, Ohio
Mission Hills, California
Peoria, Illinois

AutoCAD for Architecture is a work-text for those who wish to use AutoCAD® software to produce architectural drawings. AutoCAD® is a computer-aided drafting and design package produced by Autodesk, Inc. For information on how to obtain the AutoCAD software, contact Autodesk at (415) 332-2344.

AutoCAD is a registered trademark of Autodesk, Inc.

Send all inquiries to:
GLENCOE DIVISION
Macmillan/McGraw-Hill
3008 W. Willow Knolls Drive
Peoria, IL 61614

ISBN: 0-02-677102-0 (Work-text)
ISBN: 0-02-677101-2 (Instructor's Resource Guide)

Printed in the United States of America

3 4 5 6 7 8 9 10 CUS 96 95 94

CONTENTS

SECTION TWO DRAWING BUILDING AND WALL SECTIONS

SECTION THREE DRAWING BUILDING ELEVATIONS

SECTION FOUR DRAWING SITE PLANS

SECTION FIVE APPENDICES

ACKNOWLEDGEMENTS

A book can not be successfully completed without the aid and assistance of many dedicated people. The author is grateful to the staff of Glencoe for their many hours of assistance. A very special thanks goes to Wes Coulter, Trudy Muller, & Ardis Parker. Thanks also to Jody James for her editorial reviews, and to Dave East for his help and suggestions. A very special thanks to the many people at Autodesk who helped make this book possible.

INTRODUCTION

Constructing architectural drawings is one of AutoCAD's strongest applications. Architects and designers are finding new and unique methods of employing CAD's power.

This book is designed to step you through the methodology of constructing architectural drawings with AutoCAD. Through the use of tutorials and explanations, you will construct a set of residential plans.

The work is arranged in sessions. Each session covers a specific component of architectural CAD drawing. The "goal" drawing is shown at the beginning of each session. This drawing illustrates the finished product expected from the session. After completing all ten sessions, you will have a complete set of house plans constructed in AutoCAD!

Discussions of the available methodologies of drawing construction pertinent to the current session are discussed immediately prior to the tutorial covering the work. Many methods of drawing construction are used throughout the sessions. Alternate methods will be introduced where applicable.

It is suggested that each session be completed at one sitting. This approach helps you to understand the methodology used in the session. A thorough comprehension of the methods used will allow you to apply the principles to other circumstances.

APPENDIX

The appendix contains many helpful aids for your use. Please take time now to review the appendix. The pages at the end of the appendix are tear-out sheets. For convenience, you will want to remove these sheets when working at your computer.

WORK DISK

The work disk contains the files you need to complete each session. Each drawing will be created from a prototype drawing that is contained on the work disk. The symbols that are to be inserted are contained within the prototype drawing as resident blocks. You will be given instructions at the beginning of each session in which a new drawing is started.

Before you begin, you should back up the work disk. Next, create a directory named ACADARCH. Copy the contents of the work disk into this directory. If you are using AutoCAD Release 11, copy the file named REF.LSP into the directory where your AutoCAD program resides.

Keep the original and backup copies of the work disk in a safe place.

Section 1 Drawing Floor Plans

- Session 1: Drawing Plan Walls
- Session 2: Placing Doors and Windows in the Plan
- Session 3: Creating and Placing Library Symbols
- Session 4: Dimensioning and Titling

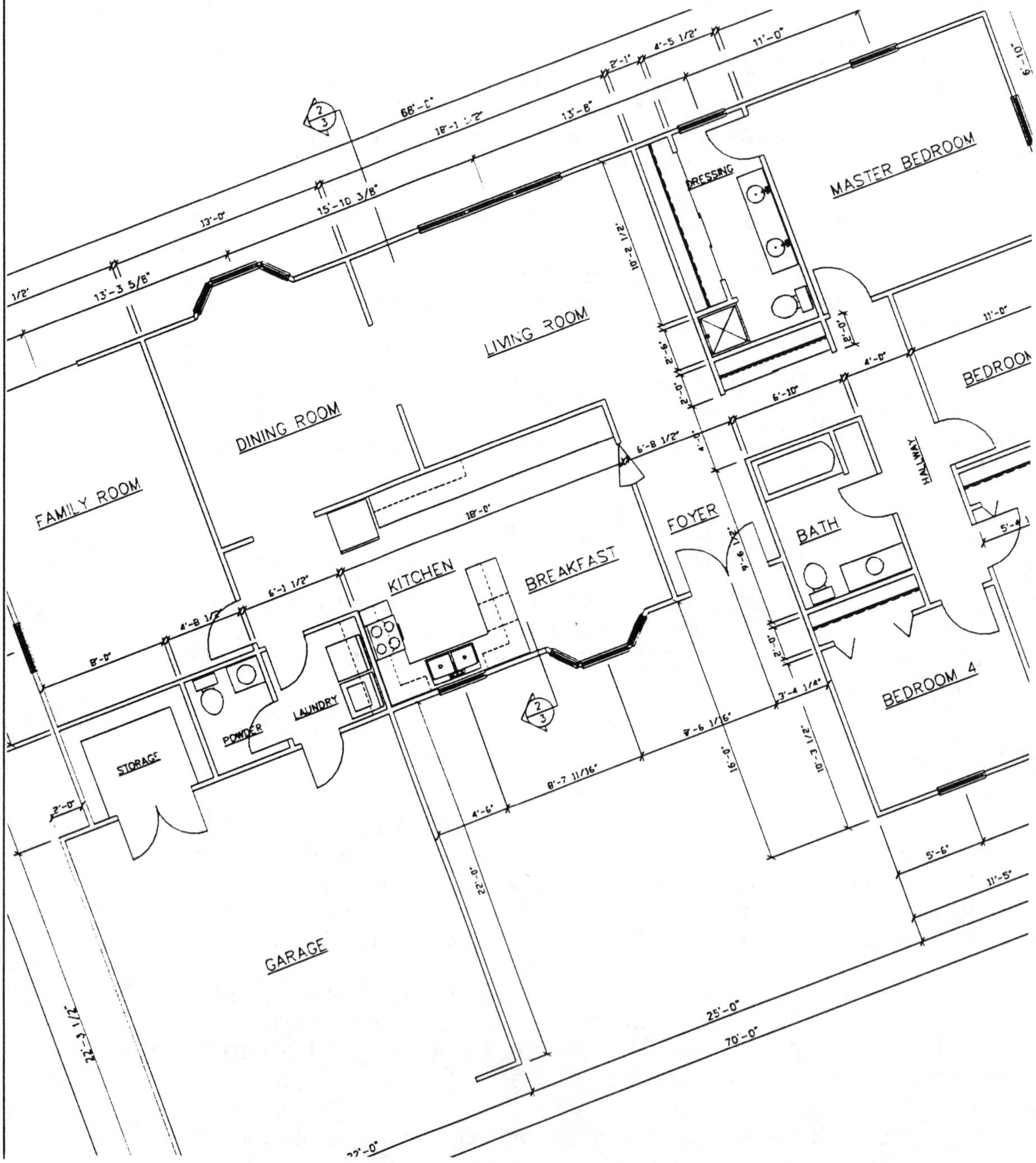

SESSION 1

Drawing Plan Walls

OBJECTIVE

The object of this session is to create the walls of the floor plan. Figure 1–1 shows how the floor plan will look at the end of this session.

YOUR NOTES
Use this space for notes about your individual plan.

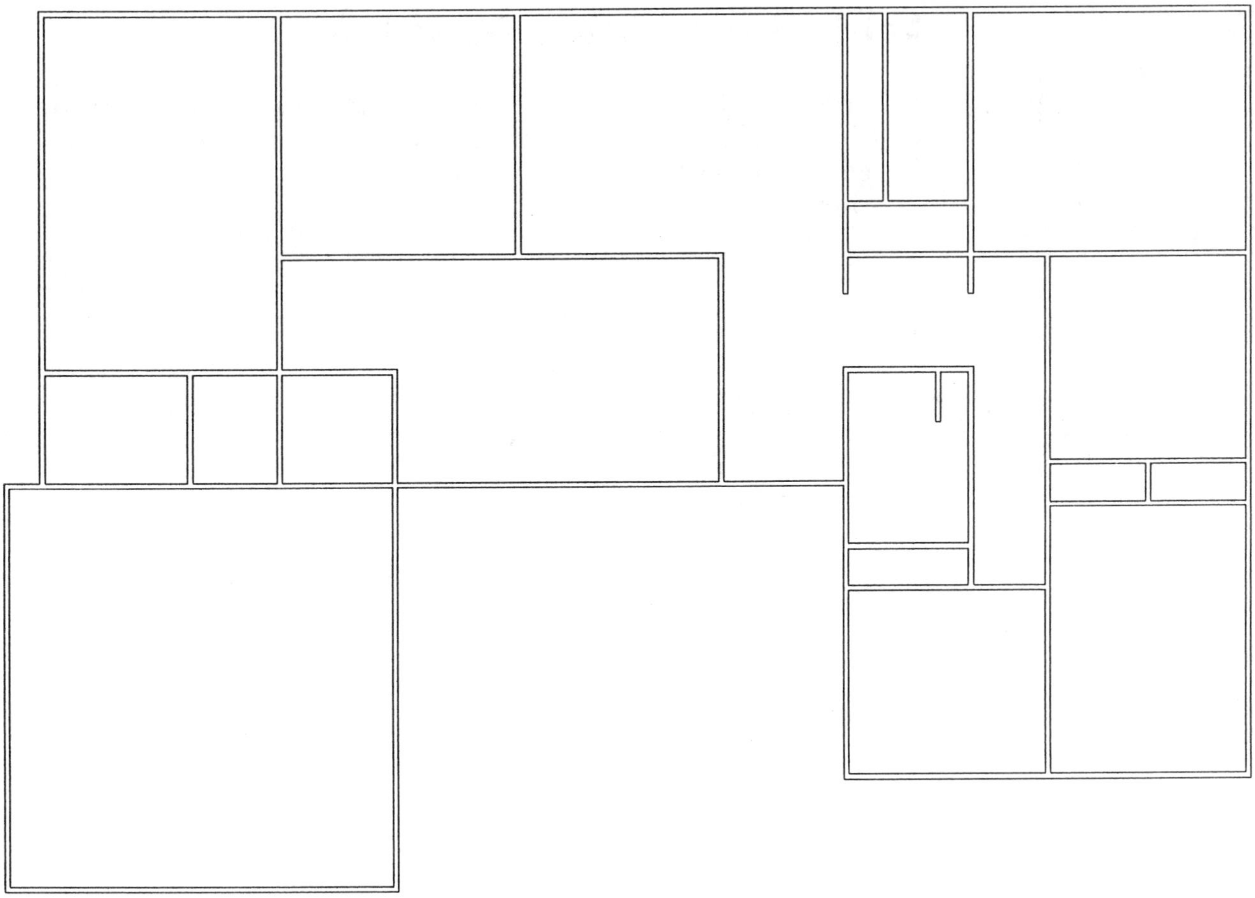

Figure 1-1

YOUR NOTES

Commands used in this session:

break	line
copy	offset
explode	pline
extend	reference lisp function
fillet	trim

Let's begin by preparing the parameters for the drawing.

SETTING THE DRAWING PARAMETERS

Before you start any drawing, you should set up the parameters for the drawing. Parameters include things such as units, limits, and snap increment. When you plan ahead and set up the drawing properly, your drawing task becomes easier and more enjoyable.

STEP 1 *Beginning a New Drawing*

The work disk contains a prototype drawing that you can use to obtain a quick start. Prototype drawings are AutoCAD drawing files that a new drawing can "equal." This means that the new drawing will contain the same parameter settings that the prototype drawing contains. To use a prototype drawing, choose option 1 from the Main menu (Begin a NEW Drawing). AutoCAD will respond 'Enter NAME of drawing:'. Enter the title of your drawing, followed by an "equals" sign and the name of the prototype drawing. For example, to create a drawing named FLPLAN that has the same parameters as an existing drawing named PROTO1, enter FLPLAN=PROTO1. If there are entities in the PROTO1 drawing, they will also be included in the FLPLAN drawing.

The prototype drawing for your floor plan drawing is PPLAN1. From the Main menu, select option 1 (Begin a NEW drawing). Respond to the 'Enter NAME of drawing:' prompt by entering \ACADARCH\FLPLAN1=\ACADARCH\PPLAN1 and ↵.

The prototype drawing has been prepared with the following settings:

Units: Architectural (to 1/16")
Limits: 0,0 (lower left) and 96′,72′ (upper right)

YOUR NOTES

Grid: 5′ and ON
Snap: 1/2" and ON
Layer: (*Make*) FLPLAN (color cyan)
Ortho: ON
Zoom All
Time: ON

Let's discuss why we chose these settings. For all the drawings except the site plan, we will use architectural units. This allows us to draw and dimension in feet and inches.

We set the limits for drawings plotted at 1/4"=1′–0" on 24"x18" (C-size) paper. To calculate the limits for a specific scale and paper size, multiply the paper dimensions by the number of units (in this case, feet) per inch desired on the plot. For example, 1/4"=1′–0" is the same as 1"=4′. This means there are 4′ per inch of plotted line. Furthermore, we wish to plot on 24"x18" paper. Multiplying 4′x24 and 4′x18 yields the upper right limits value (96′,72′). To make this easier, a table showing the limits for different combinations of scale and paper size is included in Appendix F of this book.

We set a grid so we can see the "size" of the paper on the display. As a general rule, you should choose a grid spacing that is about 1/20 of your total area. A 5′ grid is a reasonable grid to choose for this drawing. This is a good way to see the relationship between the drawing and the finished plot page size.

We will use the snap feature to help us draw accurately. We set the value to 1/2" because this value is the smallest increment we expect to use. You should never attempt to draw without setting the snap. This will become more evident when we begin to use semiautomatic dimensioning.

We created a layer named FLPLAN. We will create several additional layers later as we continue drawing our plans. These layers will allow us to make multiple use of some drawings by "freezing" and "thawing" parts of the work.

We set cyan (color 4) as the drawing color for clarity. We will assign a color to each layer as we create it, because it is easier to differentiate between work on different layers when color codes are used.

We performed a Zoom all to display the entire working area so that we can start drawing the perimeter.

YOUR NOTES

Finally, we turned on the drawing timer. In an architectural office, the timer maintains a time record for billing purposes. We won't be billing a customer for this work, but it will be interesting to see how much time we use to create the floor plan. Remember to turn the timer off if you take a break.

You may wish to turn off the UCS icon displayed in the bottom left of the screen. To turn off the icon, enter the following command sequence.

Command: **ucsicon**
ON/OFF/All/Noorigin/ORigin: **off**

If you want to check the distances between the walls you construct, you can use the Distance command. Use object snap mode near or intersection (depending on the type of "first point" to be captured) and object snap mode perpendicular or intersection to capture the second point. Using object snap when you check distances will increase the accuracy of your measurements.

DRAWING THE PERIMETER

Now that we have prepared our new drawing file, it is time to start drawing! Follow the guidelines in Step Two to create the basic outline of the house. In this session, we will draw all the walls. We will add the doors and windows in Session Two.

STEP 2 *Drawing the Plan Perimeter (Walls 1 Through 10)*

We will use numbers to designate the walls. Appendix H is a wall key plan that shows the identifying number of each wall.

Let's start by drawing the perimeter of the floor plan. This will be the logical starting place for drawing almost any plan. Refer to Figure 1–2 and Appendix K for dimensions.

From the Draw menu, select Pline. There are three ways to draw the perimeter. Use the one that best suits your purpose. In the first method, you use the screen coordinates to draw the perimeter directly from the dimensions on the reference plans. To use this method, draw from the upper left corner by placing the first point in the proximity of the 10′,60′ screen coordinates. Move your input device to the right until the coordinate readout at the top of the drawing screen reads 68′–0". If the readout shows absolute coordinates, press ctrl-D until it reads in relative coordinates. Continue drawing the perimeter, referring to the reference plans for dimensions. Use close to create an accurate closure to the beginning point. If you have entered the points correctly, the closing line should be perfectly vertical.

YOUR NOTES

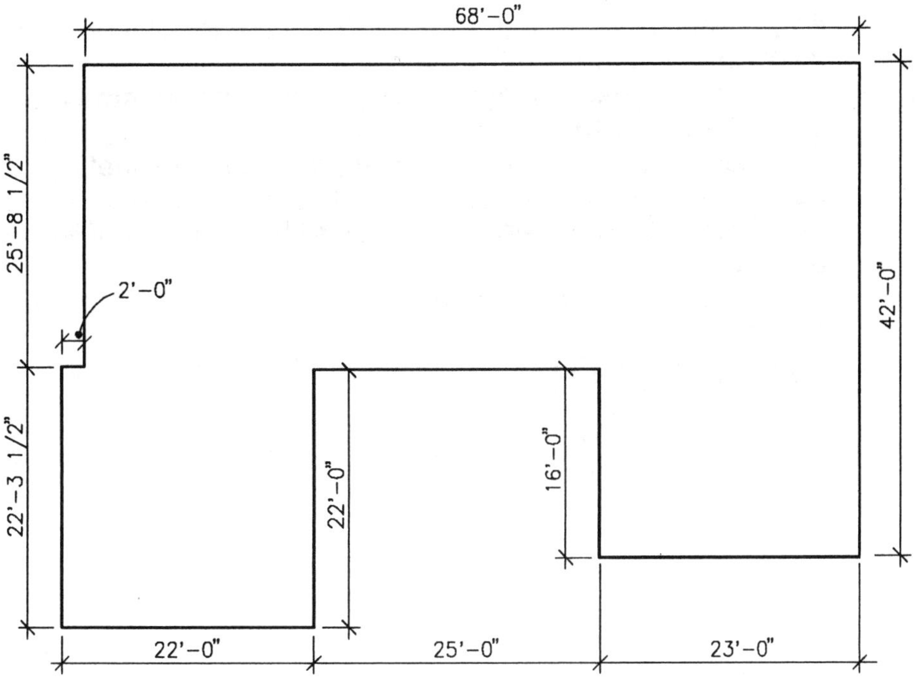

Figure 1-2

Some display systems have difficulty displaying every inch on the coordinate display. This is due to the number of pixels in the display. If this is a problem on your display, you will notice that it is difficult or impossible to place the crosshairs so that the intended dimension is indicated in the coordinate display. To remedy the problem, you may either Zoom closer or use one of the other two drawing methods to designate the line length.

YOUR NOTES

The second drawing method involves the use of polar coordinates. To use polar coordinates to construct the perimeter of the house, use the following command sequence:

Command: **pline**
From point: **10',60'** *This is an absolute coordinate.*
Current line-width is 0'-0"
Arc/Close/Halfwidth/length/Undo/Width;<Endpoint of line>:
@68' <0 *(wall [1])*
Arc/Close/Halfwidth/length/Undo/Width;<Endpoint of line>:
@42'<270 *(wall [2])*
Arc/Close/Halfwidth/length/Undo/Width;<Endpoint of line>:
@23'<180 *(wall [3])*
Arc/Close/Halfwidth/length/Undo/Width;<Endpoint of line>:
@16'<90 *(wall [4])*
Arc/Close/Halfwidth/length/Undo/Width;<Endpoint of line>:
@25'<180 *(wall [5])*
Arc/Close/Halfwidth/length/Undo/Width;<Endpoint of line>:
@22'<270 *(wall [6])*
Arc/Close/Halfwidth/length/Undo/Width;<Endpoint of line>:
@22'<180 *(wall [7])*
Arc/Close/Halfwidth/length/Undo/Width;<Endpoint of line>:
@22'3-1/2"<90 *(wall [8])*
Arc/Close/Halfwidth/length/Undo/Width;<Endpoint of line>:
@2'<0 *(wall [9])*
Arc/Close/Halfwidth/length/Undo/Width;<Endpoint of line>:
c *(wall [10])*

If you are using the AutoCAD digitizer template, the "numeric" menu area makes polar entries fast and easy.

The third drawing method involves the use of relative coordinates. If you wish to use this method, enter the following command sequence:

Command: **pline**
From point: **10',60'** *This is an absolute coordinate.*
Current line-width is 0'-0"
Arc/Close/Halfwidth/length/Undo/Width;<Endpoint of line>:
@68',0 *(wall [1])*
Arc/Close/Halfwidth/length/Undo/Width;<Endpoint of line>:
@0,-42' *(wall [2])*

YOUR NOTES

Arc/Close/Halfwidth/length/Undo/Width;<Endpoint of line>:
@-23',0 *(wall [3])*
Arc/Close/Halfwidth/length/Undo/Width;<Endpoint of line>:
@0,16' *(wall [4])*
Arc/Close/Halfwidth/length/Undo/Width;<Endpoint of line>:
@-25',0 *(wall [5])*
Arc/Close/Halfwidth/length/Undo/Width;<Endpoint of line>:
@0,-22' *(wall [6])*
Arc/Close/Halfwidth/length/Undo/Width;<Endpoint of line>:
@-22',0 *(wall [7])*
Arc/Close/Halfwidth/length/Undo/Width;<Endpoint of line>:
@0,22'3–1/2" *(wall [8])*
Arc/Close/Halfwidth/length/Undo/Width;<Endpoint of line>:
@2',0 *(wall [9])*
Arc/Close/Halfwidth/length/Undo/Width;<Endpoint of line>:
c *(wall [10])*

Your plan should now look like Figure 1–3.

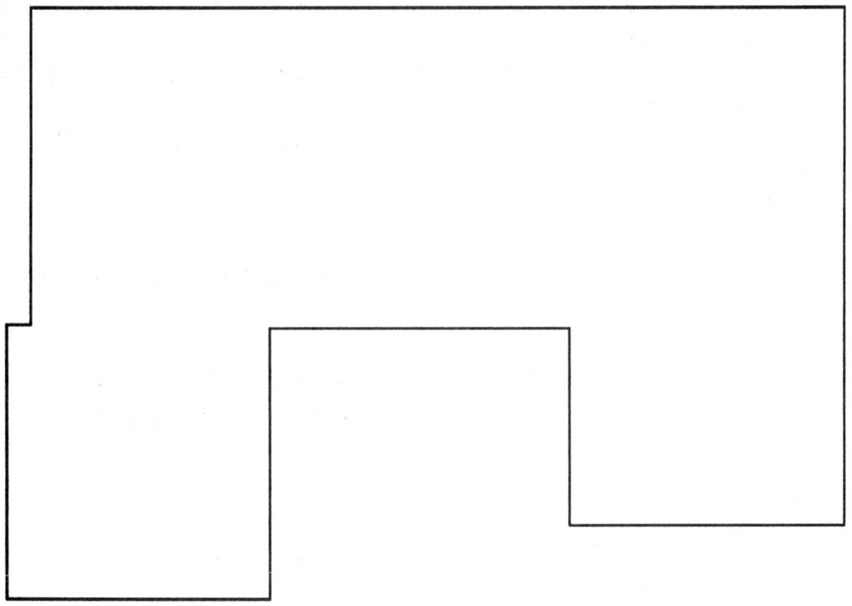

Figure 1-3

YOUR NOTES

It is now time to create the wall thickness. We will be drawing and dimensioning to the framing members. This wall is a 2x4 wall. To create the wall thickness, select Offset. Since the thickness of a 2x4 is 3 1/2", set the offset to 3 1/2". Select the polyline along one of the bottom walls. Then move the curser up and enter a point to show the direction to offset. The ortho function should still be on and will hold the line to a true vertical offset. Since this is a polyline, the walls will offset to the inside of the existing polyline. All the walls should now have a thickness of 3 1/2". Your plan should now look line Figure 1–4.

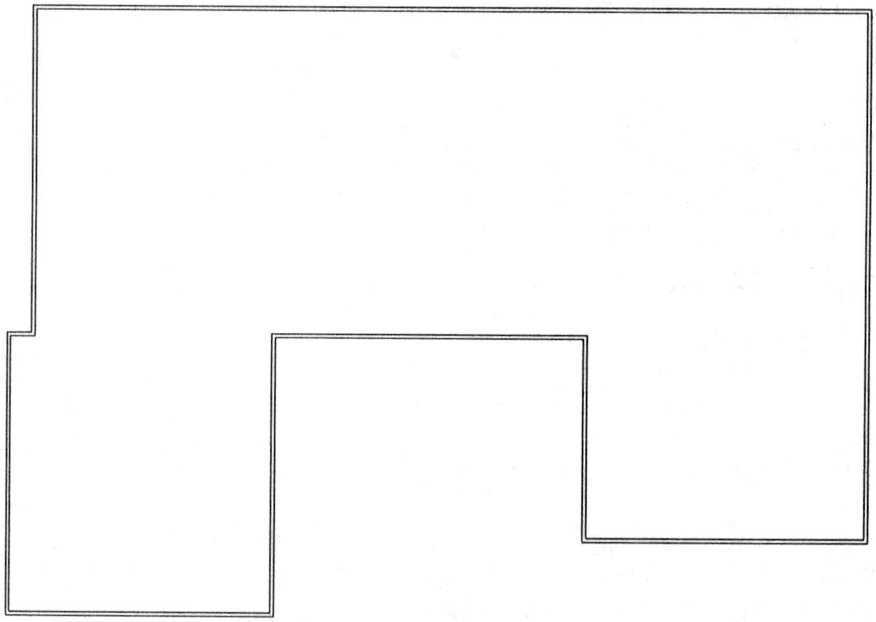

Figure 1-4

This is a good method of creating the boundary walls for a floor plan. The plan boundary is usually the best place to start drawing a floor plan. From this point you can begin to "block" in the interior walls.

YOUR NOTES

We used a polyline so that we could construct the thickness of all perimeter walls in one operation. This is a good technique to use when the same operation must be performed on several connected lines. We will use both lines and polylines throughout the construction of these plans. Note when each is used and for what purpose.

While polylines can be great timesavers, many edit commands (such as Extend) will not work properly on polylines. Use the Explode command to break each of the two polylines (the inner and outer wall lines of the perimeter) into individual line segments. After you have exploded the polylines, you may begin drawing the interior walls, but stop first and use Save to record your work to disk.

CONSTRUCTING THE INTERIOR WALLS

After the perimeter walls are constructed, the next move is to draw the interior walls. The following steps will take you through the procedures that are commonly used to do this. While you are working, note the different methods you use and think about how you can apply them to other situations. Remember, there may be more than one acceptable method for completing each step.

As we proceed, notice the "boxing in" techniques we use. At first, we don't need to worry about every nook and offset in the walls. We will begin by drawing the main walls. Then we will use AutoCAD's tools to break, offset, and otherwise construct the minor walls. This can be referred to as "drawing from the outside in."

Let's begin by drawing the interior walls for the bedrooms. Start by zooming in on the bedroom area. As we proceed, if you make a mistake, just use the Undo command and try again.

STEP 3 *Constructing Wall (11)*

For our first interior wall, we will use the simplest method of wall construction. The master bedroom is 13′–0" wide (see the reference plan in Appendix K). To draw wall [11], select Offset and set the offset distance to the width of the room plus one wall thickness, or 13′–3 1/2" (13′–0" + 3 1/2"). Select each of the exterior wall lines (wall [1]) on the north side of the master bedroom and offset them south.

YOUR NOTES

STEP 4 *Constructing Wall (12)*

Next, we are going to use an AutoCAD Lisp function called Reference to place wall [12]. This function is included with the AutoCAD software. Reference permits you to reference the first point of a command (such as a line) from a given point. You must load the Reference function before you use it. Each time you start AutoCAD, you must load the Reference function. At the command prompt, enter the following:

Command: **(load "ref")**

If a successful load is performed, AutoCAD responds with the following:

REF

Instructions on how to load the Reference function automatically each time you enter AutoCAD are given at the end of this session. Loading the Reference function automatically keeps you from having to load the command each time you enter AutoCAD.

Now let's use the Reference function to draw the next interior wall. We will draw the vertical wall between the bedrooms in the front wing (wall [12]). From this point on, Zoom as necessary to create the proper view and scale for accurate work with your display system. Refer to Figure 1–5 as you enter the following sequence.

Command: **line**
From point: **(ref)**
Reference point: **end**
of *Select point 1.*
Enter relative/polar coordinates (with @): **@11'1–1/2"<0**
To point: **per**
to *Object snap to wall [11], then cancel the line command.*

Now use Offset with a thickness of 3 1/2" to offset this line to the east, forming the completed wall.

YOUR NOTES

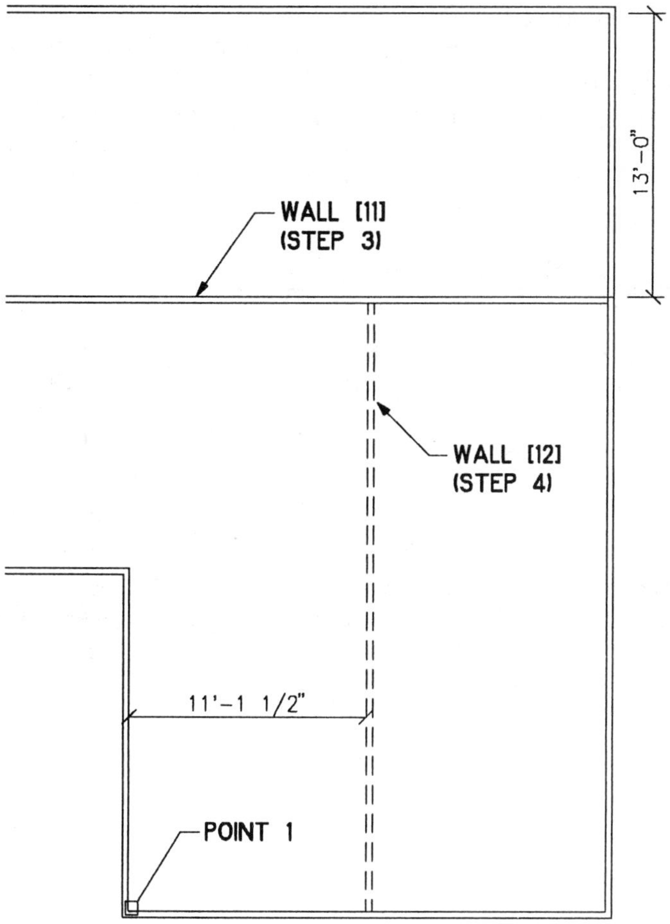

Figure 1-5

Let's take a break here and use Save to record our work to disk again. Turn the timer off if you stop now.

STEP 5 *Constructing Wall (13)*

Next we will draw the north closet wall [13] between bedrooms 2 and 3. Use the following command sequence to construct wall [13]. Refer to Figure 1–6 for the referenced points.

YOUR NOTES

Command: **line**
From point: **(ref)**
Reference point: **int**
of *Select point 1.*
Enter relative/polar coordinates (with @): **@0,-11'**
To point: **per**
to *Select point 2 at wall [2], then cancel the line command.*

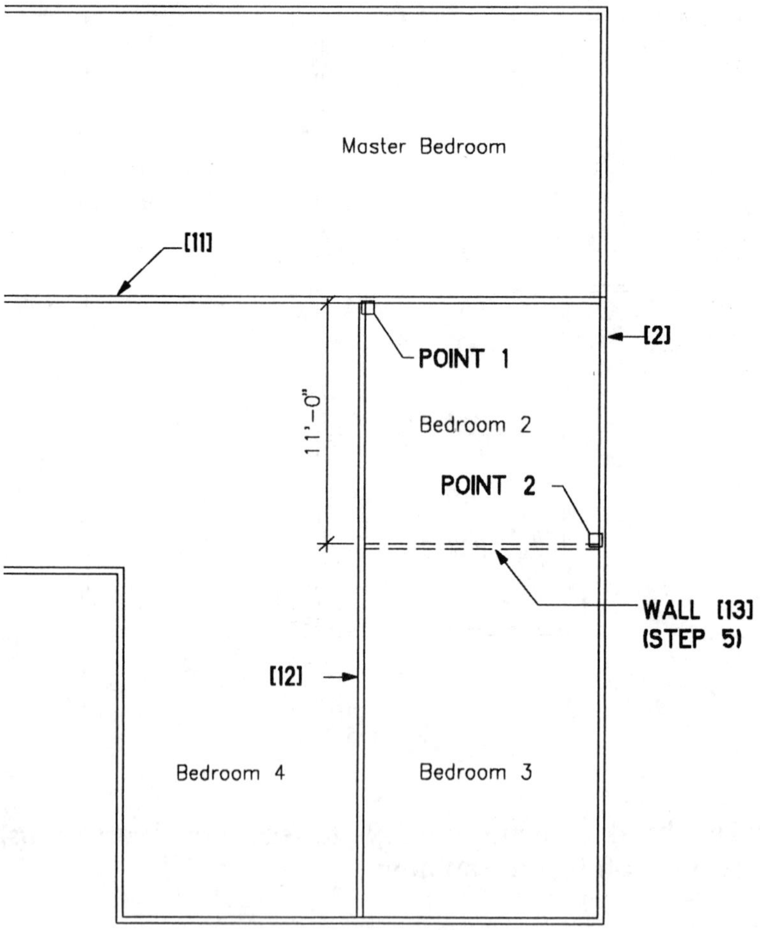

Figure 1-6

Now use Offset to offset the line south by 3 1/2".

YOUR NOTES

STEP 6 *Constructing Wall (14)*

To create the south closet wall [14], select Offset from the Modify menu and set the offset distance equal to the closet depth (2′–0") plus one wall thickness (3 1/2") for a total distance of 2′–3 1/2". Offset both of the wall lines of wall [13] south.

STEP 7 *Constructing Wall (19)*

Now we need the dividing wall that runs vertically between the closet walls (wall [19]). Select Line. Use object snap midpoint from the Tools

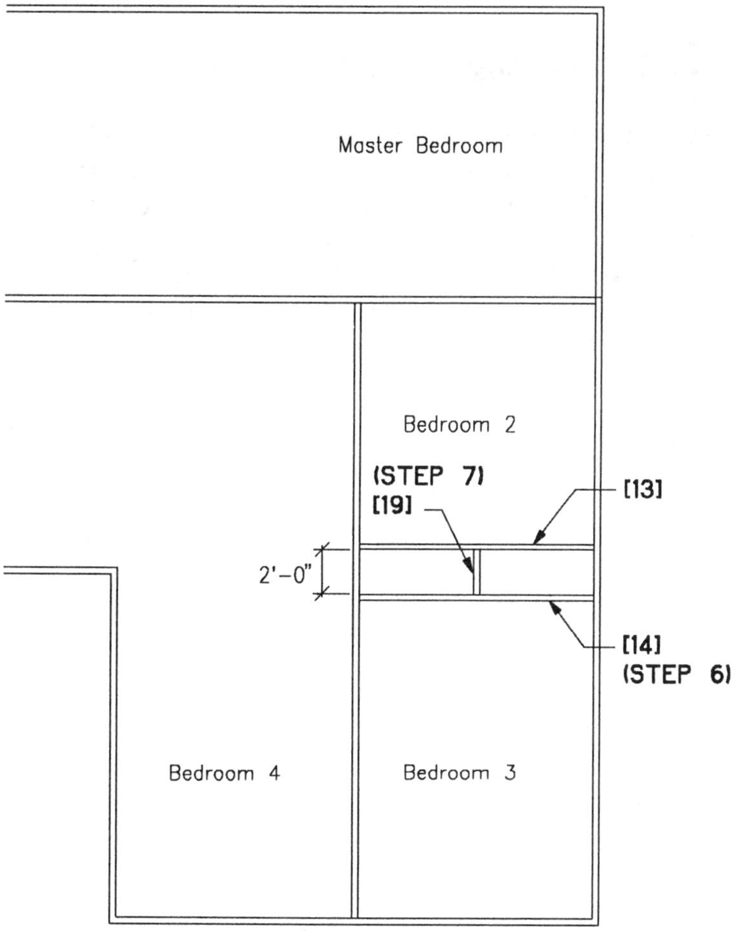

Figure 1-7

YOUR NOTES

menu to snap to the midpoint of the lower line of closet wall [13]. Use object snap perpendicular to snap to the upper line of closet wall [14]. Next, offset lines on both sides of the line you just drew at a distance of 1 3/4" (half a 3 1/2" wall width). Complete the wall by erasing the center line. Your plan should appear as shown in Figure 1–7.

STEP 8 *Constructing Wall (15)*

Next, we will construct wall [15], a 4'–0" hallway through the front wing. Use the Offset command and set a distance of 4'–3 1/2" (the width of the hall plus one wall width). Offset both lines of hallway wall [12] to the west.

STEP 9 *Constructing Wall (16)*

Since the west wall of the master bedroom (wall [16]) lines up with this wall, use the Extend command to extend both lines of wall [15] to the inner line of wall [1] at the master bedroom. To do this, select Extend from the Edit menu. Select the inner line of wall [1] as the boundary edge when prompted, then press ↵. Then select each wall line of wall [15]. The wall lines will be extended to meet the lower wall line of wall [1], which you selected as the boundary.

STEP 10 *Constructing Wall (17)*

Now let's draw the north wall of bedroom 4 (wall [17]). You may need to pan to this location. To pan, enter the Pan command, then enter two points on the screen. You can think of the first point as "attaching" to the drawing. The second point shows the location to which you "drag" the drawing. Obviously, you can only pan the distance that can be placed on the screen. If you need to pan further, use the Pan command again. When you have the correct area on your screen, use the Reference function to draw wall [17]. Use the following command sequence and refer to Figure 1–8 for the points to enter.

Command: **line**
From point: **(ref)**
Reference point: **int**
of *Select point 1.*

YOUR NOTES

Enter relative/polar coordinates (with @): **@0,10'**
To point: **per**
to *Select point 2 at wall [12], then cancel the line command.*

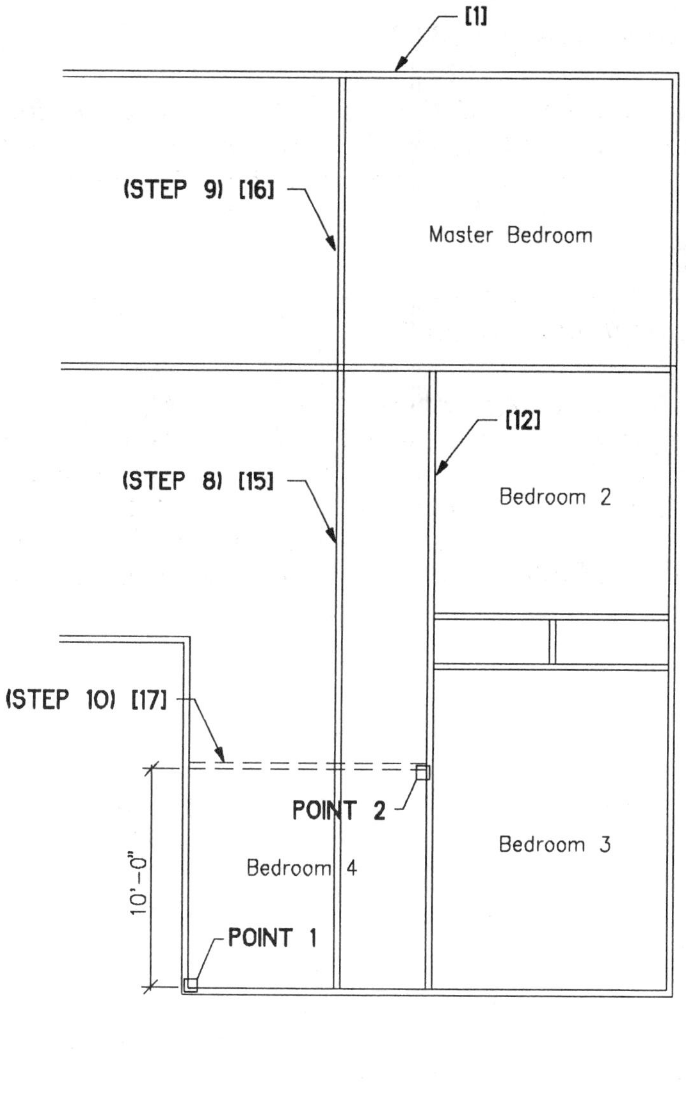

Figure 1-8

Offset the line 3 1/2" north to create the wall thickness. Then Trim the lower part of the west hallway wall [15] from the interior of bedroom 4 as shown in Figure 1–9.

YOUR NOTES

To trim the wall, select Trim from the Edit menu. Select the upper line of wall [17] as the cutting edge and press ↵. Then select each of the wall lines of wall [15]. The selection point must be below wall [17] to identify the correct part of the lines to trim.

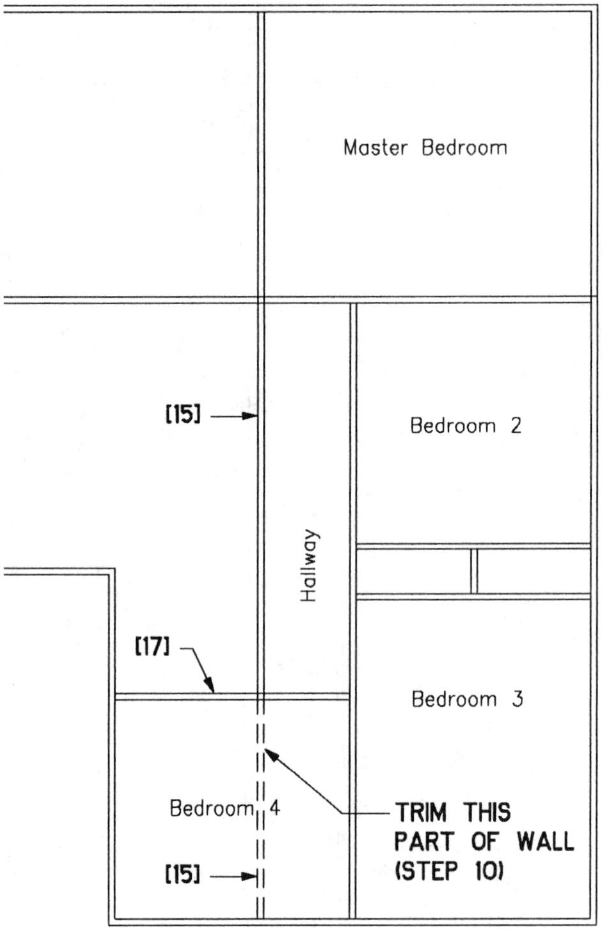

Figure 1-9

STEP 11 *Constructing Wall (18)*

Now, draw the north wall ([18]) of the closet in bedroom 4 by offsetting wall [17]. The closet is 2′ deep. Offset the wall the depth of the closet plus a wall thickness (a total of 2′–3 1/2") to the north. Since the wall

YOUR NOTES

extends into the hallway, use the Trim command to trim it as shown in Figure 1–10.

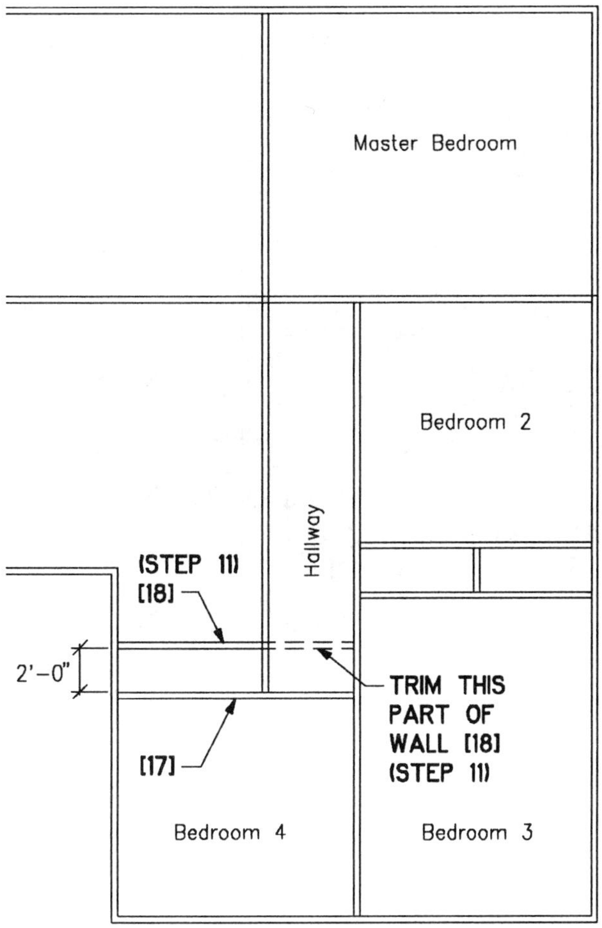

Figure 1-10

STEP 12 *Constructing Walls (20) and (31)*

Use the Offset command again to create the north bathroom wall [20]. You can do this by offsetting wall [18] to the north to create wall [20]. The length of the bathroom is 9'–3" plus one 3 1/2" wall, making a total offset thickness of 9'–6 1/2".

YOUR NOTES

Next, use Fillet (radius 0) to fillet the north bathroom wall [20] with the exterior wall on the west side of bedroom 4 (wall [4]). Figure 1–11 shows the drawing after the completed operation.

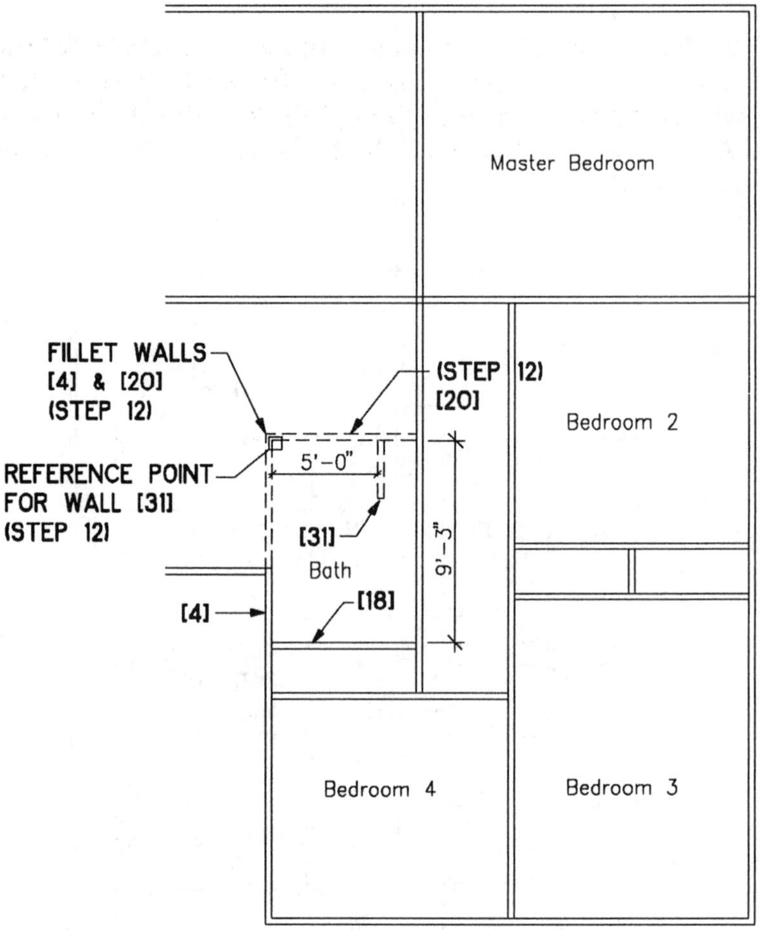

Figure 1-11

Next we will draw the side wall of the linen closet at the end of the bathtub (wall [31]). Select Line. Then call the Reference function. Place the reference point at the interior intersection of walls [4] and [20] (see Figure 1–11). Since the rough opening for our bathtub is 5′–0", enter a reference distance of @5′<0. In response to the 'To point:' prompt, enter @2′8"<270 to draw a line 2′–8" down. Next, Offset the line 3 1/2" to the east. Now cap the south end of wall [31] with the Line command, using object snap endpoint at the endpoint of each wall line of wall [31].

YOUR NOTES

STEP 13 *Constructing Wall (22)*

Let's edit the hall closet. Zoom in to obtain a good scale view of the hall closet area. Turn off the snap for this part of the work. We want to break wall [15] which currently exists at the right side of the closet (see Figure 1-12 and Appendix H). This break should be at a point 2'-0" from the outer face of wall [11].

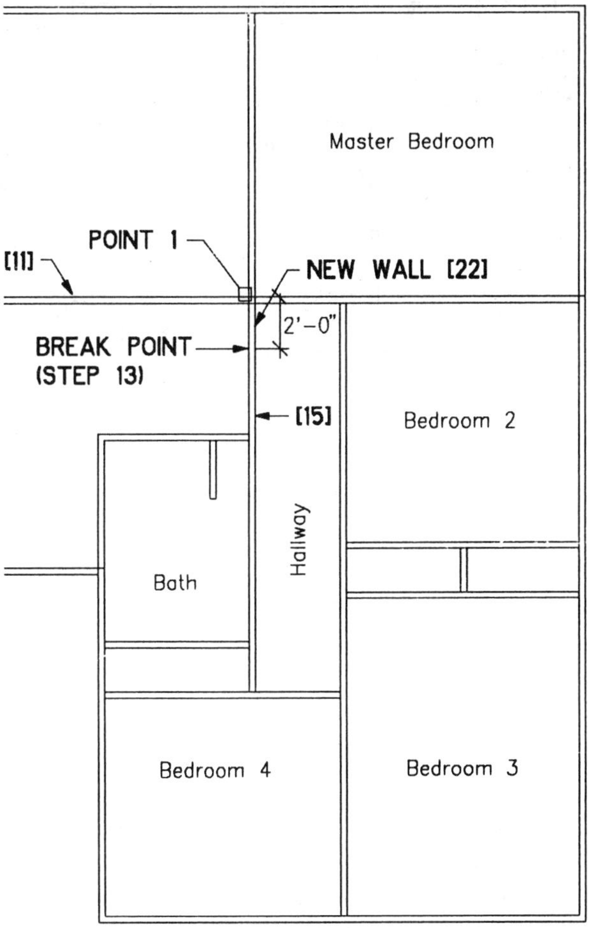

Figure 1-12

YOUR NOTES

Select the Break command and use the following command sequence.

Command: **break**
Select object: *Select the left line of wall [15].*
Enter second point (or F for first point): **f**
Enter first point: **(ref)**
Reference point: **int**
of: *Select point 1.*
Enter relative/polar coordinates (with @): **@2'<270**
Enter second point: **@**

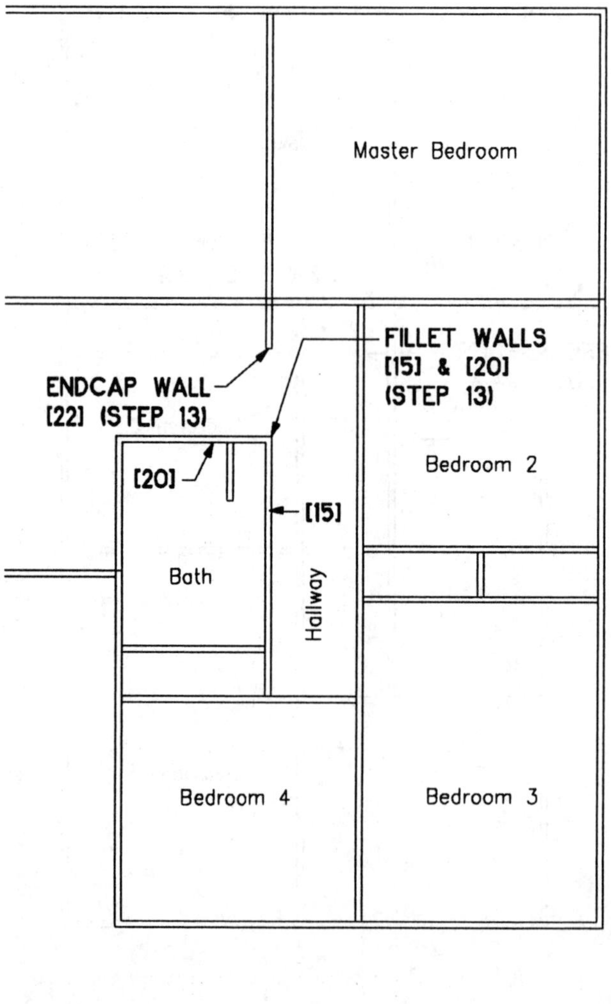

Figure 1-13

YOUR NOTES

You just used the Reference function to locate a point 2′ down the wall and the Break @ command to "split" the line. The line is now two entities. Continue by breaking (splitting) the right line of wall [15]. Then Fillet (radius 0) walls [20] and [15] as shown in Figure 1–13 The portion of wall [15] that remains attached to wall [11] now becomes wall [22].

Next, use the Line command and object snap endpoint to endcap the short closet wall [22] (see Figure 1–13).

STEP 14 *Constructing Walls (23) and (21)*

Our next step is to create the west wall for the master bedroom dressing area and bath (wall [23]). This wall is identical to wall [16], so we do not need to draw it from scratch.

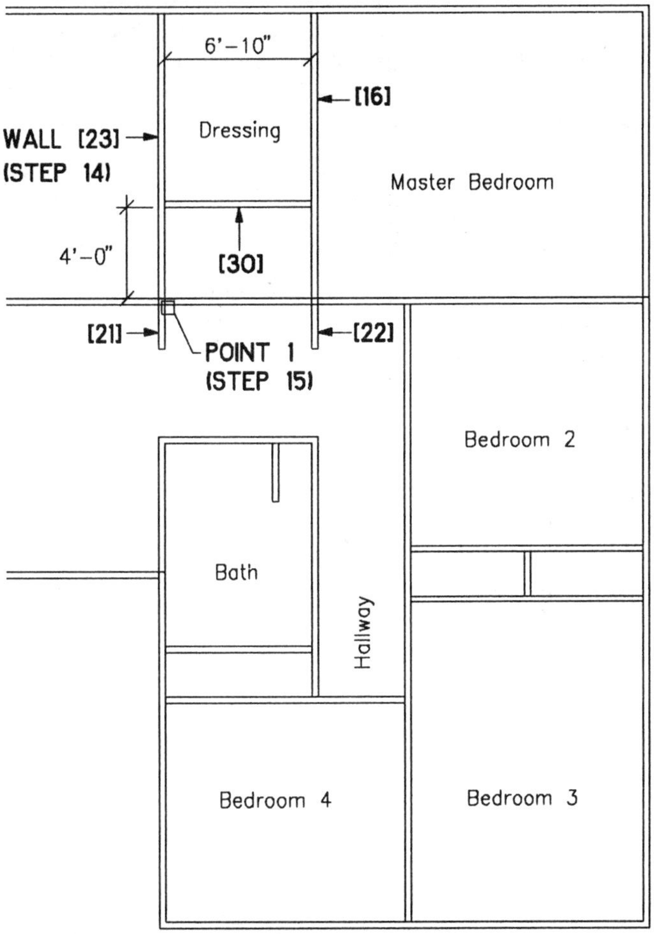

Figure 1-14

YOUR NOTES

Select Copy. Choose the east dressing room wall (walls [16] and [22]). Don't forget the endcap. Use the following command sequence and refer to Figure 1–14 to copy this wall.

Command: **copy**
Select objects: *Select the wall and endcap.*
<Base point or displacement>/Multiple: **nea**
to *Select right wall line of east dressing room wall [16].*
Second point of displacement: **@-7'1–1/2",0**

You should now have a wall on the west side of the dressing/bath area and a west wall for the hall closet.

Notice here we used the Copy command instead of Offset. Both commands are acceptable. You may use either command, depending on the type of wall construction you wish to perform.

STEP 15 *Constructing Wall (30)*

Now we will create wall [30]. Use the following sequence, and refer to Figure 1–14 to create the wall.

Command: **line**
From point: **(ref)**
Reference point: **int**
of *Select point 1.*
Enter relative/polar coordinate (with @): **@0,4'**
To point: **per**
to *Select a point on wall [16].*

Offset the line 3 1/2" north to complete the wall.

There are still some minor wall constructions and some intersection cleanups to perform, but first let's finish the main interior wall "block-ins."

YOUR NOTES

STEP 16 *Constructing Walls (24), (26), and (32)*

Verify that snap and ortho are on. Then Zoom into the family room/dining area so that we can construct wall [24].

The family room is 13'–0" wide. Select Offset with a 13'–3 1/2" offset distance (13' plus a 3 1/2" wall width). Offset both lines of the west family room wall [10] to the east. Then use the Trim command with wall [24] as a cutting edge to remove the part of wall [11] that extends into the family room (see Figure 1–15).

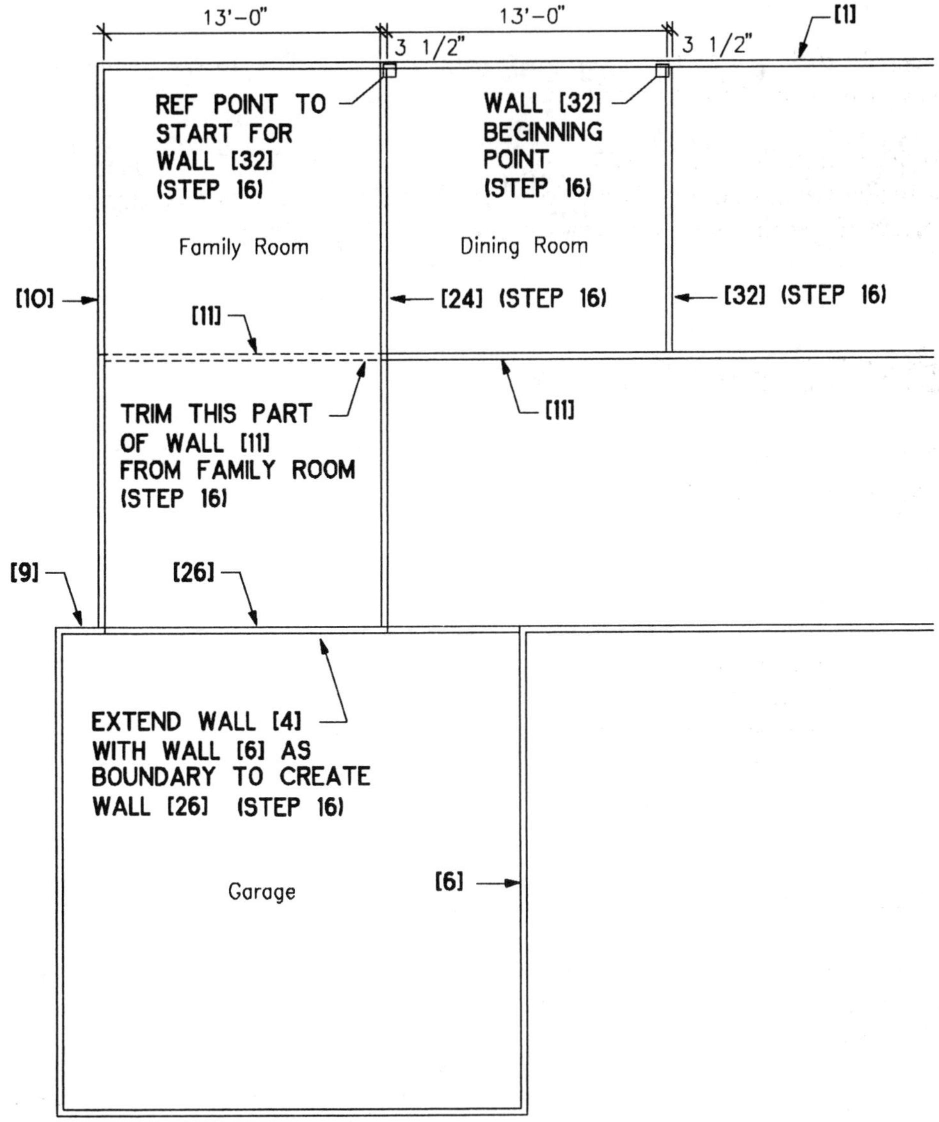

Figure 1-15

YOUR NOTES

To create wall [26], use Extend with the left line of wall [6] as a boundary to properly extend wall [9] to wall [6]. Be sure to select the right side of wall [9] so that the extension is performed in the correct direction.

Next we will create wall [32]. Select Line, then call the Reference function. Place the reference point at the intersection of the east line of wall [24] and wall [1] (see Figure 1–15). Enter @13'<0 for the reference length. From the line start point, draw the wall line to the north wall line of wall [11]. Snap to this point with object snap perpendicular. Then Offset this line 3 1/2" to the east to complete wall [32] (see Figure 1–15).

STEP 17 *Constructing Wall (25)*

Now let's construct wall [25] at the north of the laundry/powder room areas. Offset both lines of wall [26] 6'–1 1/2" (5'–10" + 3 1/2") to the north (see to Figure 1–16). Trim wall [25] with the Trim command, using wall [10] as a cutting edge.

STEP 18 *Creating an Intersection at Walls (6) and (25)*

Use Fillet (radius 0) to create the wall intersection at the northeast corner of the laundry (walls [6] and [25]).

STEP 19 *Constructing Wall (27)*

Next, we will construct the wall between the garage storage and powder room (wall 27). Use the following command sequence. Refer to Figure 1–17 for the location of point 1.

Command: **line**
From point: **(ref)**
Reference point: **int**
of *Select point 1.*
Enter relative/polar coordinates (with @): **@8',0**
To point: **per**
to *Select a point on the lower line of south family room wall [25].*

YOUR NOTES

Cancel the Line command and Offset the last line 3 1/2" to the east to complete the wall.

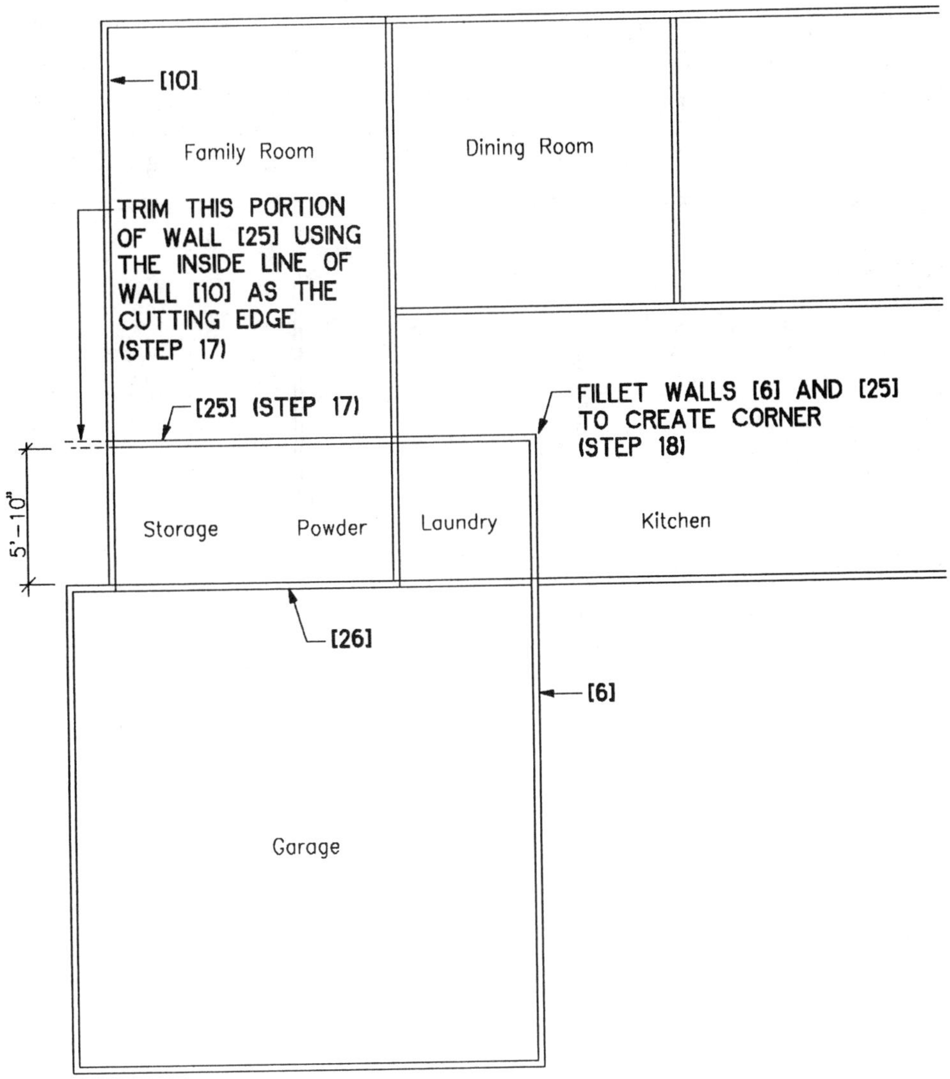

Figure 1-16

STEP 20 *Constructing Wall (29)*

Now let's create the west entry wall [29]. Zoom in on the entry hall area. Use the following command sequence. Refer to Figure 1–18 for the points referred to in the sequence.

YOUR NOTES

Command: **line**
From point: **(ref)**
Reference point: **int**
of *Select point 1.*
Enter relative/polar coordinates (with@):
@6'8-1/2"<180
To point: **per**
to *Pick upper wall line of wall [11].*

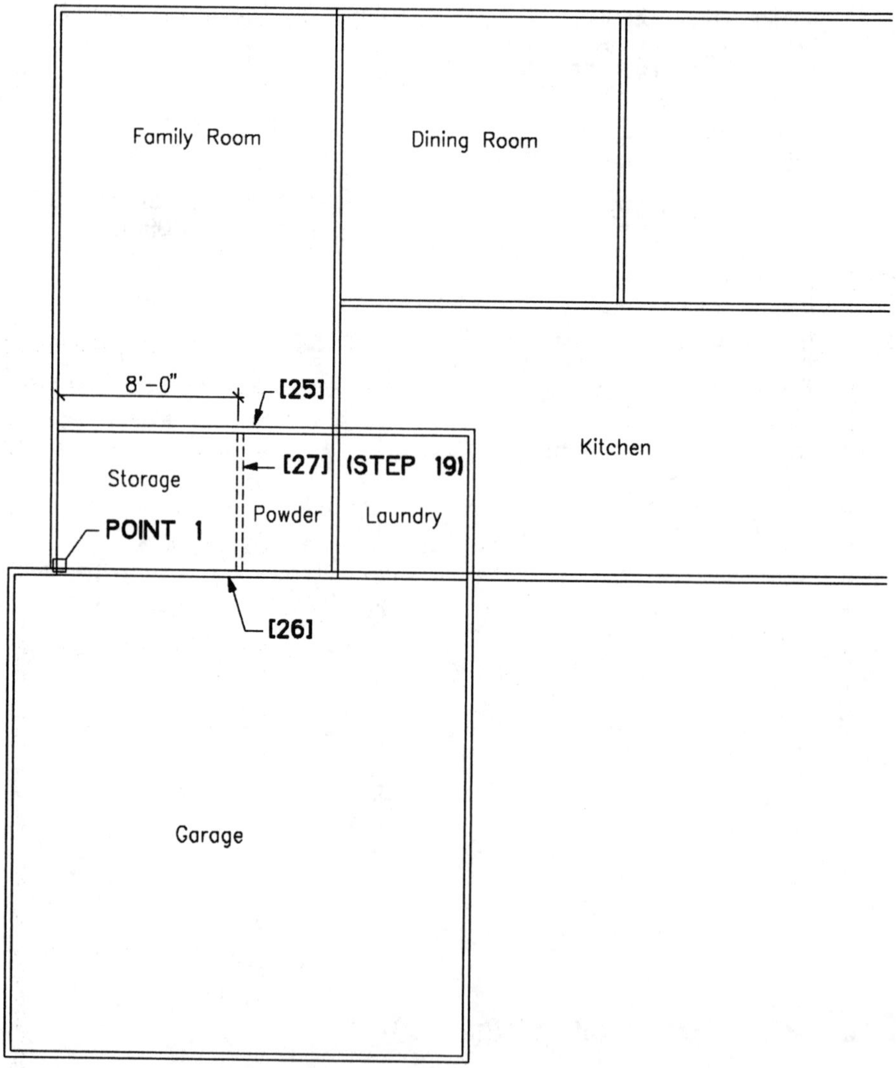

Figure 1-17

YOUR NOTES

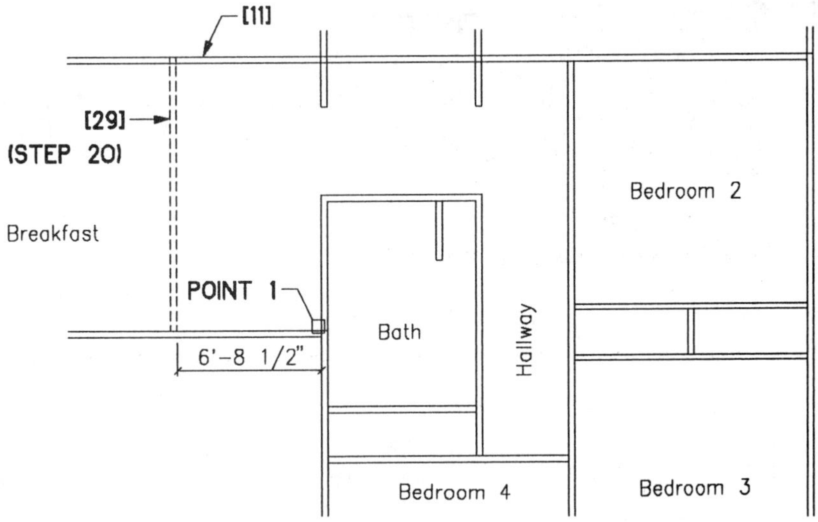

Figure 1-18

Now cancel the Line command and Offset the vertical wall line you just drew 3 1/2" to the west. Use Trim with walls [21] and [29] as cutting edges to trim the wall [11] opening between the entry and living room. You may want to Save your work again before you continue. Your drawing should now look like the one in Figure 1–19.

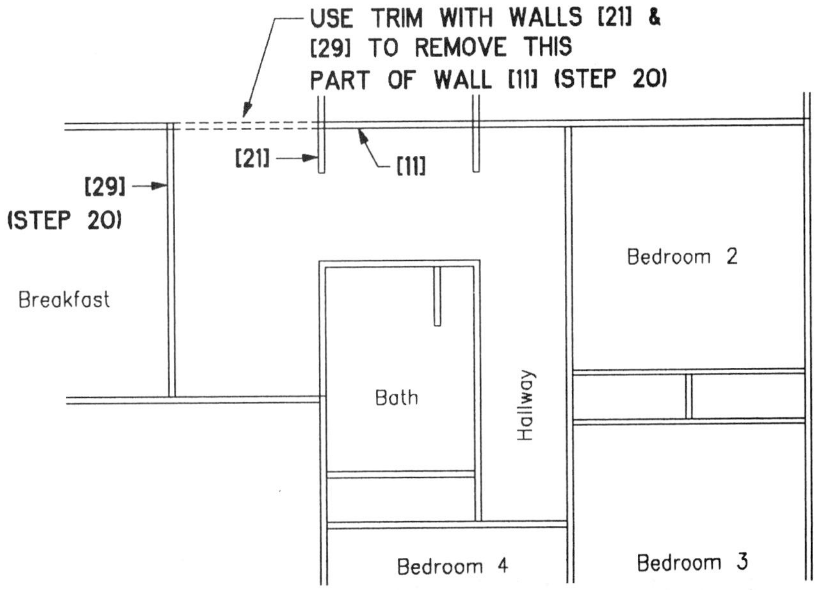

Figure 1-19

YOUR NOTES

STEP 21 *Constructing Wall (33)*

Next we will create wall [33] in the dressing room. Select the Offset command and set the offset distance to 2′–4 1/2″. Offset both lines of wall [23] to the east. Refer to Figure 1–20.

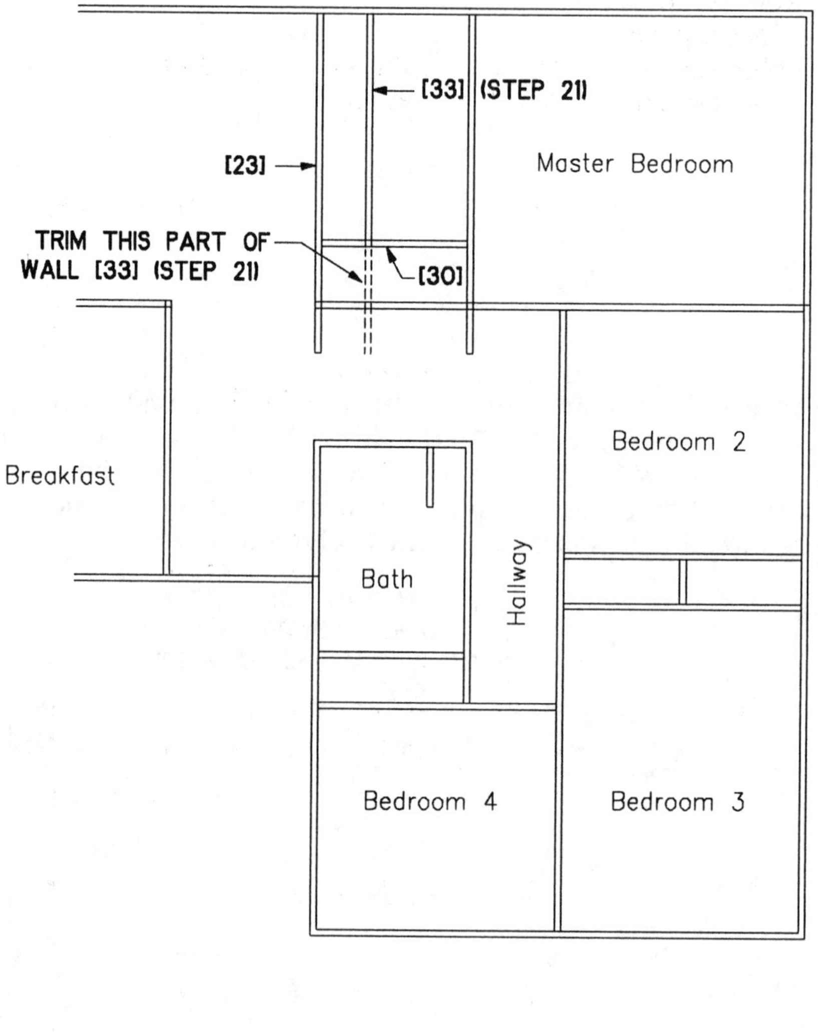

Figure 1-20

Select Trim, and use the bottom line of wall [30] as the cutting edge. Pick the parts of the new wall lines that extend below wall [30] to be trimmed.

Next we will create the opening in wall [30]. Use the following command sequence to break the lines, refer to Figure 1–21.

YOUR NOTES

Command: **break**
Select object: *Select the upper line of wall [30].*
Enter second point (of F for the first point): **f**
Enter the first point: **(ref)**
Reference point: **int**
of *Select point 1.*
Enter relative/polar coordinates (with @): **@5"<0**
Enter second point: *Select point 2.*

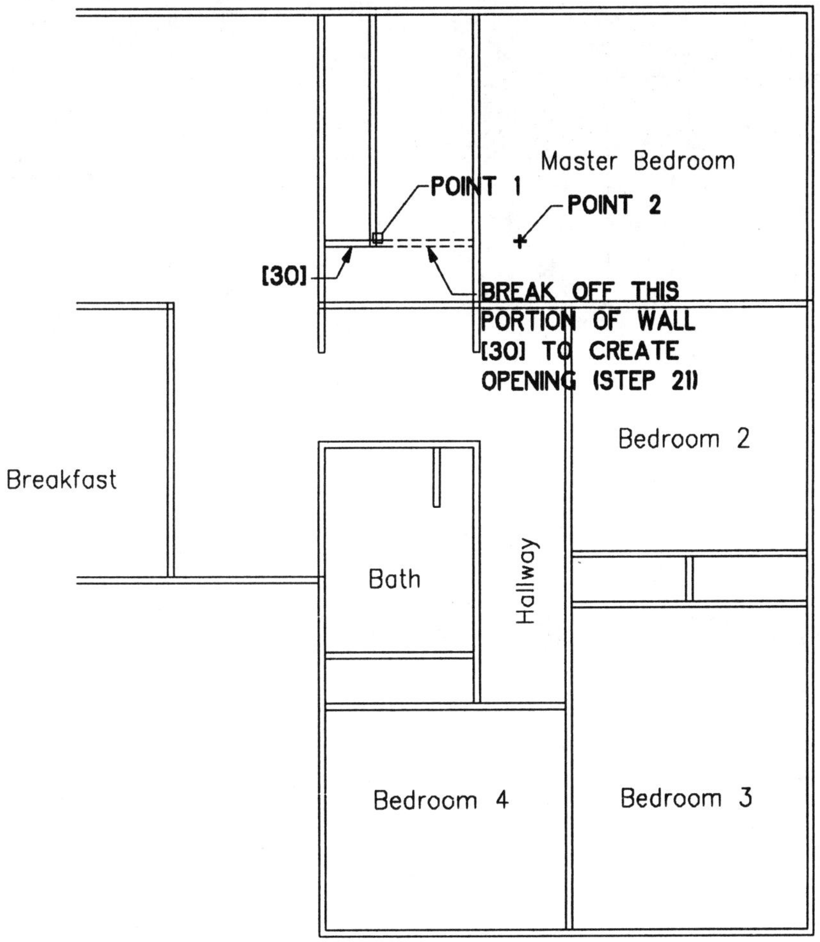

Figure 1-21

YOUR NOTES

Repeat the process for the lower line, then endcap the new wall section.

Now perform a Zoom extents and look things over. This is a good time to use the Save command again. Your drawing should look like the one in Figure 1–22. Turn off the timer and check your cumulative drawing time.

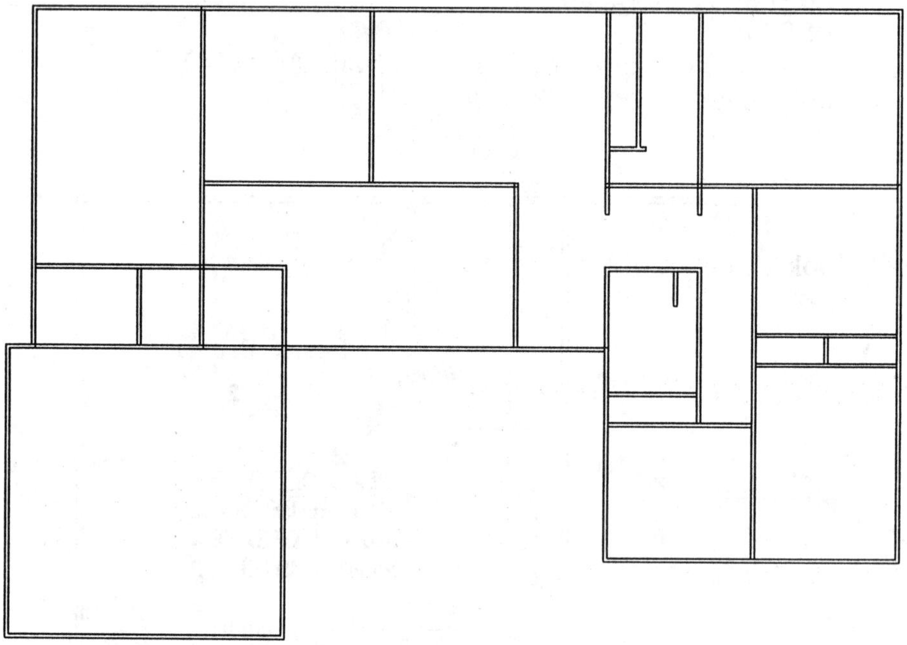

Figure 1-22

TRIMMING INTERSECTIONS

We still need to trim the intersections to finish the wall lines properly. Before we begin trimming the intersections, however, let's look at some effective methods to use.

When trimming intersections, you will encounter three types of conditions. They are as follows:

"T" intersections
"L" intersections
"+" intersections

YOUR NOTES

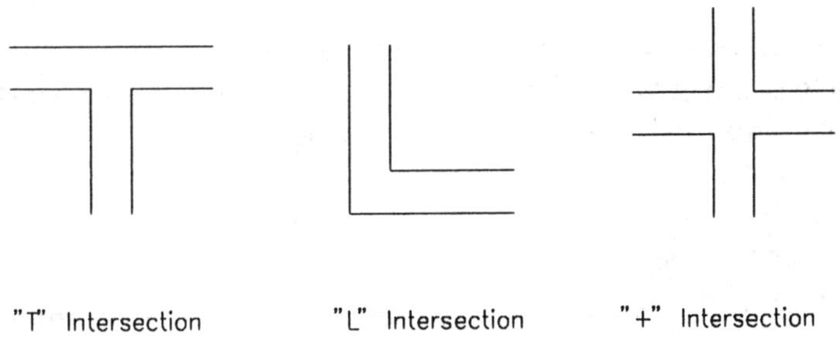

Figure 1-23

Let's look at methods of trimming each type of intersection.

Trimming a "T" Intersection

A "T" intersection can be trimmed in two ways. After using each method, you should be able to determine the best method for a given situation. Use either of the following sequences for the the type of intersections shown in Figure 1–24 and 1–25.

1. Use the Trim command.
2. Select both lines of one wall as cutting edges.
3. Trim the line between the wall lines.

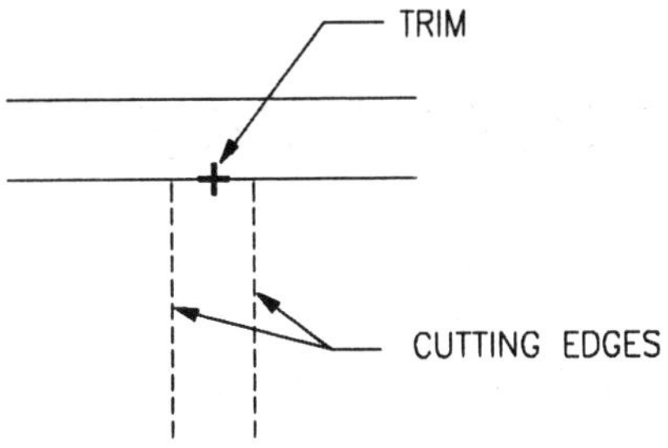

Figure 1-24

OR

YOUR NOTES

1. Use the Break command.
2. Select the wall line to be broken. Then enter F to select the first break point.
3. Enter @ to split the line into two entities.
4. Use Fillet (radius 0) to fillet both corners.

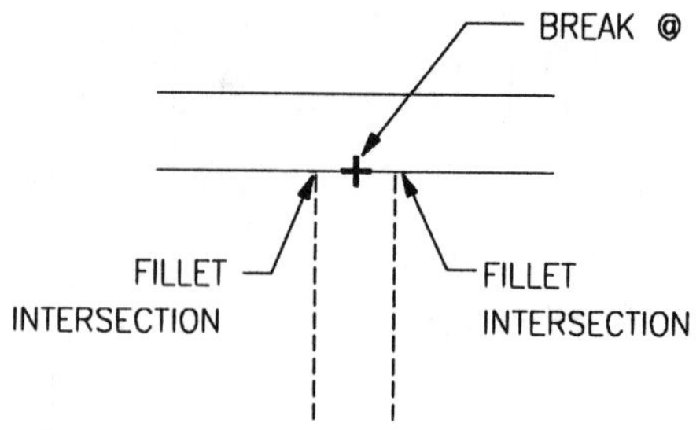

Figure 1-25

In some cases, one or two wall lines will extend into the other wall, as shown in Figure 1–26. The following sequence is recommended.

1. Use the Trim command.
2. Use a crossing window to select all the lines as cutting edges.
3. Select the line segments to be trimmed.

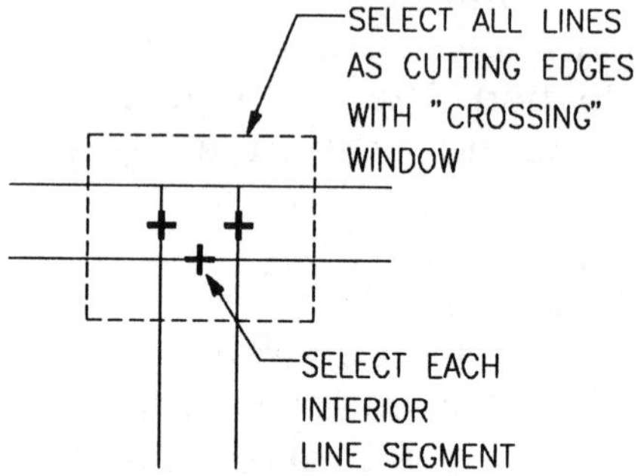

Figure 1-26

Trimming an "L" Intersection

The easiest way to trim an "L" intersection is to use the Fillet (radius 0) command to fillet each wall line. Refer to Figure 1–27 to see which wall lines to fillet.

YOUR NOTES

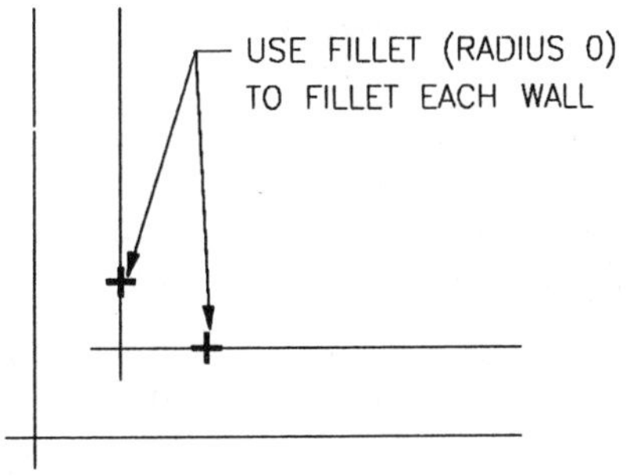

Figure 1-27

Trimming a "+" Intersection

A "+" intersection is one that is made up of walls that intersect and cross (see Figure 1–28). Use the following sequence to trim a "+" intersection.

1. Use the Trim command.
2. Use a crossing window to select all lines as cutting edges.
3. Select the interior line segments to trim.

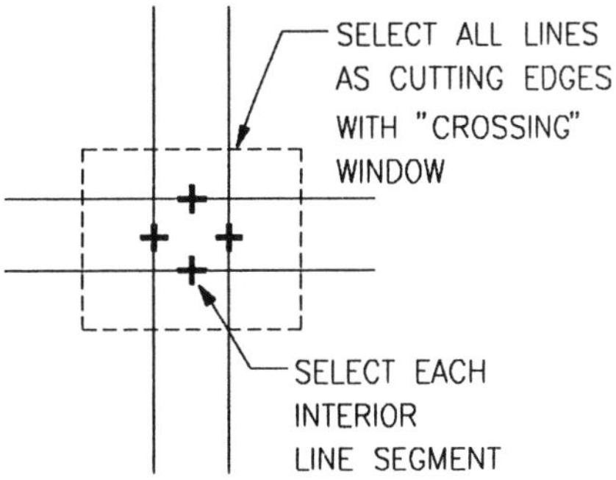

Figure 1-28

STEP 22 *Trimming the Wall Intersections*

Now it is time to trim the wall intersections on your floor plan. Use the methods you have learned to trim all the intersections in the floor plan.

YOUR NOTES

Be sure to turn the timer on again before you begin. The completed floor plan should look like the one in Figure 1–29.

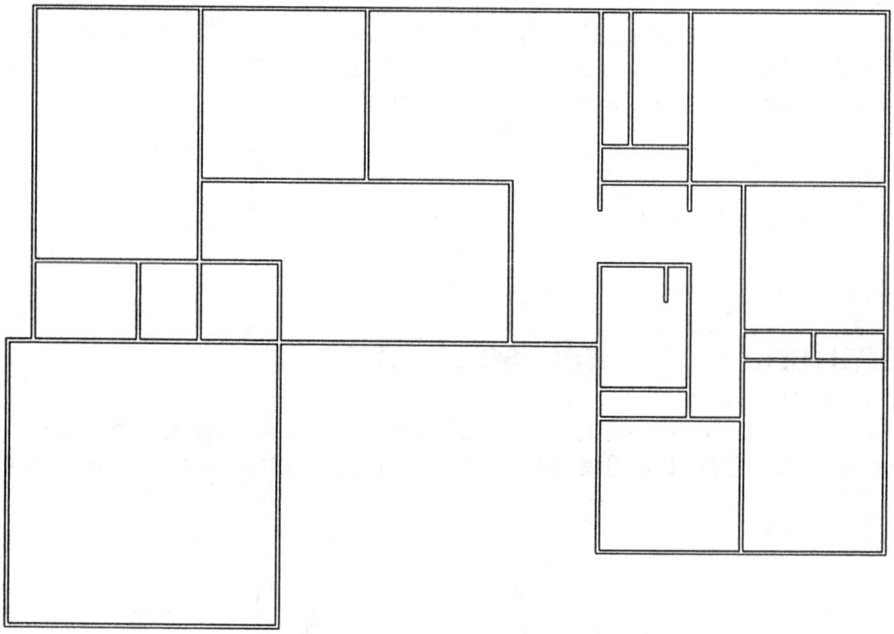

Figure 1-29

Loading the Reference Function Automatically

You may configure AutoCAD to load the Reference function automatically each time you enter the program. This is done with a file named ACAD.LSP (Reference is a LISP language function). If the ACAD.LSP file exists when you enter AutoCAD, the file is loaded automatically. The following shows the contents of the ACAD.LSP file.

```
(defun ref ()
  (setvar "LASTPOINT" (getpoint "Reference point: "))
    (getpoint "\nEnter relative/polar coordinates (with @): "
)
```

YOUR NOTES

You must use a text editor that creates ASCII files to make this file. For your convenience, an ACAD.LSP file is included on the work disk for your use. You will use the reference function several times over the next sessions, so you may want to create the file. To use the ACAD.LSP file, simply copy it into your AutoCAD directory.

Warning! If a file named ACAD.LSP already exists, it will be overwritten by this process. Check your directory for the existence of another file by this name. If such a file exists, the Reference function can be added to it by editing the existing file.

USING DLINE.LSP *(For Release 11 Users)*

If you are an AutoCAD Release 11 user, the lisp routine DLINE.LSP can be used to draw the walls for your plan. Dline draws double lines that are a specified distance apart. You can also endcap and trim intersections automatically!

Using Dline can greatly enhance the speed of floor plan construction. Let's first learn how to use Dline by drawing a simple plan. After we are used to the program, we will examine the Dline options.

Using Dline to Construct a Floor Plan

Start a new drawing of any name. Set the units to Architectural. Set the limits to 0,0 and 44',34', then zoom all.

Let's now load the Dline lisp program. Enter the following at the command line.

Command: **(load "dline")**
C:Dline loaded. Start command with DL or DLINE

The Dline program is now loaded and ready for use. The illustration in Figure 1–29 shows the plan that we will draw. Dimensions have been added for your use.

Let's start by blocking in the perimeter walls.

YOUR NOTES

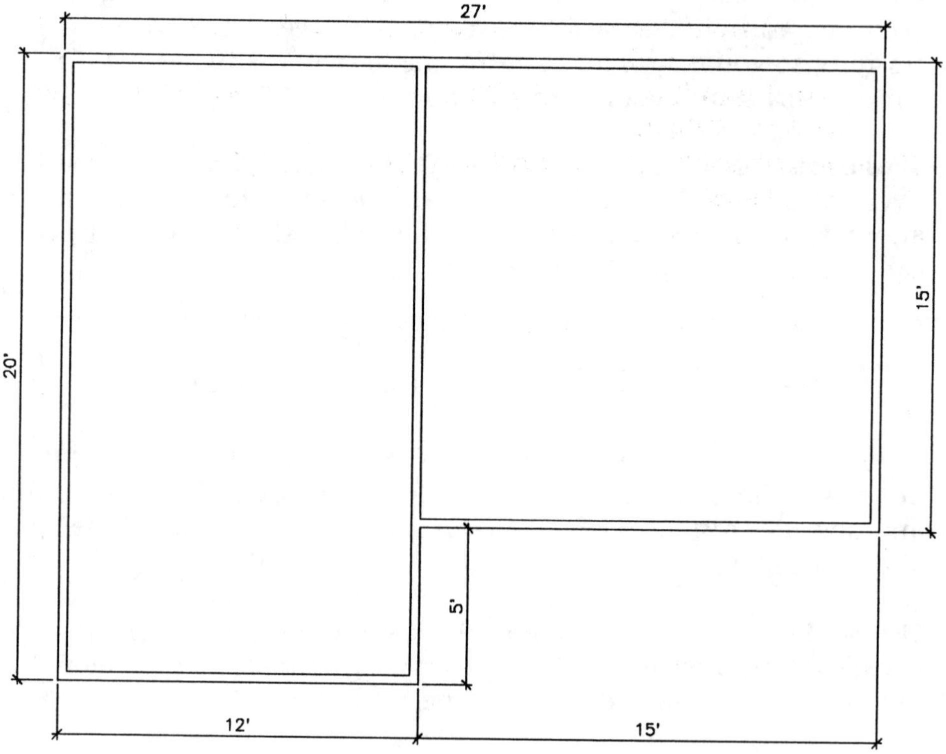

Figure 1-29

Command: **dl**
Break/Caps/Dragline/Offset/Snap/Undo/Width/<start point>: **w**
New DLINE width <*default*>: **3 1/2"**
Break/Caps/Dragline/Offset/Snap/Undo/Width/<start point>: **8',7'**
Arc/Break/CAps/CLose/Dragline/Snap/Undo/Width/<next point>: **d**
Set dragline position to Left/Center/Right/<Offset from center = x>: **r**
Arc/Break/CAps/CLose/Dragline/Snap/Undo/Width/<next point>: **@12'<0**
Arc/Break/CAps/CLose/Dragline/Snap/Undo/Width/<next point>:**@5'<90**

YOUR NOTES

Arc/Break/CAps/CLose/Dragline/Snap/Undo/Width/<next point>: **@15'<0**
Arc/Break/CAps/CLose/Dragline/Snap/Undo/Width/<next point>:**@15'<90**
Arc/Break/CAps/CLose/Dragline/Snap/Undo/Width/<next point>: **@7'<90**
Arc/Break/CAps/CLose/Dragline/Snap/Undo/Width/<next point>: **cl**

Figure 1-30

Your drawing should now look like Figure 1–30. Notice how the Dline function closed the perimeter wall lines and trimmed the “L” intersection.

Now let's draw a wall from the interior wall intersection to the back wall. Refer to Figure 1–31.

Command: **dl**
Break/Caps/Dragline/Offset/Snap/Undo/Width/<start point>: **int**
of *Select point 1.*

YOUR NOTES

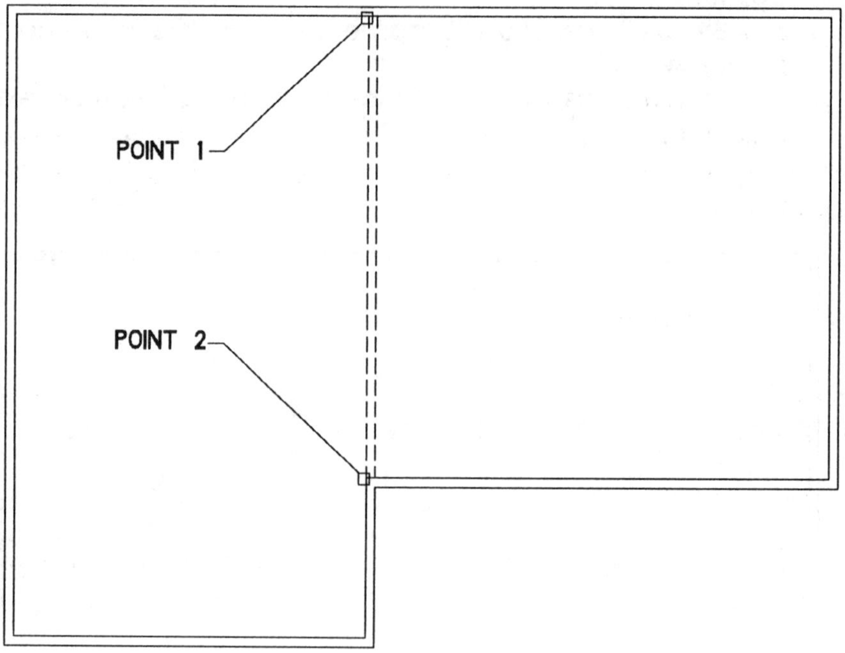

Figure 1-31

Let's interrupt the command sequence at this point and look at what we wish to do. We have just captured a point that is on the left side of the wall we wish to draw. We can set the Dline command to draw the wall relative to this point by using the dragline option. We can set the dragline (the line from which the wall is drawn) as either the left, right, or center line of the wall. Left and right is determined by looking in the direction you are drawing the wall. In our case this is the left side of the wall. Let's continue the command sequence and set the dragline to the left side of the wall.

Arc/Break/CAps/CLose/Dragline/Snap/Undo/Width/<next point>: **d**
Set dragline position to Left/Center/Right/<Offset from center = 1 3/4">: **l**

YOUR NOTES

Let's now continue and finish drawing the wall.

> Arc/Break/CAps/CLose/Dragline/Snap/Undo/Width/<next point>: **per**
> to *Select point 2.*

Notice how the "T" intersection is automatically trimmed! Continue by drawing some walls to fill in the floor plan. Experiment with the dragline option and object snap modes to create the walls you want.

Dline Options

You can control the manner in which the Dline command functions by it's options. Let's look at each of the options.

Break: Controls whether the intersections are trimmed.

CAps: Controls the endcapping of wall lines. You can choose to cap the beginning point, the end point, both, or none.

> Draw which endcaps? Start/End/Both/None/<Auto>:

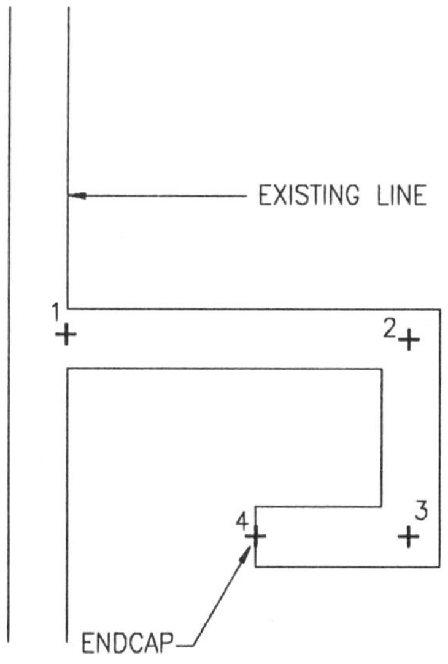

Figure 1-32

YOUR NOTES

If you select capping, endcaps are placed even if snapping is on (see the following explanation on snap). If you select auto, however, only endpoints that are not snapped are capped.

Dragline: Sets the line along which the double wall line will be drawn.

Set dragline position to the Left/Center/Right/<Offset from center *<default>*:

Figure 1–33 shows the options.

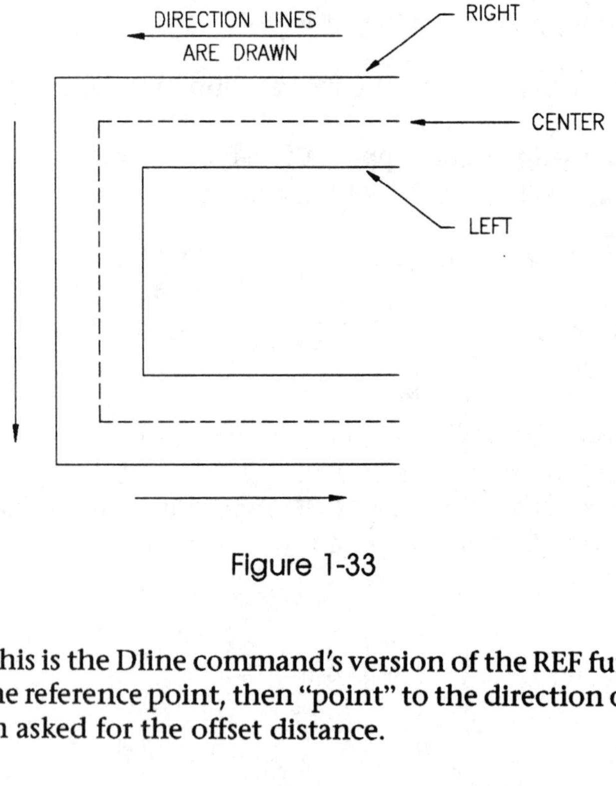

Figure 1-33

Offset: This is the Dline command's version of the REF function. You first select the reference point, then "point" to the direction of the offset. You are then asked for the offset distance.

Break/Caps/Dragline/Offset/Snap/Undo/Width/<start point>: **o**
Offset from:
Offset toward:
Enter the offset distance *<default>*:

YOUR NOTES

Snap: If the snap option is on, AutoCAD will search the area around the beginning or end of the double line and snap to an object, if present, within that area. The area is defined in screen pixels. The snap area is set by the value of the maxsnp variable. This variable is listed near the top of the Dline.lsp file. You can use a text editor to change the value.

Undo: This option works in the same way as the AutoCAD line undo option. You can undo backwards, undoing each segment of double lines.

Width: Sets the width of the double lines. This is the distance between the lines. You can set the width while between double line segments. Note that the dragline will remain the same, resulting in an increased or decreased width that can be offset from either side, or both.

Arc: Used to draw double line arcs. When you select the arc option, the last point entered automatically becomes the first point of the arc. Select Arc will display the following prompt:

```
Break/CAps/CEnter/CLose/Dragline/Endpoint/Line/Snap/Und
o/Width/<second point>:
```

The methods of arc construction apply from this point. You may, for example, select endpoint as the next point to enter to construct the double line arc.

Close: Works in a similar manner to the AutoCAD line close option. Intersection trimming is determined by the setting of the Break option. The double line is closed with a double line or double arc, depending on the function currently being used at the time the close option is used.

YOUR NOTES

SUMMARY

- Set the drawing parameters as the first step when starting a new drawing, or create a prototype drawing for each plan type. Maintain these settings as standards for all future plan drawings. Settings should include units, limits, grid spacing, snap increment, and layers.

- Start the drawing by constructing the perimeter with a polyline. Offset the polyline the width of the exterior wall. Explode the polyline for subsequent edit operations.

- Begin constructing interior walls by drawing "primary walls" first. Candidates for primary walls are those that run the full length or width of the plan or can be created by a simple offset.

- Continue by boxing in the major rooms. Use the most convenient method of wall construction. Among these methods are the Reference Lisp function, Offset command, Copy command, and the centerline/Offset method. Use Offset to create the wall thickness.

- Set all points using object snap for accuracy. The importance of accuracy will become more evident when dimensioning the plan begins.

- Use the Distance command with object snap to check room dimensions as you draw.

- Trim the intersections after all walls are constructed. Be sure all wall joints are properly filleted if you plan to hatch the walls later.

- Draw the plan using snap, ortho, the Extend command, relative coordinates, and other AutoCAD drawing aids to ensure accuracy.

- Doors, windows, and openings can be added after the wall construction process is completed.

QUESTIONS

YOUR NOTES

1. What is a prototype drawing? How could you use prototype drawings to make creating architectural drawing easier?

2. What is the advantage of using a polyline to construct the initial building perimeter?

3. What is meant by "boxing in" the plan?

4. What are the three types of wall intersections?

YOUR NOTES

5. Why would you want to construct walls using relative/polar input and object snap?

6. How would you check dimensions between walls?

PROBLEMS

YOUR NOTES

1. Select one of the plans from Appendix M and draw the perimeter.

2. Create a simple plan of your own design and "box in" the walls.

A Model Solution

Traditionally, architects have drawn separate drawings for plans, elevations and sections. Many AutoCAD users do the same, even through AutoCAD's three-dimensional capabilities offer new opportunities.

Andrew Whitman's small architectural firm is taking full advantage of these opportunities. By using ASG Architectural software and some do-it-yourself AutoLISP routines, the firm designs and draws each project as a set of interconnected 3D files. As a result, a project can be viewed as an accurate electronic 3D model at any time, even during working drawing production.

When Whitman uses ASG Architectural to design a building, he works mostly in plan view, but he also uses the automatic 3D capabilities of the software. He always keeps a 3D view displayed in a viewport, often rendered with the Shade command. He careful ly aligns each floor level at its actual height above the previous floor. In addition to being able to see what the building looks like, he can check to see that walls, columns, and windows are aligned on different floors.

When the project reaches the working drawing phase, Whitman splits each floor into its own file. All of these files, which are still aligned in the same coordinate system, can be viewed at once using AutoCAD's Xref capability. Elevations are drawn in their own file, but they are drawn "in place" on each face of the building, again using Xref to view the models walls as a "base" for the drawing.

Created by Rob Bernstein, Cadet, Inc. and rendered with ASG Model Vistion

The firm has found that ASG Architectural makes it easy to model everything in 3D with no more effort than drawing plans. By carefully using layers, user coordinate systems, Xrefs, views and viewports, the firm keeps the model manageable. Whitman feels that they are able to eliminate many of the inconsistencies that crop up in disconnected drawings.

Whitman also uses ASG's Model Vision for viewing models. Model Vision enables the firm to view a project with realistic full- color smooth shading, shadows, and materials that are "texture mapped" onto surfaces. "Quick and dirty" images can be made for design studies, while much more carefully polished renderings are made for client presentations. Model Vision can also create animated walkthroughs of a building that can be replayed on the computer or stored on videotape. Whitman has found computer renderings and animations to be equally valuable for finding unforeseen design problems and for helping a client understand a design.

SESSION 2

Placing Doors and Windows in the Plan

OBJECTIVE

YOUR NOTES
Use this space for notes about your individual plan.

The object of this session is to place doors and windows in the walls we created in Session One. The finished product of this session is shown in Figure 2–1.

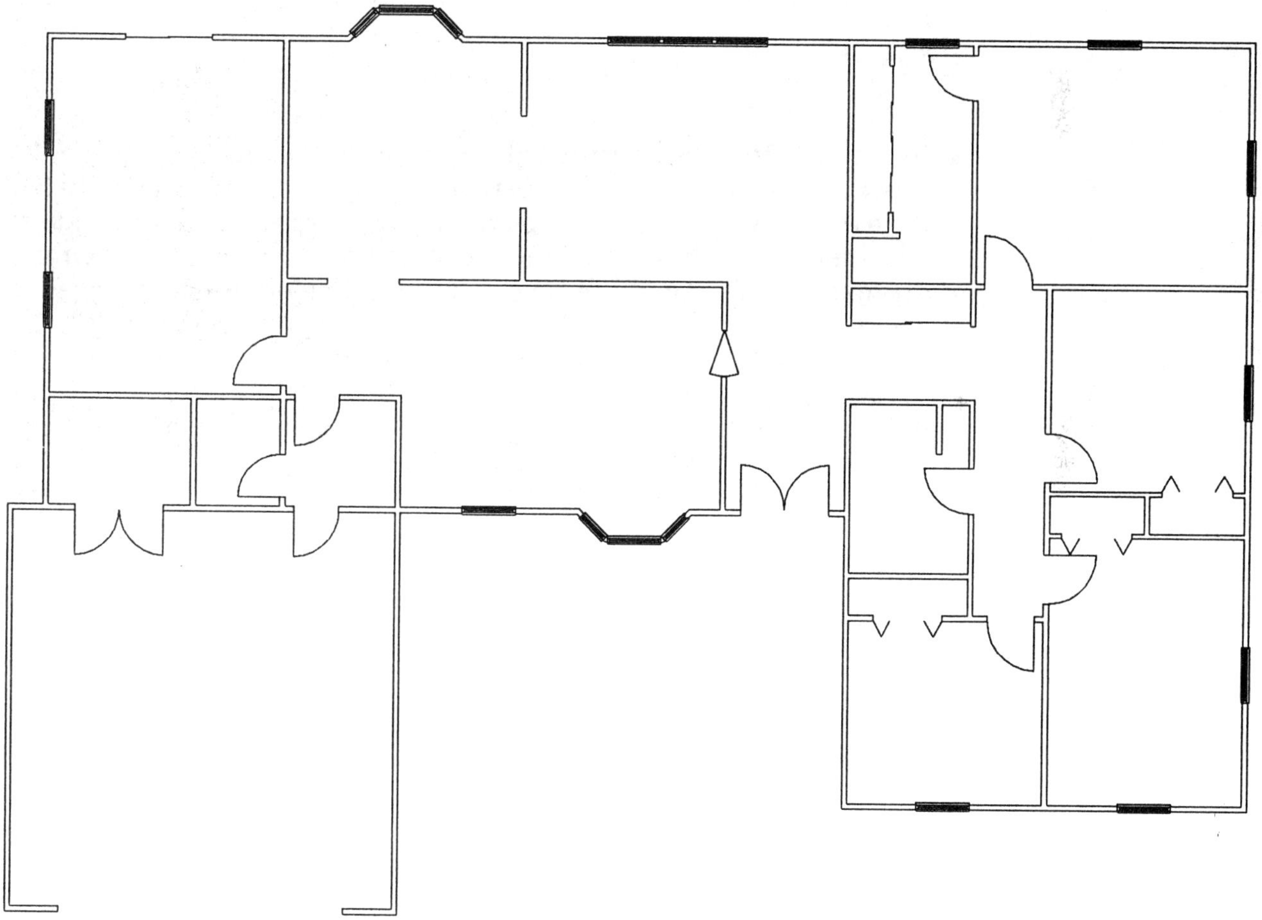

Figure 2-1

YOUR NOTES

Commands used in this session:

base
block
change
insert
ltscale
move
regen
rotate
scale
wblock

In Session One, we constructed all the walls for the floor plan. We constructed walls without doors and windows because it is more efficient to create the walls first, then create the openings in them for the doors and windows. Several techniques can be used to create the openings. These techniques are made up of several individual methodologies. If you understand the methodologies, you can use the combination that works best in each particular drawing situation.

Before we begin, let's establish our objectives. Each window is dimensioned to its center line. We should be able to place a window that is referenced to its center line.

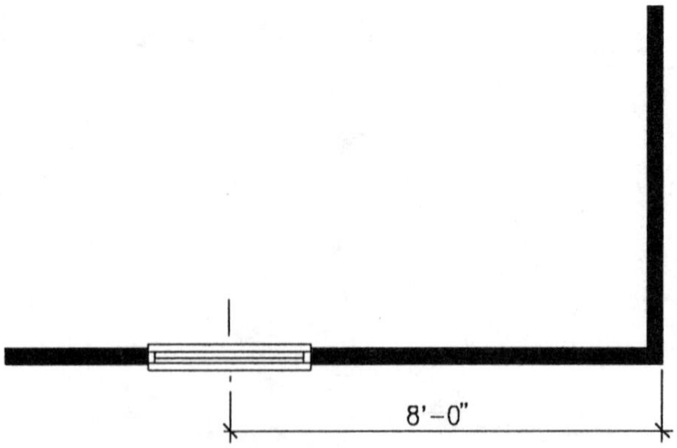

Figure 2-2

Doors are placed at a specified distance from a reference point in the drawing. If no dimension is present and the door is shown next to a

YOUR NOTES

wall intersection, a 4" to 8" offset from the intersection is usually used. We want to be able to place the door at any specified distance from a given point.

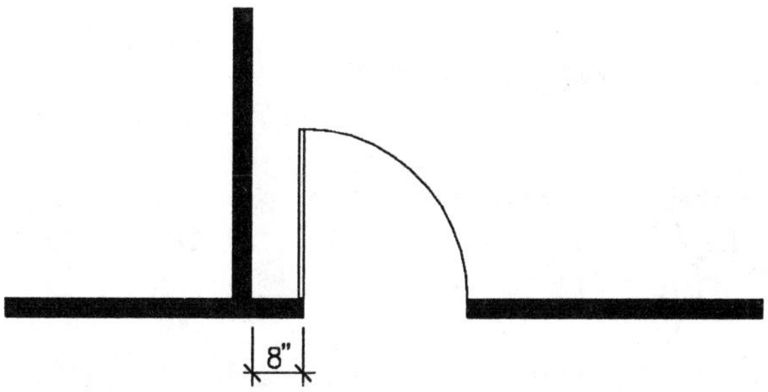

Figure 2-3

Simple doors have four door-swing possibilities: left- or right-hand, and into the room or out of it.

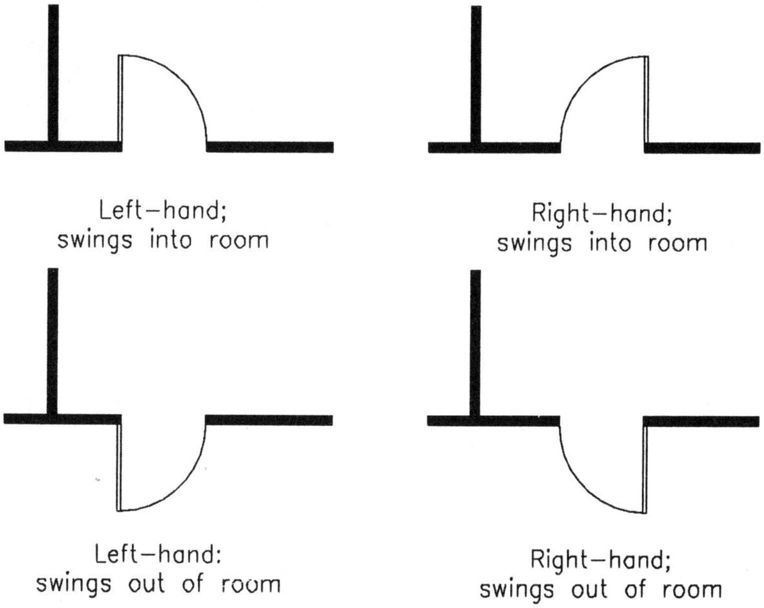

Figure 2-4

The wall must be "broken" where the door or window is placed. If we plan to hatch the walls later, we must make sure that the remaining wall segment and the door and window jambs form perfect intersections. We

YOUR NOTES

also need to be able to "freeze" the layer containing the doors and windows without leaving the wall ends open.

To meet all of our objectives, we must carefully plan the methodologies we will use to place our doors and windows. Let's begin by looking at the methodologies available to us.

INSERTING WINDOWS

The most efficient way to place several windows in a plan is to create a block that can be inserted at each location. The method used to construct the window from which the block is formed is very important.

The window must fit the opening perfectly. If it does not, extra steps will be required to create perfect intersections for the wall hatch. The ends of the jamb must be exactly the same as the wall width. Our windows will be placed into a 2x4 wall, so the width will be 3 1/2". Figure 2–5 shows a window block we will use with our plan.

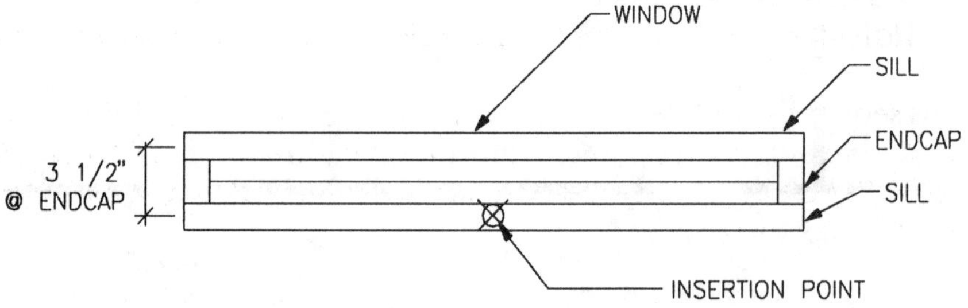

Figure 2-5

This window is a resident block named WDW1 in the prototype drawing. The window is 36" wide and has both interior and exterior sills. The circle in Figure 2–5 shows the insertion point. The insertion point is located at the center of the window horizontally and at the exterior wall line vertically. The insertion point (defined as the "base point") is located at the position shown so that different methodologies for placement can be used.

Locating Window Positions

Let's try locating some windows in a wall. We will practice on a work disk drawing named WDPLAN1 (Window and Door Plan One) before

YOUR NOTES

we begin drawing on the floor plan we constructed in Session One. Start by entering WDPLAN1 now.

If we want our floor plan to be accurate, we must place the windows at the exact points shown by the dimensions on the plans. To do this, we must first locate the center point of the window opening in our plan. Then we can insert the center point of the window at that exact location.

An accurate method of doing this is to use the reference function to locate a point on the wall line where the base point of the window should go. For example, you can locate the insertion base point of a window that is 5'–0" from a corner by using the following sequence (see Figure 2–6).

Command: **insert**
Block name (or ?): **wdw1**
Insertion point: **(ref)**
Reference point: **int**
of *Select point 1.*
Enter relative/polar coordinates (with @): **@-5'<0**
X scale factor <1> / Corner / XYZ: **1**
Y scale factor (default=X): **1**
Rotation angle <0>: *Use input device to rotate to proper position.*

Try this sequence for placing the window in the plan named WDPLAN1. After you have performed the insertion, use Undo to undo the window insertion. Then practice by placing windows on both walls, at different distances from the corner.

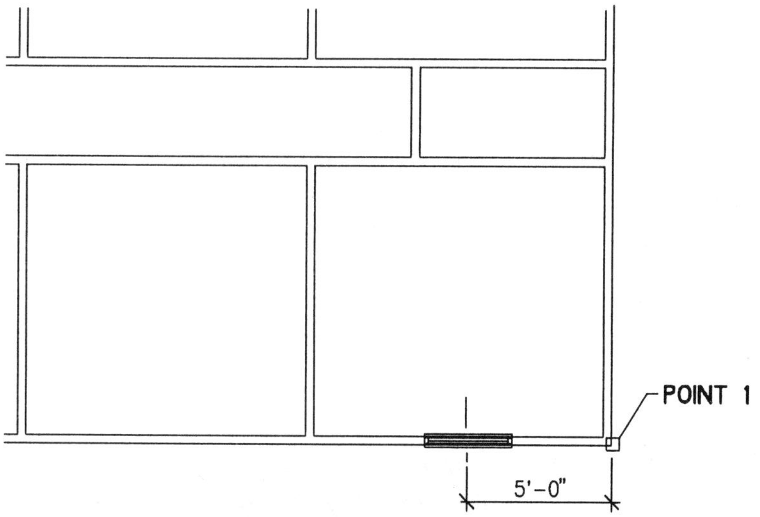

Figure 2-6

YOUR NOTES

Let's look at another method that has some particular advantages. This method uses point entities and the node object snap mode.

Let's use the last example. First, Undo the previous window insertion. Then place a point at the center line of the window location (see Figure 2–8). Use the following command sequence.

Command: **point**
Point: **(ref)**
Reference point: **int**
of *Select point 1.*
Enter relative/polar coordinates (with @): **@-5'<0**

You have just placed a point entity located 5'–0" to the left of the corner.

We will now insert the window. We will use the node object snap mode to "capture" the exact center point of the window location. Note that the point is hidden by the wall line. Since it is difficult to capture a point when it is located on a line, we can use the Setvar command and the variable pdmode to make the point visible. The pdmode is currently set to a value of 0 in the drawing. Let's use the following command sequence to change pdmode.

Command: **setvar**
Variable name or ?: **pdmode**
New value for PDMODE: **35**

Now, use the Regen command to regenerate the drawing and look at the point. The point has changed to a "target." Now you can see the point easily. You may use the pdsize variable of the Setvar command to adjust the size of the new point type. The aperture varible can be used to increase the size of the aperture box to make point selection easier. The size is listed in pixels and will vary according to the display type we are using. Adjust the variable settings according to your own drawing preferences.

You can change the points back to dots before the drawing is plotted. Do not erase the points, because we will use them later. The dots will not be visible on the plot, since they are superimposed on the wall and window lines.

YOUR NOTES

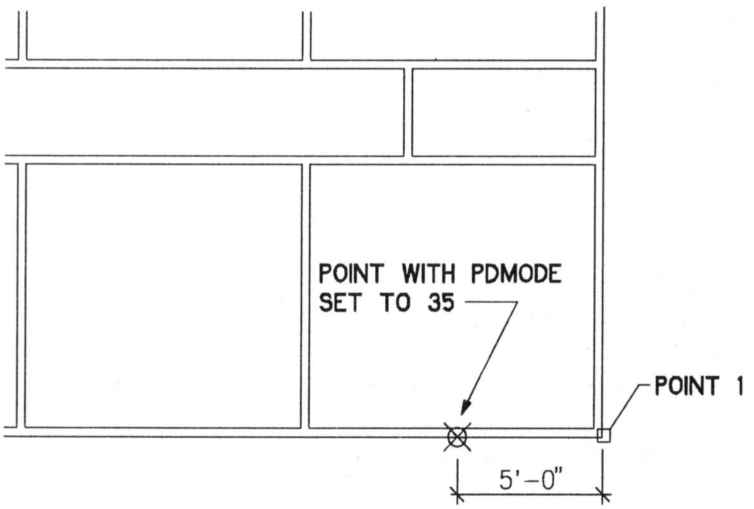

Figure 2-7

All the points you place in the drawing now will appear as targets. The Regen command is only necessary if you have changed the pdmode or pdsize and want to update the display to show the new point type or size.

Now use Insert to place the block WDW1 into the wall using object snap node to capture the points.

Placing Multiple Windows

Using points as placement markers has other advantages. If you have a series of evenly spaced windows, you can array the first point along a wall to create several quick and easy reference points. You may also use the Copy command to place the new point at the next window center line. For example, to copy a point 10′ "up," enter @10′<90 in response to the <Base point or displacement>/Multiple: prompt in the Copy command.

Verify that ortho is on. Place another reference point 12′ to the left of the last point. Insert a window at that location, as shown in Figure 2–8 (remember to use object snap node).

YOUR NOTES

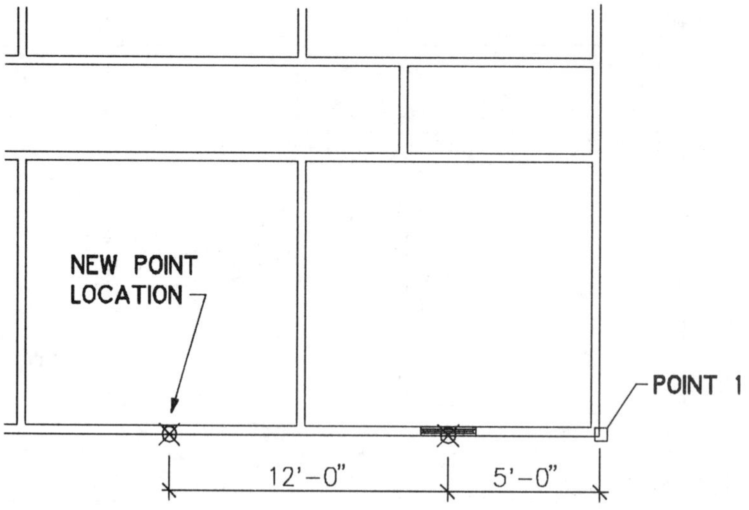

Figure 2-8

When you are finished, convert the points back to "dots" by changing the value of variable pdmode back to 0. Then perform a Regen.

The point method of window placement is recommended if you plan to dimension the plan at a later time. To dimension to the center line of the window, just use object snap node to locate the extension line. The dimension line will be perfectly placed at the window center line. We will use this method when we dimension the plan in Session Four.

Trimming the Wall

Now that we have placed the windows in our practice drawing, it is time to create the openings in the wall lines. It is efficient to use the Trim command to create the openings.

The window drawing was designed to create a line at the jambs for trimming purposes. Since we can't use a block as a cutting edge, use the Explode command to break the window block into single components. Use the jamb lines as cutting edges (see Figure 2–9) and trim the wall lines from the window area. Note that once the window block has been

YOUR NOTES

exploded, the insertion point can no longer be used as a reference point for other windows.

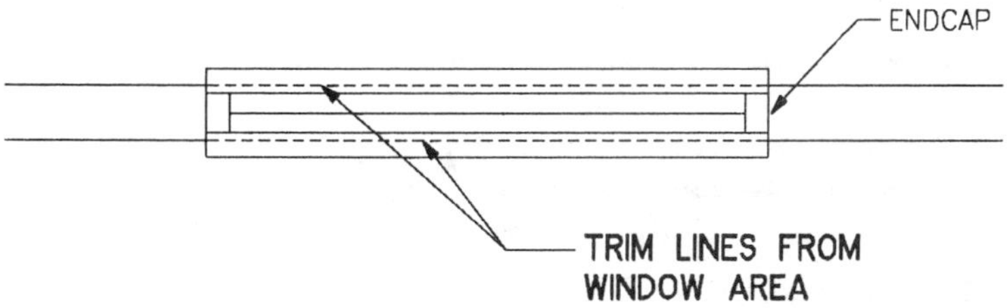

Figure 2-9

ALTERNATE WINDOW PLACEMENT METHODS

Often, it is not necessary to place windows in such an exact manner. You may be drawing a design plan that you do not intend to convert to a construction drawing. You may even need a quicker method to place a window so that you can "play" with some ideas. In these cases, you may use polylines to create "filled" walls to save time.

Let's try some methods of placing windows less precisely. First, if you are still in WDPLAN1, use Quit to exit the drawing. Use the work disk drawing WDPLAN2 (Window and Door Plan Two) for this exercise. This plan is drawn with polylines.

Using the Break Command

Insert the block WDW1 outside of a wall as shown in Figure 2–10. Next, use the Break command to create an opening in the wall for the window.

Create the opening by selecting the wall under the Break command, then entering F to reselect the first point. Line up the screen crosshairs with each end of the inserted window to locate the first and second break points.

Next, use the Move command to move the window into position. Ortho will help if the movement is in a true *X* or *Y* direction (instead of, for example, along a diagonal wall).

YOUR NOTES

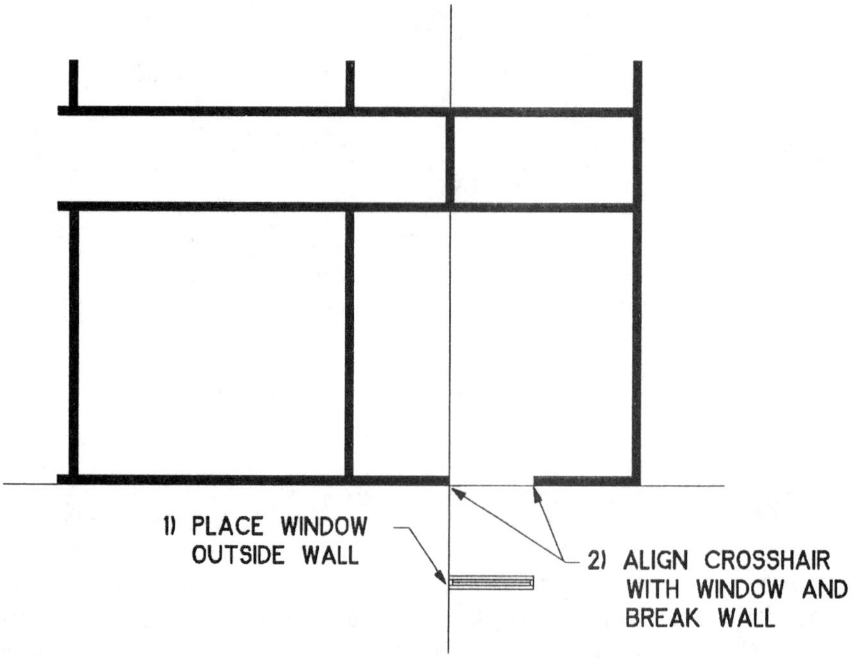
1) PLACE WINDOW
OUTSIDE WALL
2) ALIGN CROSSHAIR
WITH WINDOW AND
BREAK WALL

Figure 2-10

Using a Trim Box

Another method is to use a "trim box." You can construct a trim box by drawing a box with a Polyline. The box should be the same width as the window. (You may want to construct several boxes; one for each window width. Just insert the appropriate box, then explode it for use as a trim box). Use this box with the Trim command to create the window opening in the wall. Let's take a look at how this works.

The box in the corner room in drawing WDPLAN2 has been constructed as a trim box. Referring to Figure 2–11, Insert WDW1 just outside the wall. Move the box to a position over the wall as shown.

Now select the Trim command and pick the box as a cutting edge. Since you constructed it with a Polyline, you only have to point to any part of it (or select previous after moving it) to select the box as a cutting edge. Trim the wall from the interior of the box.

YOUR NOTES

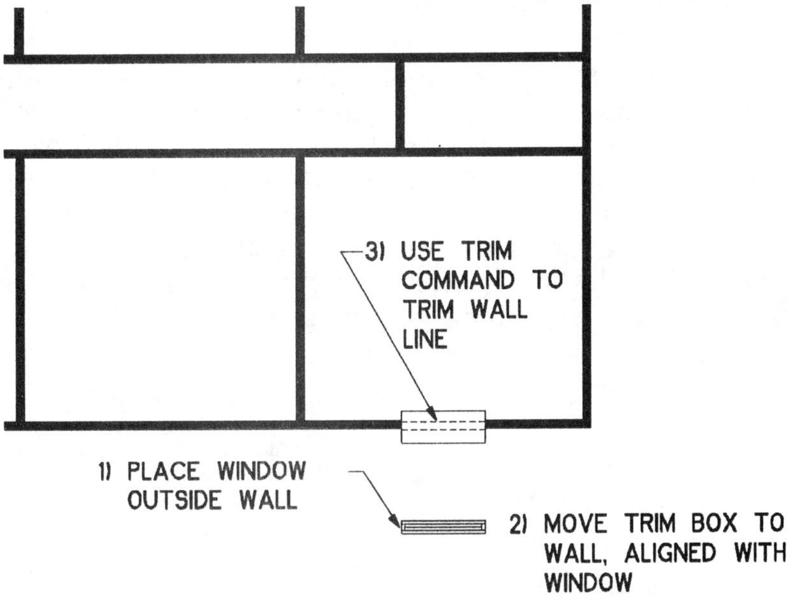
3) USE TRIM COMMAND TO TRIM WALL LINE
1) PLACE WINDOW OUTSIDE WALL
2) MOVE TRIM BOX TO WALL, ALIGNED WITH WINDOW

Figure 2-11

Now move the box to another location (or to the next window location) and move the window into place in the wall.

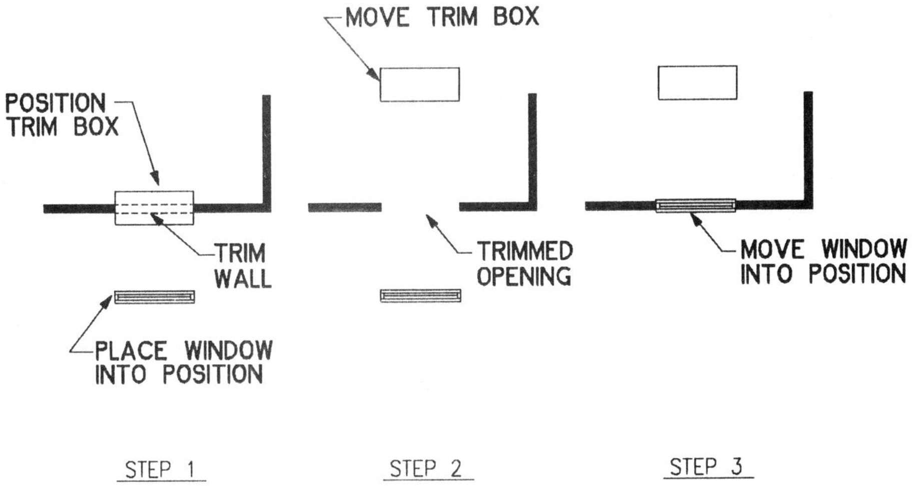
MOVE TRIM BOX
POSITION TRIM BOX
TRIM WALL
PLACE WINDOW INTO POSITION
TRIMMED OPENING
MOVE WINDOW INTO POSITION
STEP 1
STEP 2
STEP 3

Figure 2-12

YOUR NOTES

Using a Simplified Window Block

You can use yet another method of window placement if you do not wish to place a hatch in the wall. Figure 2–13 shows a window that is designed to fit into the wall without breaking the wall lines. The figure shows the window design with the window both inside and outside the wall to show how this can work. Constructing and placing a window of this design eliminates the necessity of breaking the wall lines. However, this window design precludes the ability to place a hatch in the wall properly without doing additional editing.

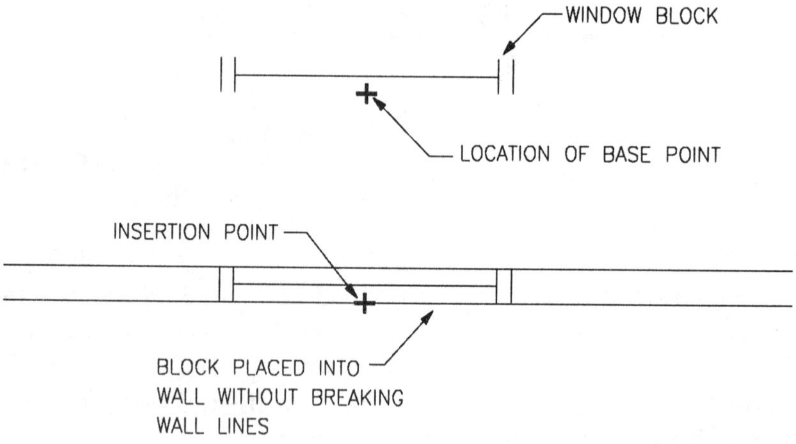

Figure 2-13

CONSTRUCTING A WINDOW FOR INSERTION

When you draw a window for insertion into a wall, you should consider several objectives.

As we will see later, hatching is easier if we can eliminate everything from the drawing except the wall lines. We accomplish this by placing the wall lines on their own layer and freezing, or turning off, all the other layers. Part of the window (the end lines) must remain to endcap the walls after the layer containing the windows is turned off or frozen. When you draw the window, place the end lines on the FLPLAN layer, which contains the wall lines. Place all other lines of the window on the layer you specified for windows. When you insert and explode the window, the lines will reside on the correct layers.

YOUR NOTES

When you draw the sill lines, use separate line segments where the sills connect to the end lines of the window (see Figure 2–14). This allows you to place the endcaps on the FLPLAN layer and the rest of the window on the WINDOWS layer. This permits the end line to form a perfect intersection with the wall lines after you explode and trim the window insertion.

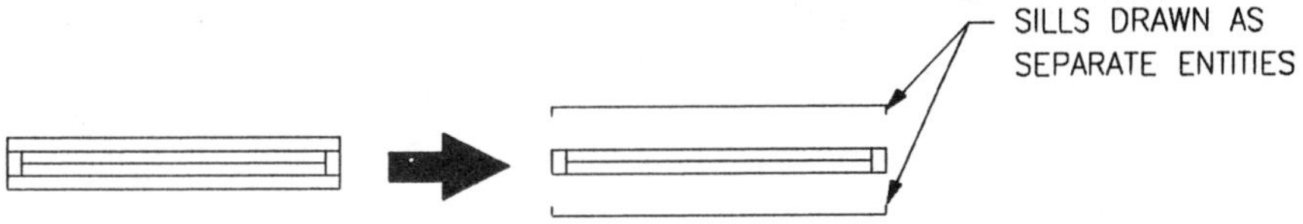

Figure 2-14

A window is best drawn in the actual drawing, using a constructed wall section as a guide. For accuracy, always use relative or polar coordinates for distances. Use object snap to draw the end lines between the wall lines (nearest for the From point: prompt and perpendicular for the To point: prompt.

When you create the block, place the base point on the wall line. Center it in the width of the window, as shown in Figure 2–13.

INSERTING DOORS

The methods for inserting doors into a drawing are similar to those for inserting windows. The same methodology for placement and wall line breaks can be applied.

Using the Reference Function

Most door placements can be performed by using the Reference function. Let's try inserting a door in our practice floor plan. Start the practice drawing named WDPLAN1. Use the following command sequence to insert a block named DOOR1 from the work disk (see Figure 2–15).

YOUR NOTES

Command: **insert**
Block Name (or ?): **door1**
Insertion point: **(ref)**
Reference point: **int**
of *Select point 1.*
Enter relative/polar coordinates (with @): **@4"<0**
X scale factor <1 /Corner / XYZ: ↵
Y scale factor (default=X): ↵
Rotation angle <0>: ↵

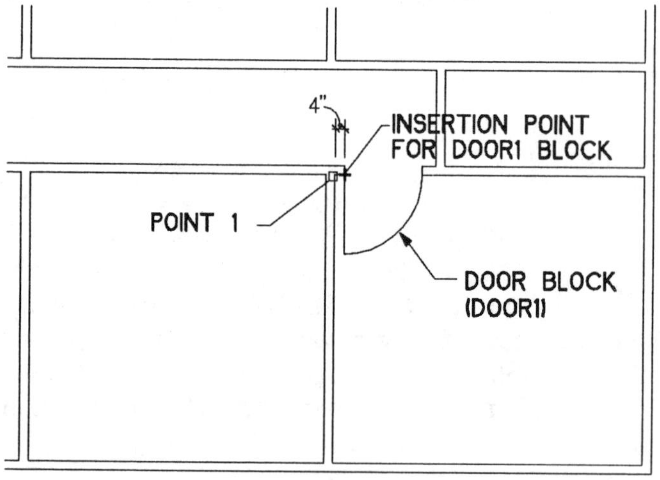

Figure 2-15

Now explode the door block and trim the wall lines. If you have a color display, you can see that the door and the endcaps are on different layers. The door is on the DOORS layer, and the endcaps are on the FLPLAN layer. This, again, is because we want all the wall lines and endcaps on the same layer.

One difference between window blocks and door blocks is orientation. As we discussed earlier, doors can have several orientations. It is easy to use the Mirror command on a door, but mirroring precludes exploding the block for trimming purposes. To avoid this, you can use doors of two orientations. These orientations are designated as "left-hand" and "right-hand" doors. An easy way to remember the difference is to think of entering a doorway with the door swinging away from you (see Figure 2–16). The hand you use to open the door is the "door hand" (left or right).

YOUR NOTES

Figure 2-16

Alternate Door Placement Methods

If you are using AutoCAD to create a design drawing, you may not need a precise door placement. If this is the case, you can place the door by inserting the door block outside the wall, lined up with the desired location. Then use the Break command to break an opening for the door. This is similar to the method you practiced for placing simple windows in a design drawing or in a plan in which the walls will not be hatched.

With doors, an additional method can be used for sizing. If the original drawing of the door is constructed so that the actual door length is 1", the door can be inserted as any size. To do this, draw a door that is 1" wide in plan. The door swing arc will also have a 1" radius. When you insert the door, you will be prompted for the *X-scale* factor. Simply enter the door width, in inches, as the scale factor. When you are prompted for the *Y-scale* factor, press ↵, since the *Y-scale* default is equal to the *X-scale* factor.

For example, if your door size is 3'–0", use 36 as the *X-scale* factor. The door will be inserted to the exact size you specify. Note that you cannot use endcaps with this type of insertion, since the endcaps will scale incorrectly for the wall width.

INSERTING DOORS AND WINDOWS IN YOUR DRAWING

Practice time is over. It is time to place all the doors and windows in your drawing!

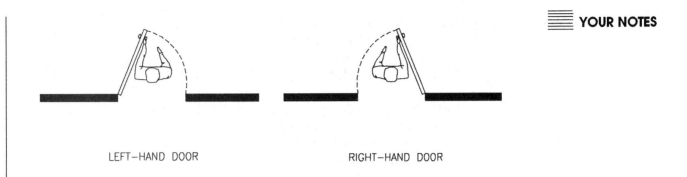

YOUR NOTES

STEP 1 *Getting Started*

Start the FLPLAN1 drawing you constructed in Session One. Use the Time command to turn on the timer. Zoom into the bedroom area of the plan. Figure 2–17 shows the dimensions for the windows on the end wall.

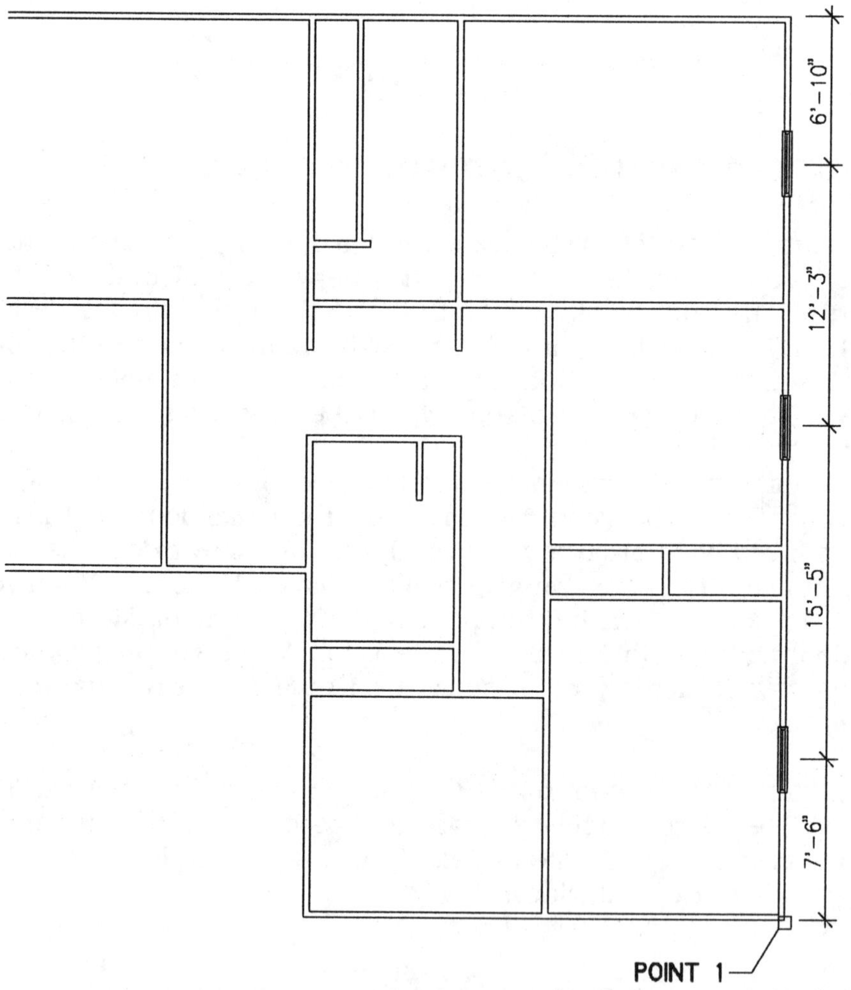

Figure 2-17

Let's put windows in the wall. (Refer to the window dimensioning plan in Appendix I as necessary.)

YOUR NOTES

STEP 2 *Placing the First Window*

Let's start by placing a point at the window location for bedroom 3. Use the following command sequence, referring to Figure 2–18.

Command: **point**
Point: **(ref)**
Reference point: **int**
of *Select point 1.*
Enter relative/polar coordinates (with @): **@7'6"<90**

The point is hard to see. Use the Setvar command to change the pdmode setting to 35, as you did during practice. Now Regenerate the drawing. The point should now be visible.

Let's set the second and third points by using a multiple Copy command.

Command: **copy**
Select objects: **last**
1 found
Select objects: ↵
<Base point or displacement>/Multiple: **m**
Base point: **nod**
of *Select the point entity.*
Second point of displacement: **@15'5"<90**
Second point of displacement: **@27'8"<90**

Now Insert the block named WDW1. Explode the block and trim the wall lines for the windows you just inserted, as you did in the practice drawing.

STEP 3 *Completing the Wall*

Repeat the insert sequence for each of the other two points you just placed. When you are finished, you should have three windows in the end wall of the building, as shown in Figure 2–18.

Next, change the pdmode back to 0. Finally, regenerate the drawing. The points will regenerate to the new value of 0, displaying as single "dots."

YOUR NOTES

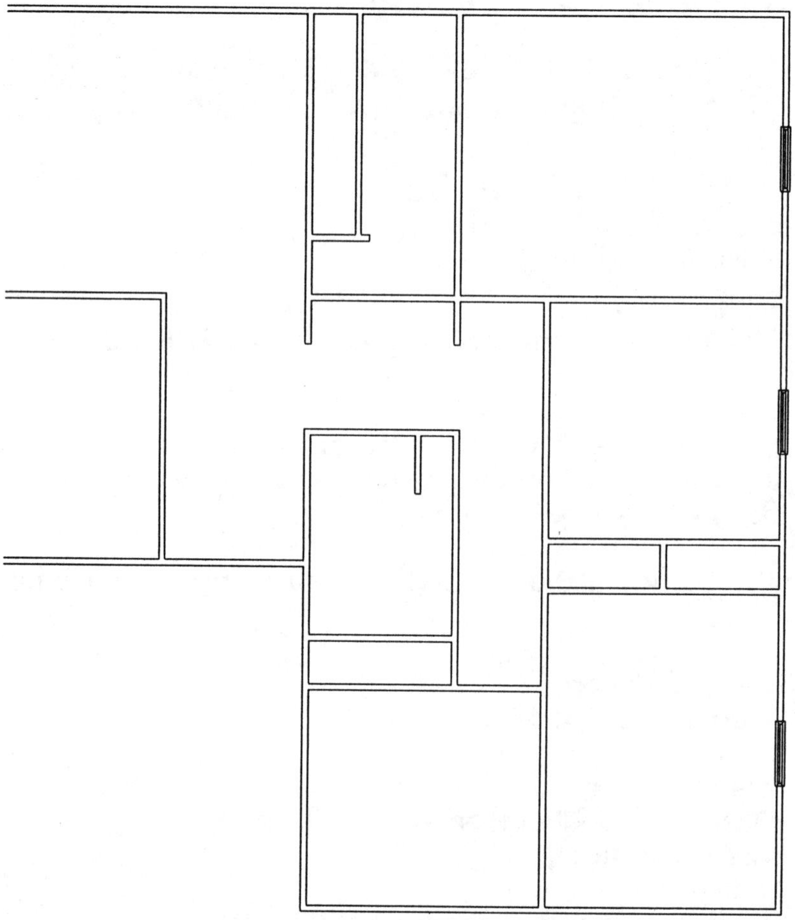

Figure 2-18

STEP 4 *Inserting the First Door*

Now let's insert a door. We will insert the door from the hallway into the master bedroom. You will notice that the door is inserted with attributes. We are going to use these attributes to construct a door schedule right on the drawing! If your display system is capable of displaying dialogue boxes (it is if you can activate pull-down menus), you can set the attribute values with a dialogue box. To do this, use the Setvar command as follows.

Command: **setvar**
Variable name or ?: **attdia**
New value for ATTDIA <0>: **1**

YOUR NOTES

The following command sequence will step you through the process, including the response to attribute prompts. If your display system does not display dialogue boxes, the values will appear on the command line at the bottom of the screen. (If you wish to set up your own attributes, follow the explanation given at the end of this session.) Refer to Figure 2–19 as you proceed.

Command: **insert**
Block name (or ?): **dr2-81**
Insertion point: **(ref)**
Reference point: **int**
of *Select point 1.*
Enter relative/polar coordinates (with @): **@6"<0**
X scale factor <1>/Corner/XYZ: ↵
Y scale factor (default=X): ↵
Rotation angle <0>: 90

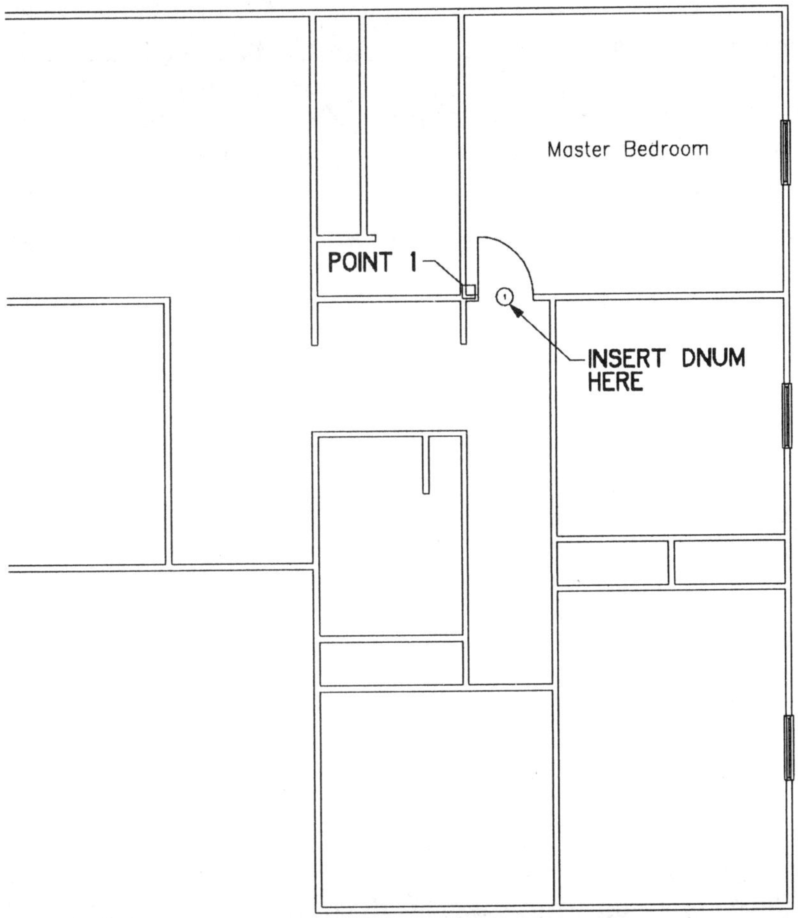

Figure 2-19

YOUR NOTES

Notice that you can rotate the door block with your input device (mouse, digitizer, etc.) when you are prompted for the rotation angle. If you are placing a door in a wall that is oriented either horizontally or vertically, use ortho for accuracy.

After you have placed the door into position, use the Explode command to explode the block. You must do this if you want to use the door entities as cutting edges when you edit the wall opening.

STEP 5 *Inserting the Door Icon*

Next, insert the door icon approximately in the middle of the wall opening. The icon is a circle with a door number in the center. We will use the door numbers to create a table showing the door size, height, thickness, and so on. The door icon to be inserted is a resident block in the drawing and is named DNUM (Door Number).

After the last insertion command prompt, a dialogue box will appear on the screen (see Figure 2–20). (Again, if your display system is not capable of displaying a dialogue box, or if you do not have the variable ATTDIA set to 1, the attribute dialogue will appear on the command line at the bottom of the screen.)

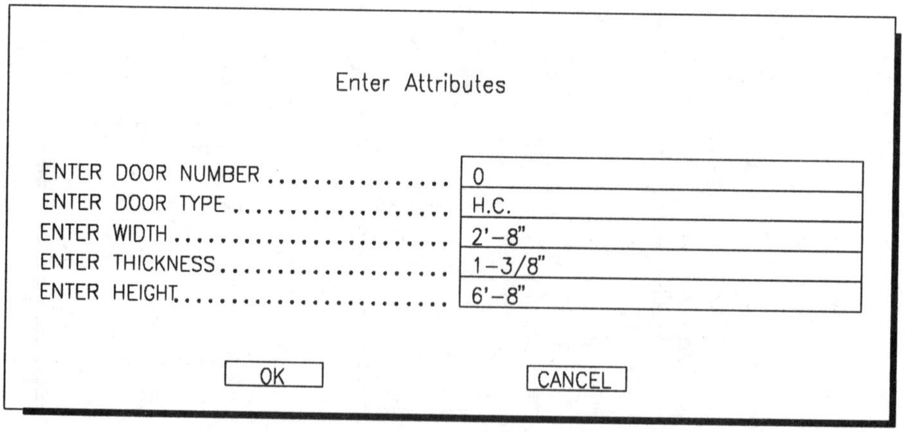

Figure 2-20

From the dialogue box, use your input device to click on the 0 that shows up as the door number. Enter 1 and click on the OK box that is displayed to the right of the ENTER DOOR NUMBER line. We will accept the rest of the door values. Click on the OK box at the bottom of the dialogue box. The door icon will appear on the drawing, with the door number shown in the circle.

YOUR NOTES

STEP 6 *Completing the Doors and Windows*

It is time to finish placing the doors and windows in your drawing. Proceed, using the procedures you have just learned. Insert a door icon for each door, changing the door number each time you insert a number icon. Your next door is number 2; the next is 3, and so forth.

Doors to insert are included as resident blocks in the prototype drawing. They are named according to door width and swing. For example, a 2′–8" left-hand door is named DR2–8L (Door, 2′–8", left hand). Figure 2-21 shows the door swing designations, as well as "specialty" doors, such as bifold, bypass, and exterior doors. A door and window key plan, showing specific door locations and designations, is provided in Appendix I. Use this plan as a guide for placing doors in your plan. Insertion points are shown in Figure 2–21 and in Appendix L. After inserting each door, insert the door number icon named DNUM and set the attributes.

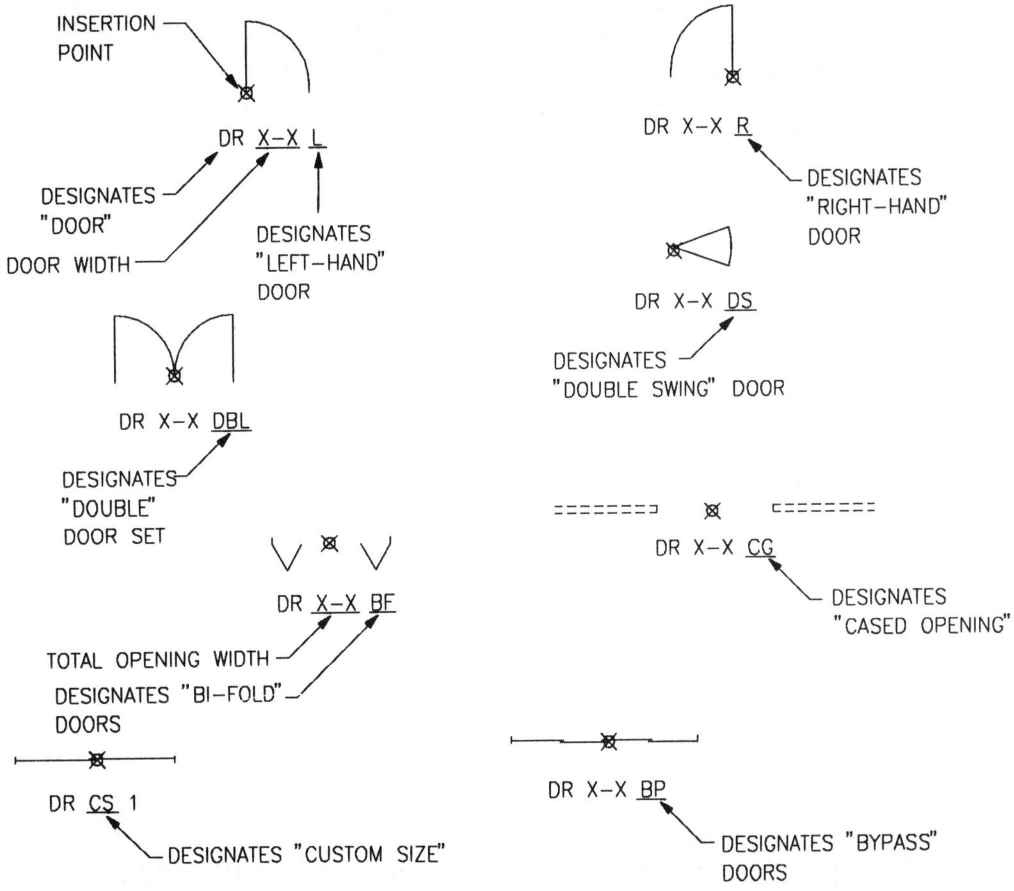

Figure 2-21

YOUR NOTES

CONSTRUCTING THE DOOR SCHEDULE

Before we can construct the door schedule, we must extract, into a file, the attributes associated with the door insertions. To do this, we will use a predefined template file named DOORS.TXT.

STEP 7 *Constructing the Extract File*

Use the following command sequence to construct the extract file.

Command: **attext**
CDF,SDF OR DXF attribute extract (for Entities) <C>: **s**
Template file: **a:doors**
Extract file name: **sched1.txt**
22 records in extract file

This command sequence causes a text file to be written to disk. The text file contains a list of the door attributes. It can be used to construct a door schedule on the drawings. Because our floor plan sheet fills most of the sheet, we will be placing the door schedule on the building section sheet.

To see the contents of the extract file you made, use the following command sequence now.

Command: **type**
File to list: **sched1.txt**

You should see a listing that shows the door number, type, width, thickness, and height in a column format.

USING BLOCKS WITH ATTRIBUTES

It is very easy to create attributes to be associated with blocks. Attributes are useful when you want to maintain database-type information with the drawing, because the attributes are stored in the blocks. AutoCAD's attribute capabilities can be used to store serial numbers for furniture shown in institutional floor plans, information about parts used in an assembly, data for doors and windows in construction drawings, and so on.

Defining Tags

YOUR NOTES

Before you can to store the attributes, you must define categories, or tags. After you define a tag, you can choose a prompt to be displayed when the block containing the attributes is inserted. Attributes can be visible or invisible on the drawing. You may wish to review the attributes section of the AutoCAD reference manual to become more proficient before you attempt to design blocks with attributes for your own use.

The DNUM drawing was created with attributes. First, the circle was drawn. Then, the Attdef command was used to create the tags. Attdef must be used for each tag. For example, the following command sequence was used to create the tag named Height (see Figure 2–22).

> Command: **attdef**
> Attribute modes -- Invisible:**n** Constant:**n** Verify:**n** Preset: **n**
> Enter (ICVP) to change, RETURN when done: ↵
> Attribute tag: **height**
> Attribute prompt: **enter door height**
> Default attribute value: **6'–8"**
> Start point or Align/Center/Fit/Middle/Right/Style:*Select point 1.*
> Rotation angle <0>: **0**

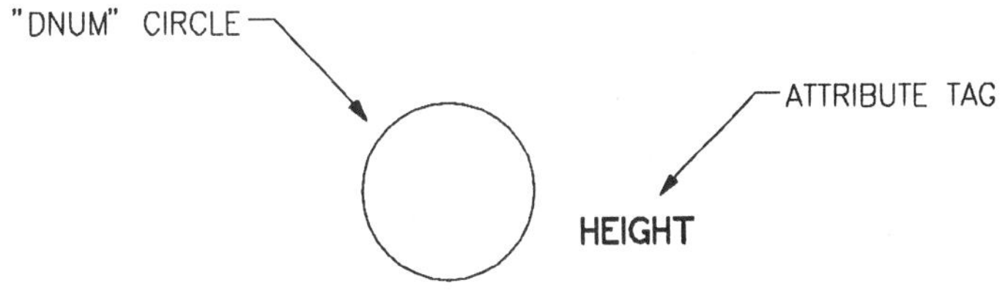

Figure 2-22

CREATING THE BLOCKS

The circle and the tags were then blocked together, then write-blocked to disk (using the Wblock command) as the desired file name. You can also save the drawing as a whole and insert it into another drawing (don't forget to use the Base command to set the insertion point).

YOUR NOTES

The door and number icon were not blocked together for three reasons. First, if the door were rotated, the door number would not be vertically oriented. Also, if the door block were exploded for trimming purposes, the attribute tags would become visible. Finally, we may want to insert all of the doors first, then place the icons with the doors in a particular order.

When you insert a drawing containing attributes into another drawing, AutoCAD prompts for the values of each tag. The variable setting Attdia determines whether a dialogue box is displayed when a drawing containing attributes is inserted. A setting of 0 suppresses the dialogue box and a setting of 1 displays it. If your display system cannot display dialogue boxes, or if the ATTDIA is set to 0, the prompts will appear on the command line at the bottom of the screen.

Extracting Attributes from the Drawing

To extract the attributes from the drawing, use the Attext command. The extract is in the form of a text file. To obtain an extraction, you will need a template file. This template file determines the order and spacing in which the attribute information will be written. The template file named DOORS.TXT, which is contained on the work disk, assigns the following attributes.

NUMBER	N005000
TYPE	C008000
WIDTH	N010000
THICKNESS	N008000
HEIGHT	N008000

You may wish to review attribute template files in the AutoCAD reference manual.

The output text file is in ASCII text format. A sample listing for a door schedule follows.

1	H.C.	2′-8"	1-3/8"	6′-8"
2	H.C.	2′-6"	1-3/8"	6′-8"
3	H.C.	3′-0"	1-3/8"	6′-8"
4	H.C.	2′-8"	1-3/8"	6′-8"

YOUR NOTES

This text file can be printed, merged into a spreadsheet, or placed back into your drawing using a supplied AutoCAD utility. The file you extracted from the door blocks will be used in Session Six to create a door schedule on the section sheet.

YOUR NOTES

SUMMARY

- Doors and windows are inserted after all the walls have been drawn and finalized.
- Doors and windows should be located on their own layers.
- Placement of windows is critical, since their locations are dimensioned.
- Openings are "cut" in the walls for doors and windows. If the wall is to be hatched later, an endcap must be placed precisely at the edge of each wall opening. The endcaps should be part of the door or window block, but they should reside on the walls layer.
- When you create door and window drawings for insertion, place the entities on the correct layers (do not use layer 0). The drawings will "float" to the correct layer in the drawing into which they are inserted. If the proper layers do not exist in the target drawing, they will be created automatically.
- Attributes may be associated with any block for recordkeeping purposes.

QUESTIONS

YOUR NOTES

1. How many door swing possibilities are there?

2. Why should door and window end jambs form a perfect intersection with the wall lines? Why should they reside on the same layer as the wall lines?

3. How would a design drawing benefit from using a simplified window block?

4. When you create a window block, why is the location of the base point important?

YOUR NOTES

5. Why would you insert the door number icon as a separate operation?

6. What is the advantage of using attributes with the door and window icons?

7. Why should doors and windows reside on their own layers?

PROBLEMS

YOUR NOTES

1. Create your own window block and insert it into a sample wall. You may use any of the methods discussed in this session.

2. Create blocks of each door swing type. Place the doors in sample wall sections you create.

3. Create a simple floor plan and place doors and windows into it.

AutoCAD in the Kitchen

Kitchen designer Susan Goldblatt used to draw her designs with a pencil and vellum. It was straightforward--draw a plan and eleva tion; then, if necessary, a few perspective sketches. Then she discovered CADkit from Computer Workstations Inc.

Goldblatt has never used AutoCAD by itself. She feels it would slow her down. CADkit, on the other hand, is geared specifically to designing cabinets and interiors. The software helps in every aspect of her work. She can use it to design a rough layout, then refine the layout by adjusting cabinet dimensions to fit a room. CADkit enables her to switch cabinet door styles by selecting them from a menu--the program can replace all the doors in a kitchen with a single command. Countertops and toekicks can be drawn in seconds. Appliances and plumbing fixtures are selected from menus.

When she has finished a design, Goldblatt can automatically create a list of all the parts of the kitchen--cabinets, coun ters, appliances, fixtures, and accessories--and the software can even produce a dimensioned list of all the pieces of each cabi net, for use in a cabinet shop. She uses the CADkit's cost estimating features to compare the costs of cabinets from different manufacturers.

CADkit's most impressive feature is that it creates fully three- dimensional models while you draw in plan view. Everything--fixtures, upper cabinets, countertops--is automatically placed a the proper height. When you want to see an elevation view of your project, a menu pick will display it--the software had drawn it even if you've never looked at the elevation before. CADkit can also dimension and label all the cabi nets, counters, and accessories automatically in each view. Finished plan and elevation drawings can easily be plotted straight from the 3D model.

Of course, a kitchen model can also be viewed in perspective and rendered with shading software. CADkit draws all its components automatically using a complex layering software. As a result, each part of a cabinet--doors, handles, countertops, toekicks, appliance panels--can be assigned a different color when rendered. Goldblatt is able to create extremely realistic renderings for her clients.

Goldblatt feels that CADkit eliminates the tedious drafting from her work, enabling her to spend more time on design. She's able to create more design alternative and show them off more effectively.

Courtesy of CADKIT

SESSION 3

Creating and Placing Library Symbols

OBJECTIVE

YOUR NOTES

Use this space for notes about your individual plan.

The object of this session is to learn how to create library symbols and place them into your drawing. Placing symbols into a drawing with AutoCAD's Insert command is very simple. However, you should be careful to set up the symbols properly. A good architectural symbol library is very valuable when it has been created in the proper manner.

Figure 3–1 shows the result of this session. Your plan may differ, however, since you are the designer here!

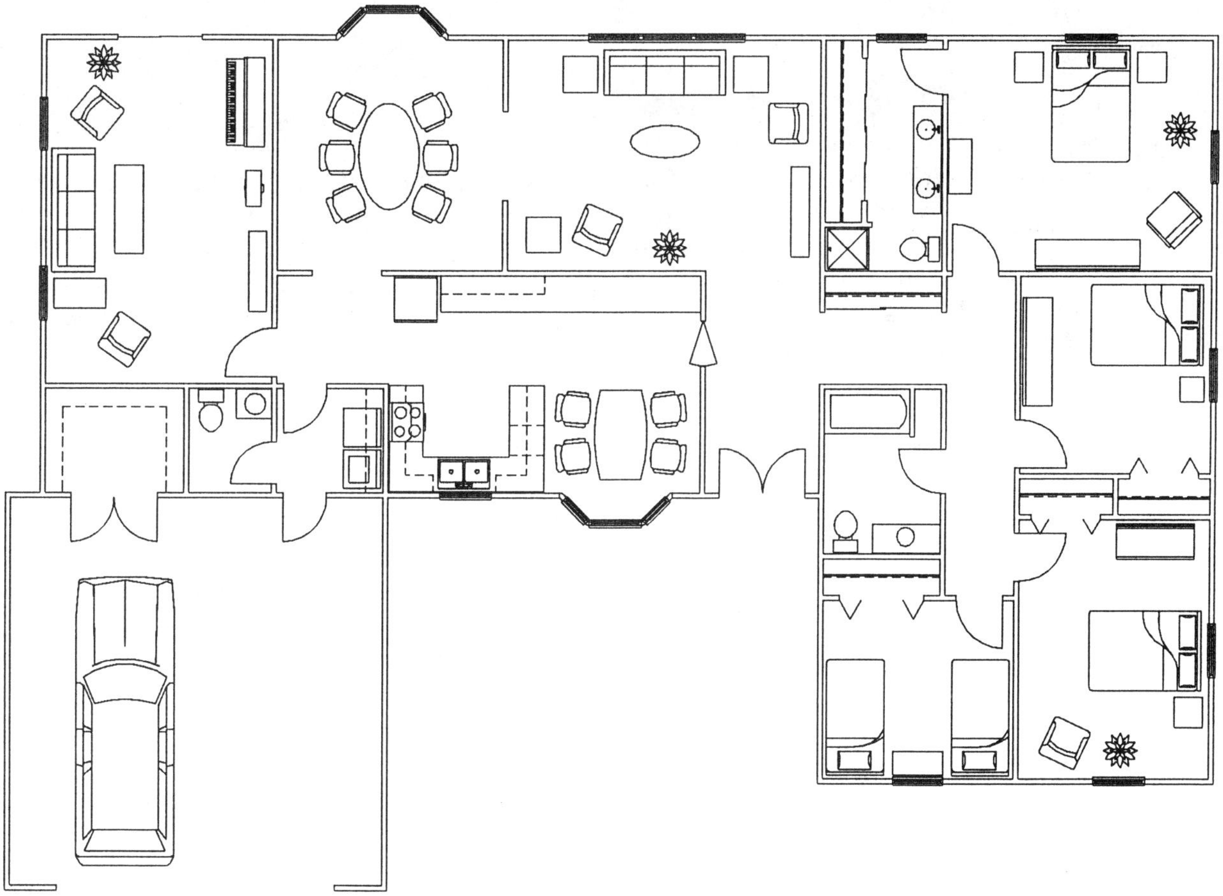

Figure 3-1

YOUR NOTES

Commands used in this session:

base	**move**
block	**regen**
change	**rotate**
insert	**scale**
ltscale	**wblock**

CREATING SYMBOLS

Symbols are created as separate AutoCAD drawings. You use the Insert command to place symbols in your current drawing. Let's look at some points you should consider when you create symbols.

Detail and Layering

You need to consider the size of the final (plotted) drawing when you create symbols for drawing. For example, keys on a piano will not plot clearly on a drawing that is plotted at 1/8"=1'–0". It would be nice, however, to have such detail in the symbol if it were to be plotted at 1/2"=1'–0". One example of this is a plot of a single room that shows a sample furniture layout.

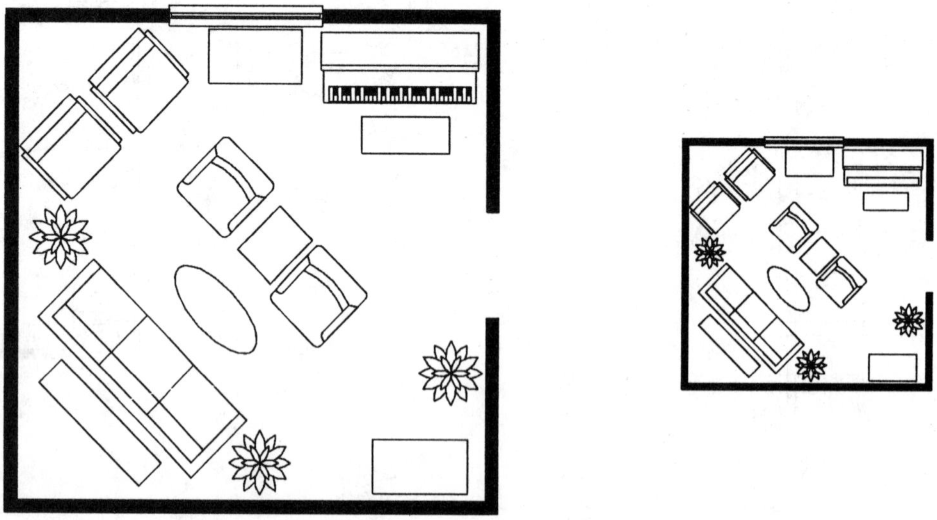

Figure 3-2

YOUR NOTES

Another example is tree symbols. You may want to use the same tree in drawings that are plotted at different scales. A tree in plan view that will be plotted at 1/8"=1'-0" can contain more detail than one that will be plotted at 1"=50'. You must also consider the possibility that the drawing, or part of the drawing, may be plotted at different scales in the future.

The solution to scale differences is to create the symbol on more than one layer. Layering techniques can add great versatility to a symbol library. If the symbol resides on its own layer, you can turn it off when you don't want to see or plot it. This allows you, for example, to use the same floor plan for a furniture layout, base floor plan, and so on. Just turn off the furniture layer when you don't want it!

The detail problem can be resolved by using two separate layers for the symbol. Place the primary details of the symbol on one layer and the secondary details on a second layer. You can freeze the secondary details layer when the plot scale is too small to show them properly. For example, if you wanted to draw the piano referred to earlier, you could create the primary piano details on a layer named FURNITURE. You could then place the piano keys on a layer named FURNDET (Furniture Detail).

When you insert the piano symbol into another drawing, the layers will be updated (layers named FURNITURE and FURNDET will be added) and the symbol will be placed on the two layers. You now have the ability to freeze the layer containing the intricate detailing for a small scale plot or a check plot.

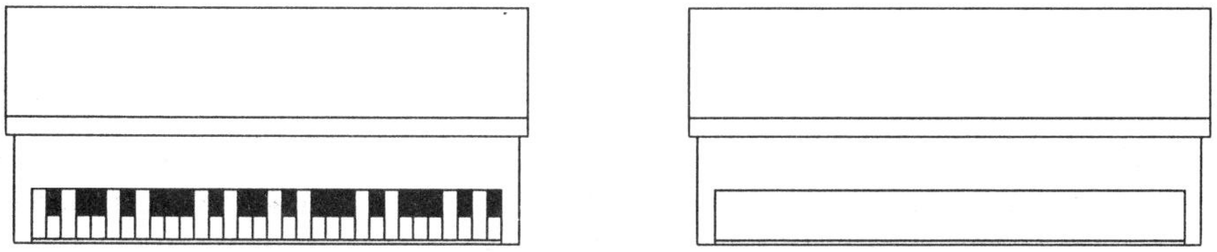

Figure 3-3

YOUR NOTES

You can use a third layer to speed up the symbol insertion process. You should set up this layer when you first create the symbol. Create a layer named OUTLINE. Make the outline layer the current layer and draw a simple polyline around the perimeter of the symbol. When you insert the first symbol into another drawing, freeze the symbol and symbol detail layers, leaving only the outline layer (in addition to your previously defined drawing layers) showing on the screen. This will allow you to zoom, pan, and place symbols in the drawing without regenerating the symbols and details. You can think of this as the symbol equivalent to the Qtext command.

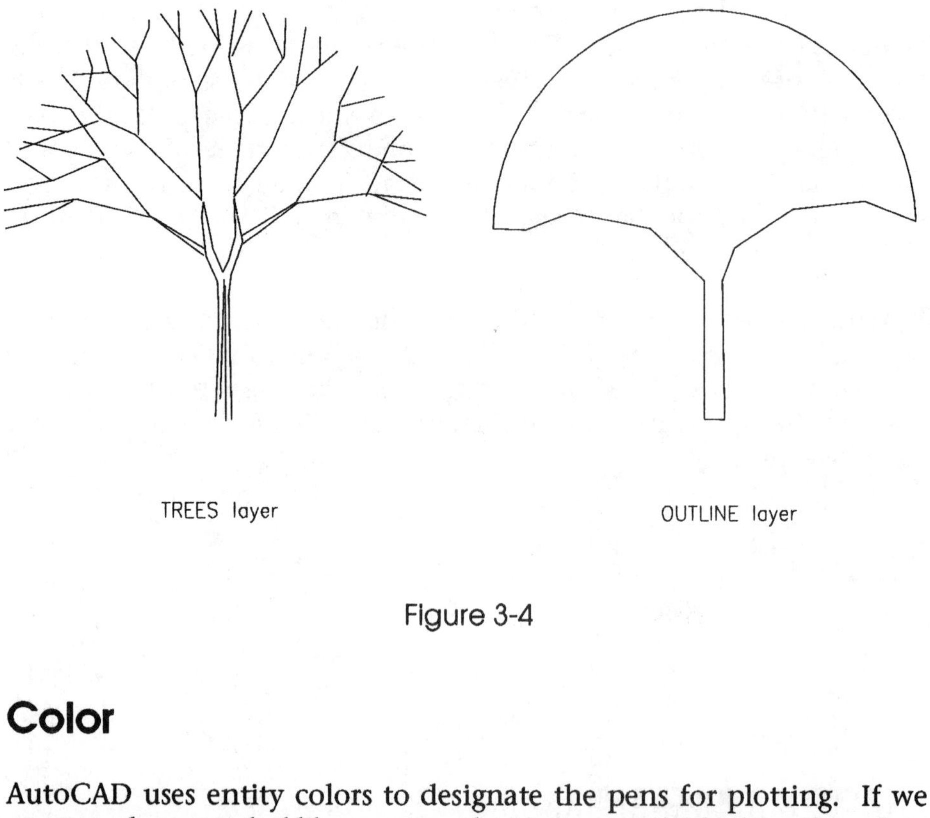

Figure 3-4

Color

AutoCAD uses entity colors to designate the pens for plotting. If we want to plan a symbol library properly, we must consider how the colors we choose for the entities that make up our symbols will work with our other color standards. For example, cyan (color 4) may be used for both the floor plan and the dimensions. If you set up the plot so that a thick pen is designated by cyan, then the dimensions will be plotted in the same thick pen.

YOUR NOTES

Since many displays are limited in the number of colors they can display, color planning is essential. Even if you are printer-plotting drawings in "single pen monochrome," your future may include a pen plotter that can use multiple and colored pens. Also consider that a symbol library has great value and may be shared with (or even sold to) other people who use pen plotters.

Therefore, when you plan colors for your symbols, think of the colors in relation to the pen widths they will represent at plot time. Some symbols may look better plotted in a thin pen, while others will require a thicker pen.

What if you have a symbol that requires both thick and thin pens? Many architectural section details fall into this category. For example, you may want to create a series of wall sections that you can insert and edit. You may want to create a detail on a single layer, but use different colors—or pen thicknesses—for particular entities. To do this, you can create the drawing on the desired layer and use the Change command to change the colors for the particular entities. The symbol will reside on the specified layer, but it will retain the different colors you choose. Note that the Change command can change the color of an entity, regardless of the color assigned to the layer on which it resides. When you plot, the entity color—not the color assigned to the layer on which it resides—determines the pen used to plot that entity.

Linetypes

Linetypes, such as dashed, hidden, dotted, and center lines, are frequently used in architectural drawings. You will want to include these in some of your symbols.

When you place different linetypes in your symbols, you select the scale of each linetype by using the AutoCAD Ltscale (linetype scale) command. You can adjust the linetype scale in the original symbol drawing. When you insert it into another drawing, however, the linetype scale of the destination drawing is used for the linetypes in the symbol.

Note: The linetype scale is updated only after the next drawing regeneration. If you set the linetype scale and the drawing does not automatically regenerate, you can force a regeneration by using the Regen command.

YOUR NOTES

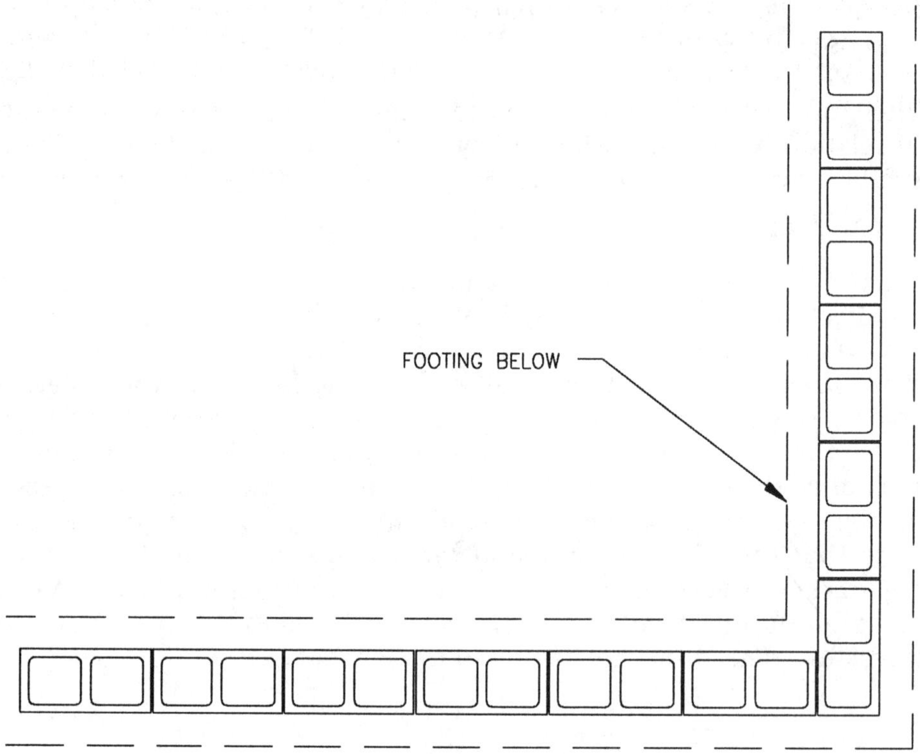

Figure 3-5

You will want to set a linetype scale for the drawing scales at which you will plot. If the linetypes in your symbols appear too large or too small, you can write your own linetypes for use in your symbols. This is very easy and is covered in the AutoCAD manual.

Orientation Angle

You will insert some symbols at the same angle that they were originally drawn. An example of such a symbol is a window detail. Other symbols, such as pieces of furniture, must be rotated to the desired angle.

YOUR NOTES

When you draw the original symbol drawing, you will find that proper planning will ease the insertion/rotation process. Let's look at an example. Consider a symbol drawing of a chair. You want to be able to insert the chair, then rotate it to a specific angle. The default AutoCAD angle of 0 is to the right (east). When you create the chair, face it to the 0-angle (right) position. Then when you insert the chair into a drawing, you can move your input device (mouse, digitizer puck, etc.) in the direction you want the chair to face and press ↵. The chair will be inserted facing the specified direction.

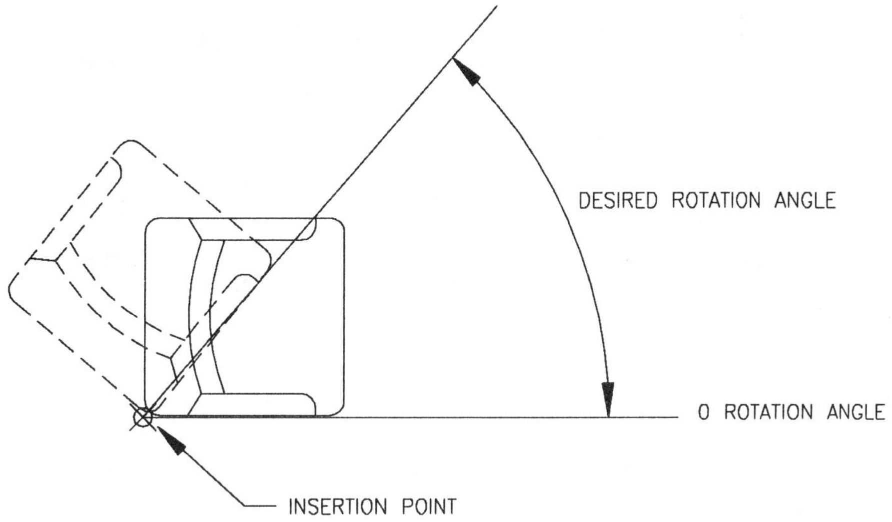

Figure 3-6

In the case of a symbol that will be inserted in the same direction each time, draw the symbol in the correct position. When you insert the symbol, simply insert it with an angle of 0 for proper orientation. You can toggle ortho on when you set the angle if you want to place the symbol precisely along the *X*- or *Y-axis*.

YOUR NOTES

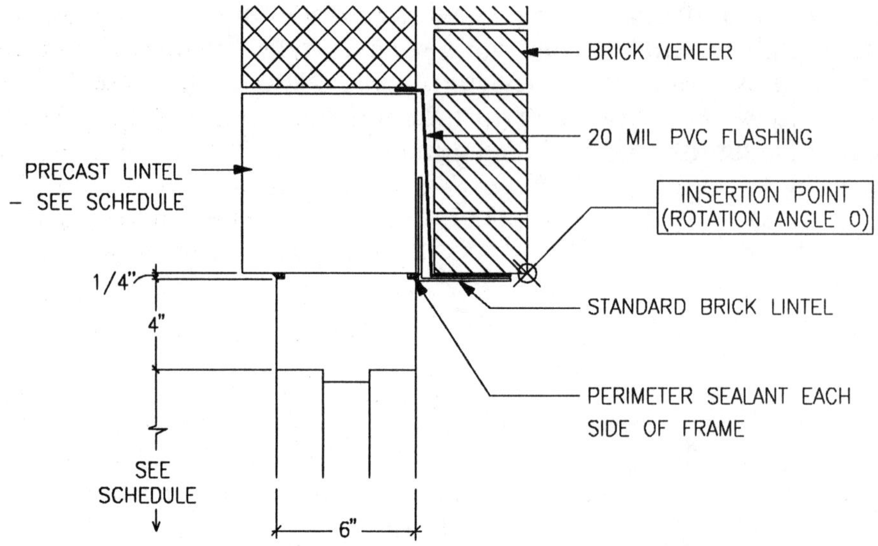

Figure 3-7

Scale

AutoCAD drawings are constructed in "real world units." This means that a building that is 50'–0" long is actually drawn that size. The display simply reduces the magnification so that the entire drawing can be displayed on the screen. It is not until you plot that the scale is important.

Because of this, you should draw your symbols at actual scale. When the symbol is inserted into another drawing, it will be correct in size. It does not matter if the limits of the destination drawing are different from those of the symbol drawings.

There is a difference, however, if the *units* setting of the symbol drawing is different from the *units* setting of the destination drawing. The most frequent example of this occurs on the site drawing. The site drawing is usually drawn in decimal units, and the rest of the plans are drawn in

YOUR NOTES

architectural units. In decimal units, it is common for one unit to equal one foot. In architectural units, AutoCAD designates that a unit is equal to one inch.

Let's look at a common situation. We can draw a site plan using decimal units. Next, we want to insert the floor plan into the site plan to show the relationship of doors and windows to the sidewalks and site views. If the drawing is inserted at a scale of 1, the floor plan will appear to be 12 times its actual size in relation to the site plan. This is because the units of the destination drawing prevail. Since the units of the site plan are set to decimal, each unit equals one foot. In the case of our floor plan, each unit equals one inch. To insert the symbol (in this case, our floor plan drawing) at the correct scale, we can use a scale factor of .08333, which is the decimal equivalent of the fraction 1/12.

If you want to draw some of your plans in decimal units, there is another alternative. Make a second copy of your symbol drawings. Then rename each drawing. Use the Scale command to rescale the symbol for decimal use and change the units. You now have a second set of symbols drawn to the proper scale, with the desired units.

When you insert symbols drawn in decimal units into a drawing using architectural units, simply use a scale factor of 12.

LIBRARY DRAWING MANAGEMENT

Architectural symbol libraries tend to grow over time. You may eventually build a library that requires many megabytes of disk space to store. One solution to this situation is a large-capacity hard drive. Another solution is to store the symbols on floppy disks by category. When you need a symbol, place the disk in the floppy drive. For example, if you wanted to insert a drawing named SECT-1A from a disk in the A-drive, simply enter the following in response to AutoCAD's request for the block name:

A:SECT1-A

Once you have inserted the symbol into the drawing, it is no longer necessary to have the symbol drawing file available. AutoCAD stores the symbol in the destination drawing's database as a block reference.

YOUR NOTES

Symbols stored on a hard drive should reside in their own subdirectory. To eliminate the necessity of entering the full DOS path name when you refer to the symbol drawing, use the DOS path statement in your AUTOEXEC.BAT file to enable AutoCAD to find it. Since it is normal to erase all AutoCAD files from the AutoCAD subdirectory before installing a new version, this also allows you to change versions without having to erase all your symbol files from the AutoCAD directory at the same time.

As your symbol library grows, you will need to do a bit of bookkeeping to keep track of your drawings. An excellent way to do this is to create a ring binder with the drawings categorized by type. The following list contains common categories for architectural symbols.

Architectural markers
Cornice details
Doors (elevation)
Doors (plan)
Fixtures
Furniture
Gutters
Material legends
North arrows
Site items
Trees (elevation)
Trees (plan)
Wall sections
Windows (elevation)
Windows (plan)

Placing the Base Point

When you create a symbol drawing, use AutoCAD's Base command to place the base point. This is the "insertion point" referred to when you insert a drawing. Proper placement of the base point is essential. In Session Two, you placed the base point of a window symbol at a point on the exterior wall. We selected this location because we wanted to be able to snap to a point (node) located in the exterior wall line. The base point was located so that the window was perfectly placed in the wall and centered on the point when the point was captured with object snap.

BUILDING A SYMBOL LIBRARY

YOUR NOTES

It is not always practical for a designer, drafter, engineer, or architect to stop work to create a special symbol library. Many libraries of excellent architectural details are available for purchase. These libraries, however, do not always have the details you prefer, or the sections and other details drawn to your personal specifications.

Creating Your Own Symbols

An excellent way to create a personal library is to capture your details "on the fly." When you are drawing a plan that requires a detail you do not have in your library, draw it directly on the plan. Then use AutoCAD's Block command to capture the desired parts in a block. Next, use Wblock (write block) to write the detail to disk. Also, look through your previous drawings for symbols that you have already drawn. You may already have an extensive library just waiting to be captured! Block these symbols and write them to disk.

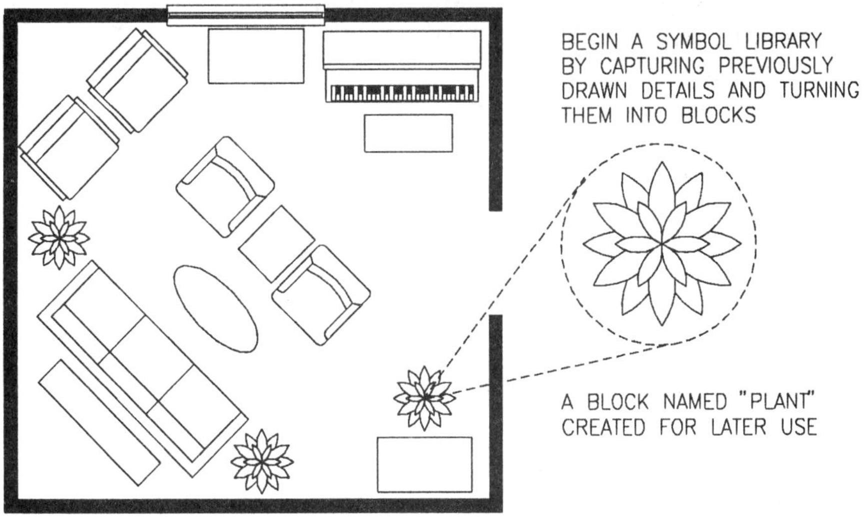

Figure 3-8

Note that it is not necessary to enter the new drawing file created by the Wblock command to place the base point. When you block the

YOUR NOTES

drawing, AutoCAD requests the insertion base point. This is the same as setting the base point. On your newly created drawing, the specified insertion base point will be located at the 0,0 absolute coordinate point of the drawing.

Editing Symbols

Many architectural detail symbols (such as wall sections) are not designed to be used "as is" in drawings. These details are created as "boilerplate" details and are almost always edited after insertion. To edit an inserted symbol, first use AutoCAD's Explode command to break the symbol into its individual entities.

If you want to edit some parts of the block, but not others, you may want to create the symbol with nested blocks. To do this, use a combination of blocks and individual entities when you create the original symbol. When you insert the symbol into a destination drawing and explode it, the individual entities will be "unblocked," but the blocks that were used in the original symbol drawing will remain blocked. You may use the Explode command again if you need to unblock these blocks back to their individual entities.

ADDING CLOSET, BATH, AND KITCHEN ITEMS

Before we insert our symbols, let's complete some detail items in the floor plan. We are going to draw the rods and shelves for the closets, then add the cabinets, fixtures, and appliances for the kitchen and baths.

Closet rods are shown as double lines. The closet shelving is shown as a hidden line. This is because the floor plan is actually a horizontal section. Our section is cut at a level between the closet rods and shelves. We can look down and see the two edges of the closet rods, but can not see the shelving that is above the section plane. We dash the edge line of the shelving to indicate it's position.

Figure 3–9 shows the dimensions used to construct the rods and shelves. Use the Layer command to change to the Millwork layer. Now use the Offset command to offset the rods and shelves from the rear wall of each closet as shown in Figure 3–1. Use the Change command to change the linetype of the shelf to Hidden.

YOUR NOTES

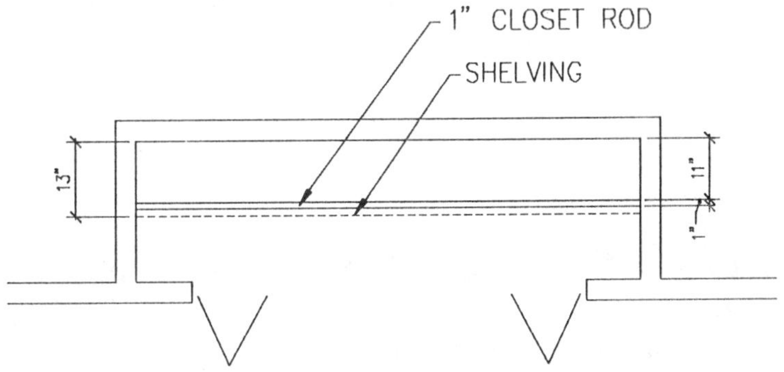

Figure 3-9

Now let's draw the kitchen cabinets. The cabinet tops are 24" deep. Figure 3–10 shows the kitchen and the cabinet dimensions. You can start by using the Offset command to offset the cabinet edges 24" from the wall.

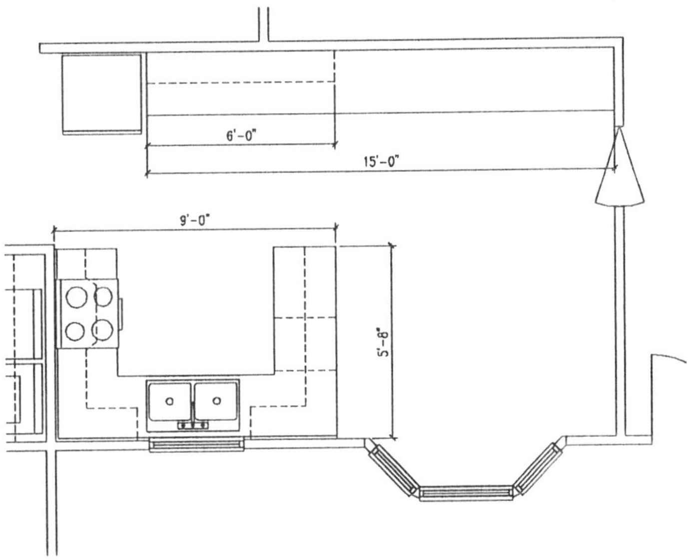

Figure 3-10

YOUR NOTES

Next, use the Layer command to change to the Fixt layer. Now use the Insert command to insert the fixtures and appliances. Refer to Appendix L and Figure 3–1 for the symbol names, insertion points, and positions.

Use the Save command to record your additions to disk. Now it is time to add the furniture to your drawing.

INSERTING SYMBOLS IN YOUR DRAWING

It is time to stop reading and start doing! A symbol library has been provided for your use. In this session, you will use the symbol library to insert the furniture, kitchen appliances, and bathroom fixtures in the house, and cars in the garage. These symbols are block references in the prototype drawing on your work disk.

Let's use some of these symbols. Start AutoCAD and enter the floor plan drawing named FLPLAN1. This is the drawing you created in Session One. Zoom into the family room. Next, execute the Insert command and enter the name CHAIR1. It is not necessary to enter the file type (.dwg) when you specify the name.

Next, place the cursor at the desired position and "click" your input device. Press ↵ twice to accept the default scale value of 0 for both the X-axis and Y-axis. Finally, move the cursor away from the chair and rotate it to turn the chair into position. You may want to verify that the ortho mode is off. The function key F8 toggles the ortho mode on and off. When the chair is at the desired angle, click your input device to position the chair. You can now leave the chair in its present position or use the Move and/or Rotate command to reposition the chair.

Note that with the exception of layer 0, it does not matter which layer you are on when you insert the symbol. The symbol entities "float" to the layers on which they were created when they were originally drawn. If the layers on which the symbols were created do not exist in your floor plan drawing, they will be created automatically. Execute the Layer command and enter a question mark (?) in response to AutoCAD's Layer: prompt to see a listing of the new layers.

Continue to place the symbols in your drawing. You may use the symbols in any room you wish. Be creative with your placements, using Move and Rotate to try different combinations and layouts. With a little practice, you can master AutoCAD's interior design potential!

Appendix L contains the symbol drawings and names. The "target" on each symbol shows the insertion point for that symbol.

YOUR NOTES

YOUR NOTES

PLOTTING INSTRUCTIONS

You may want to stop at this point and plot your work. If you have a pen plotter capable of plotting a C-size (24"x18") drawing, you can plot the drawing at a scale of 1/4"=1'-0". If you have a dot matrix printer configured to AutoCAD, you can printer plot the drawing. The following is an explanation for each type of plotting.

Pen Plot

From the AutoCAD Main menu, select option 3 (Plot a drawing). Respond to Enter NAME of drawing: with \ACADARCH\FLPLAN1 and ↵.

Next, AutoCAD prompts you for the part of the drawing to be plotted. Enter L for limits.

AutoCAD will now display the plot parameters. The last line on the screen asks if you want to change anything. Enter Y for yes. Then use the following settings.

Plot NOT written to a file
All entity colors plotted with pen 1
Size in inches
Plot origin at 0.00,0.00
Plotting size: C
Plot NOT rotated
Pen width 0.010
Area fill boundaries NOT adjusted for pen width
Hidden lines NOT removed
Scale: 1/4"=1'-0"

Before you proceed, make sure the plotter is ready to plot. A pen of 0.25mm will yield acceptable results. When you are ready, press ↵ and watch your drawing being plotted!

Printer Plot

YOUR NOTES

To printer plot, select option 4 (Printer Plot a drawing) from AutoCAD's main menu. When AutoCAD asks for the drawing name, type \ACADARCH\FLPLAN1 and press ↵. You will be prompted for the part of the drawing to plot. Enter L for limits and ↵. A listing of the plot parameters will be displayed. The last line on the screen asks if you want to change anything. Respond with Y for yes and use the following settings.

Plot NOT written to a file
Size in inches
Plot origin at 0.00,0.00
Plotting size: A
Plot rotated: YES
Hidden lines NOT removed
Scale: F (for fit)

Now prepare the printer and press ↵ to printer plot your drawing. Note that the printer plot will not be plotted to a particular scale.

YOUR NOTES

SUMMARY

- Symbols can be created as separate AutoCAD drawings, or they can be write-blocked from an existing drawing.

- You must consider the final plotted size when you determine the amount of detail to include in a symbol.

- One symbol can show differing amounts of detail if you place some details on layers that can be frozen when they are not desired.

- Outlines of details can be placed on a different layer. The layer containing the outline can be turned on, and the detail layers can be frozen. This allows for fast symbol handling by speeding up drawing regenerations when you Zoom and perform other operations that force drawing regenerations.

- The linetype scale (Ltscale) is determined by the drawing receiving the symbol, not by the symbol drawing.

- Build symbols with the "normal 0-angle" to the right (standard AutoCAD 0-angle orientation). This allows easy cursor-pointing to determine the angle when you insert the symbol into a drawing.

- Draw symbols at actual size. The symbol will insert into other drawings at the proper scale. The only exception to this is when you interchange between architectural and engineering/decimal scales. When you insert a symbol between these unit types, use the appropriate scale factor.

- Designate the symbol's base point at a location that will be appropriate when you insert the symbol into a drawing. For example, a window base point might be located where the window lines up with a wall line.

- Use the Explode command to explode a symbol for editing. If you want to explode part of a symbol while keeping other parts "glued" together, use nested blocks when you create the symbol.

- Create a symbol library system to organize your symbols properly. You may also want to create a symbol catalog to keep beside your workstation.

YOUR NOTES

YOUR NOTES

QUESTIONS

1. Why would you create a symbol block that contained more than one layer?

2. Why should the use of color be carefully considered when creating a symbol library?

3. What is the advantage of drawing symbols at a particular rotation angle?

4. What would be the effect of inserting a symbol that was created in decimal units into a drawing that is set up for architectural units? How would you convert the symbol for use?

5. How does AutoCAD store symbols in the "destination" drawing?

____

____

____

6. What must you do before you can edit an inserted symbol?

____

____

____

7. What would be the advantage of creating an outline on a separate layer for a symbol?

____

____

____

YOUR NOTES

YOUR NOTES

PROBLEMS

1. Create a symbol drawing. Place different levels of detail on two layers. Place the symbol into another drawing.

2. Create a floor plan layout of your drawing lab. Create blocks for each type of furniture. Place the furniture into the room to create a new layout.

YOUR NOTES

Making Connections on a Network

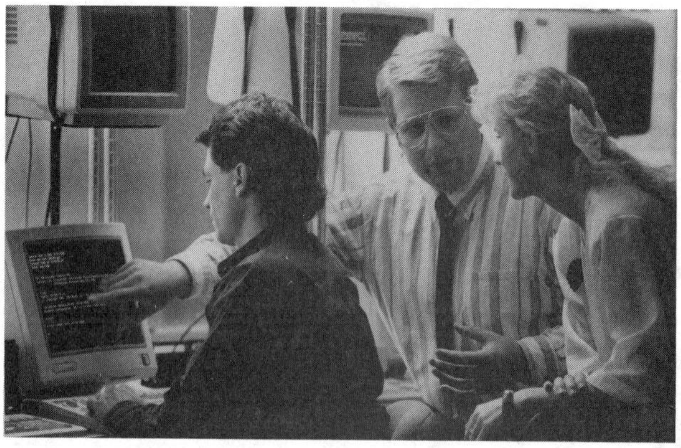

Courtesy of Novell Network

Vickerman Zachary Miller (VZM) is a firm that includes architects and structural, civil, mechanical, and industrial engineers. The VZM staff has grown from three to over fifty since 1980, and they have taken great care to maintain the kind of team attitude that is possible in a small office. They view their computer system as an important tool in achieving this goal.

VZM installed the first three AutoCAD systems in 1985. It soon became clear that passing disks around was not a good way to coordinate work. When VZM renovated new quarters, the firm installed cabling for a Novell Netware network. Now they have twelve 386-based AutoCAD stations, other PC's for non-CAD work, and Macintoshes for graphic design. Each is linked to the office file server, a computer with several large hard disks where all the firm's data is stored. The software glue that holds the network together is Netware.

Virtually all the professional staff are "CAD literate." Will Gortner, the Director of Architecture, says, "We have designers and engineers, not 'CAD operators.' It's essential to have a computer on every desk--people use them for everything. And they need to share access to the same files." With Netware, the files stored on the server are available as readily as if they were on a disk in each PC.

The key to VZM's successful CAD networking according to CAD coordinator Rose Vigdal, is the firm's use of standards. She has established conventions for layers, symbols, plotting, and other CAD issues. Extensive standards have also been set up for workstation configuration. As a result, any designer can work on any drawing without having to decipher someone else's work, and people can easily sit down at any workstation and begin working. "This is important," adds Gortner. "People wear more than one hat here: they do design one minute and engineering the next. The network and CAD system have support this kind of mode-switching and file-sharing."

Network management is shared among several people, so that no full-time administrator is required. A consultant is responsible for installing, maintaining, and upgrading hardware. The data files on the server are backed up automatically every night, and maintenance is performed on weekends. The server has only been "down" for four working hours in the past several years, though production manager Ed Castillo points out that they realized how dependent they were on the network during those four hours.

Netware has made it easier for VZM to use AutoCAD Release 11's reference file capabilities. "We use them to divide large projects into chunks that can be worked on by individuals" Vigdal says. Some retraining is required: "People aren't used to the idea of seeing more than one file at a time."

Gortner emphasizes that VZM is a democratic kind or firm--the people are "networked" in every manner. The links between the computers are, he says, a natural extension of a network that would exist without any computers.

SESSION 4

Dimensioning and Titling

YOUR NOTES

Use this space for notes about your individual plan.

OBJECTIVE

The object of this session is to learn commonly accepted techniques of dimensioning and titling a floor plan. Figure 4–1 shows the result of this session.

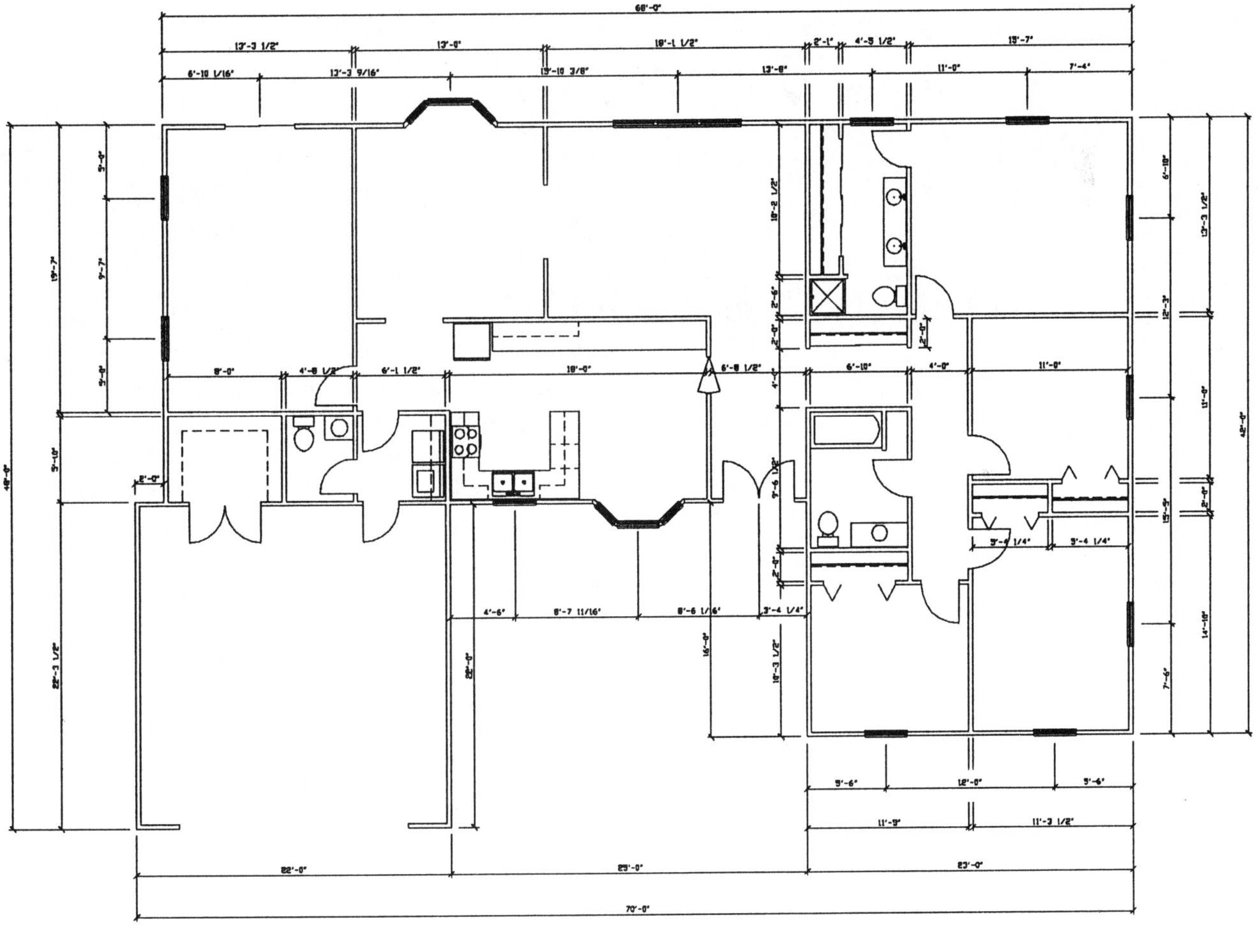

Figure 4-1

Appendix K is a detailed dimensioning plan that you will use during this session. You should familiarize yourself with Appendix K and with AutoCAD's dimensioning basics before you begin this session.

YOUR NOTES

Commands used in this session:

dim	dimzin
dimdli	erase
dimexe	explode
dimexo	layer
dimscale	line
dimsoxd	osnap
dimtad	setvar (pdmode)
dimtih	style
dimtix	text
dimtoh	trim
dimtsz	

DIMENSIONING BASICS

Dimensions form an important part of a drawing. They provide the builder with essential construction information. The most important task, other than providing correct dimensions, is to construct clear, concise dimensions that are easy to work from. The dimensions should be easy to read, precise to the points they are measuring, and consistent in their layout.

Dimensions are calculated to the "rough" frame. In residential construction plans, the rough frame is usually the foundation block and the face of the wood studs. The reason for this is apparent to those who have participated in the actual construction process. When you are framing from a dimensioned plan, the wall finishes (gypsum board, etc.) are not present. You can only measure to the rough frame.

Several dimensioning techniques may be argued successfully. For our plan, we will use some of the most commonly accepted techniques for architectural plans. After you learn the basic techniques, you may want to establish your own standards for your plans.

Components of Dimensioning

Dimensions consist of several named components. Figure 4–2 shows the components we will use in this session.

YOUR NOTES

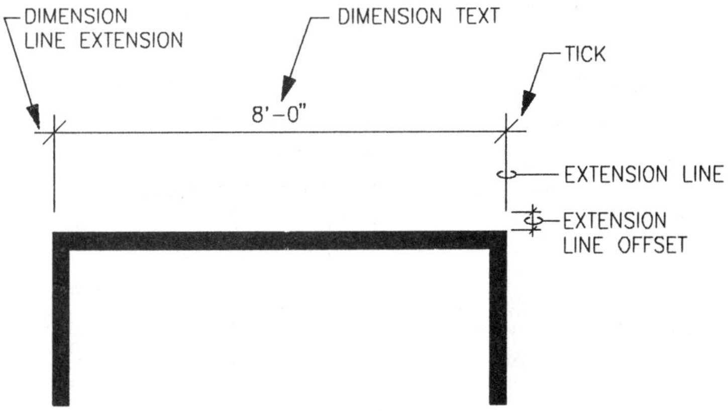

Figure 4-2

Preparing for Dimensioning

Before you begin to dimension any drawing, you should decide on a dimensioning style. AutoCAD includes dimension variables that allow you to create dimensions in any style. The settings are stored with the drawing. The default settings are determined by the settings stored in your prototype drawing. We will change the settings of some of the dimensioning variables to create the custom look we want for our floor plan. Later, we will use the same settings for all our dimensioned drawings.

The best way to create a new look for your dimensions is to experiment with different settings. A good way to find the look you want is to experiment with a sample dimension. Place the sample dimension in your drawing. Next, change a variable and use the dimension update command to see the effects of the change immediately. Once you have found a look you like, make sure the components are in the right proportion to each other. Then use the global dimscale command to size all the dimension components in relation to the drawing scale.

YOUR NOTES

The dimscale command also allows you to change the size of dimension components before you plot at a different scale. Many first-time dimension users make the mistake of trying to control the overall scale by changing each dimensioning component individually. The dimscale command will perform the same task quickly and more efficiently.

For our dimensioning, we want to achieve the look shown in Figure 4–3.

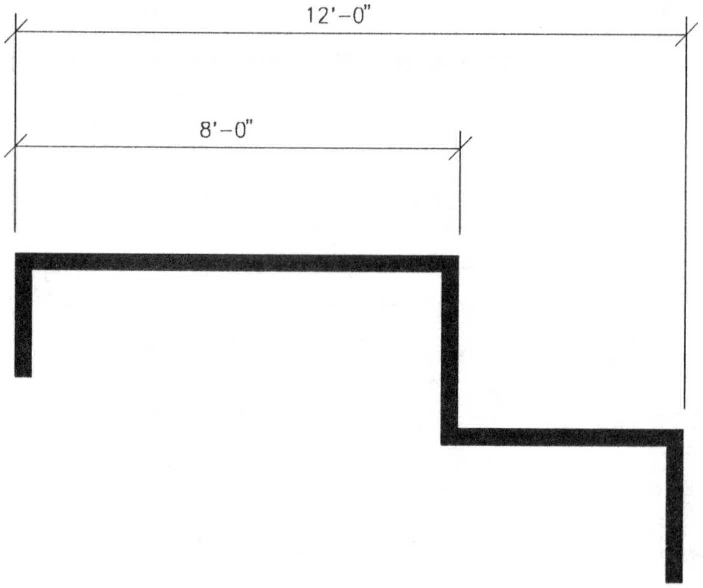

Figure 4-3

Placing a Test Dimension

Let's start by editing our floor plan drawing (FLPLAN1). Since our dimensioning plan will not show furniture, the first thing we'll do is freeze the layers named FURNITURE and FURNDET. We also want to dedicate a layer to the dimensions, so that they may be frozen and thawed as necessary. Usually layer 0 is used to place the dimensions on, so we will make 0 the current layer.

Command: **layer**
?/Make/Set/New/ON/OFF/Color/Ltype/Freeze/Thaw: **f**
Layer name(s) to Freeze: **FURNITURE,FURNDET**
?/Make/Set/New/ON/OFF/Color/Ltype/Freeze/Thaw: **s**

YOUR NOTES

New current layer <*default*>: **0**
?/Make/Set/New/ON/OFF/Color/Ltype/Freeze/Thaw: ↵

Zoom into the north end of the family room (see Figure 4–4). Use the following command sequence and Figure 4–4 to construct a single horizontal dimension line. (Initially, your dimension will not look like the one in the illustration).

Now we will enter AutoCAD's dimensioning mode. All dimension commands are issued under the dimensioning mode. To enter the mode, select Dim: from the root menu. You may also enter the dimension mode by typing Dim from the keyboard. When you are in the dimensioning mode, you will see a prompt of Dim: instead of the usual Command: prompt.

Command: **dim**
Dim: **horiz** *(if you are using the screen menu, choose* Linear *to display the screen menu panel containing* Horiz*)*
First extension line or RETURN to select: **int**
of *Select point 1.*
Second extension line: *Select point 2.*
Dimension line location: *Select point 3.*
Dimension text <13′–3 1/2">: ↵

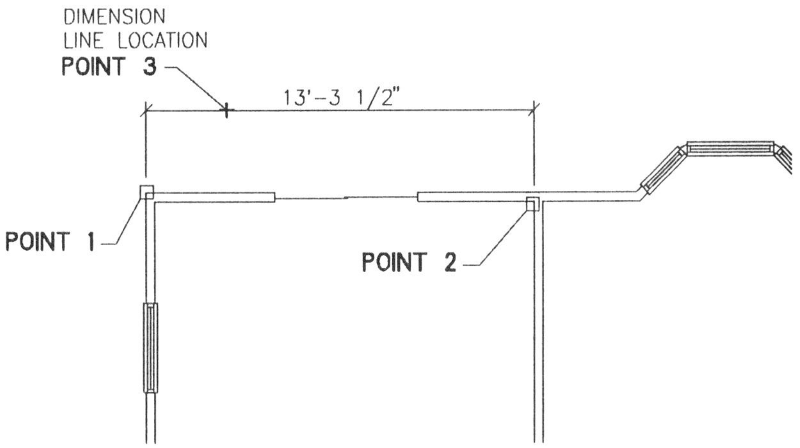

Figure 4-4

YOUR NOTES

Creating the Dimension Appearance

Now let's use the dimension variable commands to create our dimensioning appearance. First, let's use the dimscale command to enlarge the dimension so we can see the effects of our changes better. Use the following dimension command sequence to set the dimension scale.

Dim: **dimscale**
Current value <default> New value: **24**

Now use the update command and select the dimension (pick on any point of the dimension) to show the change in global scale. Use the update command after you change each of the following variable settings if you want to see the changes immediately.

Dim: **update**
Select objects: *Select the dimension.*

We now want to set AutoCAD to use ticks instead of arrows where the dimension line intersects the extension lines. Use the following sequence to do this.

Dim: **dimtsz**
Current value <default> New value: **.1**

Next, we will use the dimtad variable to place the dimension text above the dimension line.

Dim: **dimtad**
Current value <default> New value: **on**

We want the dimension text to follow the dimension lines that are placed vertically. By default, the text for vertical dimensions is placed horizontally, splitting the line, as shown in Figure 4–5.

YOUR NOTES

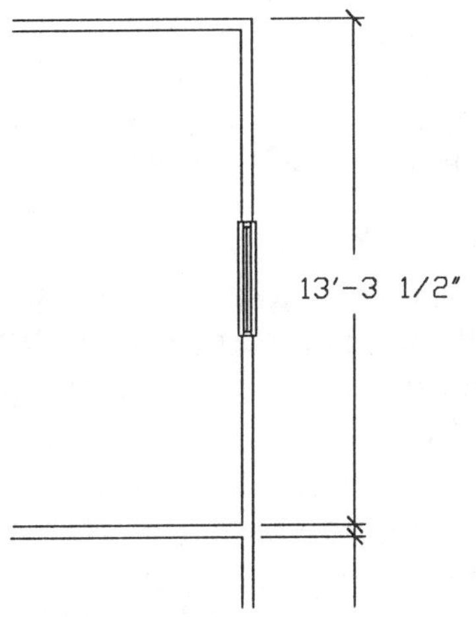

Figure 4-5

We will use the dimtoh and dimtih dimension variable commands to set the text to follow the dimension lines.

Dim: **dimtoh**
Current value <default> New value: **off**
Dim: **dimtih**
Current value <default> New value: **off**

When we dimension, we will use object snap to locate the dimension points precisely. This will sometimes involve snapping to an intersection that occurs on the inside of the wall. This was the situation with the second extension line you placed earlier in this session. We want the extension line to offset a sufficient distance to clear the outside wall line. To do this, use the dimexo variable.

Dim: **dimexo**
Current value <default> New value: **1/4"**

YOUR NOTES

When ticks are used, dimensions often look better if the dimension line extends slightly beyond the extension lines. Let's use the dimexe variable to adjust this distance.

Dim: **dimexe**
Current value <default> New value: **1/8"**

We want the default dimension text to display in feet and inches, as opposed to just feet. If the distance is less than one foot, we want the text to show inches only. We can force this type of default text display with the dimzin variable.

Dim: **dimzin**
Current value <default> New value: **3**

The dimension line increment is the distance between dimension lines. It is controlled with the dimdli variable. Let's set the increment to 1.0.

Dim: **dimdli**
Current value <default> New value: **1"**

Let's review the list of dimension variable settings we have specified for our drawings. The following list is a summary of the settings we changed.

Dimscale:	24	Dimension overall scale
Dimtsz:	.1	Tick size
Dimtad:	On	Text placed above dimension line
Dimtoh:	Off	Text outside dimension lines not horizontal
Dimtih:	Off	Text inside dimension lines not horizontal
Dimexo:	.25	Extension line offset
Dimexe:	.15	Dimension line extension past extension line
Dimzin:	3	Default number display
Dimdli:	1.0	Repeating dimension line increment

If you want to check all the values, enter the dimension mode by typing Dim. Then use the Status command. Note that the Status command in the dimensioning mode is not the same as the Status command outside the dimensioning mode.

YOUR NOTES

Saving the Dimension Variable Settings

It would be prudent to use the Save command to record your settings at this time. Once you have established a set of variables that reflects your personal preferences, you may want to make a record of it. If you want to change the default settings to your own personal set, just set each variable in the prototype drawing named ACAD and use the Save or End command to record the changes.

You may want to create a series of prototype drawings. For example, you can create prototype drawings that contain settings for particular limits, units, scales, and page sizes. You can adjust the dimension components for the particular scale of each prototype drawing. When you want to use the settings, start a new drawing that "equals" the appropriate prototype. For example, if your prototype drawing is named P1 and you want to start a new drawing named FLPLAN2, enter FLPLAN2=P1 when you are prompted for the new drawing name. Your new drawing will contain the same settings as the P1 prototype drawing.

DIMENSIONING YOUR PLAN

New let's start dimensioning and labeling our floor plan. Follow these steps to dimension the plan.

STEP 1 *Preparing to Dimension*

First, erase the test dimension you used to set the dimensioning variables. Use the Layer command to set the current layer to 0. Verify that the color is set to white (color 7).

We will start dimensioning at the north wall of the family room. Since we want to snap to precise points, let's use object snap intersection to capture our points.

Command: **osnap**
Object snap modes: **int**

YOUR NOTES

STEP 2 *Placing the First Dimension Line*

Zoom to a comfortable magnification. Use the following sequence to construct the first dimension line. If you make a mistake, press U and ↵ to undo the dimension. It is not necessary to leave dimensioning mode to use Undo because the dimension mode contains its own Undo command. Note that you must select Dim:, then Linear from the screen menu to display the Horiz, Vertical, and other dimension options. Use the following sequence and the points shown in Figure 4-6.

Command: **dim**
Dim: **horiz** *(If you are using the screen menu, you will first pick* Linear *to display the menu panel containing the* Horiz *selection)*
First extension line origin or RETURN to select: *Select point 1.*
Second extension line origin: *Select point 2.*
Dimension line location: *Select point 3.*
Dimension text <13'–3 1/2">: ↵

AutoCAD will now construct the dimension line. If you constructed your walls according to the instructions from the earlier sessions, your default dimension should read 13'–3 1/2". To accept the default dimension value, just press ↵. If you want to enter a different dimension, type the desired dimension text before you press ↵ for the last prompt.

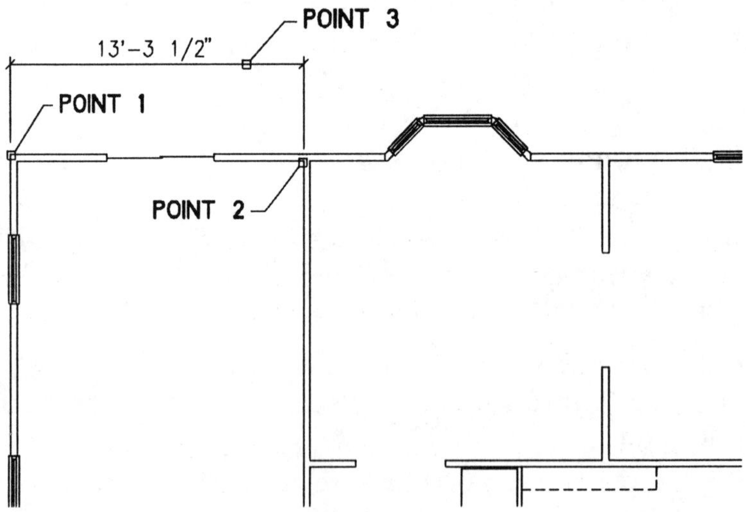

Figure 4-6

STEP 3 *Placing a Second Dimension Line*

YOUR NOTES

Under most dimensioning situations, we would now use the continue function to place the next linear dimension line. We can't do that on a floor plan, however, because the wall thickness does not allow enough room to contain the dimension text. We will have to place the text for wall thickness outside the extension lines, as shown in Figure 4–7.

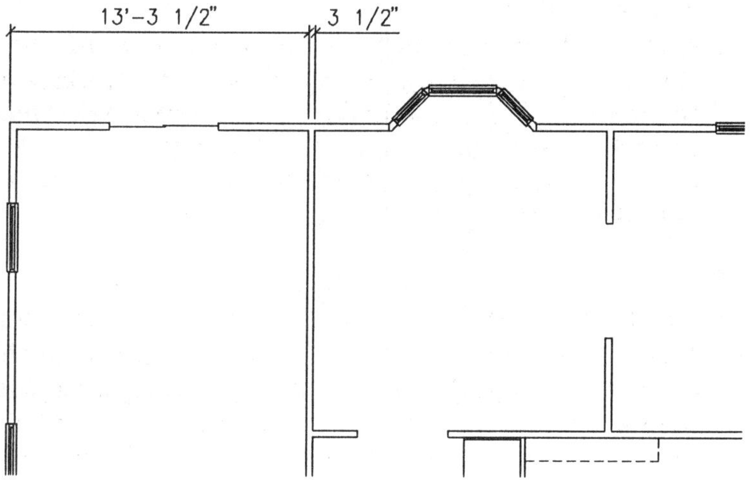

Figure 4-7

This text will interfere with the placement of the next dimension line. If we continue the dimensioning, AutoCAD will place the dimension line above the existing lines at the distance set by the dimdli variable, as shown in Figure 4–8. To avoid this, we will place the dimension lines for each room segment separately.

Now let's place the dimension for the dining room. Select Horiz again, and place the two extension line origins as shown in Figure 4–9. When AutoCAD prompts you for the dimension line location, enter object snap nearest. Place the crosshairs on the previous dimension line and pick. Press ↵ to accept the dimension text of 13'–0".

YOUR NOTES

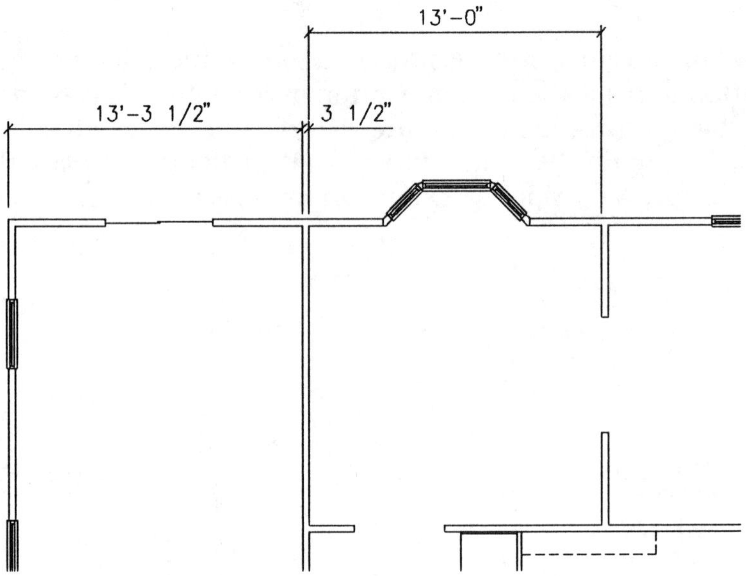

Figure 4-8

Dim: **horiz**
First extension line origin or RETURN to select: *Select point 1.*
Second extension line origin: *Select point 2.*
Dimension line location: **nea**
to *Select point 3.*
Dimension text <13'–0">: ↵

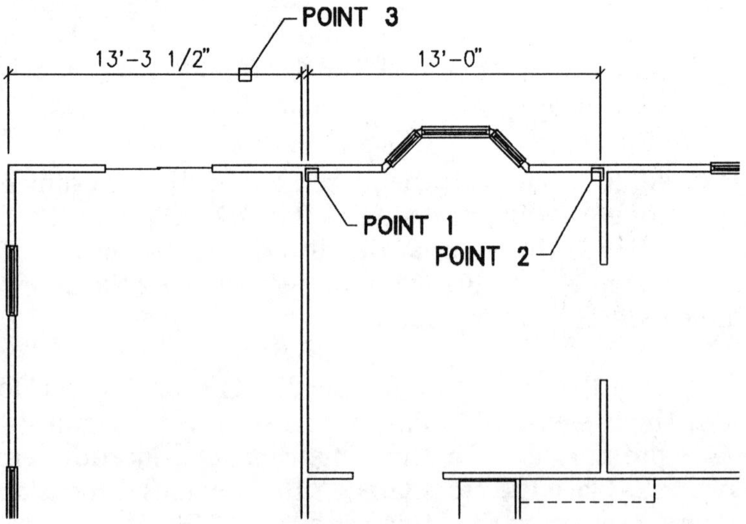

Figure 4-9

STEP 4 *Placing the Remaining Rear Wall Dimensions*

YOUR NOTES

Continue by placing dimensions across the rear wall of the floor plan. Use the dimensioning guide in Appendix K for dimension placement. If you make a mistake, use the Undo command to back up and start again. When you are finished, your plan should look like the one in Figure 4–10.

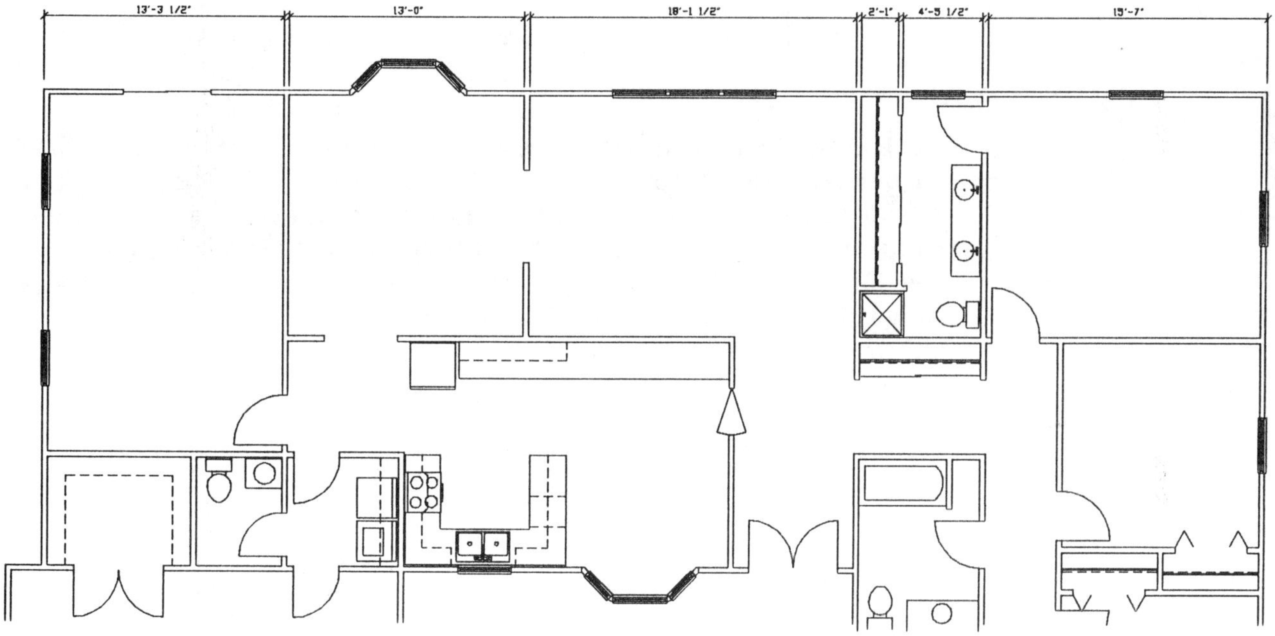

Figure 4-10

STEP 5 *Placing Window and Door Dimensions*

Next, let's place the dimensions for the windows and doors. We can place these dimensions by using object snap to snap to a point. You remember that you used points to locate the windows in the walls. Let's use the pdmode variable to see these points.

Command: **setvar**
Variable name or ?: **pdmode**
New value for PDMODE: **35**

YOUR NOTES

You should now see a point at the center of each window. If you do not, regenerate the drawing.

Now you can dimension windows and doors to their center lines. Use object snap node to snap to the points so that you can use the center lines for extension line origins. If you placed windows by another method, you may use object snap midpoint to capture the midpoint of the window sill line.

> Command: **osnap**
> Object snap modes: **node**

Next, enter the Dimension mode and select Horiz. Start by using object snap override mode (from the * * * * menu) to capture the intersection as shown in Figure 4–11. This will be the first extension line origin. Continue by selecting the point on the center line of the sliding door in the family room for the second extension line origin. Place the dimension line below the dimension lines you drew previously, as shown in Appendix K.

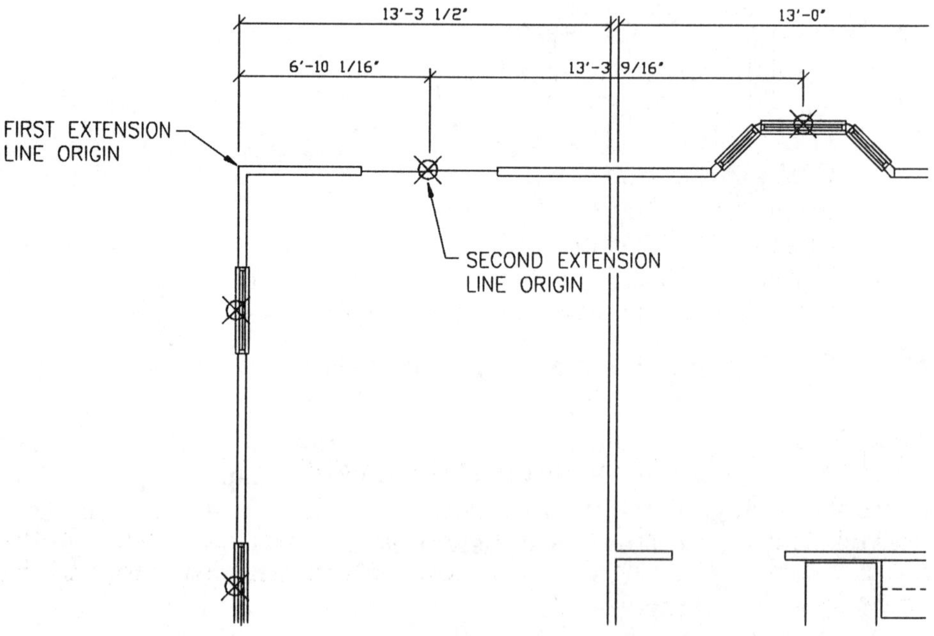

Figure 4-11

YOUR NOTES

Now use Continue to continue dimensioning. Use the aperture set up by the osnap node setting to capture the point entity for each window. When you get to the end of the wall, use object snap override to capture the intersection of the wall corner as the last extension line origin.

Next, set the object snap mode to intersection. Place a dimension line from outside corner to outside corner of the rear wall, as shown in Appendix K.

PLACING WALL THICKNESS TEXT

We will now place the wall thickness text. Our wall thickness is 3 1/2".

STEP 6 *Creating a Text Style*

Let's start by creating a text style for the wall thickness text.

Command: **style**
Text style name (or ?) <default>: **wall-thk**

New style
Font file <default>: **simplex**
Height <0'-0">: **3 1/2"**
Width factor <1.00>: **.8**
Obliquing angle <0>: ↵
Backwards <N> ↵
Upside-down? <N> ↵
Vertical? <N>↵
WALL-THK is now the current text style.

STEP 7 *Placing the Wall Thickness Dimension*

Now place the wall thickness dimension for the wall between the family room and dining room. Use the following command sequence and the point shown in Figure 4 – 12.

YOUR NOTES

Command: **text**
Start point or Align/Center/Fit/Middle/Right/Style: *Select point 1.*
Rotation angle <0>: ↵
Text: **3 1/2"**

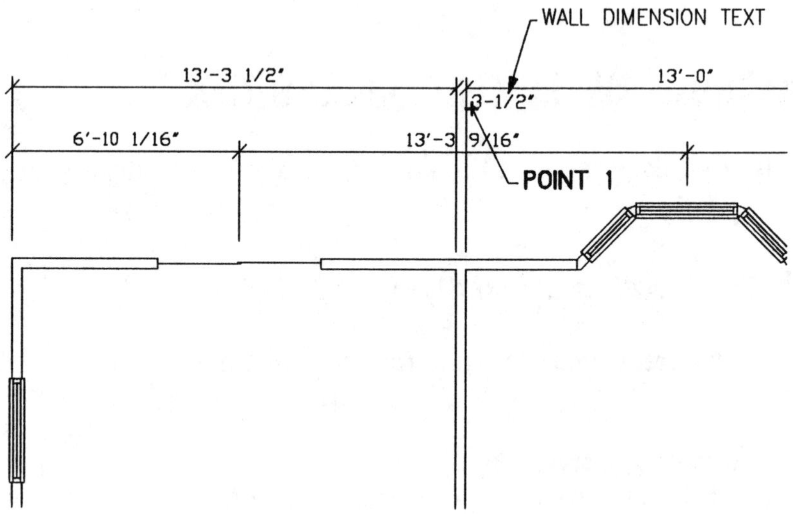

Figure 4-12

STEP 8 *Coping the Dimension Text*

Next, use multiple Copy to copy the dimension text to each wall thickness location. Use Appendix K as a guide for text placement.

CROSSING EXTENSION AND DIMENSION LINES

As you have probably already noticed, some of your dimension lines cross extension lines. This can be confusing to someone who is not familiar with your plan. It is customary to break extension lines that cross through a dimension line.

YOUR NOTES

Before you can break an extension line, you must explode the dimension. However, before you explode any dimensions, you should consider a very important point. AutoCAD dimensions can be "stretched." If you want to stretch a room, you can stretch the dimension along with it. When you stretch the dimension with the room, the dimension text automatically reflects the new distance. After a dimension is exploded, however, it loses the ability to update its dimension text when the dimension is stretched.

STEP 9 *Breaking Extension Lines*

We won't be stretching any rooms for the plan, so we can explode our dimensions. Let's look at a good way to break the extension lines that cross our dimension lines. Turn on ortho. Select the Line command and draw two lines, as shown in Figure 4–13.

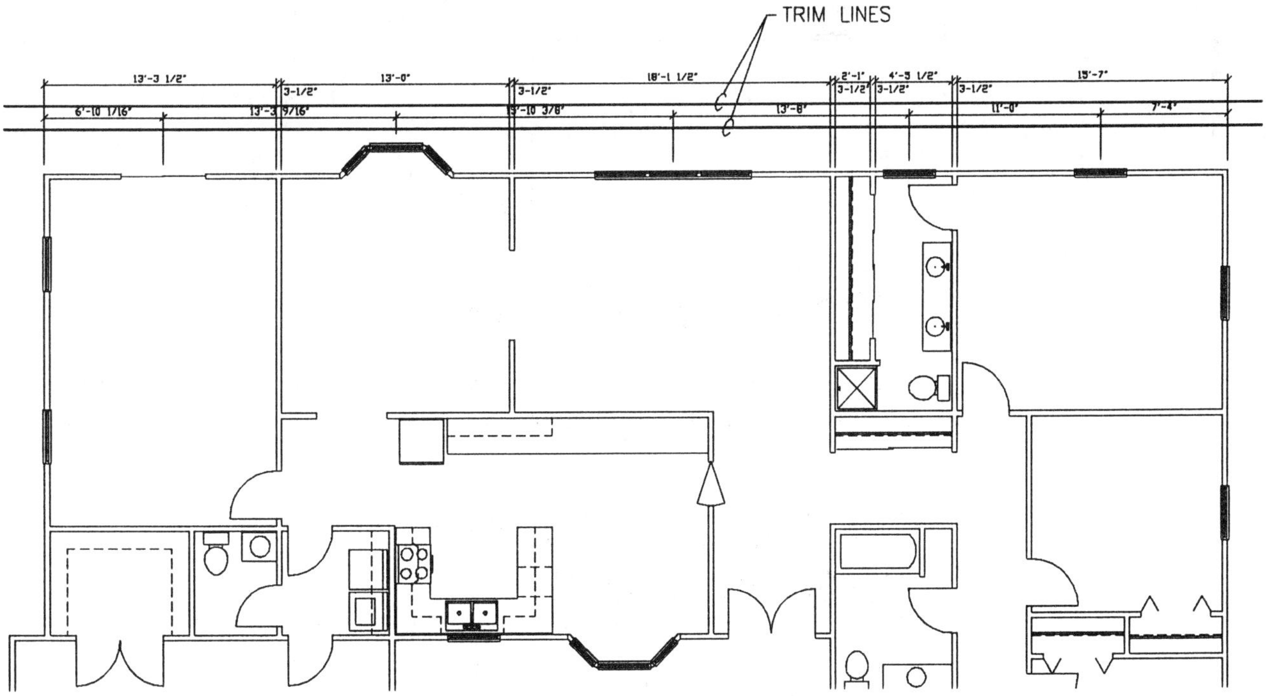

Figure 4-13

YOUR NOTES

Next, use the Explode command to explode the dimensions that describe the walls. Use the Trim command to trim the extension lines from between the two lines. Finally, use the Erase command to remove the two lines. Your dimensions should appear similar to those in Figure 4–14.

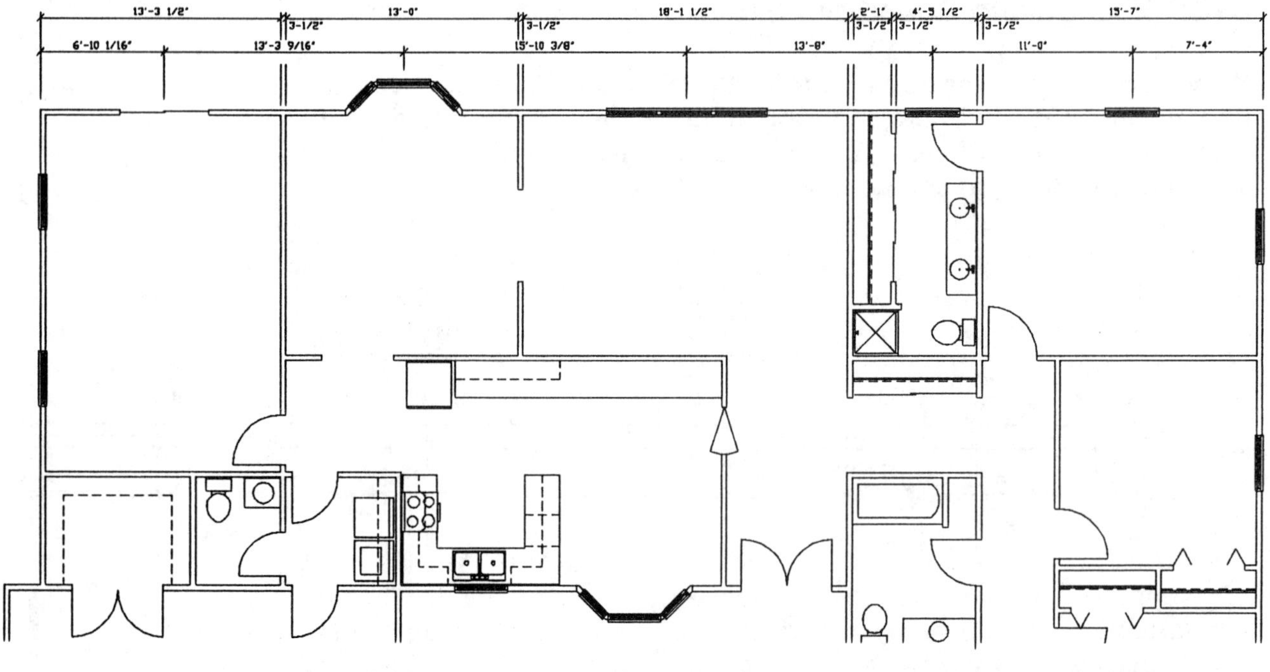

Figure 4-14

STEP 10 *Placing the Remaining External Dimensions*

Continue to place the external dimensions. Follow the dimensions shown in the dimensioning guide in Appendix K.

CONSTRUCTING INTERNAL DIMENSIONS

YOUR NOTES

Dimension lines should be constructed outside the plan whenever possible. This leaves the plan area uncluttered. When it is necessary to place dimensions inside the plan area, select a position on the plan where a dimension string can be placed through the entire distance in a continuous line.

STEP 11 *Placing the First Internal Dimension String*

In our plan, we will place a horizontal internal dimension string through the middle of the floor plan (see the dimensioning guide in Appendix K).

You can place this dimension string in almost exactly the same way you placed the external wall strings. The only difference is the selection of object snap. For the extension origins, you can use object snap near. Construct each room dimension separately. Use object snap near to capture the previous dimension line location when AutoCAD prompts you for the dimension line location. When the line passes through a doorway (for example, through the door between the breakfast room and the foyer), you can use object snap intersection to select the door jamb as the extension line origin.

If you wish, you may use the dimse1 and dimse2 variables. These stand for "suppress extension line 1" and "suppress extension line 2." When the variable is on, the suppression is in effect and the extension line is not displayed. Turning the variable off restores the extension lines for subsequent dimensions.

Architects typically use these variables when they place strings of dimensions across interior walls. If you do not use these variables, the extension lines will fall on top of the wall lines. However, you cannot normally detect them in a final plot.

STEP 12 *Placing Internal Dimensions*

Continue to place the internal dimensions. When you have finished, copy the wall thickness dimension text as you did when you constructed the external dimensions.

YOUR NOTES

TITLING YOUR FLOOR PLAN

You should wait to title your floor plan until after you have completed the dimensioning. This allows you to place the dimensions in their optimal positions, since the titles can be located anywhere in the room.

Try to make the title placements visually pleasing. Place the titles as close to the visual center of the space as possible. Also, line up the titles across the page whenever feasible.

STEP 13 *Creating a Room Name Style*

Let's create a new layer named ROOM_NAME. Make this the current layer, with a color setting of red (color 1). Next, create a new text style using the following command sequence.

Command: **style**
Text style name (or ?) <WALL_THK>: **rname**

New style
Font file <default>: **simplex**
Height <0'-0">: **8"**
Width factor <1.00>: ↵
Obliquing angle <0>: ↵
Backwards <N> ↵
Upside-down? <N> ↵
Vertical? <N> ↵
RNAME is now the current text style.

Title the family room first. Use the Text command to place the room name. If you want to underline the room name, use AutoCAD's "%" text function. For example, if you wish to underline the title FAMILY ROOM, enter the following:

%%UFAMILY ROOM%%U

YOUR NOTES

Some spaces, such as bathrooms and laundry rooms, may be too small—you may not be able to locate a room title within the available space. To title these spaces, create a text style named RNAME2, with a text height of 5".

YOUR NOTES

PLOTTING INSTRUCTIONS

You may want to stop at this point and plot your work. If you have a pen plotter capable of plotting a C-size (24"x18") drawing, you can plot the drawing at a scale of 1/4"=1'–0". Before beginning your plot, you should verify that the furniture layers are frozen. If you have a dot matrix printer configured to AutoCAD, you can printer plot the drawing. The following is an explanation for each type of plotting.

Pen Plot

From the AutoCAD main menu, select option 3 (Plot a drawing). Respond to Enter NAME of drawing: with \ACADARCH\FLPLAN and ↵.

Next, AutoCAD prompts you for the part of the drawing to be plotted. Enter L for limits.

AutoCAD will now display the plot parameters. The last line on the screen asks if you want to change anything. Enter Y for yes. Then use the following settings.

Plot NOT written to a file
All entity colors plotted with pen 1
Size in inches
Plot origin at 0.00,0.00
Plotting size: C
Plot NOT rotated
Pen width 0.010
Area fill boundaries NOT adjusted for pen width
Hidden lines NOT removed
Scale: 1/4"=1'–0"

Before you proceed, make sure the plotter is ready to plot. A pen of 0.25mm will yield acceptable results. When you are ready, press ↵ and watch your drawing being plotted!

Printer Plot

YOUR NOTES

To printer plot, select option 4 (Printer Plot a drawing) from AutoCAD's main menu. When asked for the drawing name, enter \ACADARCH\FLPLAN and press the ↵. You will be prompted for the part of the drawing to plot. Enter L for limits and ↵. A listing of the plot parameters will be displayed. The last line on the screen asks if you want to change anything. Respond with Y for yes and use the following settings.

Plot NOT written to a file
Size in inches
Plot origin at 0.00,0.00
Plotting size: A
Plot rotated: YES
Hidden lines NOT removed
Scale: F (for fit)

Now prepare the printer and press ↵ to printer plot your drawing. Note that the printer plot will not be plotted to a particular scale.

YOUR NOTES

SUMMARY

- Prepare to dimension by placing a test dimension. Set the desired dimension variables and update the test dimension to see the results.
- Use the dimension variables to obtain the appearance you want. Then use the overall scale abilities of the dimscale variable to scale the dimension to a suitable size.
- Store, either in prototype drawings or in a notebook, dimension scale and variable settings for drawings that will be plotted at different scales.
- Place all the dimensions on a dedicated layer, ususally layer 0. Freeze or thaw the layer as necesssary.
- Use Object snap when you dimension a plan. If you have constructed the drawing accurately, you can accept AutoCAD's measurement of the dimensioned distance.
- Use the Stretch command to adjust dimension lengths.
- Explode dimension lines to trim out extension lines that cross. Note, however, that exploded dimension lines can no longer be stretched or updated.
- Title the plan after you finish dimensioning so that the titles do not conflict with the dimension locations.

QUESTIONS

YOUR NOTES

1. What are some important factors to consider when you place dimensions in a drawing?

___

___

___

2. How can you control the overall size of dimensions?

___

___

___

3. What is the advantage of constructing a "test dimension" before you place dimensions in your drawing?

___

___

___

YOUR NOTES

PROBLEMS

1. Create a test dimension and experiment with different dimension variable settings. Use the Dim Update command to see the changes after each is made.

2. Create a simple floor plan and practice dimensioning different parts of the drawing.

YOUR NOTES

Section 2 Drawing Building and Wall Sections

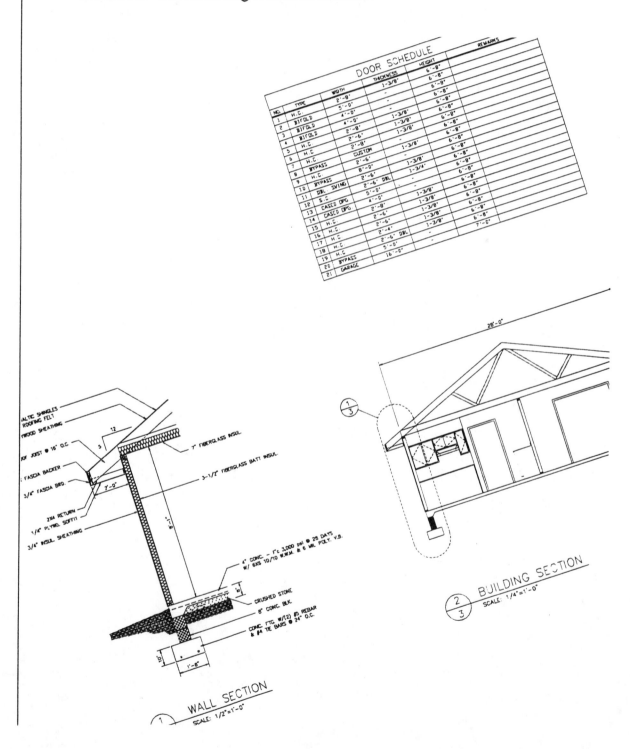

- Session 5: Drawing the Building Section
- Session 6: Constructing the Wall Section

DOOR SCHEDULE

NO.	TYPE	WIDTH	THICKNESS	HEIGHT	REMARKS
1	H.C.	2'-8"	1-3/8"	6'-8"	
2	BIFOLD	5'-0"	-	6'-8"	
3	BIFOLD	4'-0"	-	6'-8"	
4	BIFOLD	4'-0"	-	6'-8"	
5	H.C.	2'-8"	1-3/8"	6'-8"	
6	H.C	2'-6"	1-3/8"	6'-8"	
7	H.C.	2'-8"	1-3/8"	6'-8"	
8	BYPASS	CUSTOM	-	6'-8"	
9	H.C.	2'-6"	1-3/8"	6'-8"	
10	BYPASS	8'-0"	-	6'-8"	
11	DBL. SWING	2'-6"	1-3/8"	6'-8"	
12	S.C.	2'-6" DBL	1-3/4"	6'-8"	
13	CASED OPG	5'-0"	-	6'-8"	
14	CASED OPG.	4'-0"	-	6'-8"	
15	H.C.	2'-8"	1-3/8"	6'-8"	
16	H.C.	2'-6"	1-3/8"	6'-8"	
17	H.C.	2'-6"	1-3/8"	6'-8"	
18	H.C.	2'-4"	1-3/8"	6'-8"	
19	H.C	2'-6" DBL	1-3/8"	6'-8"	
20	BYPASS	5'-0"	-	6'-8"	
21	GARAGE	16'-0"	-	7'-0"	

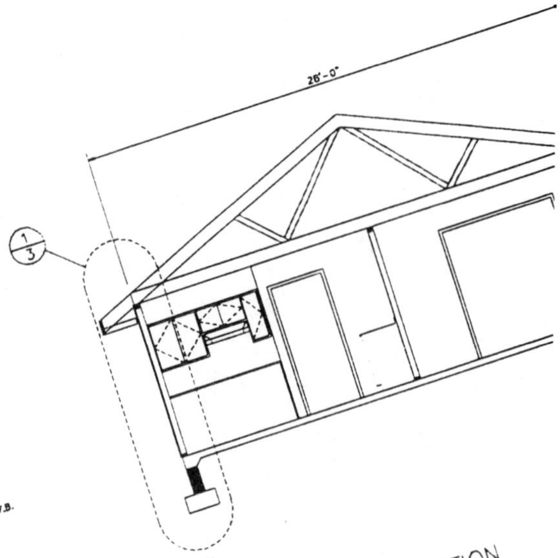

2
3
BUILDING SECTION
SCALE: 1/4"=1'-0"

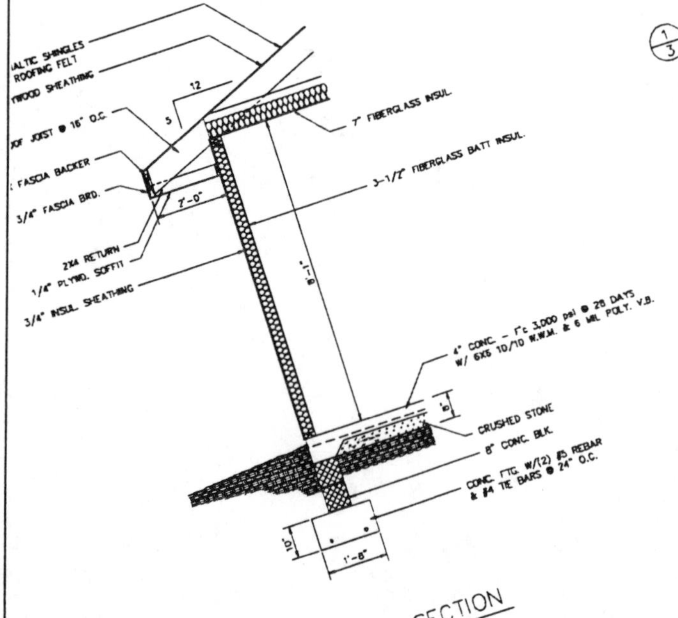

1
WALL SECTION
SCALE: 1/2"=1'-0"

SESSION 5

Drawing the Building Section

OBJECTIVE

YOUR NOTES

Use this space for notes about your individual plan.

In this session, we will draw the primary building section. Figure 5–1 shows the result of this session. This is the first part of drawing sheet number three. You will complete this drawing sheet in Session Six.

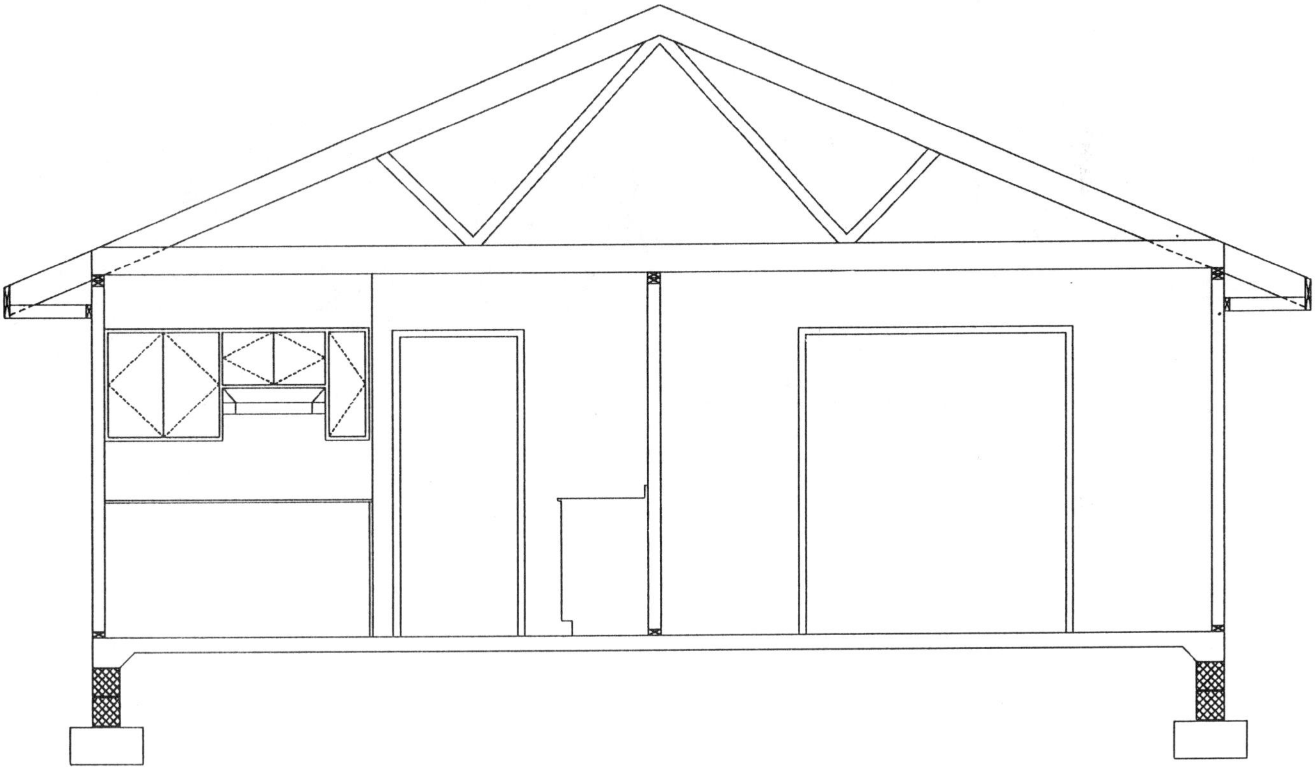

Figure 5-1

Commands used in this session:

block
copy
erase
explode
extend
fillet
insert
layer
limits
line
reference lisp function
trim
units

YOUR NOTES

A section is a drawing that shows a building as it would look if you cut it in two and removed part of it. Sections are used to explain parts of the structure that plan views and exterior views cannot show adequately.

Our section will show a "cut" through the central part of the plan. The location of this cut is shown by a section marker. Figure 5–2 shows a typical section marker.

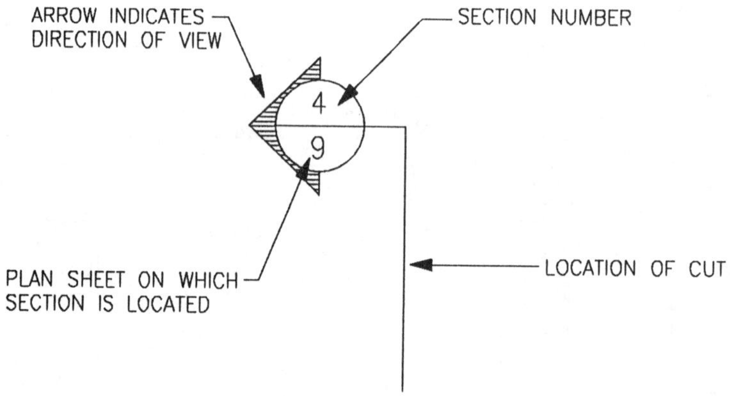

Figure 5-2

The line extending from the marker indicates the location of the cut. The marker points in the direction you are looking when you view the section. The circle part of the section marker contains further information about the section. The top number is the section number. The bottom number is the number of the drawing sheet on which the section is located. The section marker in Figure 5–2 indicates that the section can be found on drawing sheet number 9 and that it will be marked as section number 4 (four).

We will cut our section through the main part of the building. The location of the cut is shown in Figure 5–3. Note the direction in which the section marker indicates that we will be looking.

YOUR NOTES

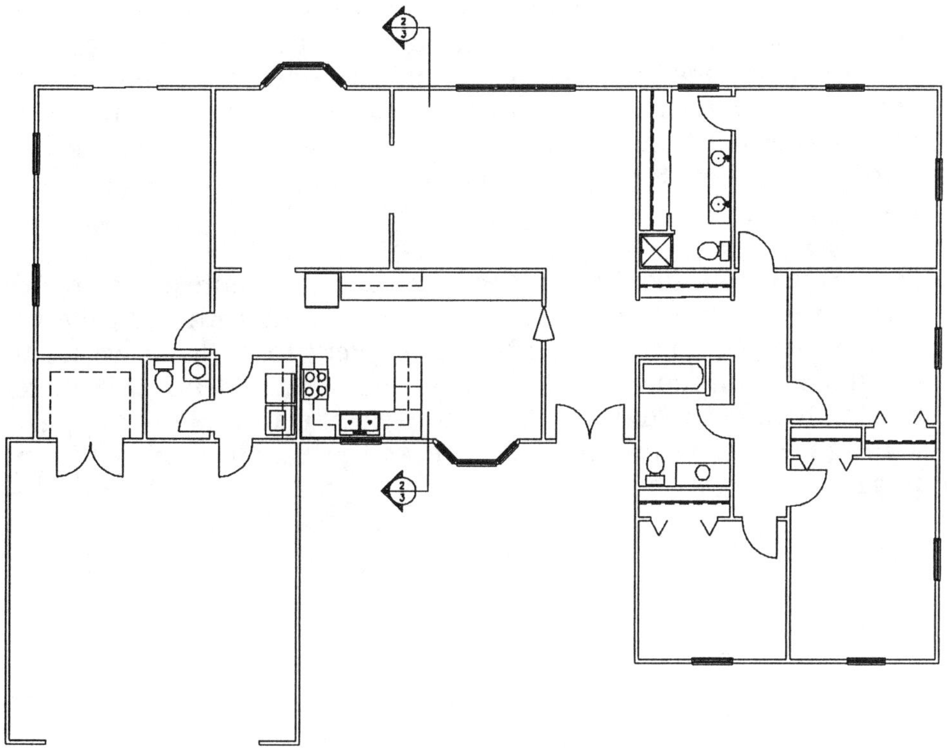

Figure 5-3

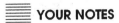

SETTING UP THE DRAWING

Let's set up our drawing. Enter AutoCAD and start a new drawing named SECTION to equal the prototype drawing named PSECTION, which is provided on the work disk. (Enter \ACADARCH\SECTION= \ACADARCH\PSECTION.) The following settings have been used to compose the prototype drawing.

Units: Architectural (to 1/16")
Limits: 0,0 (lower left) and 96′,72′ (upper right)
Snap: 1/2" and ON
(load "ref")
Layer: SECTIONS (color: cyan)
Ltscale: 12
Time: ON

YOUR NOTES

COMPONENT METHODOLOGY

Let's start our section drawing by introducing a new methodology called the *component method.* In the component method, architects use predrawn components to construct the drawing. Predrawn components differ somewhat from the typical library of details. A library detail is usually a complete form. A component is meant to be only one part of a larger detail.

Let's evaluate our requirements for the building. Figure 5–4 shows the section we will construct. Instead of seeing this drawing as a collection of lines, let's begin to look at it in a different manner. If we see the drawing as a true representation of a section, we can identify 8" concrete blocks, three 2x4 studs with one bottom (sole) plate and two top plates, a 10"x20" concrete footing, a 2'–8" doorway, and a number of other items.

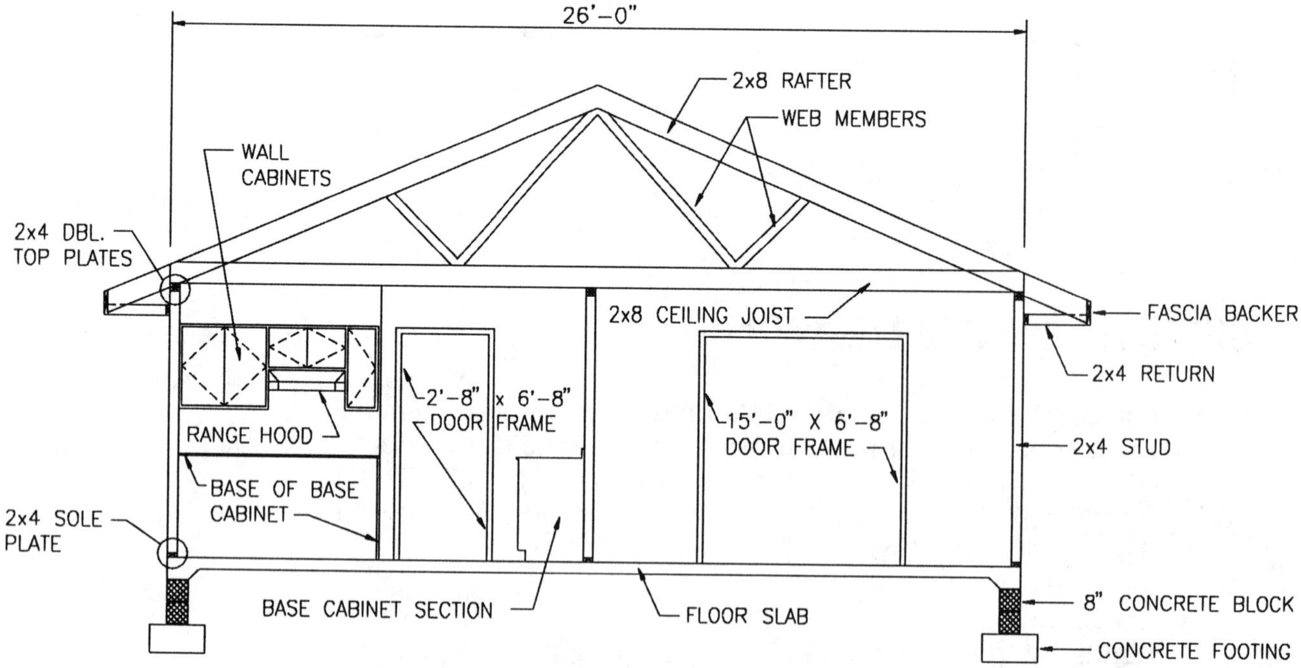

Figure 5-4

YOUR NOTES

DRAWING THE COMPONENTS

We will first draw each of these components individually. Then we will begin to "build" the section in a way that is similar to actually building the structure. Some standard line drawing will connect our components into a completed section drawing. Let's get going!

STEP 1 *Drawing the Footing*

We will start by drawing the footing. Figure 5–5 shows the footing. It is a simple rectangle drawn with lines. Draw the lines as dimensioned. Do not draw the dimensions shown for any of the components shown in this session.

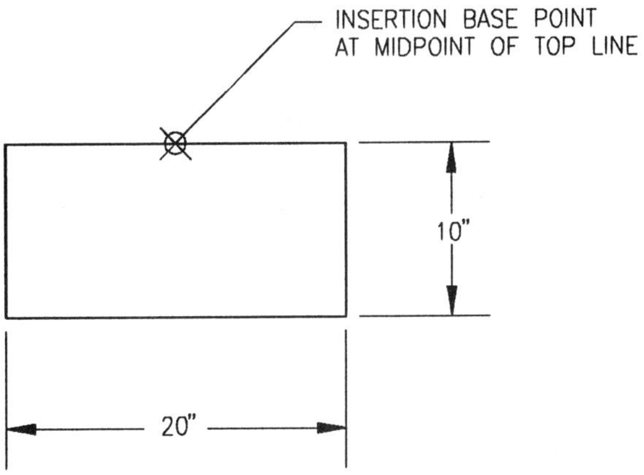

Figure 5-5

Start by selecting the Line command. Place the first point at any location on the screen. Use the following command sequence.

Command: **line**
From point: *Select any point.*
to point: **@20<0**
to point: **@10<90**
to point: **@20<180**
to point: **c**

YOUR NOTES

Next, block the footing. Use the following sequence.

Command: **block**
Block name (or ?): **footing**
Insertion base point: **mid**
of *Select the midpoint of the top line of the footing.*
Select objects: *Use window selection to select the four lines.*

The footing is now a block named FOOTING.

STEP 2 *Drawing the Concrete Block*

Now let's draw a single concrete block. The block dimensions are 7–5/8"x7–5/8". Use the following command sequence.

Command: **line**
From point: *Enter any point on the screen.*
to point: **@7-5/8<0**
to point: **@7-5/8<270**
to point: **@7-5/8<180**
to point: **c**

Now let's add a hatch to the block interior. Start by creating a new layer named HATCH. Set the color to white (color 7). Use the following command sequence to place the hatch.

Command: **hatch**
Pattern (? or name/Ustyle): **ansi37**
Scale for pattern <default>: **24**
Angle for pattern <default>: **0**
Select objects: *Select all four lines.*

Your concrete block should now look like the one shown in Figure 5–6.

YOUR NOTES

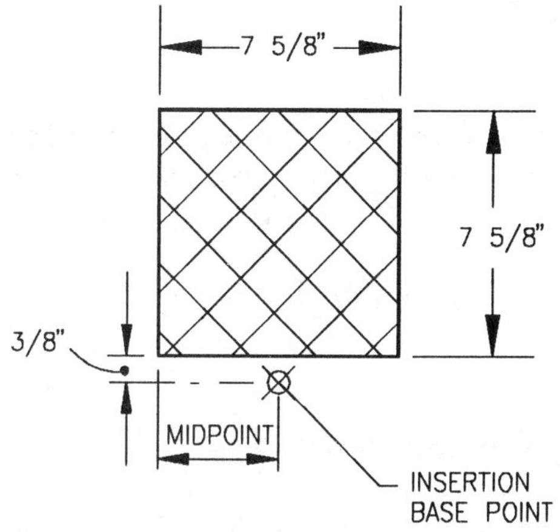

Figure 5-6

Next, we will block the concrete block under the name CBLOCK.

Command: **block**
Block name (or ?): **cblock**
Insertion base point: **(ref)**
Reference point: **mid**
of *Select midpoint of lower line.*
Enter relative/polar coordinates (with @): **@3/8<270**
Select objects: *Select the block and hatch.*

STEP 3 *Drawing the Stud Wall*

The stud wall is made up of a 2x4 that measures 1 1/2"x3 1/2"x92 1/2". The wall has one 2x4 bottom plate and two 2x4 top plates, as shown in Figure 5–7.

Before you begin to draw the stud wall, make SECTIONS the current layer of your drawing. To draw the stud wall, use the Line command to draw a rectangle 8′–1" (the total of the stud length plus 3 plates) by 3 1/2". Next, use the Offset command to offset the plates 1 1/2", as shown in Figure 5–7. Turn ortho off and draw the crossed lines on the plates.

YOUR NOTES

Next, block the stud wall under the name SWALL. Use the lower left corner of the bottom plate as the insertion point, as shown in Figure 5–7.

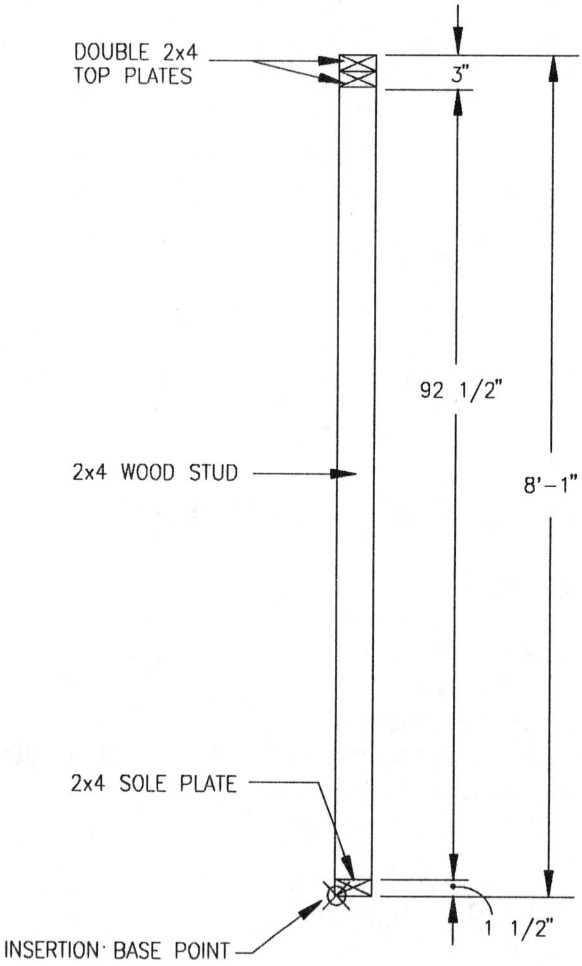

Figure 5-7

STEP 4 *Drawing the Door Frames and the 2x4*

We will now draw the door frames. Let's begin by making the DOORS layer current. Use the following command sequence.

YOUR NOTES

Command: **layer**
?/Make/Set/New/ON/OFF/Color/Ltype/Freeze/Thaw: **s**
New current layer <default>: **doors**
?/Make/Set/New/ON/OFF/Color/Ltype/Freeze/Thaw: ↵

Now let's draw the door frames. The first door is 2'–8" wide by 6'–8" high. Refer to Figure 5–8 and draw the frame, using the Line command.

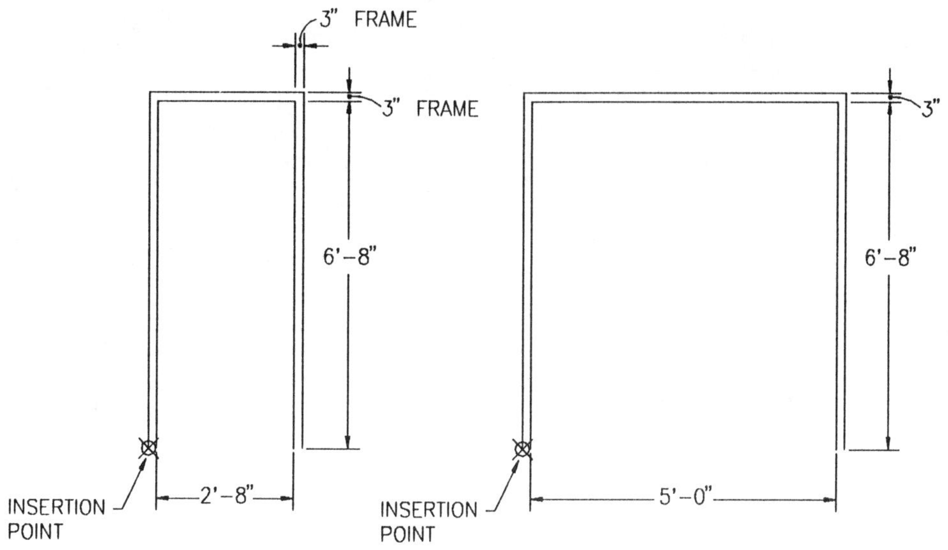

Figure 5-8

Next, block the frame under the name 28DFRAME. Use the lower left line endpoint as the insertion point. Refer to Figure 5–8 as necessary.

The second door frame is 5'–0" wide by 6'–8" high. Refer to Figure 5–8 and draw the frame, using the Line command. Block this door frame under the name 50FRAME.

We will need a 2x4 in section view. Make SECTIONS the current layer. Then use the Line command to draw the 2x4, as shown in Figure 5–9.

YOUR NOTES

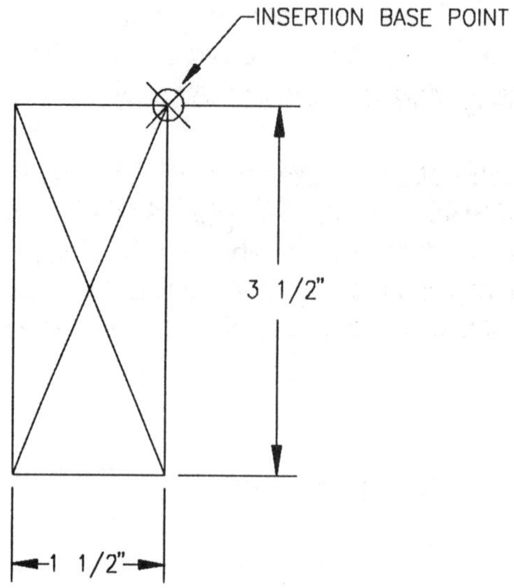

Figure 5-9

Block the 2x4 under the name 2x4, using the insertion base point shown in Figure 5–9. This would be a good time to use the Save command to record your work to disk.

CONSTRUCTING THE SECTION

Now we have the components we need. Let's use these components to construct the building section.

STEP 5 *Inserting the Footing*

Let's start the section by inserting the footing into the drawing. Use the following command sequence.

Command: **insert**
Block name (or ?): **footing**
Insertion point: **52,16**

YOUR NOTES

X scale factor /Corner/XYZ: **1**
Y scale factor (default=X): ↵
Rotation angle : **0**

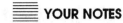

STEP 6 *Placing the Concrete Block*

Next, we will insert the concrete block. The block should be centered on the footing. Remember that we placed the insertion point 3/8" below the center of the bottom line of the block. This is because we want to leave a 3/8" mortar joint on top of the footing. Refer to Figure 5–10. Use the following command sequence to place the concrete block.

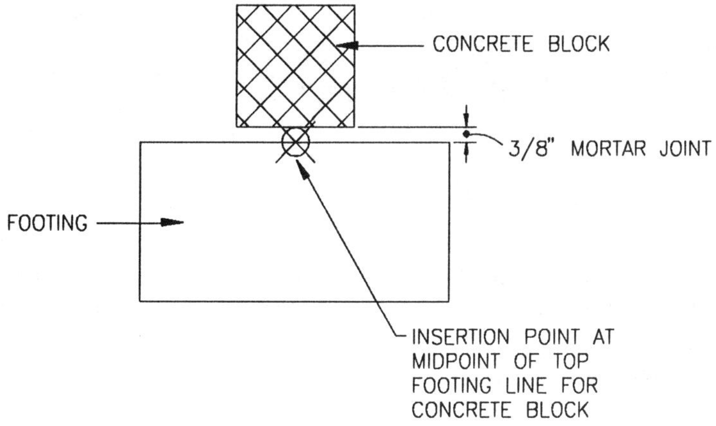

Figure 5-10

Command: **insert**
Block name (or ?): **cblock**
Insertion point: **mid**
of *Select top line of footing.*
X scale factor /Corner/XYZ: **1**
Y scale factor (default=X): ↵
Rotation angle : **0**

Now Copy the concrete block. Place the copy 8" above the first block. Since the block is 7 5/8" high, this will leave room for another 3/8" mortar joint between the blocks. Refer to Figure 5–11.

YOUR NOTES

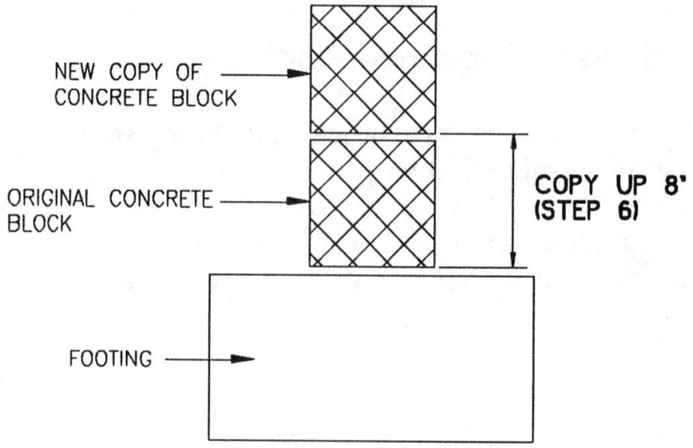

Figure 5-11

STEP 7 *Drawing the Floor Slab*

Now it's time to draw the floor slab. The slab is 4" thick, with 8" at the down-turned ends. We will draw only part of the slab now. Refer to Figure 5–12, and use the following command sequence.

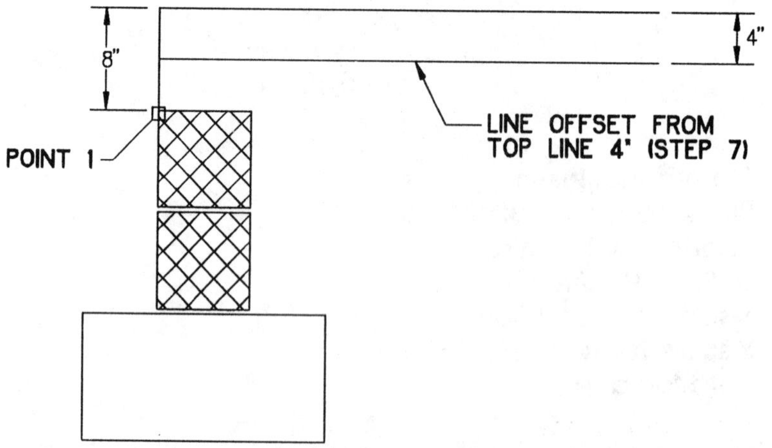

Figure 5-12

YOUR NOTES

Command: **line**
From point: **end**
of *Select point 1.*
to point: **@8<90**
to point: *For now, draw the line a short distance to the right, as shown in Figure 5–12.*

Next, offset the top line of the slab 4" to form the bottom surface.

Command: **offset**
Offset distance or Through: **4**
Select object to offset: *Select top line of slab.*
Side to offset? *Move cursor below the selected line and pick.*

We will now draw the 45° line, as shown in Figure 5–13. We can use the Distance command to approximate a distance. Then we can draw the line and fillet the 45° line to the bottom slab line. The Distance command shows that 8" is a good approximate line length. Let's draw and fillet the line. Refer to Figure 5–13.

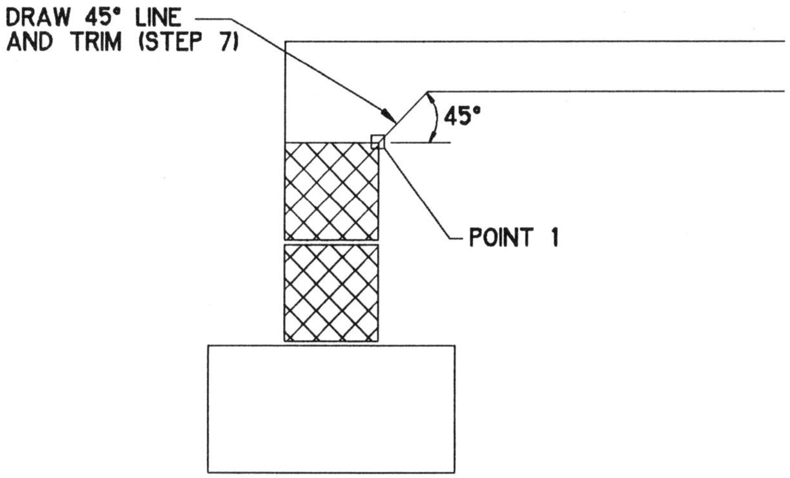

Figure 5-13

Command: **line**
From point: **int**
of *Select point 1.*
to point: **@8<45**

YOUR NOTES

Now use the Fillet command (radius 0) to fillet the two lines. Your drawing should look like the one in Figure 5–13.

STEP 8 *Placing the Stud Wall*

Now let's place the stud wall on top of the slab. Use the Insert command to place the block named SWALL on top of the slab. Refer to Figure 5–14.

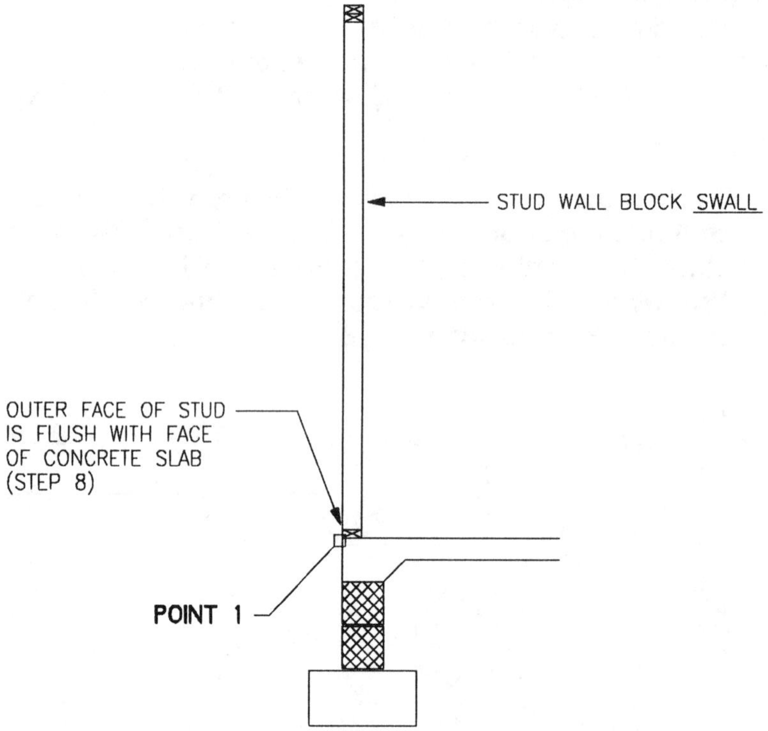

Figure 5-14

Command: **insert**
Block name (or ?): **swall**
Insertion point: **int**
of *Select point 1.*
X scale factor /Corner/XYZ: **1**
Y scale factor (default=X): ↵
Rotation angle : **0**

YOUR NOTES

Your drawing should now look similar to the one in Figure 5–14. Use the Explode command to explode the stud wall so we can edit the entities later.

STEP 9 *Setting Up a Mirror Reference Line*

An examination of the floor plan drawing reveals that the structural part of our section is symmetrical. We can save drawing time by using the Mirror command to create the right half of the section. We can set up the drawing for an accurate mirror function by placing a line at the exact center point and drawing to that line.

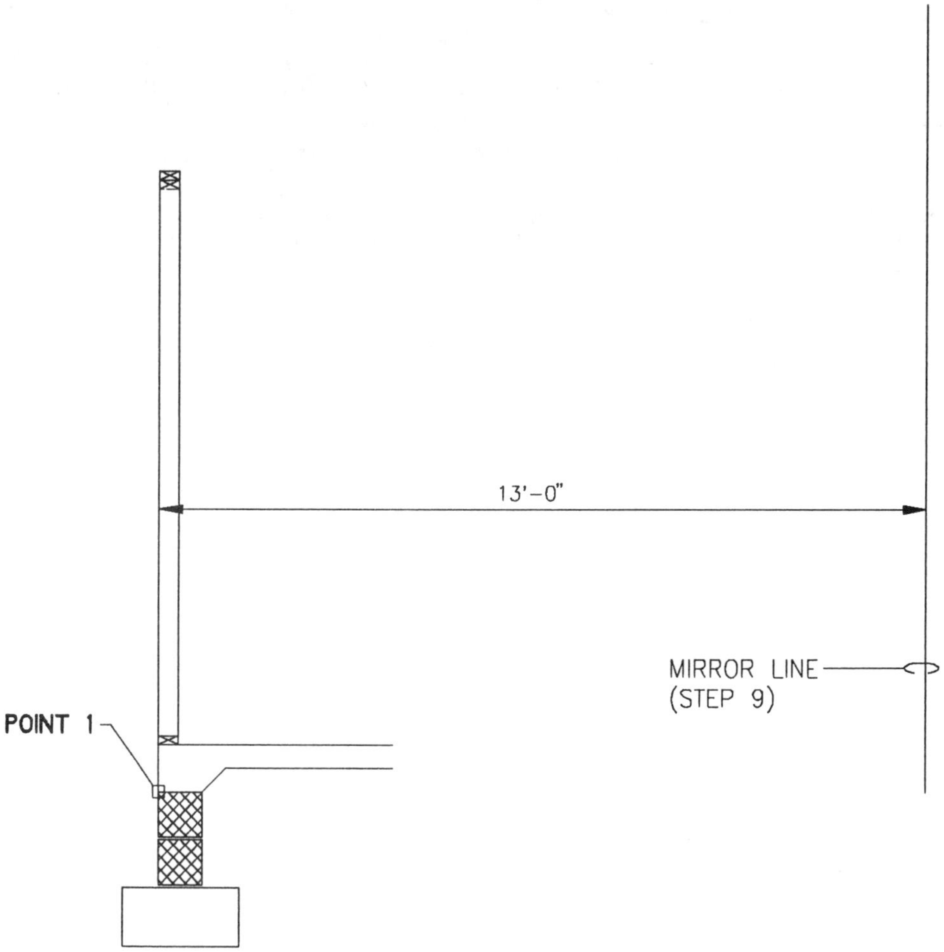

Figure 5-15

YOUR NOTES

Let's see how we might do this. A check of the dimensioned floor plan shows that the distance between the exterior faces of the studs is 26'–0". This means that we can set a line exactly 13'–0" (half the distance) from the outside face of the exterior wall stud. Refer to Figure 5–15 and the following command sequence to place this line.

Command: **line**
From point: **(ref)**
Reference point: **int**
of *Select point 1.*
Enter relative/polar coordinates (with @): **@13'<0**
To point: *Press F8 to turn on ortho, and draw a reference line approximately 16' up.*

We have now placed a reference line for a future mirror operation. Let's see how we can use this mirror reference line.

DRAWING THE ROOF COMPONENTS

The roof components are the roof joist, ceiling joist, web members, and overhang. We will start by drawing the roof joist.

STEP 10 *Drawing the Roof Joist*

The roof joist shows a 5/12 pitch. This means the roof rises 5 units for every 12 horizontal units. Let's start by drawing the bottom line of the sloping roof joist. Refer to Figure 5–16, and execute the following command sequence.

Command: **line**
From point: **int**
of *Select point 1.*
To point: **@12'<0**
To point: **@5'<90**
To point: **c**

Next, erase the horizontal and vertical lines you just drew, leaving only the diagonal line. We now have a line at a 5/12 pitch. Use the Extend command to extend the line to the mirror reference line.

YOUR NOTES

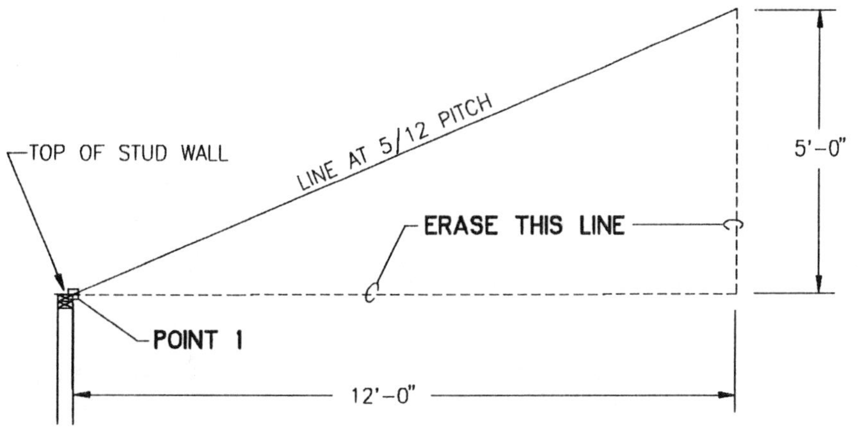

Figure 5-16

Command: **extend**
Select boundary edge(s)...
Select objects: *Select the mirror reference line.*
Select objects: ↵
Select object to extend: *Select the 5/12 pitch line.*

Now use the Offset command to place the top line of the roof joist. The joist is a 2x8. Since it is set on its edge, the 2x8 is 7 1/2" tall.

Command: **offset**
Offset distance or Through <default>: **7-1/2**
Select object to offset: *Select the 5/12 pitch line.*
Side to offset? *Select a point above the line.*

STEP 11 *Extending the Floor Slab*

Use the Extend command to extend the floor slab lines to the reference line now. Refer to Figure 5-17.

YOUR NOTES

STEP 12 *Constructing the Ceiling Joist*

We will construct the overhang after we place the ceiling joist. The joist is a 2x8 that is 7 1/2" tall. Refer to Figure 5–17 and the following command sequence to construct the ceiling joist.

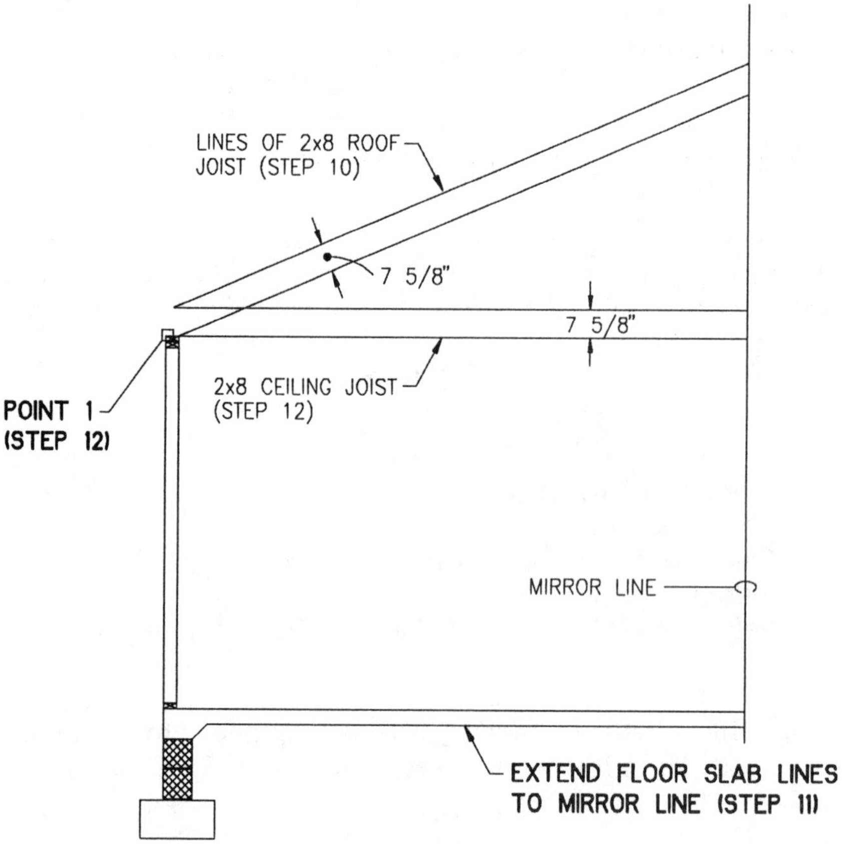

Figure 5-17

Command: **line**
From point: **int**
of *Select point 1.*
to point: **per**
to *Select the mirror reference line.*

YOUR NOTES

Next, offset the bottom face of the roof joist to create the top face. Refer again to Figure 5–17.

> Command: **offset**
> Offset distance or Through <default>: **7–5/8**
> Select object to offset: *Select the bottom line of the ceiling joist.*
> Side to offset? *Pick a point above the line.*

Let's use the Save command again to record our work.

STEP 13 *Constructing the Overhang*

Now let's construct the overhang. We will start by constructing another reference line. Refer to Figure 5–18. Select the Line command. Using object snap near, select a point on the outer face of the stud (see point 1 on Figure 5–18).

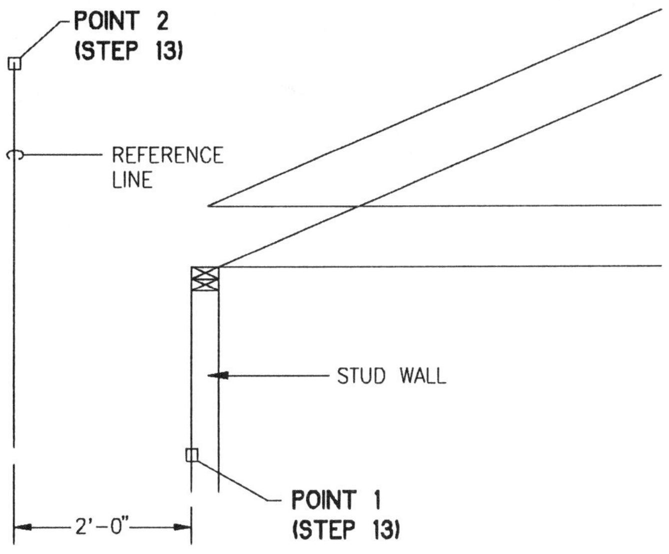

Figure 5-18

The overhang is 2'–0". We will construct a vertical reference line parallel to the wall stud and 2'–0" to the left of it. Use the following command sequence.

YOUR NOTES

Command: **line**
From point: **(ref)**
Reference point: **nea**
to *Select point 1.*
Enter relative/polar coordinates (with @): **@2'<180**
To point: *Turn on ortho, and place the endpoint of the line approximately at point 2 in Figure 5–18.*

Now use the Extend command to extend the rafter lines to the reference line. Pick the reference line as the boundary edge for the extend.

We will now Trim the reference line to make it the end line of the rafter. Refer to Figure 5–19 and the following command sequence.

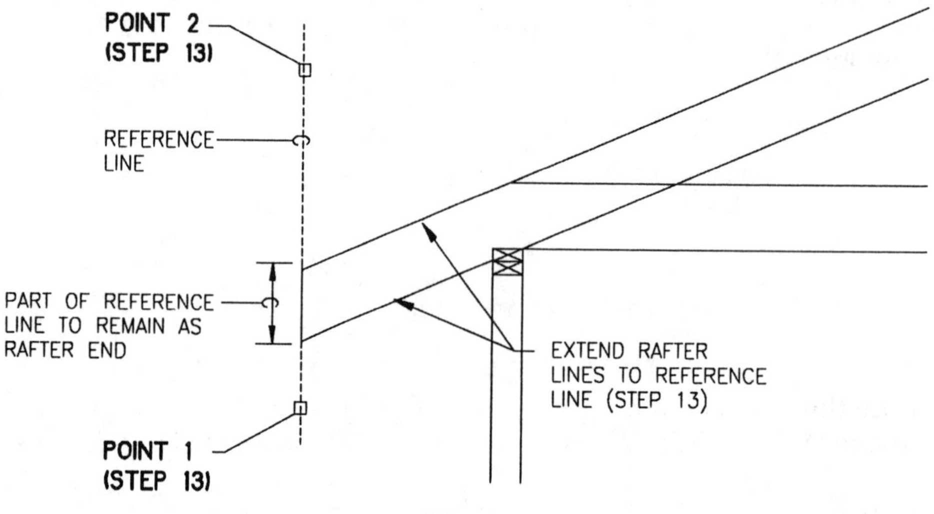

Figure 5-19

Command: **trim**
Select cutting edge(s): *Select bottom line of rafter and top line of sheathing.*
Select objects: ↵
Select object to trim: *Select reference line at points 1 and 2.*

Use the Offset command with a setting of 1 1/2" to offset the rafter end toward the house. This will create the fascia backer. Refer to Figure 5–20.

YOUR NOTES

Then use the Line command and object snap endpoint to draw a line from point 1 to the outer line of the wall stud at point 2. Use object snap perpendicular to snap to the wall stud.

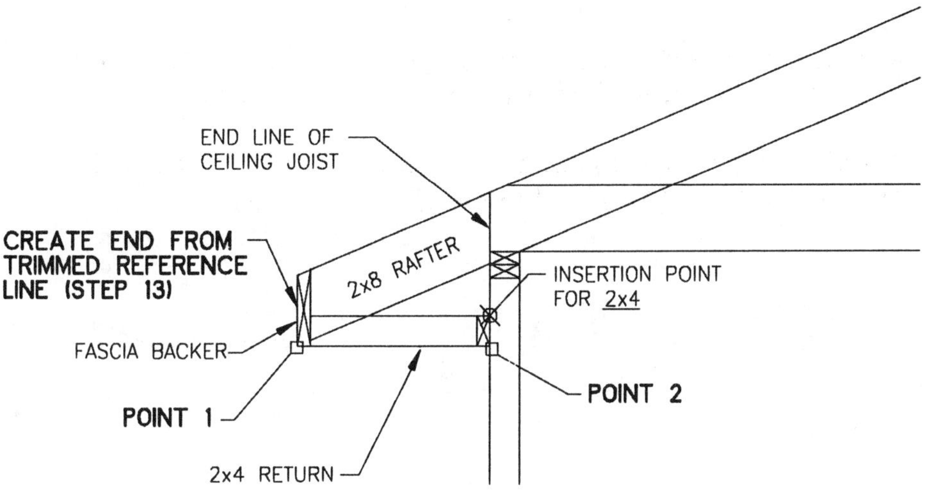

Figure 5-20

Now use the Offset command with an offset distance of 3 1/2" to offset the line to the top. This creates the 2x4 return, as shown in Figure 5–20.

Refer to Figure 5-20 to place the following details. Insert the block named 2x4 at the position shown. (You'll need to rotate the block 90°.) Then draw the end line of the ceiling joist.

Using the Line command, place the crossed lines in the fascia backer. Then use the Trim and Extend commands to make your drawing look like the one in Figure 5–20.

STEP 14 *Constructing the Hidden Lines*

Some of the lines in this section should be shown as hidden lines. We will show these lines with the linetype Hidden. Before we do this, we

YOUR NOTES

must "split" these lines so the hidden part is separated from the part that is not hidden. Let's use the Break command to split these lines. Refer to Figure 5–21 and the following command sequence.

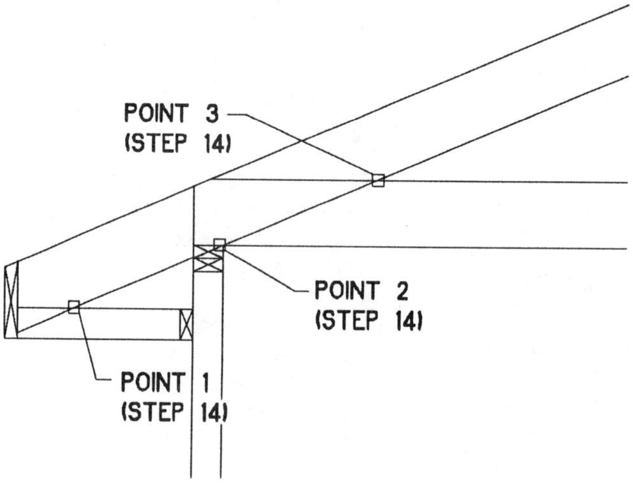

Figure 5-21

Command: **break**
Select object: *Select the bottom rafter line.*
Enter second point (or F for first point): **f**
Enter first point: **int**
of *Select point 1.*
Enter second point: **@**

Because you entered the @ symbol, the second break point was placed at the same point as the first, splitting the line. Repeat the procedure, using points 2 and 3 in Figure 5–21 to split the line.

Now let's use the Change command to change the linetypes. Refer to Figure 5–22 and the following command sequence.

YOUR NOTES

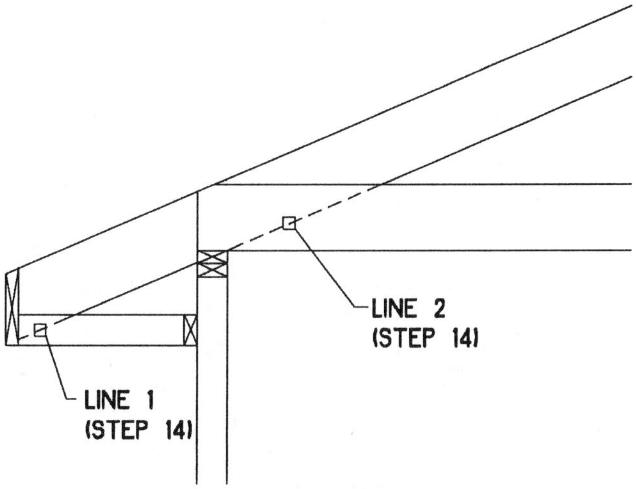

Figure 5-22

Command: **change**
Select objects: *Select lines 1 and 2 in Figure 5–22.*
Properties/change point: **p**
Change what property
(Color/Elev/LAyer/LType?Thickness) ? **lt**
New linetype <default>: **hidden**
Change what property
(Color/Elev/LAyer/LType?Thickness) ? ↵

The linetypes should now be shown as hidden. If they are not, regenerate the drawing.

STEP 15 *Mirroring the Section*

Now verify that ortho is on. Use the following sequence to mirror the section. Refer to Figure 5–23.

YOUR NOTES

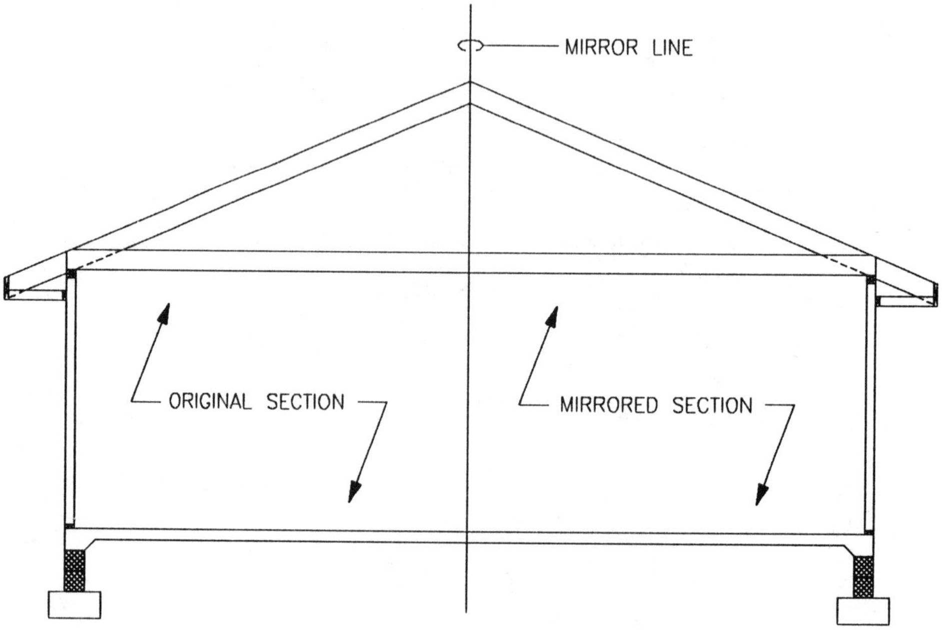

Figure 5-23

Command: **mirror**
Select objects: *Use a window to capture the entire section, minus the mirror line.*
First point of mirror line: **end**
of *Select top end of mirror reference line.*
Second point: *Move cursor down and pick.*
Delete old objects? **n**

Now erase the mirror reference line.

STEP 16 *Constructing the Web Members*

Next, we will next place the web members in the roof structure. An inspection of the design indicates a "W" web configuration. (See Figure 5–1 on the first page of this section.) This requires the web members to

YOUR NOTES

connect to two places at the ceiling truss, creating three equal spaces (see Figure 5–24).

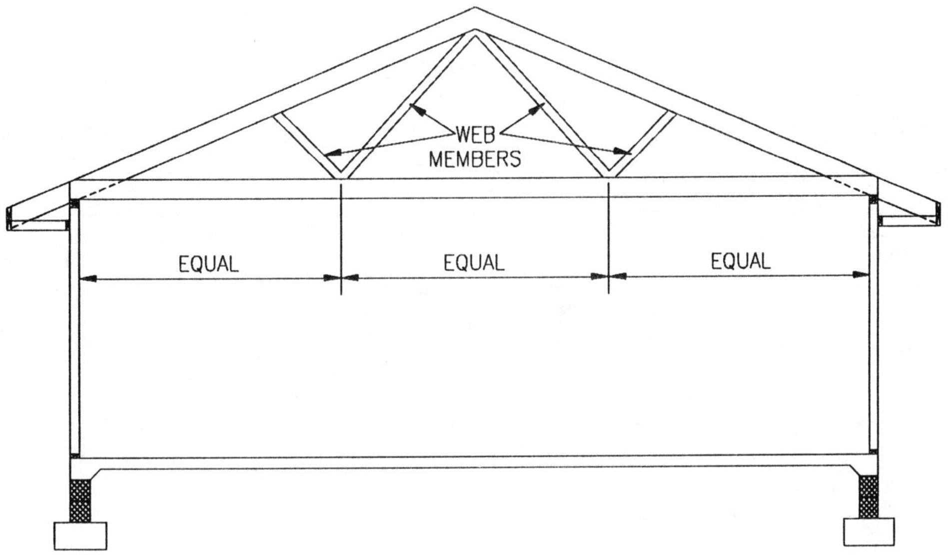

Figure 5-24

We can use the Divide command to create three equal divisions. If we pick either side of the ceiling joist to divide, however, we will see that it is in two pieces. This is because we only drew half of it. We mirrored the other half.

Let's draw a new line from point 1 to point 2, as shown in Figure 5–25. We can use the Divide command to divide this new line into three equal parts.

First set the pdmode to 35 so that we can see the dividing points.

Command: **setvar**
Variable name or ?<default>: **pdmode**
New value for PDMODE <default>: **35**

Now use the Divide command to divide the top line of the ceiling joist into 3 divisions. Use the following command sequence.

YOUR NOTES

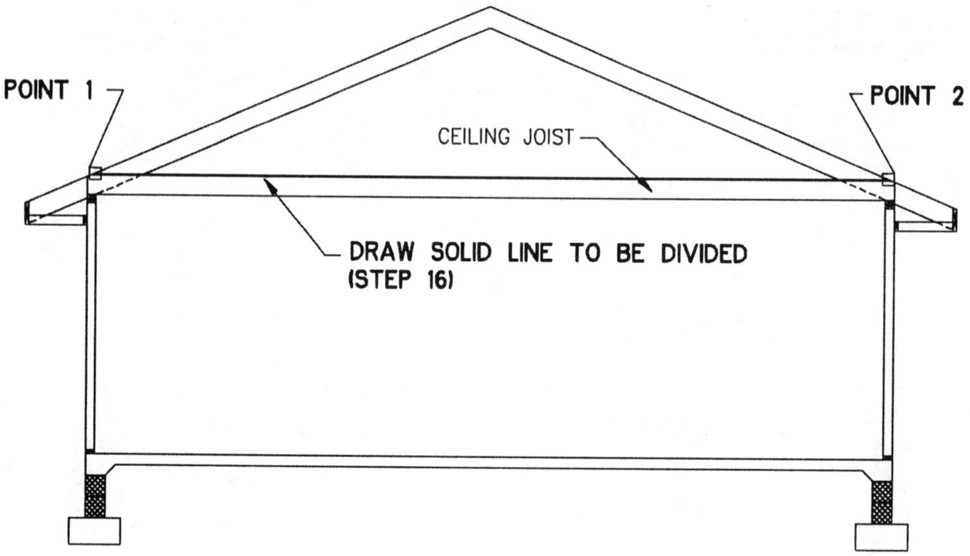

Figure 5-25

Command: **divide**
Select object to divide: *Select top ceiling joist line.*
<number of segments>/block: **3**

You should now see two points similar to those in Figure 5–26.

After you place the points, use the Erase command to delete the line you placed. Use Redraw after erasing to refresh the drawing screen so that the lines below the erased line will be properly displayed.

Now let's draw some lines to locate the web members. Follow the sequence shown in Figure 5–26 to construct the lines.

We will use these as center lines for the webs. The webs are constructed of 2x4's. Use Offset, set to 1 3/4", to offset the center line to each side.

YOUR NOTES

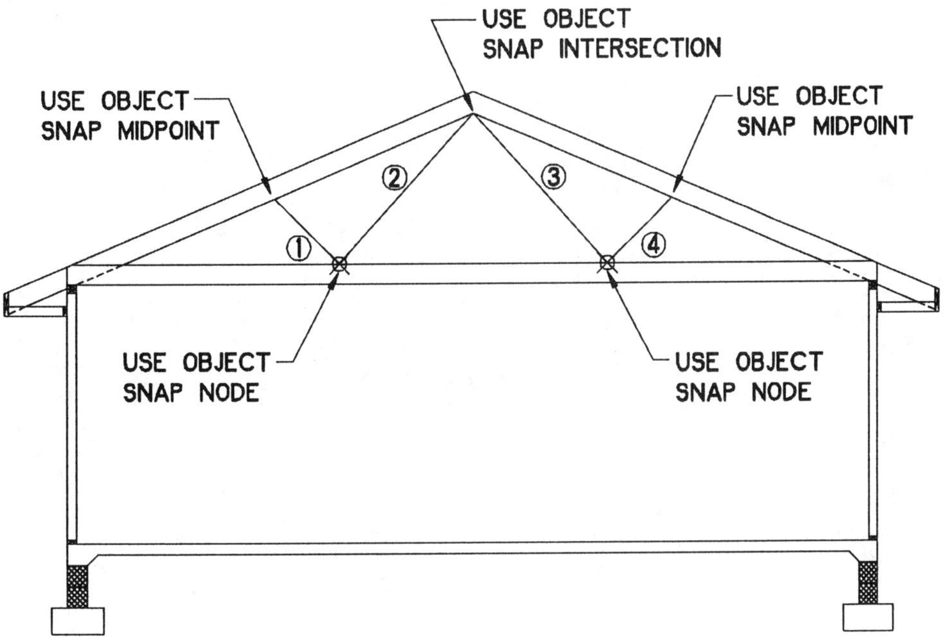

Figure 5-26

This will create the 3 1/2" width of the 2x4 web, as shown in Figure 5–27.

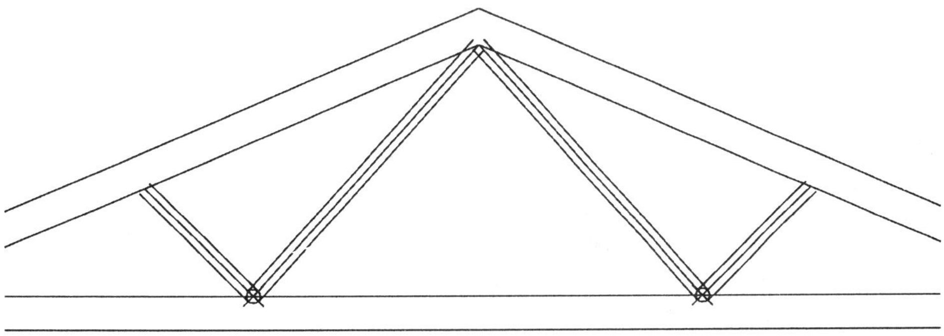

Figure 5-27

YOUR NOTES

Next, Erase the points and the center lines. Use the Extend, Trim, and Fillet commands to edit the lines so that the webs look like the ones in Figure 5–28. Use the Save command again to record your work to disk.

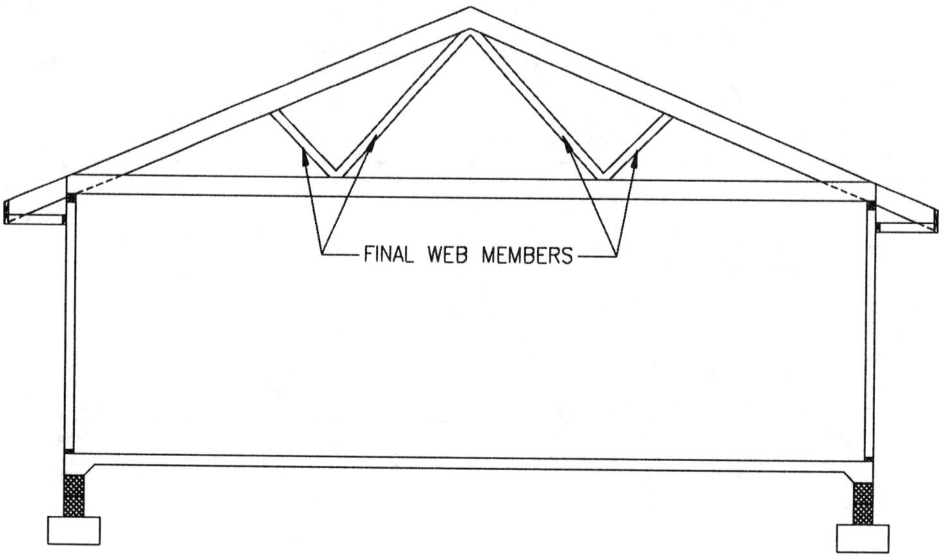

Figure 5-28

STEP 17 *Inserting the Stud Wall*

Now it is time to draw the interior parts of the house that you would see in section. Let's insert the stud wall. Use Figure 5–29 and the following command sequence.

Command: **insert**
Block name (or ?) <default>: **swall**
Insertion point: **(ref)**
Reference point: **int**
of *Select point 1.*
Enter relative/polar coordinates (with @): **@13'7"<0**
X scale factor / Corner /XYZ: **1**
Y scale factor (default=X): **1**
Rotation angle <default>: **0**

YOUR NOTES

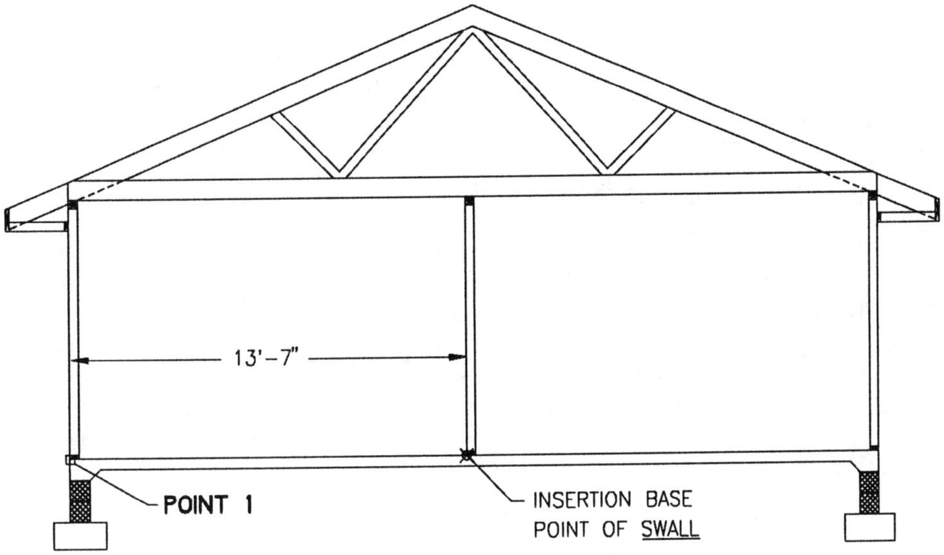

Figure 5-29

STEP 18 *Inserting the Doorways*

Let's proceed by inserting the doorways. Refer to Figure 5–30 and the following command sequence.

Command: **insert**
Block name (or ?) <default>: **28dframe**
Insertion point: **(ref)**
Reference point: **int**
of *Select point 1.*
Enter relative/polar coordinates (with @): **@6'4"<0**
X scale factor / Corner /XYZ: **1**
Y scale factor (default=X): **1**
Rotation angle <default>: **0**

YOUR NOTES

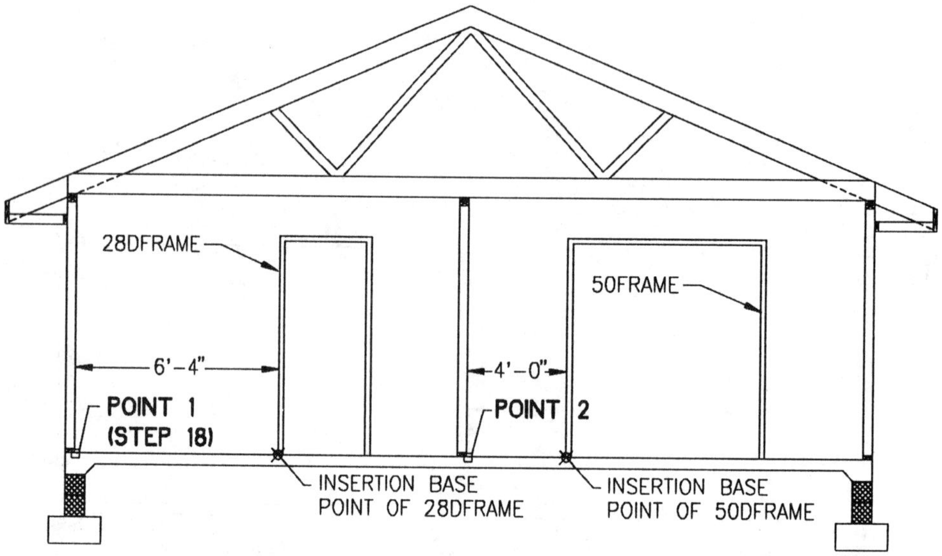

Figure 5-30

Now insert the second door frame, referring to Figure 5–30 as necessary.

Command: **insert**
Block name (or ?) <default>: **50frame**
Insertion point: **(ref)**
Reference point: **int**
of *Select point 2.*
Enter relative/polar coordinates (with @): **@4'<0**
X scale factor / Corner /XYZ: **1**
Y scale factor (default=X): **1**
Rotation angle <default>: **0**

STEP 19 *Placing the Wall Edge*

Let's place the edge of the wall that occurs between the kitchen and laundry. Refer to Figure 5–31.

YOUR NOTES

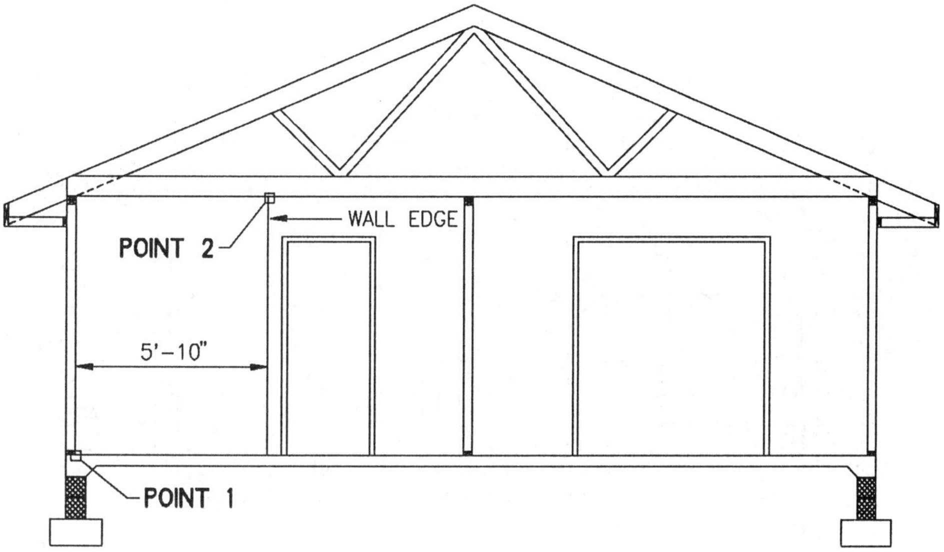

Figure 5-31

Command: **line**
From point: **(ref)**
Reference point: **int**
of *Select point 1.*
Enter relative/polar coordinates (with @): **@5'10"<0**
To point: **per**
to *Select point 2.*

STEP 20 *Inserting the Cabinets*

Now it is time to insert the cabinets. First, make a layer named CABINETS with a color of blue (color 5).

Figure 5–32 shows the layout and the block names. The cabinet drawings are resident blocks in the prototype drawing. Insert the cabinets as shown in Figure 5–32.

YOUR NOTES

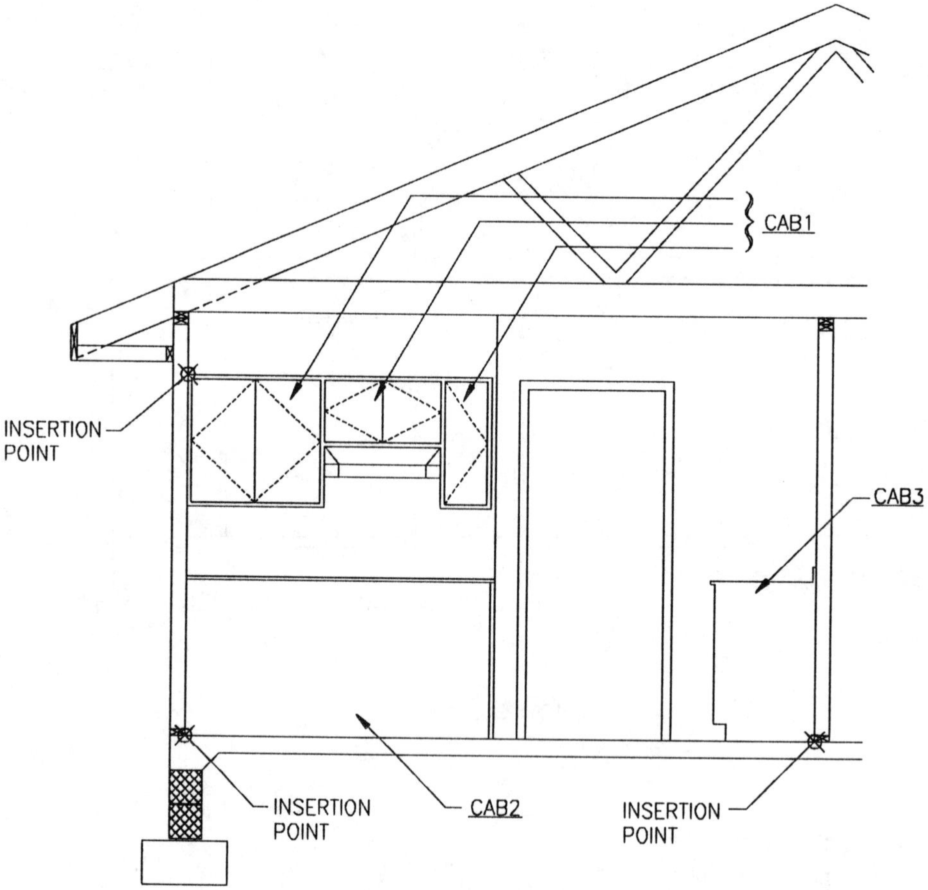

Figure 5-32

After you have finished inserting the cabinets, turn the timer off.

YOUR NOTES

YOUR NOTES

SUMMARY

- You can save drawing time on some types of drawings by using the component method of drawing construction.
- Components are distinguishable items that can be drawn and blocked, then inserted into their positions in a drawing. You can think of components as CAD building blocks.
- Components can be write-blocked to disk, or even drawn separately, to create a component symbol library.
- When you create a drawing component, think carefully about the placement of the insertion base point. This should be a point that you would normally use to insert the component.
- When you construct a component, place all entities of the component on the layer(s) on which you want them to appear after insertion.
- Use the Explode command to break component blocks into individual entities for editing.

QUESTIONS

YOUR NOTES

1. What is a building section?

2. How is the location of a section shown on a floor plan drawing?

3. What is the "component method" of creating a drawing? What are the advantages of using this method?

4. How can you save time when you are drawing a symmetrical section?

5. What is meant by the "pitch" of a roof?

YOUR NOTES

PROBLEMS

1. Create the following component blocks:

   12" x 24" footing
   7-5/8" x 7-5/8" masonry block
   2 x 10 (in cross section)
   2 x 4 wall

   Create a wall section using these components.

2. Select a floor plan from Appendix M. Locate a position for the building section and draw the section.

YOUR NOTES

The Team Approach

The Mall of America was an enormous project. The $625 million, 4.2 million-square-foot complex, which included both shopping and entertainment facilities, was to be built as a "fast-track" job. For Melvin Simon and Associates, the developer, this meant that the design and construction team had to be able to work together without a hitch. Melvin Simon's Director of Construction, Joseph Talentino, decided that the designers, engineers, and builders would all use AutoCAD to create design drawings and working drawings for the project.

The entire design team, which included a number of independent firms, set up shop in one office near the mall site. They began by selecting appropriate third-party software, choosing Sofia's AdCADD Auto-Architect, Civil, Structural, and HVAC applications. These applications enhanced the features available through Auto CAD by providing the routines for drawing buildings and architec tural symbol libraries. Several AutoLISP programmers, led by system manages Jamie Sletten, further modified the system. They ensured that a carefully planned layering system was maintained and that drawings could be easily exchanged between disciplines.

Since the job was "fast-tracked," the structural steel was being placed while the architectural design was being finished. Changes were frequent and constant. Talentino says "Using AutoCAD on a network, we made sure that everyone was working from the same sheet of music. Everyone could reference everyone else's draw ings, at any time." Since all of the applications software came from a single vendor, it was easier to make sure that compatibil ity was maintained.

Since Softdesk's AutoCAD add-ons are all three-dimensional, the Simon team created many of the mall drawings in 3D. The steel drawings and ductwork drawings were compared in 3D to prevent conflicts. The builders often referred to three-dimensional plots. The developer showed rendered images and animations to store owners who were interested in moving into the mall.

It was generally agreed that the use of AutoCAD and the Softdesk add-ons saved millions of dollars and months of time over the course of the mall design and construction. In addition, there would be significant future benefits for store owners who would have access to the original CAD drawings. Not only would they be able to locate walls, columns, and connections accurately, but they could use the three-dimensional building model to plan their own store interiors.

Courtesy of Autodesk, Inc.

SESSION 6

Constructing the Wall Section

OBJECTIVE

In this session, we will complete the section sheet we started in Session Five by constructing the wall section and the door schedule. The completed drawing sheet from sessions Five and Six is shown in Figure 6–1.

YOUR NOTES

Use this space for notes about your indivudual plan

DOOR SCHEDULE

NO.	TYPE	WIDTH	THICKNESS	HEIGHT	REMARKS
1	H.C.	2'-8"	1-3/8"	6'-8"	
2	BIFOLD	5'-0"	-	6'-8"	
3	BIFOLD	4'-0"	-	6'-8"	
4	BIFOLD	4'-0"	-	6'-8"	
5	H.C.	2'-8"	1-3/8"	6'-8"	
6	H.C.	2'-6"	1-3/8"	6'-8"	
7	H.C.	2'-8"	1-3/8"	6'-8"	
8	BYPASS	CUSTOM	-	6'-8"	
9	H.C.	2'-6"	1-3/8"	6'-8"	
10	BYPASS	8'-0"	-	6'-8"	
11	DBL. SWING	2'-6"	1-3/8"	6'-8"	
12	S.C.	2'-6" DBL	1-3/4"	6'-8"	
13	CASED OPG.	5'-0"	-	6'-8"	
14	CASED OPG.	4'-0"	-	6'-8"	
15	H.C.	2'-8"	1-3/8"	6'-8"	
16	H.C.	2'-6"	1-3/8"	6'-8"	
17	H.C.	2'-6"	1-3/8"	6'-8"	
18	H.C.	2'-4"	1-3/8"	6'-8"	
19	H.C.	2'-6" DBL	1-3/8"	6'-8"	
20	BYPASS	5'-0"	-	6'-8"	
21	GARAGE	16'-0"	-	7'-0"	

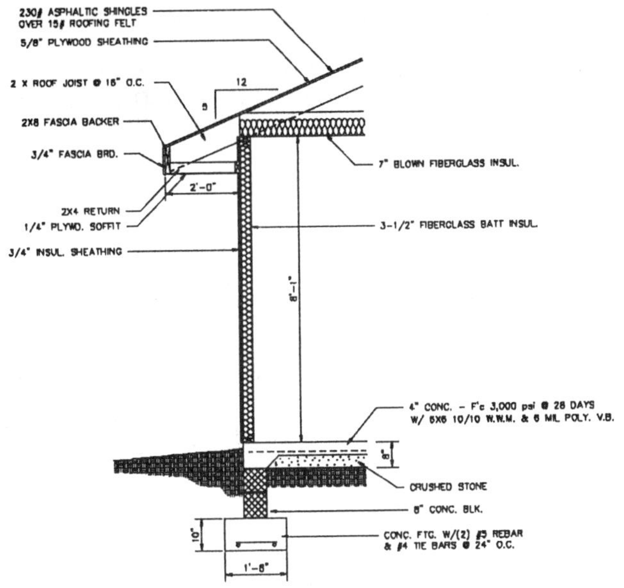

1/3 WALL SECTION

SCALE: 3/4"=1'-0"

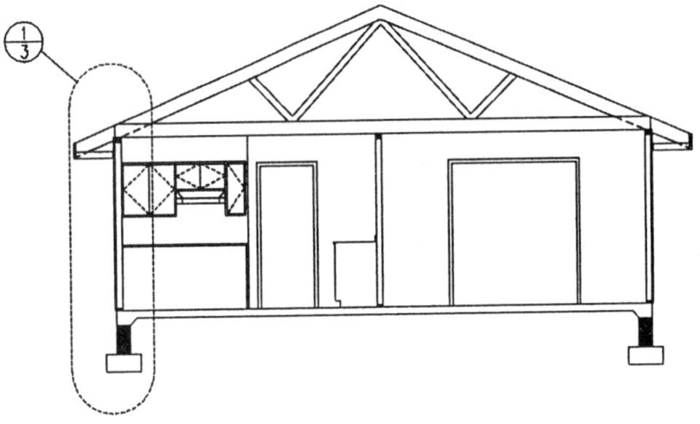

2/3 BUILDING SECTION

SCALE: 3/8"=1'-0"

Figure 6-1

YOUR NOTES

We will cut the wall section at the location shown in Figure 6–2. Note that the numbers in the section marker indicate that it is Section 1 and is located on drawing sheet three.

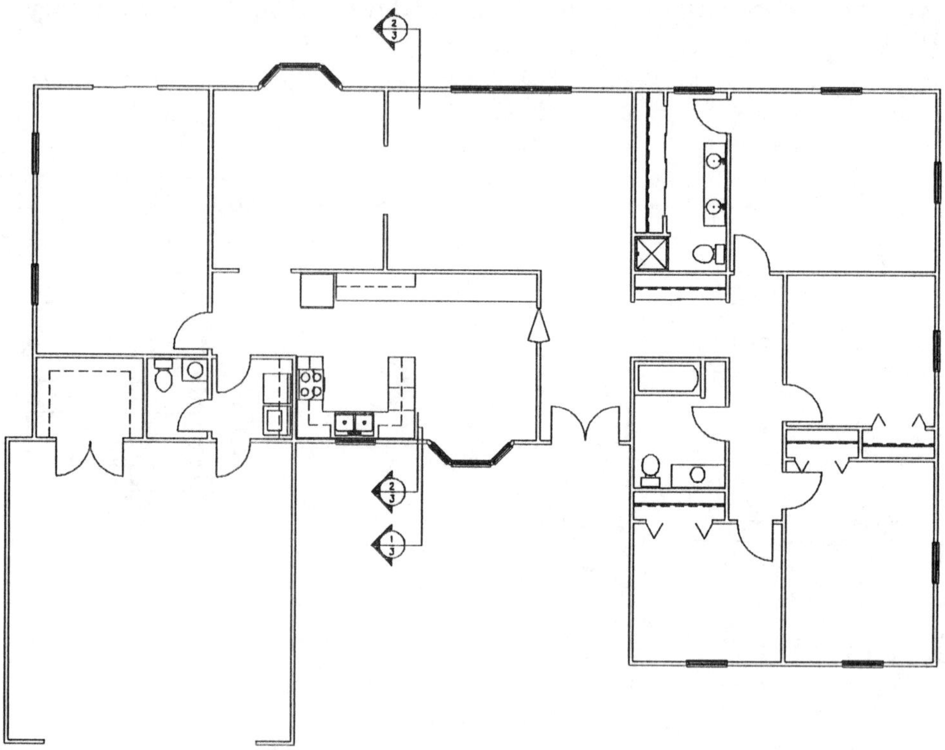

Figure 6-2

Commands used in this session:

- **array**
- **asctext (autolisp program)**
- **break**
- **change**
- **copy**
- **dim**
- **erase**
- **explode**
- **hatch**
- **insert**
- **layer**
- **line**
- **osnap**
- **pline**
- **scale**
- **sketch**
- **style**
- **text**
- **trim**
- **zoom**

CREATING THE WALL SECTION

YOUR NOTES

As we discussed in Session Five, a section is a drawing that shows details of an object by "cutting" it in two so that we can view the cut area. A wall section is used to show details of a wall.

A wall section differs from a building section. A wall section shows details of a single wall, whereas a building section shows the width of an entire building. Items such as materials, vertical and horizontal dimensions, and the relationship of materials to each other are noted on the wall section.

Splitting the Building Section

We will use the building section we constructed in Session Five as a starting place. Start the drawing named SECTION, which you drew in Session Five.

Since the wall section is a larger, more detailed part of the of the building section, you can use part of the building section to obtain a quick start for the wall section. This is one of the methodologies that makes CAD very efficient.

STEP 1 *Drawing a "Cut" Line*

Start by turning on the timer with the Time command. Next, select the Line command and draw a line, as shown in Figure 6–3. We will use this line as a "cut" line to separate our wall section from the building section.

STEP 2 *Breaking the Section Lines*

We will now use the Break command to "split" the wall section from the building section. Move the screen crosshairs to the top of the screen to access the pull-down menus. (Alternate instructions will follow for those whose displays are not capable of displaying pull-down menus.) Select the Tools menu. From the pull-down menu, select osnap. The command line prompts:

YOUR NOTES

Command: **osnap**
Object snap modes:

Now highlight intersection on the menu and press the button on your input device. You have just set object snap intersection in continuous mode.

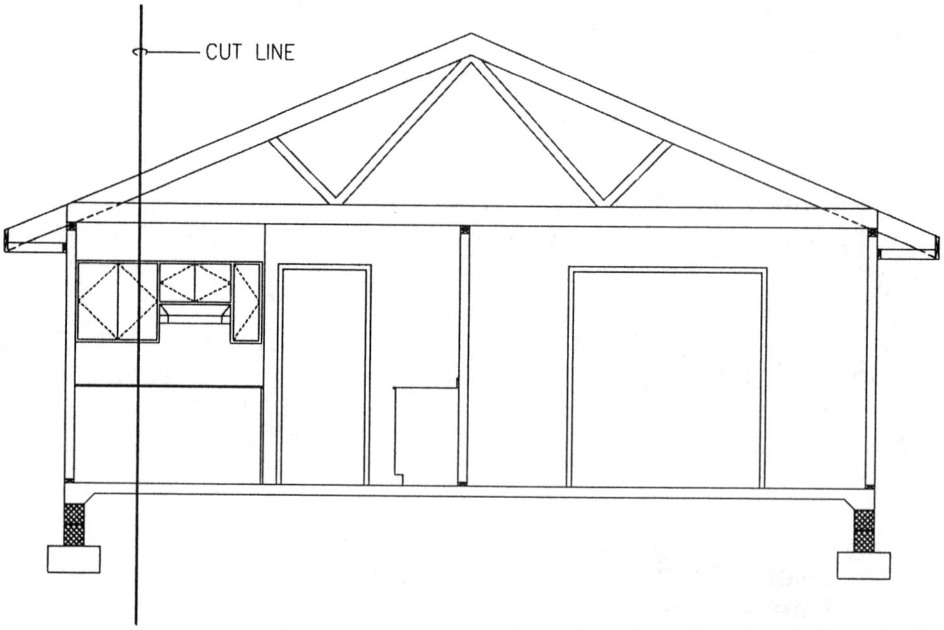

Figure 6-3

If your display system can not display pull-down menus, use the following command sequence to set the object snap.

Command: **osnap**
Object snap modes: **int**

Now it is time to split the wall section. Select the Break command. Refer to the following command sequence and Figure 6–4.

YOUR NOTES

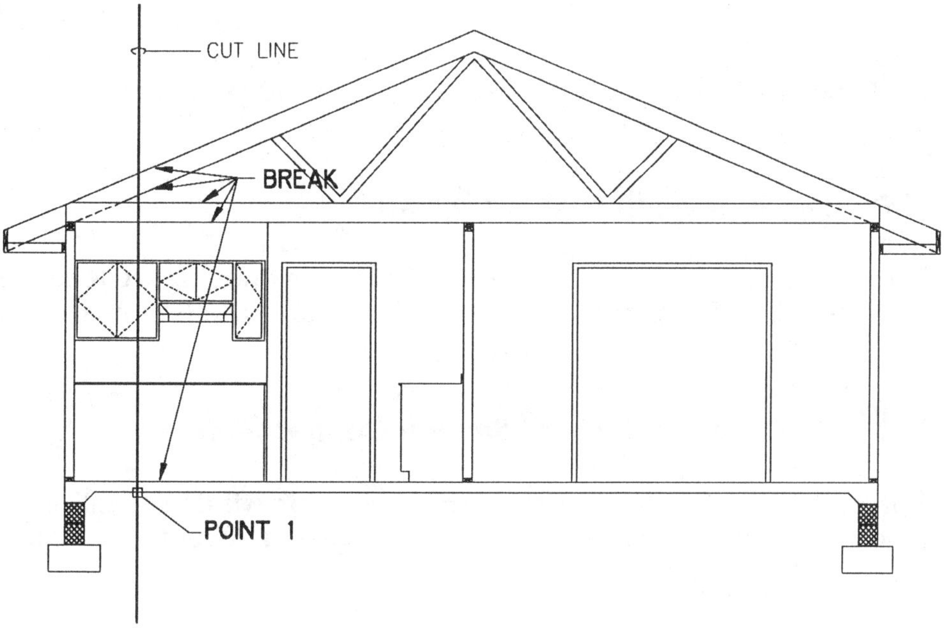

Figure 6-4

Command: **break**
Select object: *Select the bottom line of the floor slab.*
Enter second point (or F for first point): **f**
Enter first point: *Enter point 1.*
Enter second point: **@**

By entering an @ symbol, you place the second point at the same place as the first point. Alternately, you may use the object snap aperture on your crosshairs to capture the same point you captured for the first break point. Note that you will not see a change in the drawing at this time. This operation separates the bottom floor slab line into two entities. This will allow us to separate a copy of the building section later.

Continue to use the Break command in the same manner to split each line that intersects the cut line we placed in the building section. After you have split each intersecting line, use the following command sequence to cancel the object snap intersection mode.

YOUR NOTES

Command: **osnap**
Object snap modes: **none**

Finally, erase the cut line. Your building section should appear unchanged. Use the Save command now to record your edits.

Placing the Split-Away Section

Now it is time to copy our wall section from the building section. We will resize the wall section to a larger scale to show details more readily.

STEP 3 *Copying the Wall Section Components*

Select the Copy command. Use an object selection window to select the objects to the left of where the cut line was placed. Refer to Figure 6–5 and use the following command sequence.

Command: **copy**
Select objects: **w**
First corner: *Place window corner at point 1.*
Other corner: *Place window corner at point 2.*
Select objects: ↵
<Base point or displacement>/Multiple: *Select a point near point 3.*
Second point of displacement: *Select a point near point 4.*

You should now have a copy of the wall section part of the building section.

STEP 4 *Scaling the Wall Section*

Remember from Session Five that we set the limits for a plot scale of 1/4"=1'–0". We want our wall section to be plotted at a scale of 1"=1'–0". We can use the Scale command to enlarge the section so it will plot larger. Appendix B contains a table of scale factors you should use to enlarge or reduce part of a drawing to achieve different scales. By checking the table, we see that if the rest of the drawing is plotted at a scale of

YOUR NOTES

1/4"=1′–0", and we want our section to be plotted at 1"=1′–0", we can use a scale factor of 4. Use the following command sequence to enlarge the section.

> Command: **scale**
> Select objects: *Use a window to select the entire wall section.*
> Select objects: ↵
> Base point: *Pick a point at the bottom line of the footing.*
> <Scale factor>/Reference: **4**

Your drawing should now look like the one in Figure 6–5.

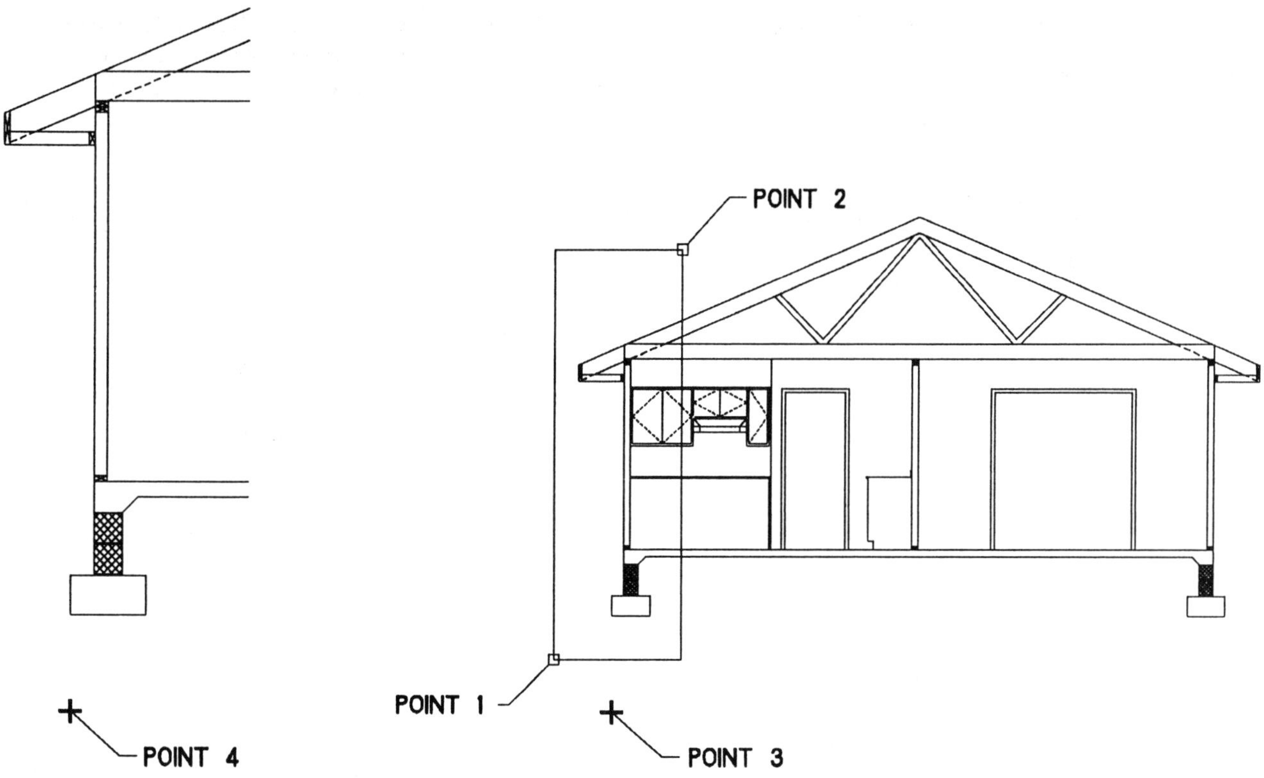

Figure 6-5

YOUR NOTES

Constructing the Ground Lines

Since some of the wall section will be underground, we need to show a ground level. To show ground level, we will draw a ground line. We will use the Sketch command to place the ground line.

STEP 5 *Using the Sketch Command*

To draw the ground line, use the following command sequence. Refer to Figure 6–6 for the finished sketch.

Command: **sketch**
Record increment <default>: **1**
Sketch. Pen eXit Quit Record Erase Connect .

Check the status line at the top of your screen to be sure that ortho is off. If ortho is on, press F8 to turn it off before you start sketching.

Place the cursor at point 1 as shown in Figure 6–6 and pick. Carefully move the cursor to the left, drawing a ground line that slopes slightly downhill. Don't worry if the ground line looks a bit rough, since we want such a look to represent the ground surface. When you have reached a point approximately at point 2, press the pick button on your input device again. Note that the command line shows <pen down> and <pen up> messages when you push the pick button. This means the sketch pen is "up" off the paper (not drawing) or "down" on the paper (drawing).

If you are satisfied with the ground line you have drawn, press R to record the sketch line. If you are not satisfied, press Q to quit and try again. After you have recorded the sketch, press X to exit the sketch command mode.

Step 6 *Drawing the Straight Ground Line*

Next, use the Line command to draw a straight ground line below the concrete floor slab as shown in Figure 6–6.

YOUR NOTES

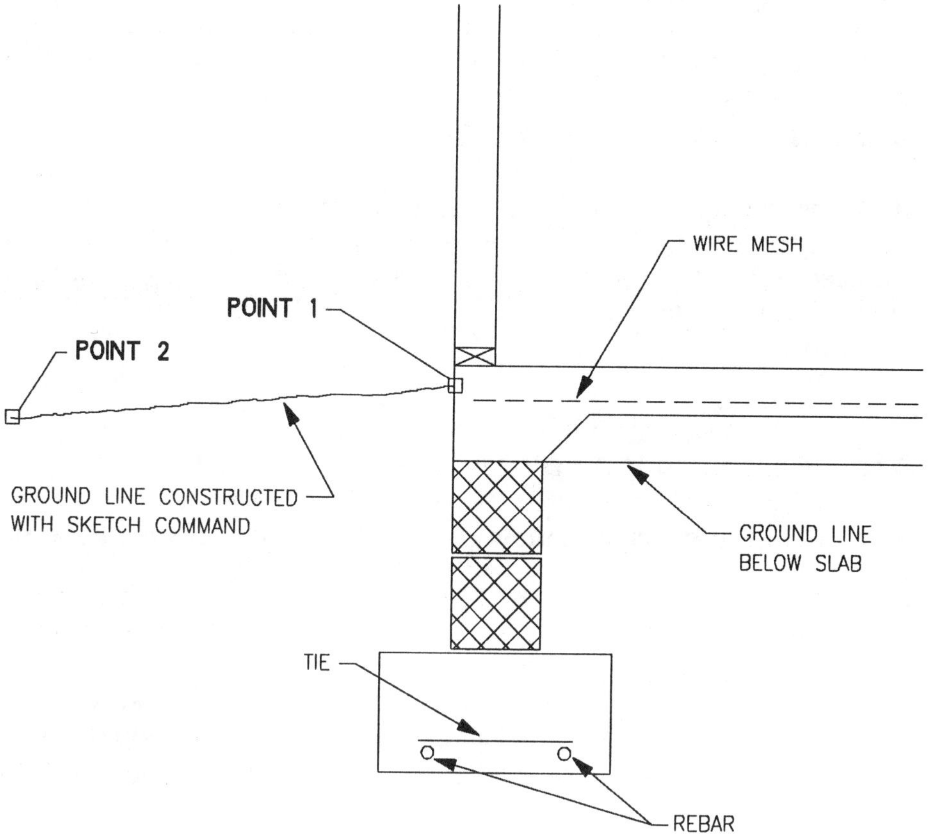

Figure 6-6

Note the line designating wire mesh in Figure 6–6. It is a hidden line, represented by dashes. Offset the upper line of the floor slab 3" to the south to create the line representing the mesh. Change the linetype to Dashed using the following command sequence:

Command: **change**
Select objects: **!**
Select objects: ↵
Properties/<default>: **p**
Change what property(Color/Elev/LAyer/LType/Thickness)? **lt**
New linetype <default>: **dashed**
Change what property (Color/Elev/LAyer/LType/Thickness)? ↵

YOUR NOTES

Now choose the method you find most efficient, and draw the rebar and tie as shown in the footing. Refer again to Figure 6–6.

Constructing the Hatches

It is time to construct the hatches in the section drawing. Hatches are normally drawn inside a boundary area. As you can see from Figure 6–7, we need to hatch an area that does not normally contain a boundary. However, we can use a methodology to place the hatch that makes the operation very simple.

STEP 7 *Setting the Hatch Layer*

First, change to the layer named HATCH, which you created in Session Five.

Command: **layer**
?/Make/Set/New/ON/OFF/Color/Ltype/Freeze/Thaw: **s**
New current layer default: **hatch**
?/Make/Set/New/ON/OFF/Color/Ltype/Freeze/Thaw: ↵

Verify that layer HATCH is listed on the status line at the top of the screen.

STEP 8 *Constructing a Hatch Boundary*

Let's now use the Polyline command to construct a temporary hatch boundary for the earth hatch below the exterior ground line. Use the following command sequence, and refer to Figure 6–7.

Command: **pline**
From point: *Select point 1.*
Current line-width is 0'-0"
Arc/Close/Halfwidth/Length/Undo/Width/<Endpoint of line>:
Select point 2 and subsequent points, using Close *to close from point 8 to the beginning point.*

YOUR NOTES

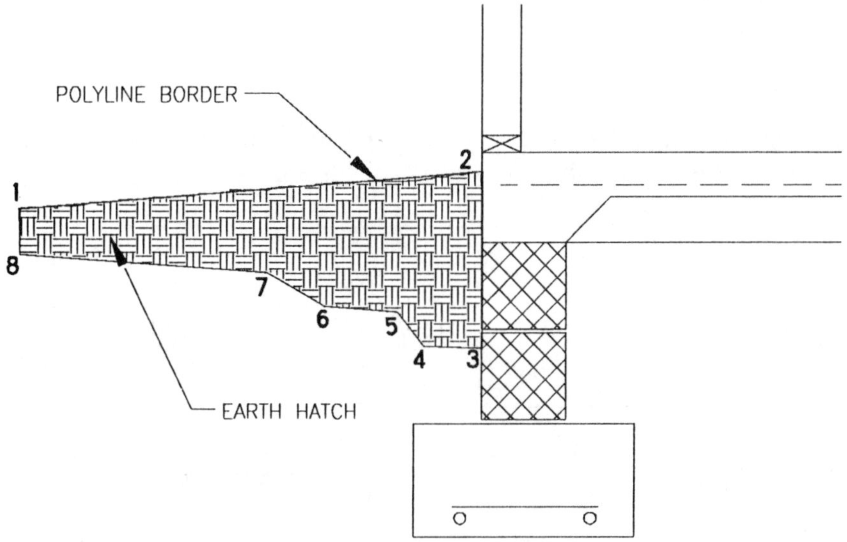

Figure 6-7

STEP 9 *Placing the Earth Hatch*

Now we will place the hatch in the polyline boundary we constructed. Follow the command sequence carefully.

Command: **hatch**
Pattern (? or name/U,style): **earth**
Scale for pattern <default>:**12**
Angle for pattern <default>: **0**
Select objects: **l**
1 found
Select objects:↵

Your hatch should now appear within the polyline boundary. Now we can erase the boundary. Notice that we are using "Previous" to select the polyline boundary. If we used "Last," we would select the hatch.

YOUR NOTES

Command: **erase**
Select objects: **p**
1 found
Select objects ↵

Next, use the same technique to place the earth hatch in a polyline boundary beneath the slab, as shown in Figure 6–8.

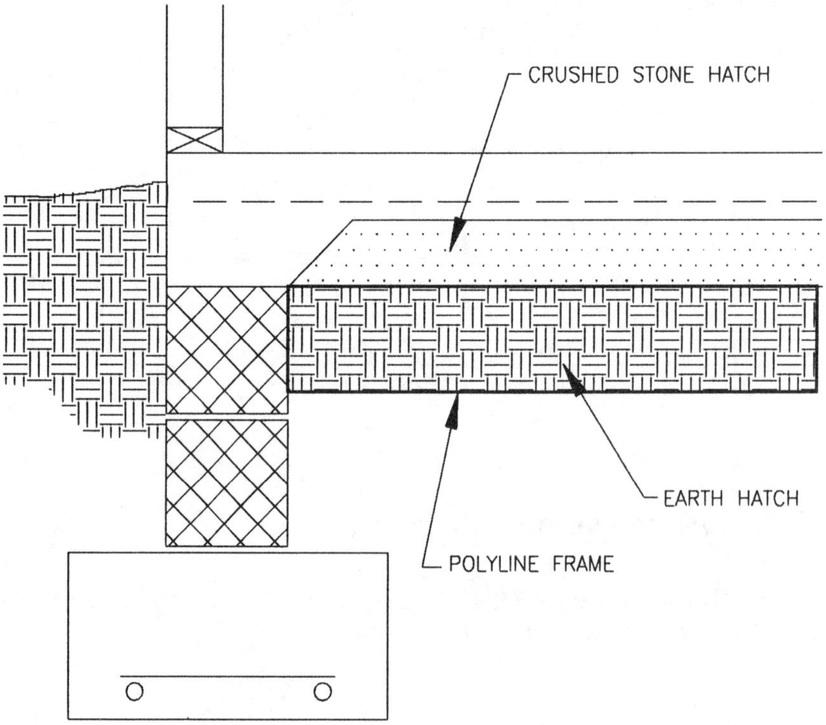

Figure 6-8

STEP 10 *Placing the Crushed Stone Hatch*

Now place the hatch that represents the crushed stone beneath the concrete slab, as shown in Figure 6–8. The name of the hatch is Dots, the scale is 12, and the rotation angle is 0.

YOUR NOTES

Placing a "Quick Hatch"

We should now place the wall insulation. A check of the hatch patterns available in AutoCAD, however, does not reveal a hatch that could be satisfactorily used for an insulation hatch. Let's look at another methodology.

Figure 6–9 shows a hatch pattern that is typically used for insulation. Upon close inspection, we can see that the pattern, like all hatch patterns, is a shape that is repeated over an area.

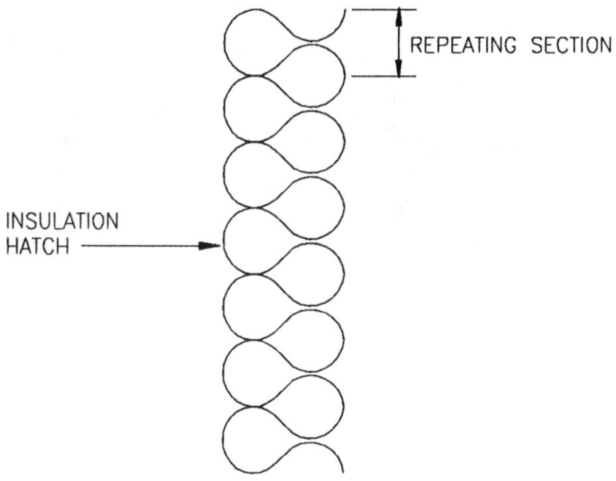

Figure 6-9

STEP 11 *Inserting the "Quick Hatch" Component*

We can draw the repeating part of the hatch and array it to create the hatch for the wall insulation. The prototype drawing contains a resident block named INHAT (Insulation Hatch). Let's insert this symbol. Use the following command sequence, and refer to Figure 6–10.

YOUR NOTES

Command: **insert**
Block name (or ?): **inhat**
Insertion point: **int**
of *Select point 1.*
X scale factor <1> / Corner / XYZ: **1**
Y scale factor (default=X): ↵
Rotation angle <0>: ↵

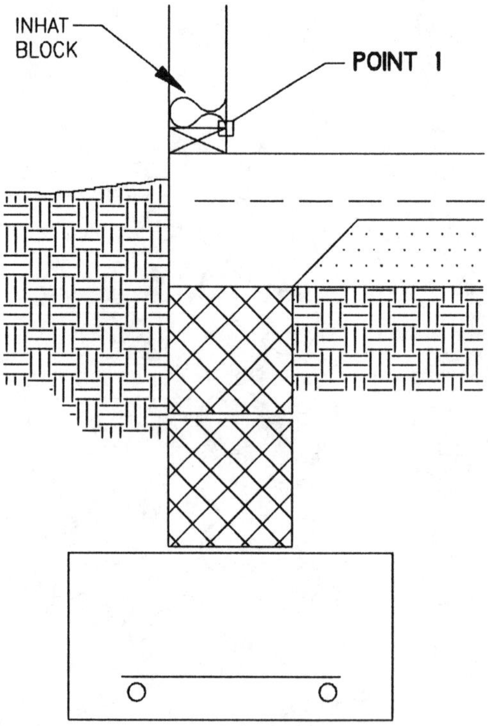

Figure 6-10

STEP 12 *Arraying the "Quick Hatch" Component*

Notice that the "partial hatch" you inserted is one cycle of an insulation hatch. All we need to do now is array the item up the wall. To do the array, we need to know how many copies of the item we need to make.

YOUR NOTES

We can use the distance command to measure of the height of the item and of the overall vertical distance in the wall cavity where it goes. Then we simply divide the overall distance by the item height.

A check of our insulation partial hatch and the wall cavity indicates that we will need an array that contains 50 vertical copies. Let's use the Array command to place the insulation hatch in the wall. Use the following command sequence, and refer to Figure 6–11.

Command: **array**
Select objects: **l**
Rectangular or Polar array (R/P): **r**
Select objects: ↵
Number of Rows (---) <1>: **50**
Number of columns (| | |) <1>: **1**
Unit cell or distance between rows (---): **end**
of *Select point 1.*
Other corner: **end**
of *Select point 2.*

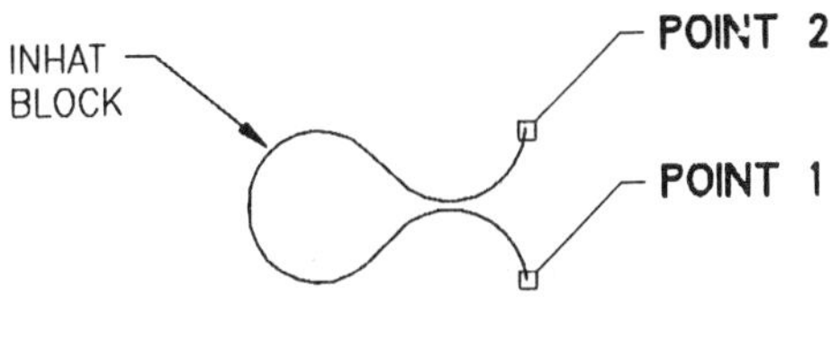

Figure 6-11

Now zoom into the area of the top wall plate and the top of the insulation hatch. Notice that the last copy of the item you arrayed protrudes above the bottom line of the wall plate.

Use the Explode command to break apart the last item (the one at the top). Next, refer to Figure 6–12 and use the Trim command to trim the parts of the item that are above the wall plate.

YOUR NOTES

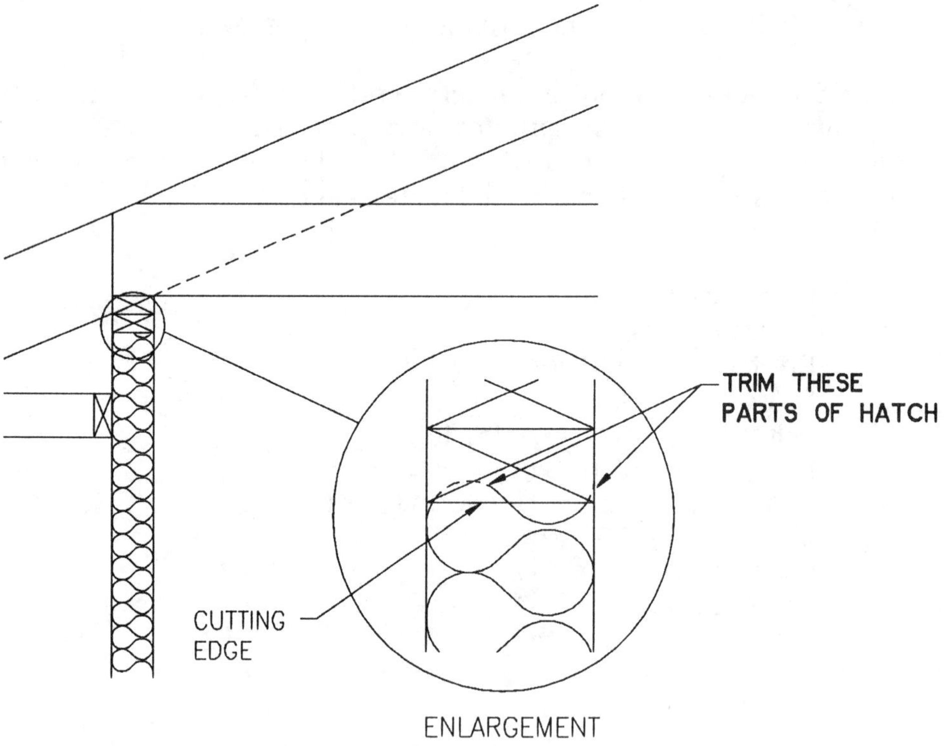

Figure 6-12

STEP 13 *Placing the Ceiling Insulation Hatch*

Next, we want to place 7" of insulation in the attic. We will use the same technique we used to place the wall insulation. We will also use the same INHAT block. Use the following command sequence and refer to Figure 6–13 to place the block in the proper location and to the right scale. (Be sure to note the scale factors used in the sequence.)

Command: **insert**
Block name (or ?) <default>: **inhat**
Insertion point: **int**
of *Select point 1.*
X scale factor <1> / Corner / XYZ: **2**
Y scale factor (default=X): **1**
Rotation angle <0>: **270**

YOUR NOTES

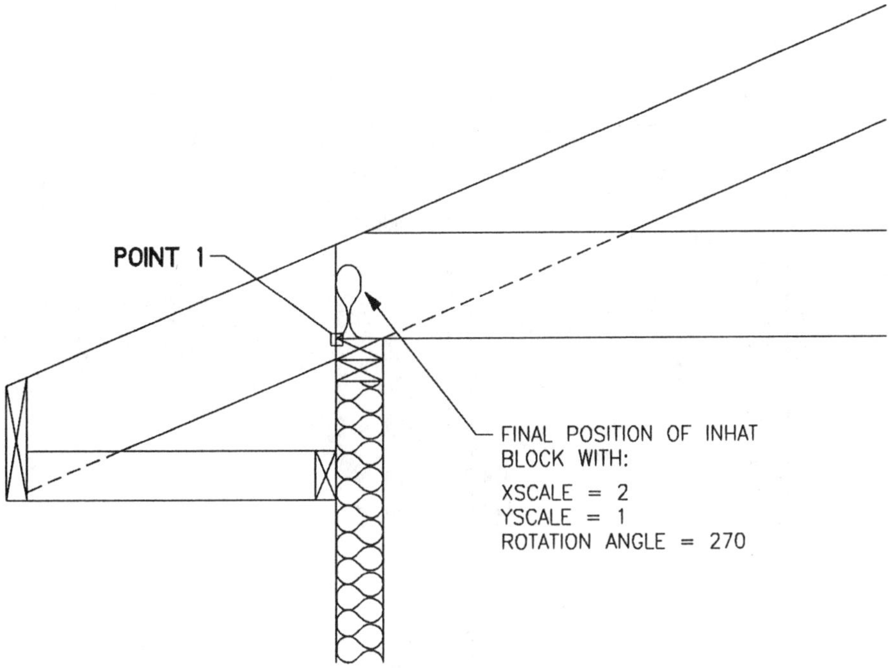

Figure 6-13

Now measure the distance you want the insulation to fill and divide the measurement by the width of the item you want to insert. Finally, use the Array command and specify the number of items you calculated as the number of columns in the array. If you need to review, refer to the previous section on placing the wall insulation.

STEP 14 *Completing the Trim Details*

Next we will complete the trim details, as shown in Figure 6-14. Create the 3/4" fascia board, the 1/4" soffit, and the 5/8" roof sheathing using the appropriate methods you have learned. Add the 3/4" insulated wall sheathing and rendering lines at 1/4" intervals, using Figure 6-14 for reference. Finally, be sure all of the proper corners have been drawn and trim unwanted line segments.

YOUR NOTES

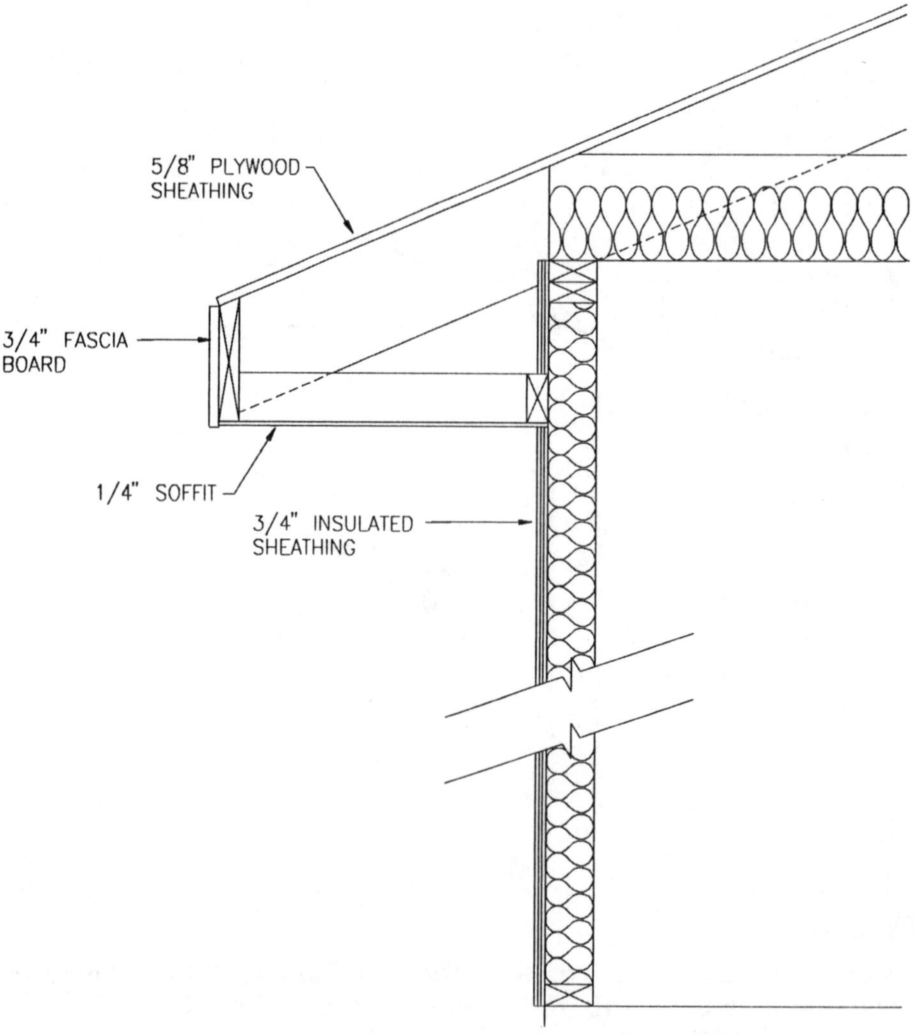

Figure 6-14

This would be a good time to stop and save your drawing edits with the Save command.

PLACING THE DIMENSIONS AND NOTES

Before we place any dimensions or notes, let's set up the dimensioning variables. The following is a list of the variable settings you can use for this drawing.

YOUR NOTES

dimalt	off	dimlim	off	dimtix	on
dimaltd	2	dimrnd	0"	dimtm	0"
dimaltf	25.400	dimsah	off	dimtofl	off
dimaso	on	dimscale	24.000	dimtoh	off
dimasz	3/16"	dimse1	off	dimtol	off
dimcen	3/32"	dimse2	off	dimtp	0"
dimdle	0"	dimsho	off	dimtsz	0"
dimdli	3/8"	dimsoxd	off	dimtvp	0"
dimexe	3/16"	dimtad	on	dimtxt	3/16"
dimexo	1/16"	dimtih	off	dimzin	1
dimlfac	1.000				

STEP 15 *Setting a Layer for Notes and Dimensions*

Make a new layer named NOTES.

Command: **layer**
?/Make/Set/New/ON/OFF/Color/Ltype/Freeze/Thaw: **m**
New current layer <default>: **notes**
?/Make/Set /New/ON/OFF/Color/Ltype/Freeze/Thaw: ↵

STEP 16 *Creating a Text Style*

Next, create a style for the text used in the dimensions and notes. Use the following command sequence.

Command: **style**
(Text style name (or ?) <default>: **notes**
New style
Font file <default>: **simplex**
Height <0'-0">: **4"**
Width factor <1.00>: ↵

Obliquing angle <0>: ↵
Backwards? <N>: ↵
Upside-down? <N>: ↵
Vertical? <N>: ↵

NOTES is now the current text style.

YOUR NOTES

STEP 17 *Placing Dimension Leaders and Notes*

Now use AutoCAD's dimensioning mode to construct the dimensions, the dimension leaders, and the "arrowed notes," as shown in Figure 6–15.

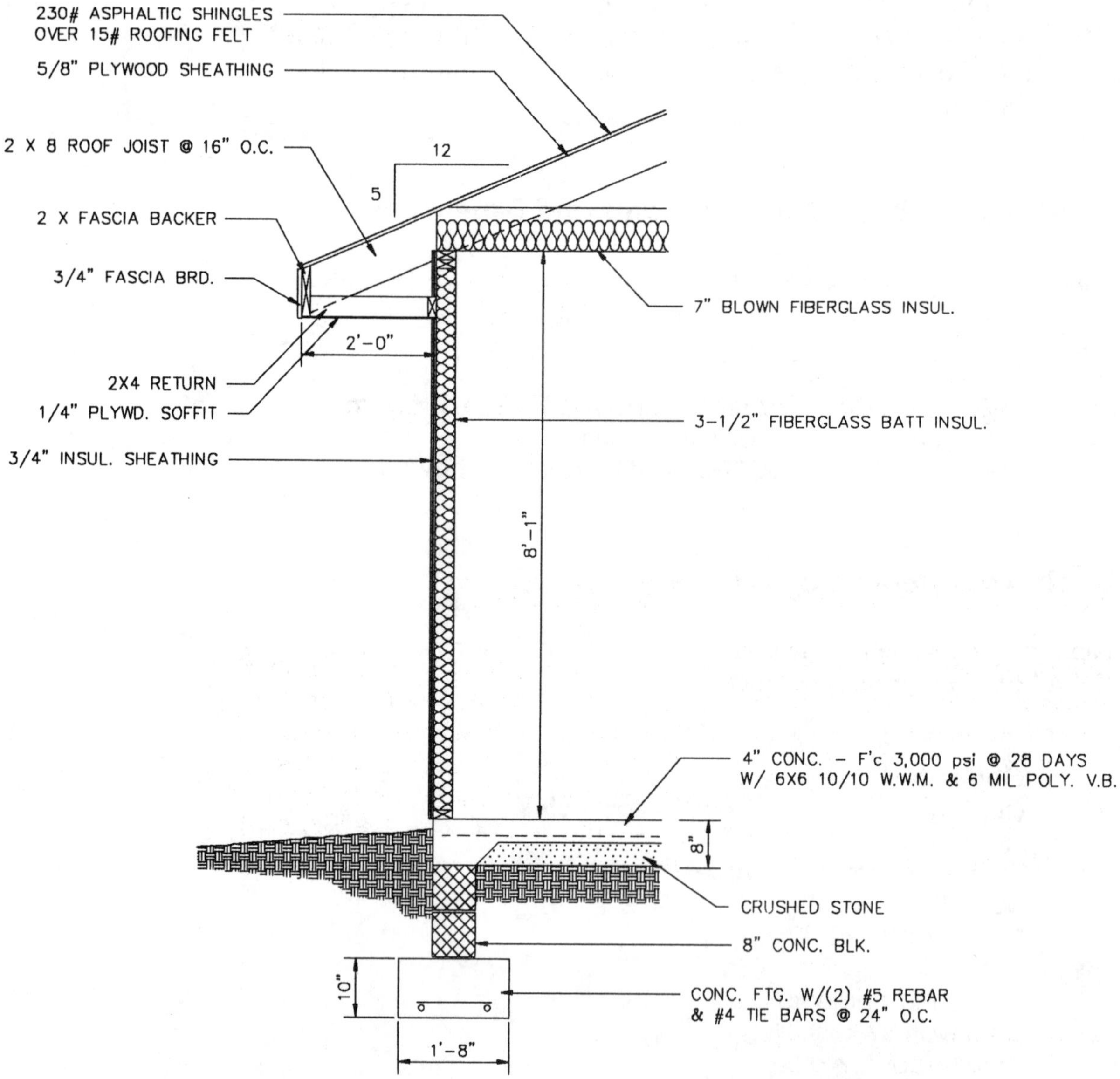

Figure 6-15

YOUR NOTES

STEP 18 *Placing the Titles*

Create a new text style named TITLE for the titles below the sections, as shown in Figure 6–16. Use a text height of 10". Construct the scale line below the title name in the NOTES text style. The radius of the section circle is 2′.

Note: You can change the style with the S option when you select the Text or Dtext command.

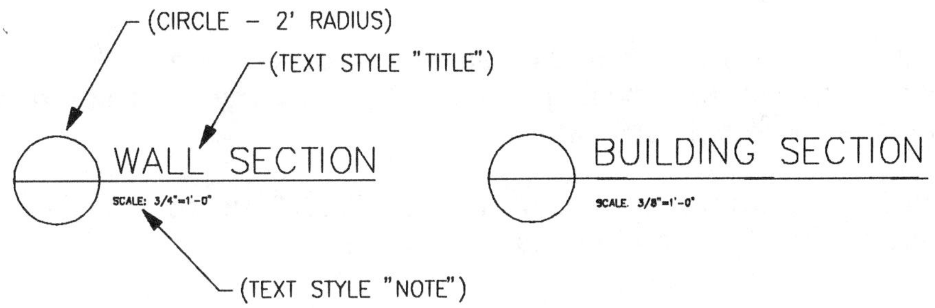

Figure 6-16

CREATING THE DOOR SCHEDULE

When you placed your doors in the floor plan in Session Two, you used AutoCAD's attribute abilities to create a database of door information. After you were finished, you extracted this information in the form of a text file named SCHED1 (Schedule One). We will now use this file to place a door schedule on the drawing sheet. (Don't worry if your schedule did not work out like the one in Figure 6–17. A file named SCHED2 is available on the work disk. It is ready to use if you need it.)

STEP 19 *Using ASCTEXT.LSP*

First, create a new text style named TABLE.

Command: **style**
(Text style name (or ?) <default>: **table**

YOUR NOTES

New style
Font file <default>: **monotxt**
Height <0'-0">: **4"**
Width factor <1.00>: ↵

Obliquing angle <0>: ↵
Backwards? <N>: ↵
Upside-down? <N>: ↵
Vertical? <N>: ↵

TABLE is now the current text style.

We are using the Monotxt font because it is a constant-spaced font. This will make your tables line up properly. If you use the Simplex font for your tables, they will align "crooked."

Next, load an AutoLISP program named ASCTEXT. (Be sure to enter the parentheses and quotation marks as shown.)

Command: **(load "asctext")**
C:ASCTEXT

Now execute the Asctext command.

Command: **asctext**
File to read (including extension): **sched1.txt** *(Be sure to include any subdirectory paths needed to locate your file.)*
Start point or Center/Middle/Right: **48,60**
Rotation angle <0>: ↵
Change text options? <N>: **y**
Distance between lines/<Auto>: **10**
First line to read/<1>: ↵
Number of lines to read/<All>: ↵
Underscore each line? <N>: ↵
Overscore each line? <N>: ↵
Change text case? Upper/Lower/<N>: ↵
Set up columns? <N>: ↵

The text should now appear on the screen, as shown in Figure 6–17.

YOUR NOTES

1	H.C.	2'-8"	1-3/8"	6'-8"
2	BIFOLD	5'-0"	-	6'-8"
3	BIFOLD	4'-0"	-	6'-8"
4	BIFOLD	4'-0"	-	6'-8"
5	H.C.	2'-8"	1-3/8"	6'-8"
6	H.C.	2'-6"	1-3/8"	6'-8"
7	H.C.	2'-8"	1-3/8"	6'-8"
8	BYPASS	CUSTOM	-	6'-8"
9	H.C.	2'-6"	1-3/8"	6'-8"
10	BYPASS	8'-0"	-	6'-8"
11	DBL. SWING	2'-6"	1-3/8"	6'-8"
12	S.C.	2'-6" DBL	1-3/4"	6'-8"
13	CASED OPG.	5'-0"	-	6'-8"
14	CASED OPG.	4'-0"	-	6'-8"
15	H.C.	2'-8"	1-3/8"	6'-8"
16	H.C.	2'-6"	1-3/8"	6'-8"
17	H.C.	2'-6"	1-3/8"	6'-8"
18	H.C.	2'-4"	1-3/8"	6'-8"
19	H.C.	2'-6" DBL	1-3/8"	6'-8"
20	BYPASS	5'-0"	-	6'-8"
21	GARAGE	16'-0"	-	7'-0"

Figure 6-17

STEP 20 *Constructing Schedule Box Lines*

Use the Line command to draw the bottom line of the schedule below the last line of text. Next, use the Array command to array the line up the text.

Command: **array**
Select objects: **l**
Rectangular or Polar array (R/P): **r**
Number of rows (---) <default>: **22**
Number of columns (| | |) <default>: **1**
Unit cell or distance between rows (---): **10**

If the lines do not fall exactly between the text rows, use the Move command to place them correctly. They will fit, since both the text spacing and the line spacing is 10".

YOUR NOTES

Next, use the Line command to construct the remainder of the lines in the schedule, as shown in Figure 6–18. Fill in the headings with the Text command. Change to the TITLE style and place the title DOOR SCHEDULE at the top of the schedule, as shown. When you are finished, move the entire schedule, if necessary, to place it at a visually pleasing location on the drawing.

DOOR SCHEDULE

NO.	TYPE	WIDTH	THICKNESS	HEIGHT	REMARKS
1	H.C.	2'-8"	1-3/8"	6'-8"	
2	BIFOLD	5'-0"	-	6'-8"	
3	BIFOLD	4'-0"	-	6'-8"	
4	BIFOLD	4'-0"	-	6'-8"	
5	H.C.	2'-8"	1-3/8"	6'-8"	
6	H.C.	2'-6"	1-3/8"	6'-8"	
7	H.C.	2'-8"	1-3/8"	6'-8"	
8	BYPASS	CUSTOM	-	6'-8"	
9	H.C.	2'-6"	1-3/8"	6'-8"	
10	BYPASS	8'-0"	-	6'-8"	
11	DBL. SWING	2'-6"	1-3/8"	6'-8"	
12	S.C.	2'-6" DBL	1-3/4"	6'-8"	
13	CASED OPG.	5'-0"	-	6'-8"	
14	CASED OPG.	4'-0"	-	6'-8"	
15	H.C.	2'-8"	1-3/8"	6'-8"	
16	H.C.	2'-6"	1-3/8"	6'-8"	
17	H.C.	2'-6"	1-3/8"	6'-8"	
18	H.C.	2'-4"	1-3/8"	6'-8"	
19	H.C.	2'-6" DBL	1-3/8"	6'-8"	
20	BYPASS	5'-0"	-	6'-8"	
21	GARAGE	16'-0"	-	7'-0"	

Figure 6-18

STEP 21 *Adding Notations*

We will complete the section by adding a detail marker. A detail marker identifies a part of the drawing that is shown separately with additional notes and detail information. This part of the drawing is usually enlarged to show the details more clearly.

YOUR NOTES

In Figure 6–1, the building section annotated as section 2/3 shows a detail marker for the wall section. The dashed "bubble" shows the area to be shown in detail and is marked as detail 1/3.

After adding the detail marker, recall your floor plan drawing and add the section markers as shown in Figure 6–2. This will allow someone unfamiliar with the plan to understand where the sections have been cut and in which direction they are looking.

When you have finished, use the Time command to turn the timer off.

YOUR NOTES

PLOTTING INSTRUCTIONS

You may want to stop at this point and plot your work. If you have a pen plotter capable of plotting a C-size (24"x18") drawing, you can plot the drawing at a scale of 1/4"=1'–0". If you have a dot matrix printer configured to AutoCAD, you can printer plot the drawing. The following is an explanation for each type of plotting.

Pen Plot

From the AutoCAD Main menu, select option 3 (Plot a drawing). Respond to Enter NAME of drawing: with \ACADARCH\SECTION and ↵.

Next, AutoCAD prompts you for the part of the drawing to be plotted. Enter L for limits.

AutoCAD will now display the plot parameters. The last line on the screen asks if you want to change anything. Enter Y for yes. Then use the following settings.

Plot NOT written to a file
All entity colors plotted with pen 1
Size in inches
Plot origin at 0.00,0.00
Plotting size: C
Plot NOT rotated
Pen width 0.010
Area fill boundaries NOT adjusted for pen width
Hidden lines NOT removed
Scale: 1/4"=1'–0"

Before you proceed, make sure the plotter is ready to plot. A pen of 0.25mm will yield acceptable results. When you are ready, press ↵ and watch your drawing being plotted!

Printer Plot

YOUR NOTES

To printer plot, select option 4 (Printer Plot a drawing) from AutoCAD's main menu. When asked for the drawing name, enter \ACADARCH\SECTION and press *f*. You will be prompted for the part of the drawing to plot. Enter L for limits and *f*. A listing of the plot parameters will be displayed. The last line on the screen asks if you want to change anything. Respond with Y for yes and use the following settings.

Plot NOT written to a file
Size in inches
Plot origin at 0.00,0.00
Plotting size: A
Plot rotated: YES
Hidden lines NOT removed
Scale: F (for fit)

Now prepare the printer and press ↵ to printer plot your drawing. Note that the printer plot will not be plotted to a particular scale.

YOUR NOTES

SUMMARY

- Large-scale details of sections can be "split" away and enlarged with the Scale command.

- The Sketch command allows you to make ground lines with just the right amount of "waviness" to simulate a ground surface line.

- A single component can be drawn and then arrayed for a "quick hatch." This, of course, is not a true hatch, but it can serve as a quick and convenient method for placing one-of-a-kind patterns easily. Look for patterns that repeat and select the part that makes one full "cycle." Draw that part and array it.

- Use the Monotxt font style for tables. It will provide a properly aligned column.

- ASCTEXT.LSP is a LISP file that can be used to place ASCII text into your drawing. This feature is not restricted to attribute extract files. You can use a word processor in non-document mode to create note blocks for your drawing. Then use ASCTEXT.LSP to place the notes into your drawing. Some word processors have the ability to produce a new ASCII file from an existing file. If you are experienced in EDLIN, you can create ASCII files from DOS.

QUESTIONS

YOUR NOTES

1. Why is using the "quick hatch" method of constructing a hatch sometimes more efficient than writing a standard hatch pattern?

2. What is the ASCTEXT.LSP program used for?

3. Why would you want to "split" a wall section from a building section?

4. Describe an effective method of creating a ground line.

5. Why should you use the Monotxt font for tables and schedules?

YOUR NOTES

PROBLEMS

1. Create a text file with Edlin or a word processor in nondocument (ascii) mode. Use the Asctext.lsp program to place the file into a drawing.

2. Select an exising drawing. Use the techniques covered in this session to "split" a small detail from a larger one. Use the Scale command to increase the scale of the new detail.

YOUR NOTES

Section 3 Drawing Building Elevations

- Session 7: Drawing Building Elevations
- Session 8: Embellishing Elevation Drawings

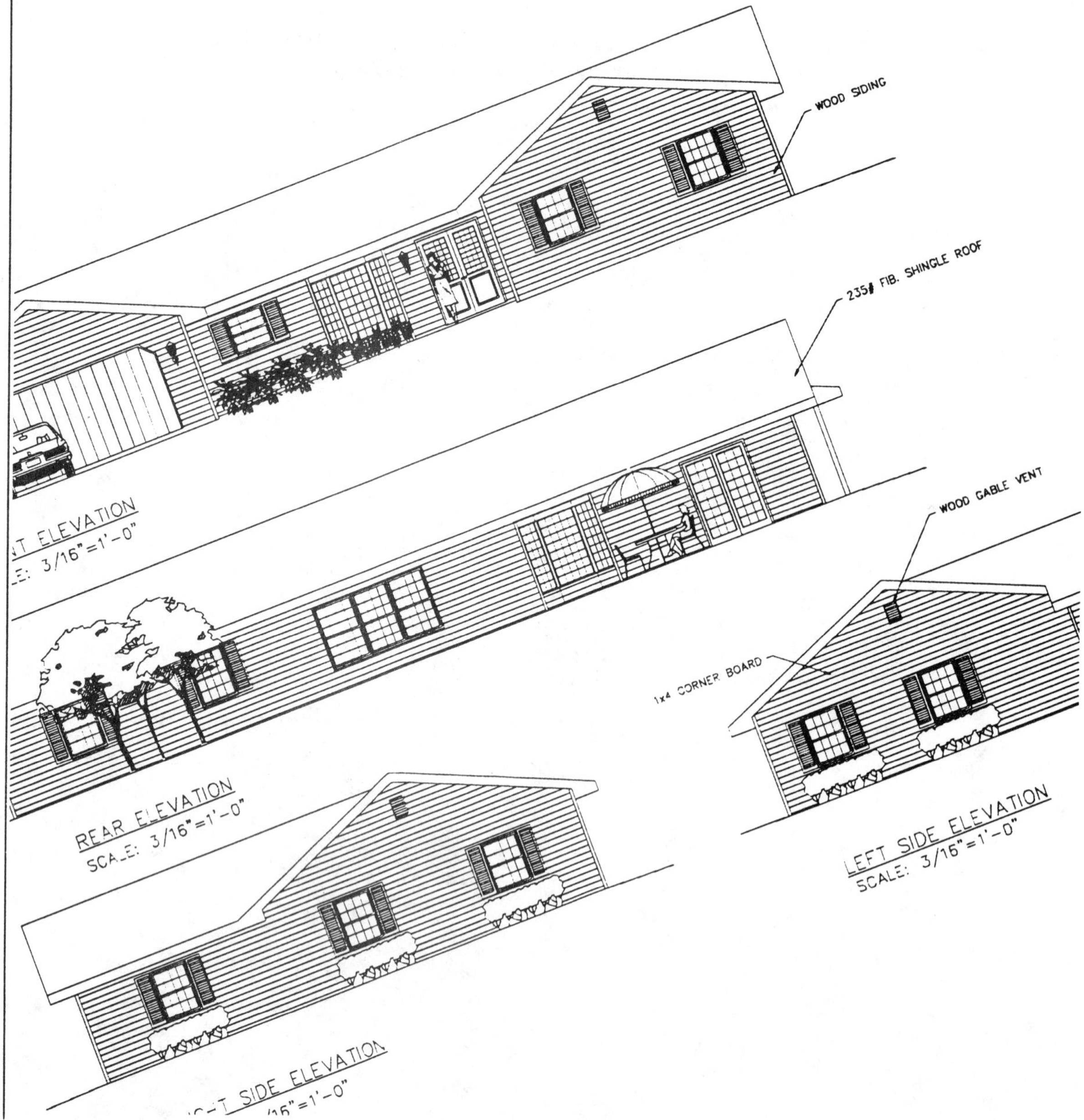

SESSION 7

Drawing Building Elevations

OBJECTIVE

YOUR NOTES
Use this space for notes about your individual plan

The object of this session is to learn the techniques of constructing building elevation drawings. You will be creating the main lines, windows, and doors of the exterior of your house. Later, in Session Eight, you will discover the procedures for adding realistic embellishments to an elevation drawing to enhance the sense of materials and scale.

Figure 7–1 shows what your drawing should look like at the end of this session. You will complete the drawing sheet in Session Eight.

Figure 7-1

YOUR NOTES

Commands used in this session:

erase
extend
fillet
insert
line
reference lisp function
trim

CREATING BUILDING ELEVATIONS

Building elevations are drawings that show the exterior "look" of a building. An elevation serves many purposes:

- As a design drawing, the elevation visually describes the exterior of a building for someone who is not trained to visualize how a plan might look as a finished product. In other words, it serves as a picture.
- As a construction drawing, the elevation shows the builder the desired exterior look and enhances the builder's understanding of the desired finished product.
- The elevation shows and labels exterior materials and shows where they should be placed.
- The elevation depicts the door and window designs graphically.
- The elevation shows the desired finished ground grade.
- The elevation shows special design features. For example, the chamfered corner of the garage door opening in your current drawing is described visually by the elevation.
- The elevation drawing is the only drawing that combines many of these elements into a single drawing that shows the relationships between the materials, design elements, ground slopes, roof relationships, and any other elements that describe the exterior of the building.

STEP 1 *Starting the Elevations*

YOUR NOTES

We are going to draw all four elevations on one sheet. Let's start a new drawing for this sheet. Our drawing name will be ELEVS (Elevations). If we add up the distances needed for the elevations, we find that the scale for our sheet should be 3/16"=1'–0". Go ahead now and start a new drawing named ELEVS to equal the prototype drawing called PELEVS. The following settings are present in the prototype drawing.

Units: Architectural
Limits: 128',96'
Snap: 1"
Grid: 5'
Layer: (*Make*) ELEV
Color: White (color 7)
Ortho: ON
Zoom All
Timer: ON

STEP 2 *Drawing the Outline*

To start any elevation, you should first check the dimensions of the floor plan to locate the building corners. Then you can construct the main outline of the building. Figure 7–2 shows the dimensions of the outline of the house.

Elevation drawings are usually made of the front, the back, and both sides (left and right) of a building. We will start with the front elevation of the house. Let's construct the outline without the roof lines for now. Select the Line command and use the following command sequence to construct the outline of the front elevation.

Command: **line**
From point: **16',78'**
To point: **@70'<0**
To point: **@8'<90**
To point: **@70'<180**
To point: **c**

YOUR NOTES

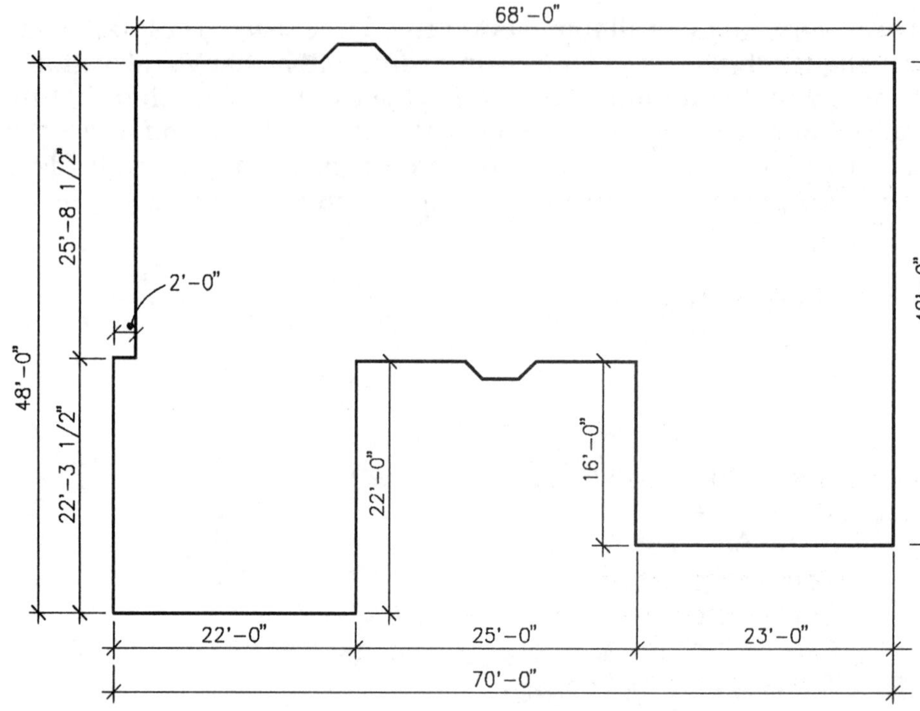

Figure 7-2

Your drawing should now contain a "box" that is 70′ wide and 8′ high. The 70′ is the width of the house, and the 8′ is the wall height.

STEP 3 *Placing the Other Corners*

Now let's place the other corners of the house. Refer to Figure 7–3 and use the Offset command to place the corners of the walls.

> Command: **offset**
> Offset distance or Through <default>: **22'**
> Select object to offset: *Select left wall line, labeled* A.
> Side to offset? *Move cursor to right of line* A *and click.*

YOUR NOTES

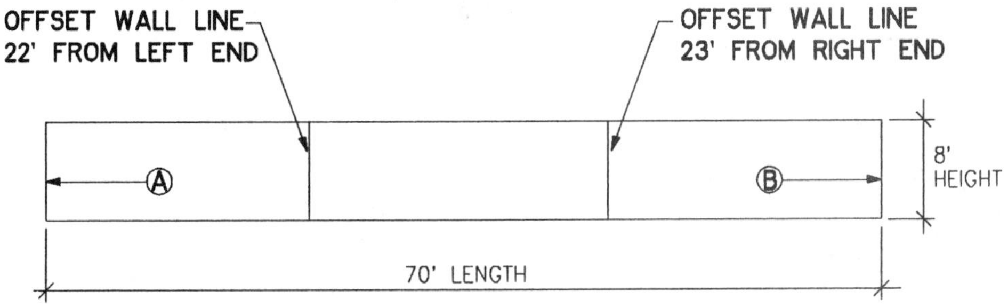

Figure 7-3

Now let's place the other corner line for this elevation.

Command: **offset**
Offset distance or Through <default>: **23'**
Select object to offset: *Select right wall line, labeled* B.
Side to offset? *Move cursor to right of line* B *and click.*

DRAWING THE ROOF LINES

It is now time to build the roof lines. We are going to construct the roof lines in much the same way we did in our section drawing. Figure 7–4 shows the method we will use to do this. Our roof slope is 5/12. We will start as though we were drawing a section. First, let's draw the roof over the garage.

STEP 4 *Constructing the Wall Thickness*

Start by using the Offset command to offset the outside wall on both sides of the garage 3 1/2" to the inside, creating the actual 2x4 wall thickness. This will give us a starting place for our roof rafter (see Figure 7–4). You may want to refer to the section drawing you created in sessions Five and Six to help you understand how the roof rafter joins to the wall.

YOUR NOTES

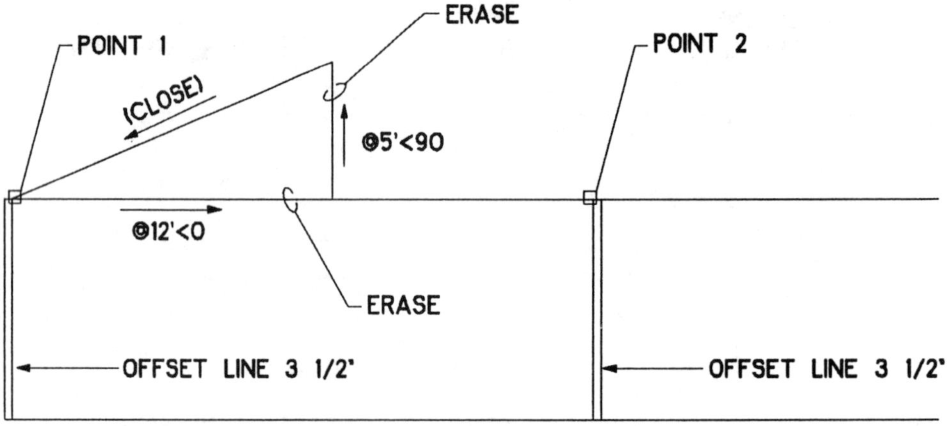

Figure 7-4

STEP 5 *Constructing the Bottom Rafter Line*

Now let's construct the bottom line of the rafter. Use the same technique you used in Session Six to create a 5/12 slope. Use the following command sequence, and refer to Figure 7–4.

Command: **line**
From point: **end**
of *Select point 1.*
To point: **@12'<0**
To point: **@5'<90**
To point: **c**

Now erase the horizontal and vertical lines, leaving just the 5/12 pitch line. Then construct another 5/12 pitch line from the other side of the garage. Using the following sequence.

Command: **line**
From point: **end**
of *Select point 2.*
To point: **@12'<180**
To point: **@5'<90**
To point: **c**

YOUR NOTES

As before, erase the horizontal and vertical lines. Now use Fillet (radius 0) to fillet the roof lines together. Your drawing should now look like the one in Figure 7–5.

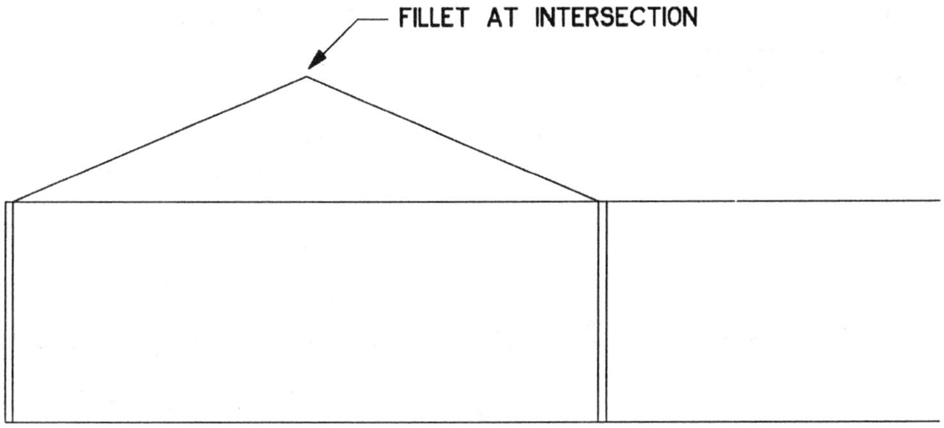

Figure 7-5

STEP 6 *Offsetting the Rafter Lines*

Next, use the Offset command to offset each line 8" up. Again, fillet the peak of the two new lines. The 8" offset creates the thickness of the rafter and roof sheathing. Now erase the inside wall lines and the top wall line you created, leaving just the outside wall edges. Your drawing should now look like the one in Figure 7–6.

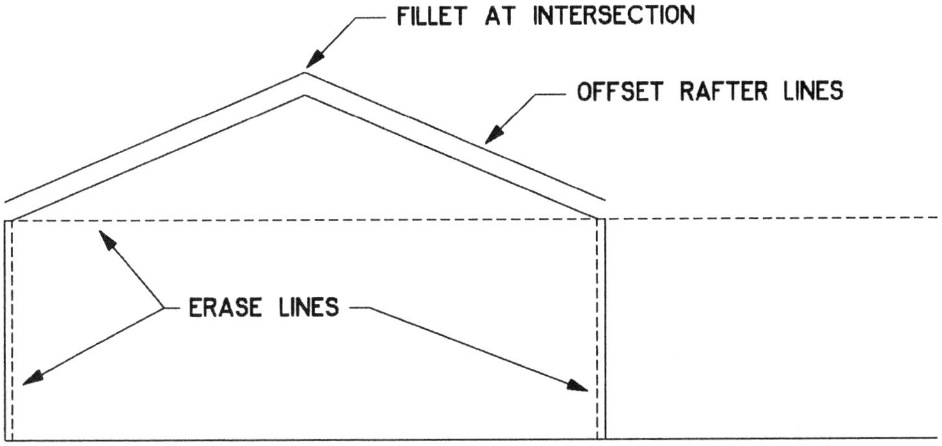

Figure 7-6

YOUR NOTES

DRAWING THE OVERHANG

Our next task is to draw the overhang. The overhang extends 2'–0" past the end of the wall. Let's use the Reference function to place a guide line 2' outside of the left garage wall. You may first need to load the Reference function.

Command: **(load "ref")**
REF

STEP 7 *Drawing a Construction Line*

Use the following command sequence and refer to Figure 7–7 to place the construction line.

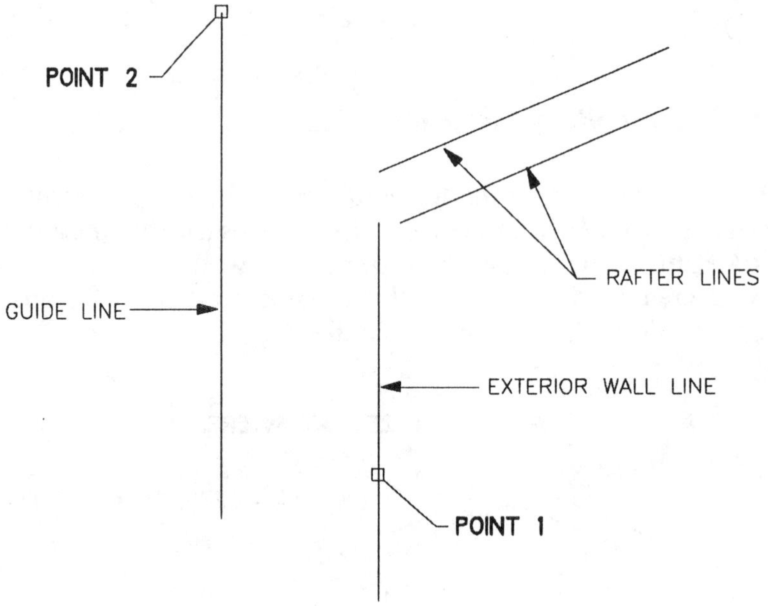

Figure 7-7

Command: **line**
From point: **(ref)**
Reference point: **nea**
to *Select a point near point 1.*
Enter relative/polar coordinates (with @): **@2'<180**
To point: *Select the line endpoint at approximately point 2.*

STEP 8 *Extending the Rafter Lines*

YOUR NOTES

Next, use the Extend command to extend the rafter lines to the guide line. Then use Trim (with the rafter lines as cutting edges) to trim the guide line, as shown in Figure 7–8.

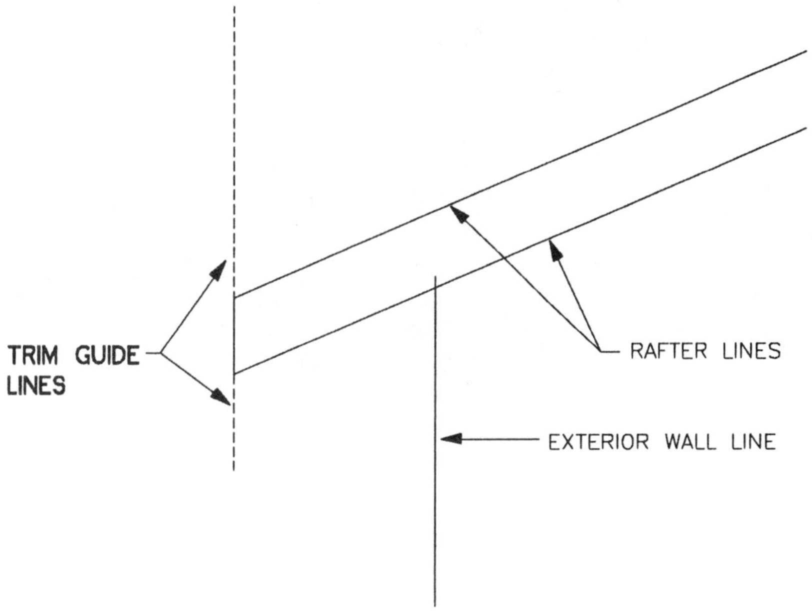

Figure 7-8

STEP 9 *Drawing the Soffit Line*

Now draw a soffit line from the bottom outer edge of the overhang to the wall line. Use object snap perpendicular to snap the line endpoint to the wall line (see Figure 7–9).

STEP 10 *Trimming the Rafter*

Use the Trim command to trim the bottom rafter line and the wall line where they extend above the bottom rafter line. Refer to Figure 7–9 as necessary.

YOUR NOTES

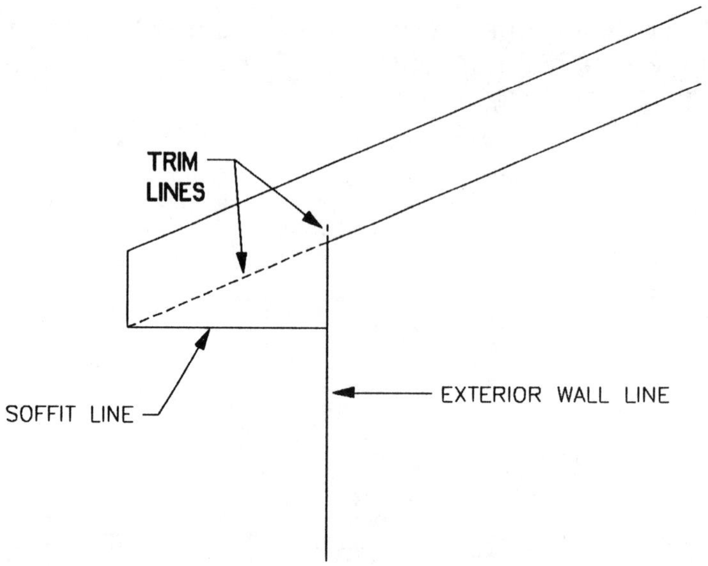

Figure 7-9

STEP 11 *Trimming the Opposite Rafter*

Next, repeat the same sequence for the opposite side of the garage. When you have finished, your drawing should look like the one in Figure 7–10.

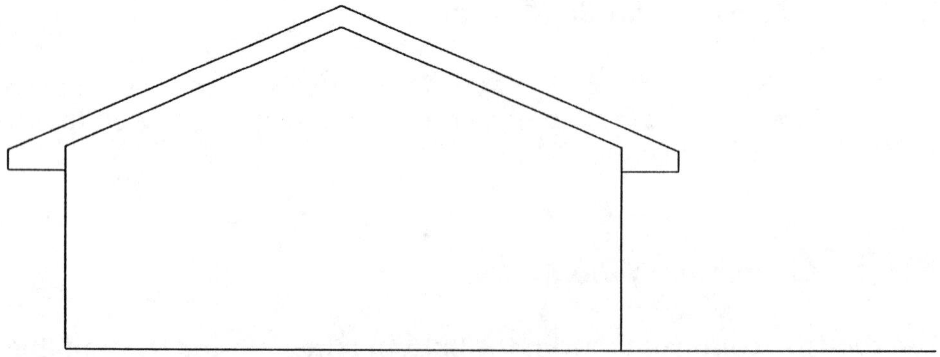

Figure 7-10

YOUR NOTES

This would be a good time to use the Save command to record your work to disk. If you take a break, be sure to use the Time command to turn the timer off.

STEP 12 *Drawing the Roof over the Bedroom Wing*

Now that you know the procedures for drawing the roof lines and overhangs, use the same techniques to construct the roof above the bedroom wing at the right side of the front elevation. Take your time, and review the procedure you just completed if you need to. The procedure is exactly the same. When you are finished, your drawing should look like the one in Figure 7–11.

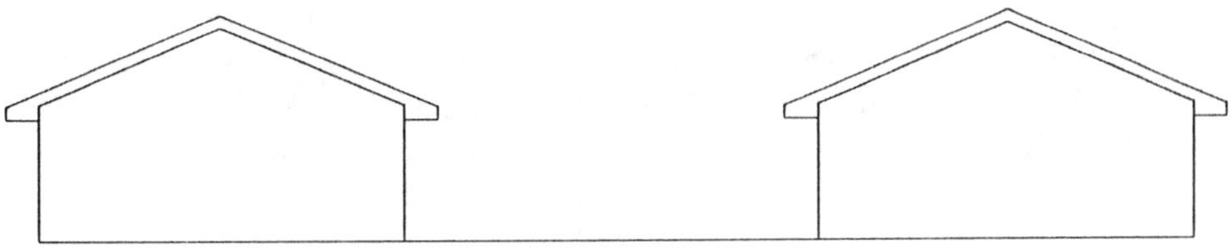

Figure 7-11

After you complete the roof over the bedroom wing, record your work to disk again using the Save command.

STEP 13 *Drawing the Front Overhang*

Next, use the Line command to draw the front overhang between the roof edges, as shown in Figure 7–12.

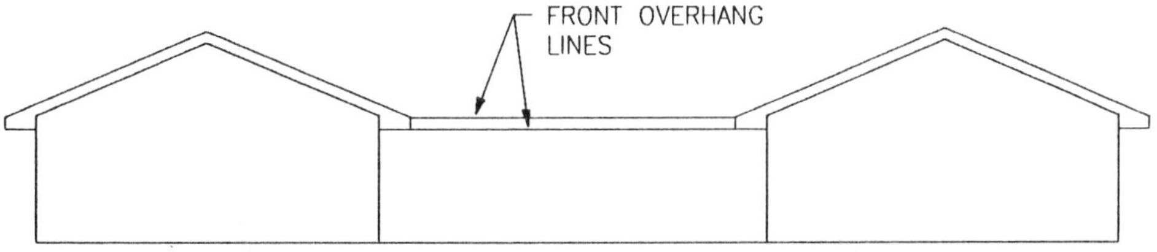

Figure 7-12

YOUR NOTES

Notice the vertical lines representing the corner boards at the building corners in Figure 7–13. Show a 4" offset from each corner, and extend the new line to meet the lower rafter edge.

Note that we are not drawing the main roof line at this time. We will place the line after we draw a side elevation that will give us the correct height for the roof peak.

Remember that when you draw an elevation that is symmetrical, you can save time by drawing half the elevation, then using the Mirror command to "construct" the opposite half.

PLACING THE DOORS AND WINDOWS

After you construct the outline of the elevation, the next step is to place the ventilation vents, doors and windows. Start by placing the vents. Refer to Figure 7–1 and use the Insert command to place the vent nmaed VENT in the front and side gables at the approximate locations shown.

Next we will place the doors and windows. The easiest procedure is to construct the doors and windows separately. Then you can insert them into your drawing. The doors and windows for your drawing have already been prepared and are on the work disk. Figure 7–13 shows the front elevation with the names of the window and door drawings, as well as the dimensions for placement.

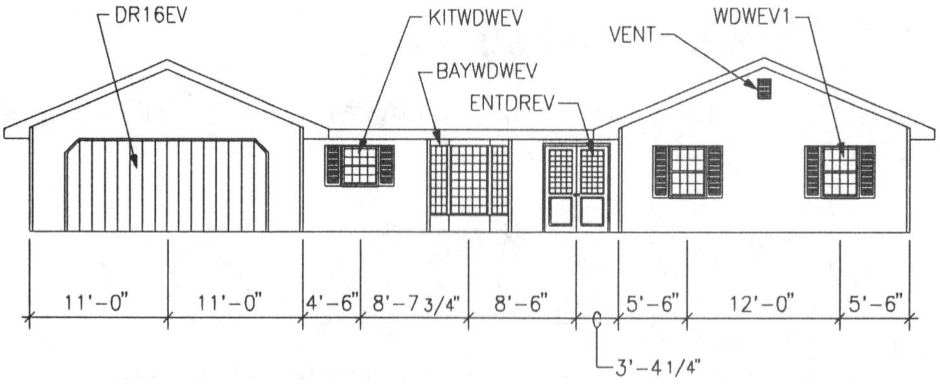

Figure 7-13

YOUR NOTES

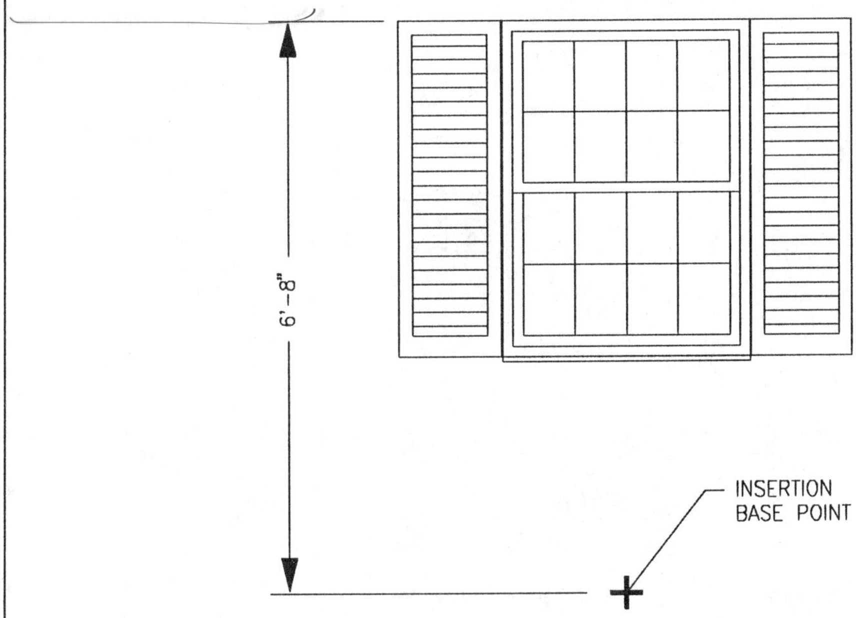

Figure 7-14

The methodology for placing the doors and windows is similar to the one we used in Session Two. Now, however, we are working in elevation instead of in plan view. The insertion point for each door and window is at the horizontal center of the item and at the floor line. Figure 7–14, for example, shows the insertion point for the window symbol named WDWEV1.

STEP 14 *Placing a Window*

Let's place a window in bedroom 3. Refer to Figure 7–15, and use the following command sequence.

Command: **insert**
Block name (or ?): **wdwev1**
Insertion point: **(ref)**
Reference point: **int**
of *Select point 1.*
Enter relative/polar coordinates (with @): **@5'6"<180**
X scale factor <default>/Corner/XYZ: **1**
Y scale factor (default=X): ↵
Rotation angle <default>: **0**

YOUR NOTES

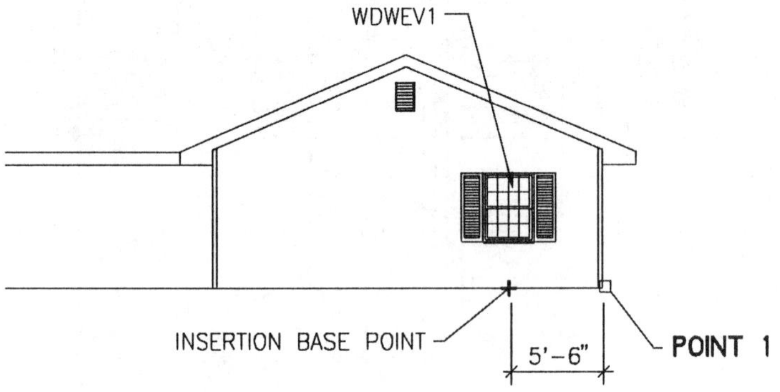

Figure 7-15

The window should now be placed as shown in Figure 7–15.

STEP 15 *Placing the Remaining Doors and Windows*

Continue to place the doors and windows in the front elevation, referring to Figure 7–13 as necessary. After you are finished, use the Save command to record your drawing to disk.

STEP 16 *Drawing the Remaining Elevations*

Construct the back and side elevations in the same manner. The elevations shown in Figure 7–16 contain the dimensions and the door and window names you need to complete each elevation. After you have completed a side elevation, remember to use the Distance command to measure the height of the roof peak. Then add the roof line to the front elevation. You have already constructed the roof for the front wings, so you can measure the peak height to use in the side elevations.

Remember to save your work periodically and to turn the timer off if you take a break. After you are finished, you will be ready for Session Eight and the fun of embellishing the elevations with symbols to make them look more realistic. Have fun!

YOUR NOTES

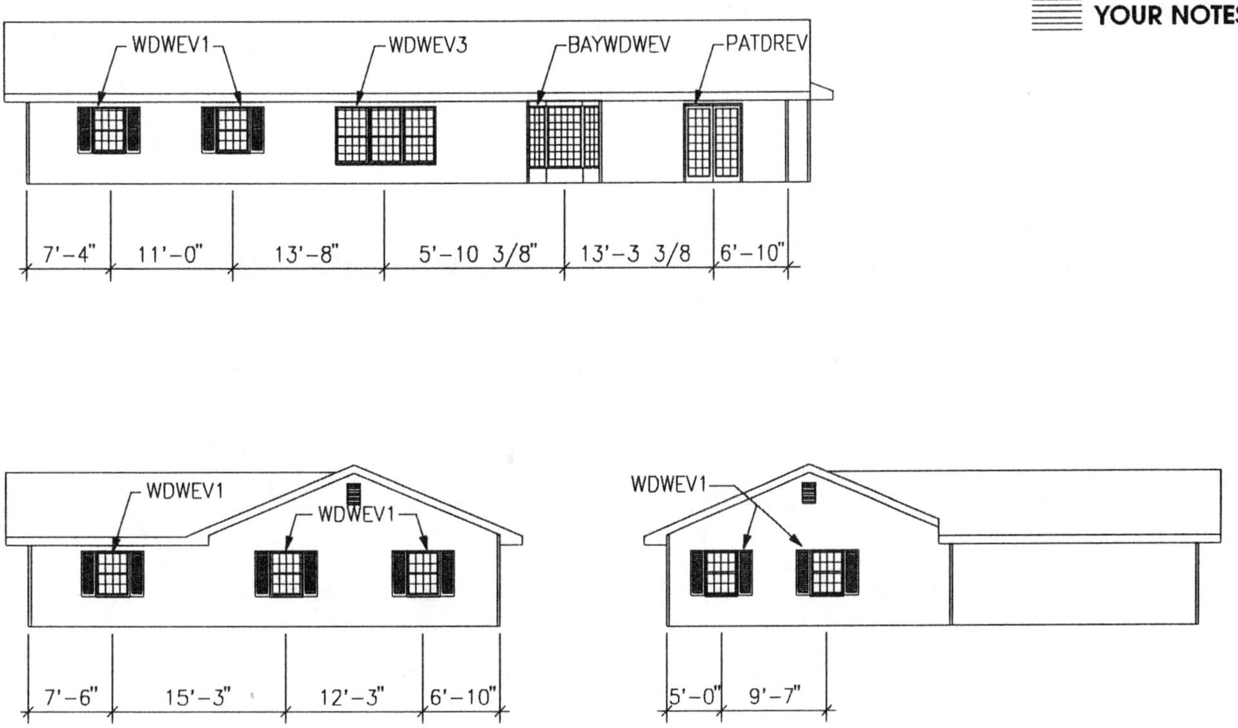

Figure 7-16

YOUR NOTES

SUMMARY

- Building elevations are drawings that show the exterior appearance of a building.
- It is usually necessary to draw sections to obtain vertical heights before you can draw the elevations.
- Start by drawing the "outline" of the elevations. Use the overall floor plan and section dimensions to obtain the distances.
- Continue by drawing the main building lines.
- Place the details into the elevation drawing last.
- It may be necessary to draw roof lines after you draw another elevation that shows the gable end of the roof. You can use the second elevation to obtain a vertical height for the roof ridge.
- If an elevation, or part of an elevation, is symmetrical, draw half of it. Then use the Mirror command with a reference line to construct the opposite half.
- Build door and window blocks with conveniently placed insertion base points. For example, our insertion points are at the floor line.

QUESTIONS

YOUR NOTES

1. What is a building elevation? What information is shown in an elevation drawing?

____

____

____

2. What is the first step in drawing an elevation?

____

____

____

3. How can you save time when you are drawing an elevation that is symmetrical?

____

____

____

YOUR NOTES

PROBLEMS

1. Select a floor plan from the Appendix and construct an elevation of your own design.

2. Create your own door and window designs. Construct blocks with the proper base points and insert them into an elevation.

YOUR NOTES

Viewing the Real Thing

The architectural firm Design Partners, Inc., was designing a theater for a particularly demanding client. In order to under stand the design, the client wanted the firm to build an extra- large model so that they could view the design from inside. The cost would be enormous.

The firm created the design using the three-dimensional capabilities of AutoCAD and Ketiv's ArchT2/3D software. With the electronic 3D model available, it seemed wasteful to build a complex model with foam board and plexiglass.

Meanwhile, DPI architect Jim Teller read about a program called Realtime that allows designers to "look around" a CAD model. Realtime , from a company called StereoCAD, shades electronic 3D models very quickly--so quickly that the viewer seems to be moving around in a model. Realtime displays a shaded image on the monitor screen, then lets you move your point of view by pointing with a mouse. The images are flashed at a rate of about five per second, fast enough to look like an animated cartoon. It's like walking through a building while looking through a TV screen, except that the viewer can walk through walls or fly.

Courtesy of StereoCAD, Inc.

When he saw Realtime, Teller was impressed enough that he tried it on the theater project. He explored the design inside and out, "flying" from one level to another. He saw the building from views he had never considered and made some design changes.

When he was ready to present the design, he was concerned that the cartoonlike quality of Realtime's images would scare the client. Realtime uses "flat" shading, that doesn't show shadows or material textures. The client was impressed anyway, and enjoyed flying through the model. Teller noted the views that the client was especially interested in, and after the client left he used Autodesk's 3D Studio to create high-quality renderings of each view. The presentation was a success, and the physical model was not needed.

Realtime is an example of a technology called virtual reality (VR). It simulates real worlds through a computer. More sophisticated VR software uses stereo video goggles to make it seem as if the viewer is actually inside a model. Some systems enable users to "grab" onto images of objects using a "data glove" and move them around the virtual world. This may be the design technology of the future, in which architects can place and move walls, windows, and doors in a virtual building, then "bring in" the client to try out different materials, colors, and lighting.

SESSION 8

Embellishing Elevation Drawings

OBJECTIVE

The object of this session is to learn the techniques of embellishing elevation drawings. You will learn how to create and insert symbols of landscaping, people, and other objects properly. We will also analyze methods of placing the hatches around the symbols to show finishes.

This session completes the elevations you drew in Session Seven. The completed drawing from this session is shown in Figure 8–1.

YOUR NOTES

Use this space for notes about your indivudual plan

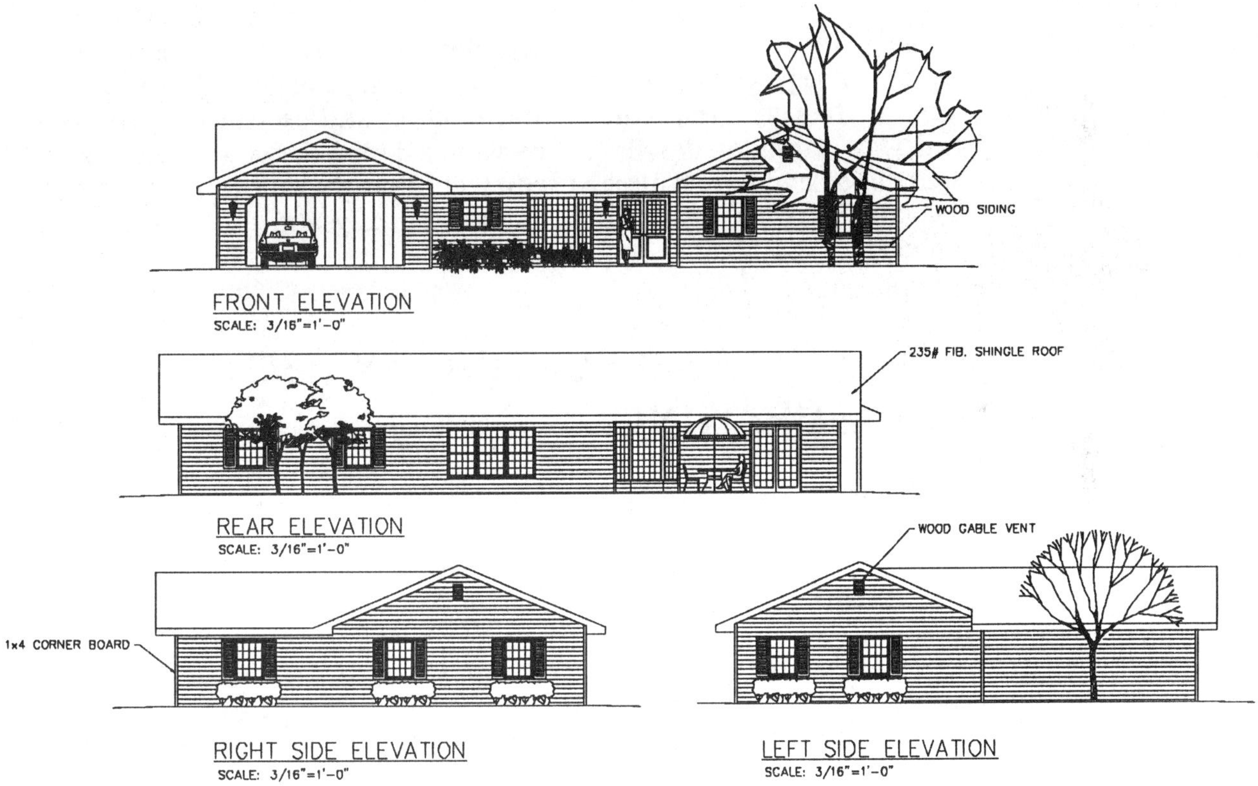

Figure 8-1

Commands used in this session:

break
ddlmodes
dimscale
dim/leader
explode
hatch
insert
layer
osnap
pline
style

YOUR NOTES

PURPOSES OF RENDERING ELEVATIONS

Elevations are "rendered," or embellished, to achieve a more realistic look. The amount of rendering we place in a drawing is determined by the type of drawing we are creating. If the drawing is meant to be used as a design drawing, we can employ any amount of rendering. Construction drawings, however, usually contain only a minimum amount of embellishment. This is because the purpose of the construction drawing is to convey construction information, not design information.

In our plan, we are going to place more embellishments than would ordinarily be placed in a construction drawing. Later, if we wish, we can turn off the layers that contain the symbols and use the drawing as a "strict" construction drawing. If we want a design drawing, we can leave the symbol layers on. This is a useful technique that allows us to employ the same drawing for both the design drawing and the construction drawing.

CREATING AND PLACING SYMBOLS IN THE DRAWING

Let's start by placing symbols in the drawing. This is a good starting point, since the surface textures (in our case, the wall siding) must "wrap" around the symbols. If it does not, the hatch used to create the texture obscures the symbols.

As we learned in Session Three, we should create symbols on their own layers. This allows us to freeze or thaw layers to control the symbols. We are going to use this capability in our drawing to create outlines to "hold" our texture hatches.

The symbols you need to complete the drawing are resident blocks on the work disk. The following layers were used to create the symbol drawings.

Layer	Symbol Parts Contained On Layer
Outline	Polyline outline of symbol
Detail	Detail parts of symbol
Shrubs	Shrubbery symbols

YOUR NOTES

Trees	Tree symbols
Humans	Human symbols
Vehicles	Vehicle symbols
Misc_symb	Miscellaneous symbols, (lights, vents, etc.)

STEP 1 *Placing Symbols in the Front Elevation*

Start the drawing named ELEVS, which you created in Session Seven. Zoom in on the front elevation. The symbols for this session are shown in Appendix L, along with their names and insertion points. These items are included as resident blocks in the prototype drawsing on the work disk

Place the symbols in the drawing as you wish. This is your place to play! Figure 8–2 shows a suggested layout to use if you prefer. All of the insertion points are placed at the ground line for easy placement. You can use object snap near to capture the ground line and achieve a perfect vertical placement.

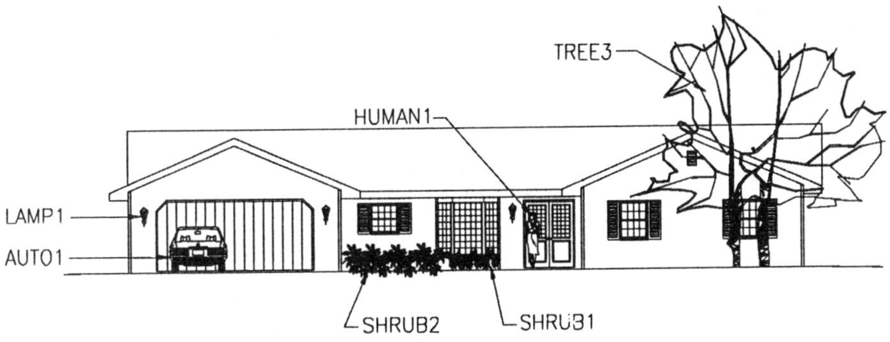

Figure 8-2

STEP 2 *Placing Symbols in the Remaining Elevations*

After you have finished placing symbols in the front elevation, place the symbols for the back and side elevations. Figure 8–3 shows suggested symbol placements for these elevations.

YOUR NOTES

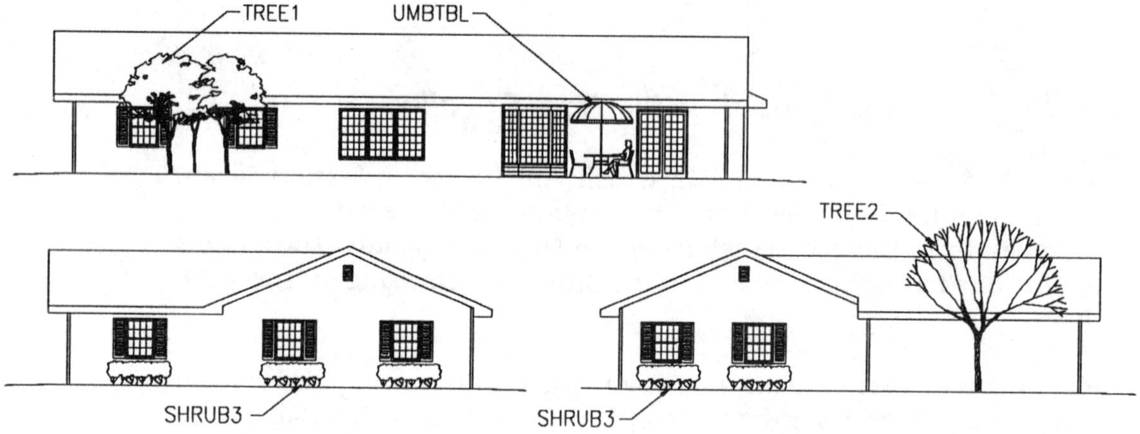

Figure 8-3

After you have completed the symbol placement, save your work to disk. If you take a break, don't forget to turn the timer off.

PLACING THE HATCHES

Our next step is to place the surface textures. We are going to place a hatch on the side of the building to indicate wood siding. Before we can place the hatch, however, we must create a boundary to hold it. As you know, the boundary must be perfectly formed. No entity making up the hatch can extend beyond an intersection. If it does, the hatch program will become confused and build the hatch improperly.

STEP 3 *Creating the Hatch Outlines*

We can create a hatch boundary by using the Polyline command to create an outline for the hatch. Let's draw a boundary for the front elevation. We will begin by setting the object snap mode for continuous operation.

YOUR NOTES

Command: **osnap**
Object snap modes: **int**

Next, change to the OUTLINE layer so the polyline will be placed on that layer. The OUTLINE layer was created in the current drawing when the symbols were inserted. Each symbol contains a layer named OUTLINE, so AutoCAD automatically created the layer in the current drawing for you. Note that you must thaw the layer named OUTLINE before you can make it the current layer.

Command: **layer**
?/Make/Set/New/ON/OFF/Color/Ltype/Freeze/Thaw: **t**
Layer name(s) to Thaw: **outline**
?/Make/Set/New/ON/OFF/Color/Ltype/Freeze/Thaw: **s**
New current layer <default>: **outline**

STEP 4 *Placing the Polyline Outlines*

Next, execute the Polyline command. Draw a frame around the perimeter of the elevation. Each symbol, window, and door that was included on the work disk already contains an outline, so it is not necessary to draw outlines for these objects.

Let's see how the outlines look. Explode the blocks, then use the Layer command to freeze all layers except the layer named OUTLINE. If your display system can display dialogue boxes, use the Ddlmodes command to display an easy-to-use dialogue box. Your elevations should look like the ones in Figure 8–4. Note that the edge of the garage that extends to the right side of the rear elevation has not been framed. Designers will often leave planes that are relatively distant unrendered. If this area were rendered, it might not appear as a distant plane.

STEP 5 *Breaking the Outlines at Intersections*

Next, we need to construct "clean" closed polygon areas for the hatch. Start by exploding each of the symbols. Then we will break the outline entities where they cross. Let's look at an example. Figure 8–5 shows a tree in front of the left side elevation. Use the Break command with the @ option to split the line into two entities where the lines cross. Use the following command sequence to break the line.

YOUR NOTES

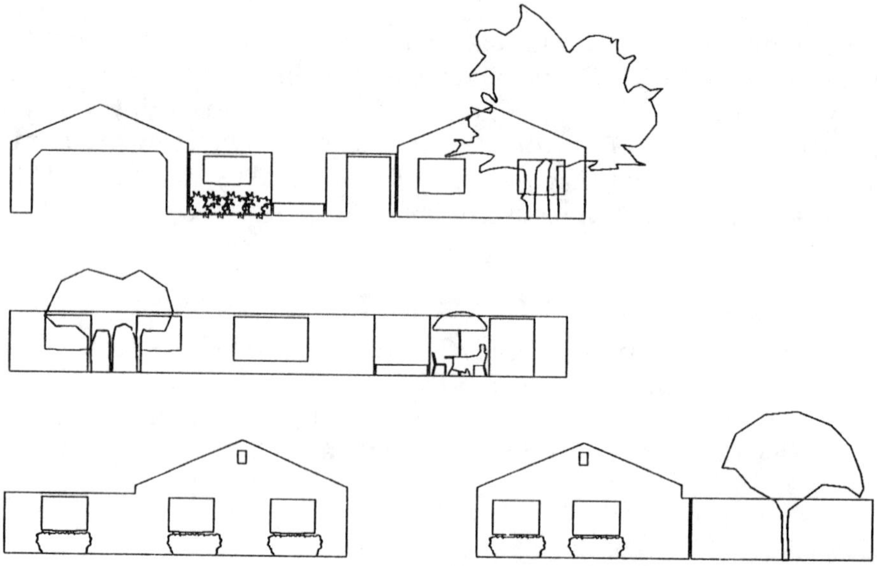

Figure 8-4

Command: **break**
Select object: *Select point 1.*
Enter second point (or F for first point): **f**
Enter first point: **int**
of *Select point 2.*
Enter second point: **@**

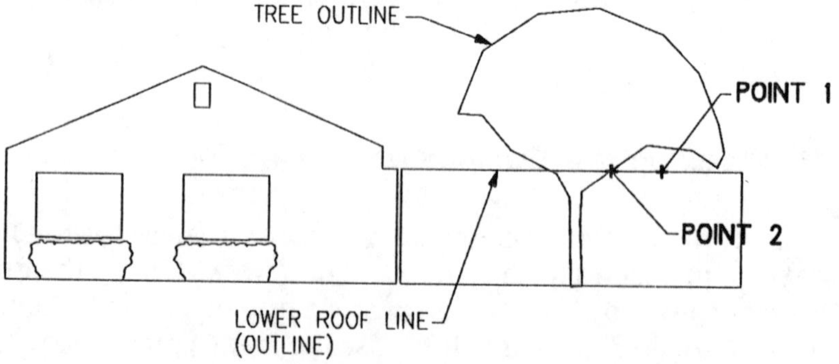

Figure 8-5

YOUR NOTES

The lower roof line is now split at the intersection of the tree outline. Continue to split the house lines where they intersect symbol outlines. Each intersection should be broken to make a closed area for the hatch. Complete the rest of the hatch boundaries now. After you have constructed all of the hatch boundaries, use the Save command to record your work to disk.

STEP 6 *Placing the Hatch*

Now let's place the hatch in the closed areas. Use the following command sequence.

Command: **hatch**
Pattern (? or name/U,style): **line**
Scale for pattern <default>: **45**
Angle for pattern <default>: **0**
Select objects: *Select all the entities surrounding one of your areas.*

Continue to place hatch patterns in all the areas you defined for a hatch. If a hatch doesn't build properly, you probably missed breaking an intersection.

Now, use the Layer command (or the Ddlmodes command) to freeze the OUTLINE layer and thaw all the remaining layers. You may want to trim the roof lines from behind the trees. Notice in Figure 8–1 that the lines have been trimmed from behind the trees full of leaves, and have been left in place when they would be visable through the barren branches.

PLACING THE TEXT

Finally, we will place the text and notes in the drawing. Since we will use dimension leaders as part of our notes, set the Dimscale dimension variable to 36.

Command: **dim**
Dim: **dimscale**
Current value <default> New value: **36**

YOUR NOTES

STEP 7 *Creating the Text Styles*

Next, create a layer named TEXT and change to the new text layer. Now use the following command sequences to create two text styles.

Command: **style**
Text style name (or ?) <default>: **notes**
New style.
Font file <default>: **simplex**
Height <default>: **10**
Width factor <1.00>: ↵
Obliquing angle <0>: ↵
Backwards? <N>: ↵
Upside-down? <N>: ↵
Vertical? <N>: ↵
NOTES is now the current text style.

We how have a new text style named NOTES. We will use this style to place the scale specifications and object descriptions in the drawing. Before we do that, though, let's create another text style to use for the titles of the elevations.

Command: **style**
Text style name (or ?) <default>: **title**
New style.
Font file <default>: **simplex**
Height <default>: **18**
Width factor <1.00>: ↵
Obliquing angle <0>: ↵
Backwards? <N>: ↵
Upside-down? <N>: ↵
Vertical? <N>: ↵
TITLE is now the current text style.

STEP 8 *Placing the Text on the Drawing*

Start by placing the titles as shown in Figure 8–6. Next, change the text style to NOTES and put the scale notation under the titles. Now use the Dim/Leader command to place the material notes as shown in Figure 8–6.

YOUR NOTES

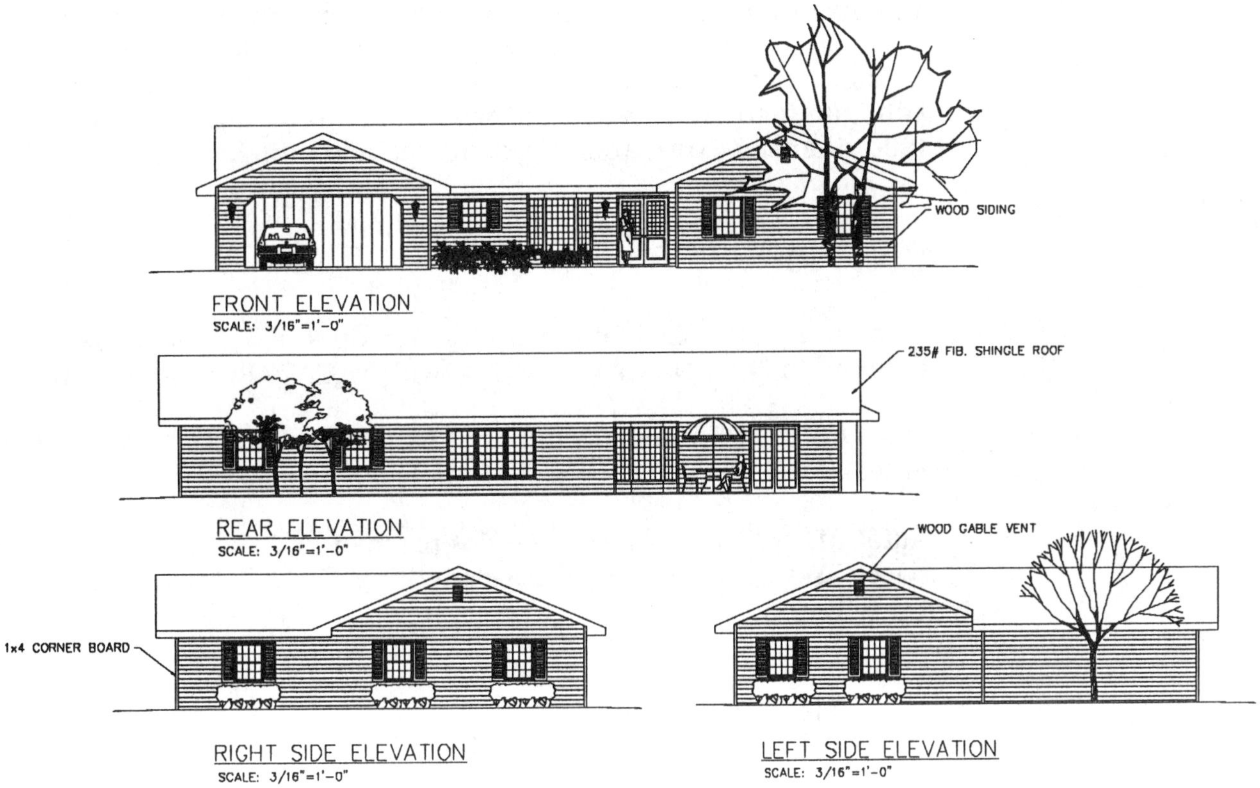

Figure 8-6

Use Save to record your work to disk again. Turn the timer off, sit back, and admire your work!

YOUR NOTES

PLOTTING INSTRUCTIONS

You may want to stop at this point and plot your work. If you have a pen plotter capable of plotting a C-size (24"x18") draw ing, you can plot the drawing at a scale of 3/16"=1'–0". If you have a dot matrix printer configured to AutoCAD, you can printer plot the drawing. The following is an explanation for each type of plotting.

Pen Plot

From the AutoCAD Main menu, select option 3 (Plot a drawing). Respond to Enter NAME of drawing: with \ACADARCH\ELEVS and ↵.

Next, AutoCAD prompts you for the part of the drawing to be plotted. Enter L for limits.

AutoCAD will now display the plot parameters. The last line on the screen asks if you want to change anything. Enter Y for yes. Then use the following settings.

Plot NOT written to a file
All entity colors plotted with pen 1
Size in inches
Plot origin at 0.00,0.00
Plotting size: C
Plot NOT rotated
Pen width 0.010
Area fill boundaries NOT adjusted for pen width
Hidden lines NOT removed
Scale: 3/16"=1'–0"

Before you proceed, make sure the plotter is ready to plot. A pen of 0.25mm will yield acceptable results. When you are ready, press ↵ and watch your drawing being plotted!

Printer Plot

YOUR NOTES

To printer plot, select option 4 (Printer Plot a drawing) from AutoCAD's Main menu. When asked for the drawing name, enter \ACADARCH\ELEVS and press ↵. You will be prompted for the part of the drawing to plot. Enter L for limits and Return. A listing of the plot parameters will be displayed. The last line on the screen asks if you want to change anything. Respond with Y for yes and use the following settings.

Plot NOT written to a file
Size in inches
Plot origin at 0.00,0.00
Plotting size: A
Plot rotated: YES
Hidden lines NOT removed
Scale: F (for fit)

Now prepare the printer and press ↵ to printer plot your drawing. Note that the printer plot will not be plotted to a particular scale.

YOUR NOTES

SUMMARY

- Architects render elevations to create a more realistic appearance.
- The amount of rendering an elevation contains depends on whether it is a design or construction drawing.
- Each symbol should contain an outline on a separate layer. This allows you to use the symbol outlines as hatch barriers. Using the outlines in this way avoids hatching through the symbols.
- To prevent AutoCAD from forming an improper hatch, you must break the outlines where they cross other hatch boundaries.
- Select symbols and hatches that enhance visual understanding of the elevation. Remember, an elevation is a visual description of the structure that is viewed by people who may not have the same imaginative capabilities that you have.

QUESTIONS

YOUR NOTES

1. What is the difference in the level of embellishment between design and construction elevation drawings?

____

____

____

2. What is the purpose of embellishing a design elevation?

____

____

____

3. How can you control the location of hatch patterns placed into an elevation drawing?

____

____

____

4. What is the purpose of creating a block that contains an outline layer?

____

____

____

YOUR NOTES

PROBLEMS

1. Create an elevation block that contains an outline layer. Place the block into a drawing. Freeze and thaw layers to view the outline and the drawing separately.

2. Create a new drawing, using the PELEVS drawing on the work disk as a prototype. Design an elevation and use the blocks provided to embellish the drawing. Create hatch boundaries and use AutoCAD hatch patterns to place hatches in your drawing.

YOUR NOTES

Section 4 Drawing Site Plans

- Session 9: Drawing Site Plans
- Session 10: Embellishment of the Site Plan

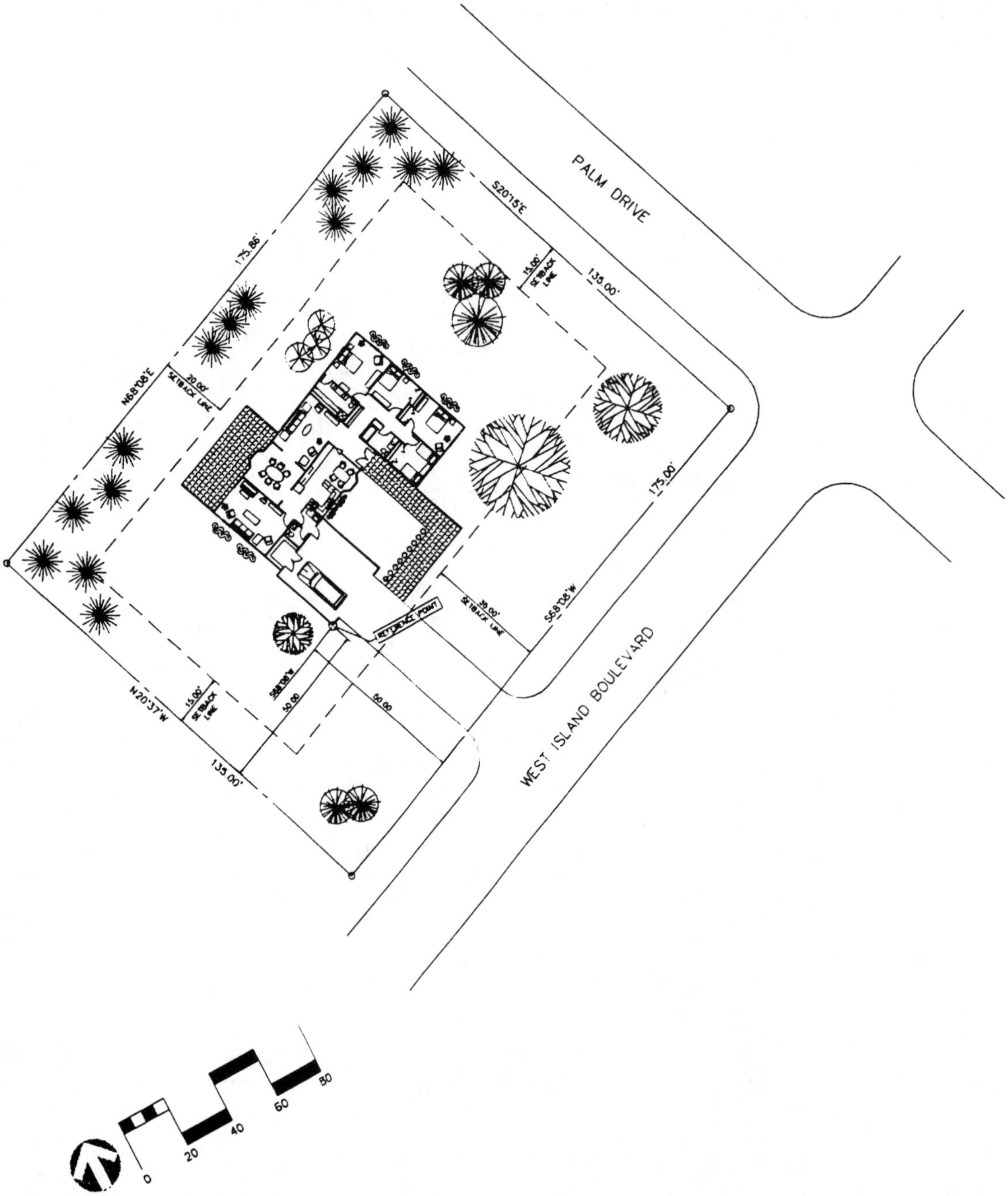

SESSION 9

Drawing Site Plans

OBJECTIVE

The object of this session is to learn the techniques of constructing a site plan. We will construct a site plan from a legal description, place the setback lines and streets, and insert the building floor plan at a specific position and compass heading. The finished drawing from this session is shown in Figure 9–1.

YOUR NOTES

Use this space for notes about your indivudual plan

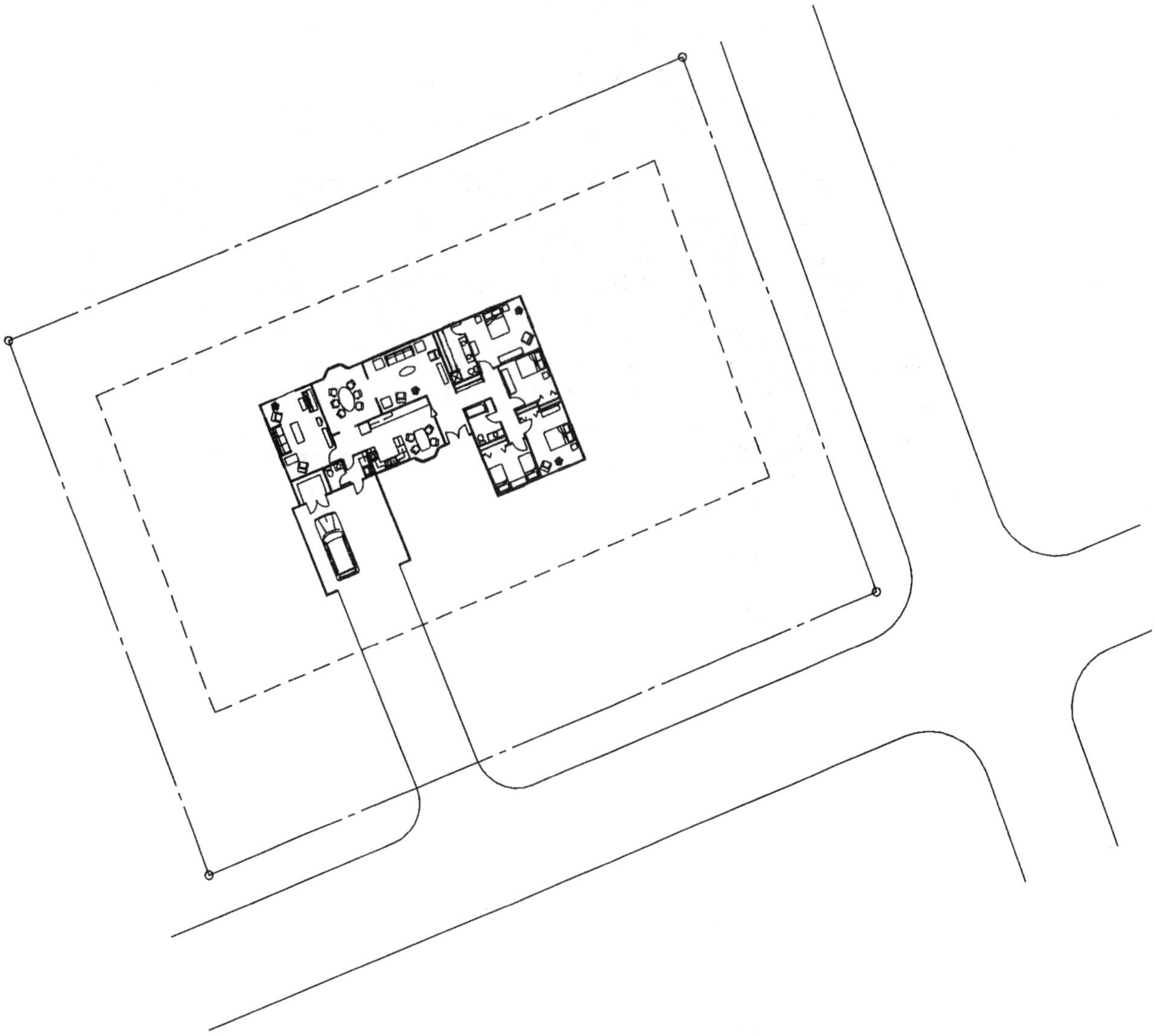

Figure 9-1

YOUR NOTES

Commands used in this session:

base	insert	offset
change	layer	point
circle	limits	setvar
ddlmodes	line	snap
erase	linetype	trim
fillet	ltscale	units

SITE PLANS

Site plans are used to show the layout of buildings, driveways, sidewalks, and other items on the property. Site plans are also referred to as plot plans, layout plans, and property plans. The plans can be drawn to either engineering or architectural scales.

Identifying Types of Lines

Site plans contain lines that describe the property. The line that shows the perimeter of the property is called the *property line*. It is also referred to as a lot line.

Site plans can also show setback lines. *Setback lines* show the distance that all building construction must be from the property line. For example, a 35′ front setback means that you can not build closer than 35′ to the front property line. Driveways and sidewalks can be built across the setback line, but no part of the building may cross the line. Setback lines are usually given from each property line (front, back, and both sides) and are typically set by local ordinances. The setback for each side of a property can be a different distance.

The "lay" of the property is described by *contour lines*. Contour lines are also referred to as topographic, or "topo," lines. Contour lines can often be recognized as many curvy lines on the plan. Each line is assigned an elevation (height in reference to a known point). The line passes through every point on the property that is the height represented by that contour line. Figure 9–2 shows an example of a site plan with property lines, setback lines, and contour lines. The numbers on the contour lines refer to the vertical elevation in relation to a known elevation.

YOUR NOTES

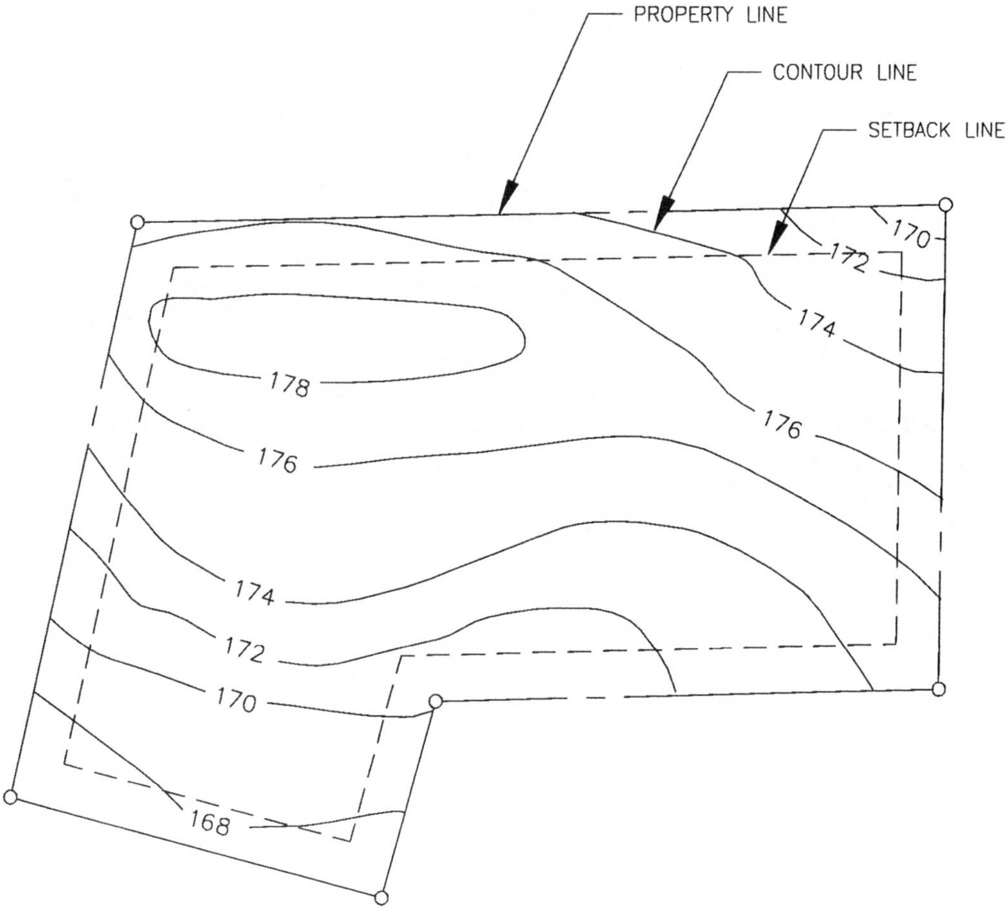

Figure 9-2

The building is located on the plan in reference to a known physical point. The most common reference point is a property line corner. A specified point on the building (usually a corner) is placed a designated distance from the reference point, and the building is "turned" in line with a defined compass heading.

Defining Property Lines

The first step in drawing a site plan is to construct the property lines. For our site plan, we will use a legal description of the property. A legal

YOUR NOTES

description is a written depiction of the site. To understand a legal description, you must first understand how property line headings are designated.

Property lines are described using a distance and a heading. The *distance* is the length of the line between the last property line segment and the next. The *heading* is the direction of the property line. For example, we could describe a property line by saying it is "100 feet North." This property line would be 100 feet long and would run straight to the north.

Real property lines, however, are rarely this simplistic. They almost always run in directions that are between the compass points. Therefore, we usually can define a direction by describing a line that runs a certain number of degrees from one compass point toward another compass point. For example, a line could run "North 45 degrees East" (see Figure 9–3). This describes a line that runs 45 degrees east from due north, as shown in Figure 9–3.

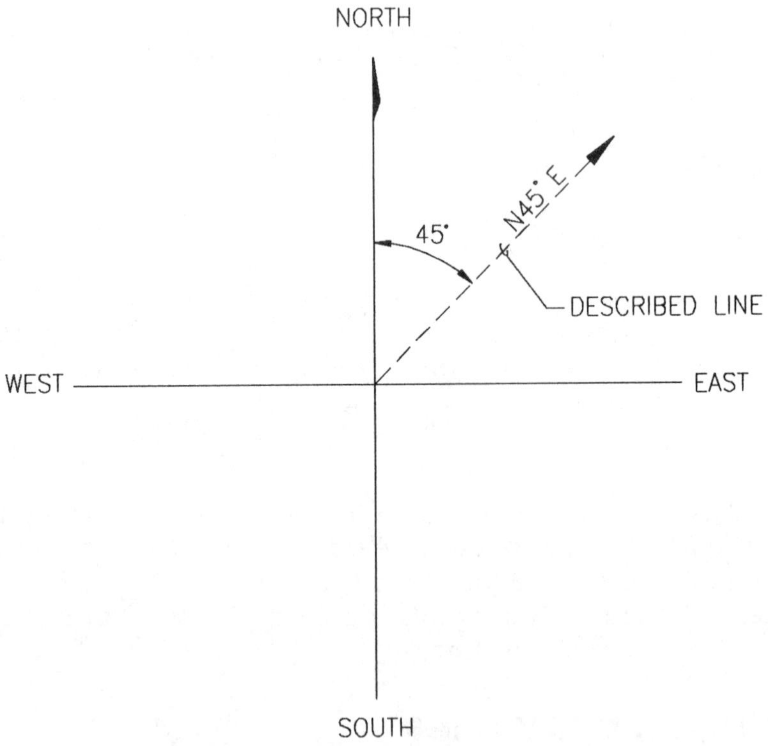

Figure 9-3

YOUR NOTES

This is the method surveyors use to describe the distance and direction of a property line. They can also break each degree down into 60 minutes (written 60′) and each minute down into 60 seconds (written 60″). A "real world" property line description might be written as "31°22′57″ at a distance of 257.89′."

DRAWING THE SITE PLAN

Let's use a legal description to construct the property lines. Start a new drawing named SITE to equal the prototype drawing named PSITE. The prototype drawing has been set up with the following drawing parameters.

Units: Decimal
- 2 digits to the right of the decimal
- Surveyor's units
- 2 fractional places for angle measurement
- Direction for angle E: E
- Angles not measured clockwise

Limits: 480,360 (1″=20′ on C-size paper)
Layer: LINES
Color: white (color 7)
Time: OFF
Ltscale: 10

Now we need a legal description. The following is the legal description for our property. Read through the description to familiarize yourself with the technique used.

> Commencing at the southeast corner of McGraw property, thence Northerly 135.00′ along a line N20°37′W thence Easterly 175.86′ along a line N68°08′E thence Southerly 135.00′ along a line S20°15′E thence Westerly 175.00′ along a line S68°08′W to the beginning.

Let's start by drawing the first property line. Turn on the timer, and let's begin!

YOUR NOTES

STEP 1 *Drawing the Property Lines*

Select the Line command, and place a beginning point at the absolute coordinate of 150,100.

Command: **line**
From point: **150,100**
To point: **@135<N20d37'W**

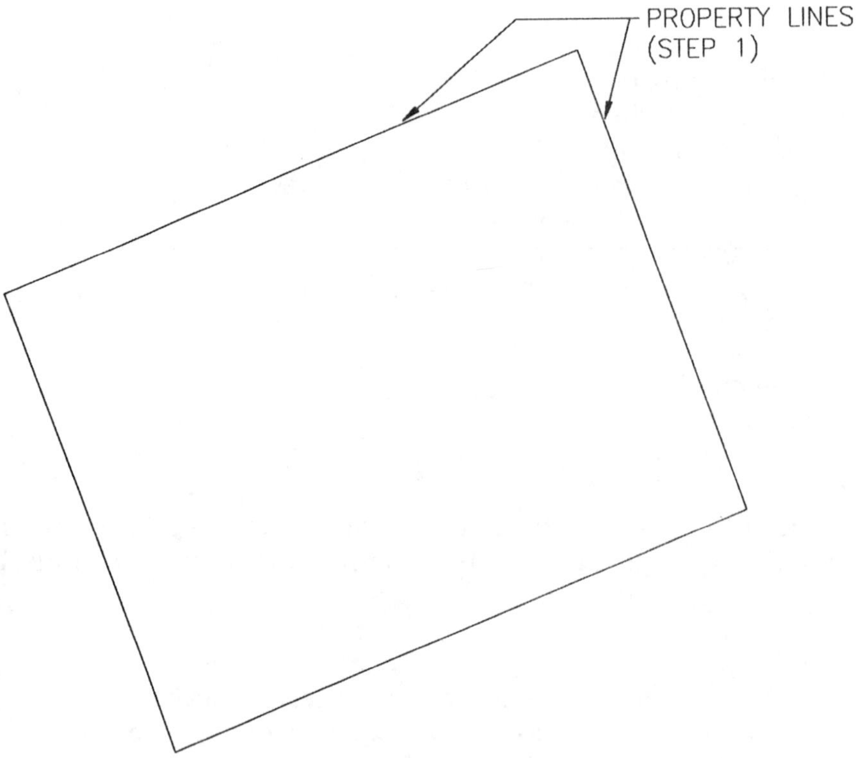

Figure 9-4

You should now see the west property line. The line is 135′ long and has a heading described by 20 degrees, 37 minutes west from north (north is straight up in the drawing). It doesn't matter whether you use upper or lower case for the compass directions and the degree *d*.

YOUR NOTES

Let's continue the command sequence and draw the remaining property lines.

To point: **@175.86<N68d08'E**
To point: **@135.00<S20d15'E**
To point: **@175.00<S68d08'W**

Your drawing should look like the one in Figure 9–4.

STEP 2 *Defining the Linetype*

Property lines are often shown as line segments with two short dashes. Let's write a linetype definition for our property line. Use the following command sequence to construct the property linetype.

Command: **linetype**
?/Create/Load/Set: **c**
Name of linetype to create: **property**
File for storage of linetype <ACAD>: ↵
Wait, checking if linetype already defined...
Descriptive text: -------- -- -- -------- *(Enter the "look" with dashes and spaces.)*
Enter pattern (on next line):
A,2,-0.2,0.2,-0.2,0.2,-0.2,2 *(Note that AutoCAD places the A on the line for you.)*
New definition written to file

STEP 3 *Changing the Linetype of the Property Line*

Now use the Change command to change the property lines to the linetype named Property.

Command: **change**
Select objects: *Select the property lines.*
Properties/<Change point>: **p**
Change what property (Color/Elev/LAyer/LType/Thickness)? **lt**
New linetype <default>: **property**
Change what property (Color/Elev/LAyer/LType/Thickness) ? ↵

YOUR NOTES

Your property lines should now be changed to the Property linetype. You may have to regenerate the drawing to display the change.

This would be a good time to use the Save command to record your work to disk.

STEP 4 *Drawing the Setback Lines*

The setback lines run parallel to the property lines. We can use the Offset command to construct them. Refer to Figure 9–5 for each setback dimension, and offset the property lines to construct the setback lines.

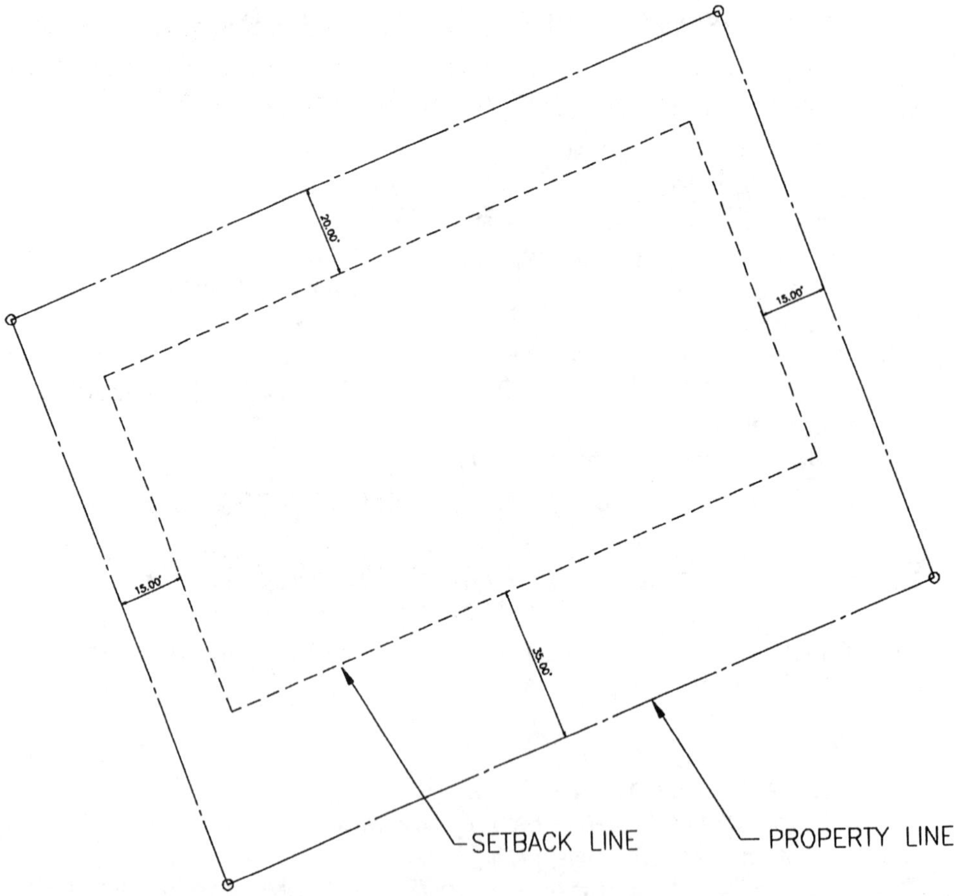

Figure 9-5

YOUR NOTES

Next, use the Change command to change the setback lines to linetype Hidden.

PLACING THE BUILDING ON THE SITE

Next, we are going to insert our floor plan into the site plan. Before we do this, however, we must go back to our floor plan drawing and set the insertion base point so we can make an accurate placement. We will also prepare the layers so that only the appropriate layers of the floor plan will show up when we insert the plan.

STEP 5 *Preparing the Floor Plan Drawing*

Use the End command to end the current drawing and start the floor plan drawing named FLPLAN1. Select the Base command and use object snap intersection to capture the point. Refer to Figure 9–6.

Command: **base**
Base point <0.00,0.00,0.00>: **int**
of *Select point 1.*

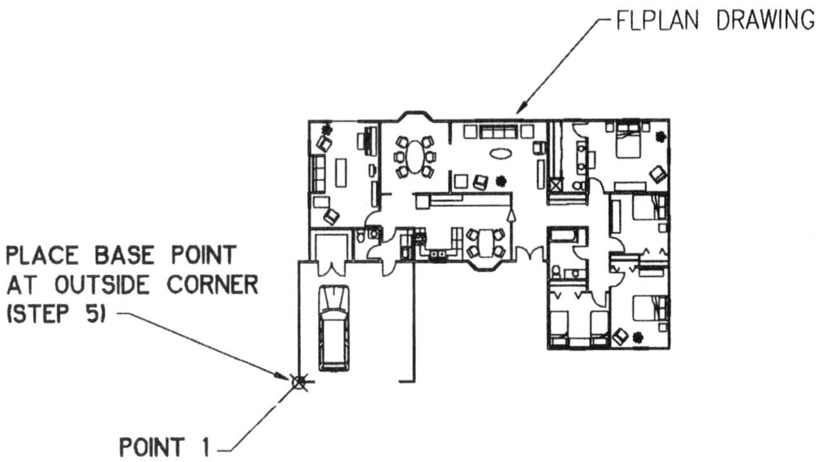

Figure 9-6

YOUR NOTES

Next, use the Layer command to freeze all the layers except FLPLAN, DOORS, WINDOWS and FURNITURE. If your display system is capable of displaying dialogue boxes, you may want to use the Ddlmodes command to display a dialogue box.

Now end the FLPLAN1 drawing, and start the drawing named SITE again.

STEP 6 *Creating a Reference Point*

We now need a reference point on the site plan to help us place the floor plan drawing correctly. Figure 9–7 shows the dimensions from a corner of the property to the corner of the house where we placed the base point.

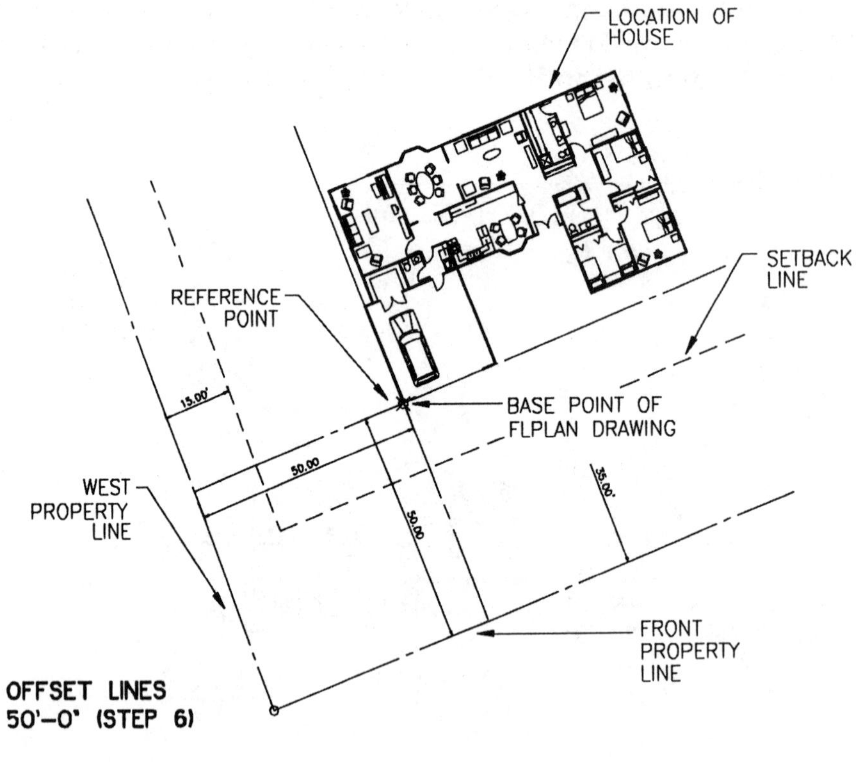

Figure 9-7

Let's offset the property lines to create an intersection at that point. Refer to Figure 9–7.

YOUR NOTES

Command: **offset**
Offset distance or Through <default>: **50**
Select object to offset: *Select the west property line.*

Repeat the same sequence for the front (south) property line, using the same 50-foot offset setting. Then use Setvar to set the pdmode to a value of 35.

Command: **setvar**
Variable name or ?: **pdmode**
New value for PDMODE: **35**

Next, select the Point command and object snap intersection to place a point entity at the intersection. Finally, erase the lines that you placed with the Offset command, leaving only the point.

STEP 7 *Inserting the Floor Plan*

Now we will use the Insert command to place the building onto the site. Since the floor plan is drawn in architectural units and the site is drawn in decimal units, we will need to use a scale factor of 0.0833 for the insertion.

Command: **insert**
Block name (or ?): **flplan**
Insertion point: **node**
of *Select the point you placed.*
X scale factor <1> / Corner / XYZ: **.0833**
Y scale factor (default=X): ↵
Rotation angle <E>: **N68d08'E**

Your drawing should look like the one in Figure 9–8.

Use the Save command to record your changes again.

YOUR NOTES

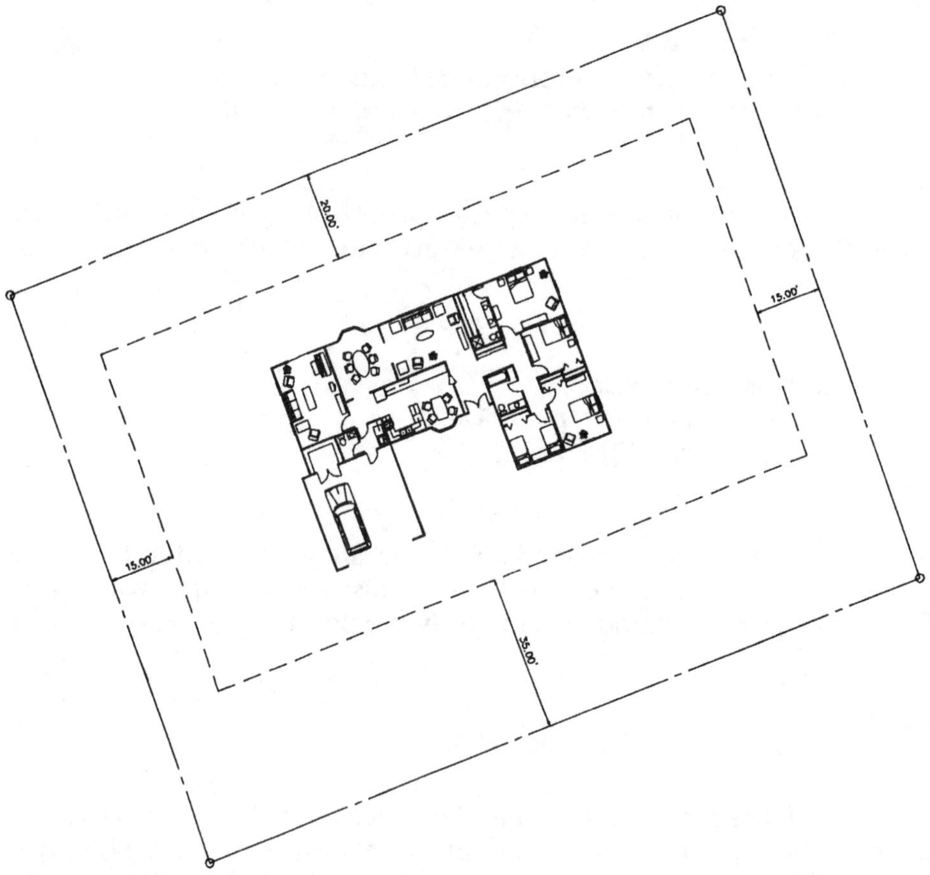

Figure 9-8

CONSTRUCTING THE STREETS

Now let's construct the streets. The edges of the streets are 10 feet from the property lines. Both of the streets are 24 feet wide.

STEP 8 *Placing the Street Lines*

Use the Offset command to offset the south and east property lines 10 feet, as shown in Figure 9–9.

Next, set the offset width to 24 feet. Offset the street edge to form the other side of the street, as shown in Figure 9–9.

YOUR NOTES

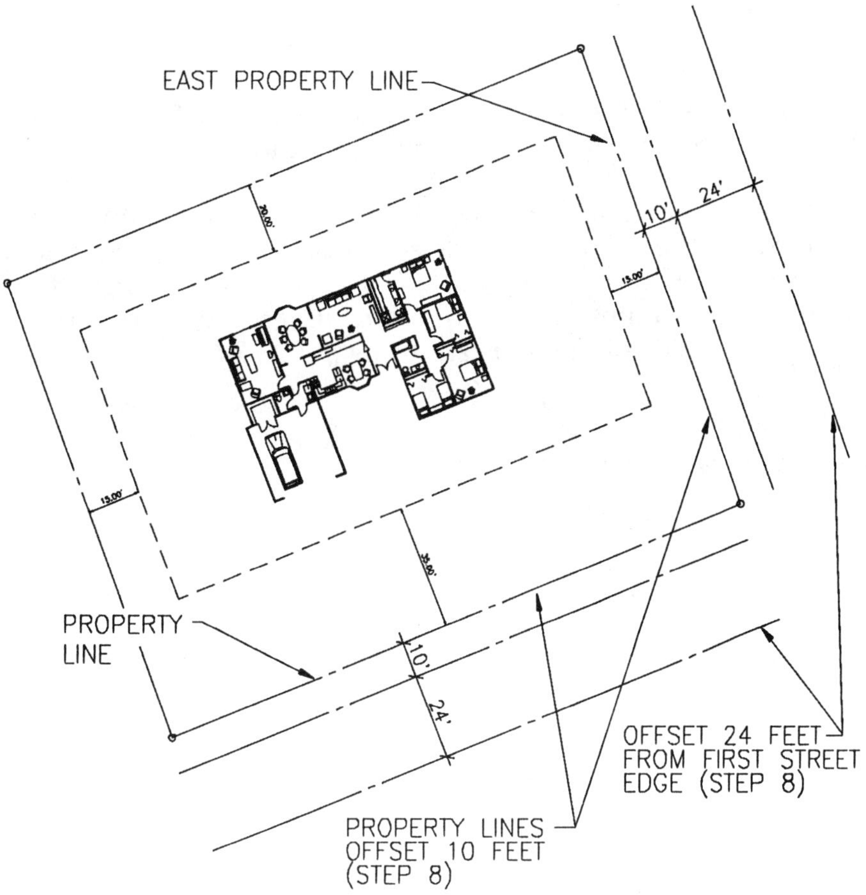

Figure 9-9

STEP 9 *Extending the Streets*

Note that the streets do not run past the property lines. If you look at Figure 9–1, you will see that the streets extend past the intersection. Let's look at a technique for lengthening the streets.

Let's start by using the Snap command to rotate the crosshairs to match the streets. Use the following command sequence to do this.

YOUR NOTES

Command: **snap**
Snap spacing or ON/OFF/Aspect/Rotate/Style <default>: **r**
Base point <0.00,0.00>: ↵
Rotation angle <E>: **S68d08'W**
Angle adjusted to N 68d8' E

Next, press the F8 key to turn on the ortho mode. Look at the status line at the top of the screen to verify that ortho is displayed.

Select the Change command and choose both the street lines along the south side of the property. Move the crosshairs to approximately the point shown as point 1 in Figure 9–10 and select. Repeat, using point 2 as the change point. Repeat the same procedure for the street lines along the east side of the property, using points 3 and 4 in Figure 9–10.

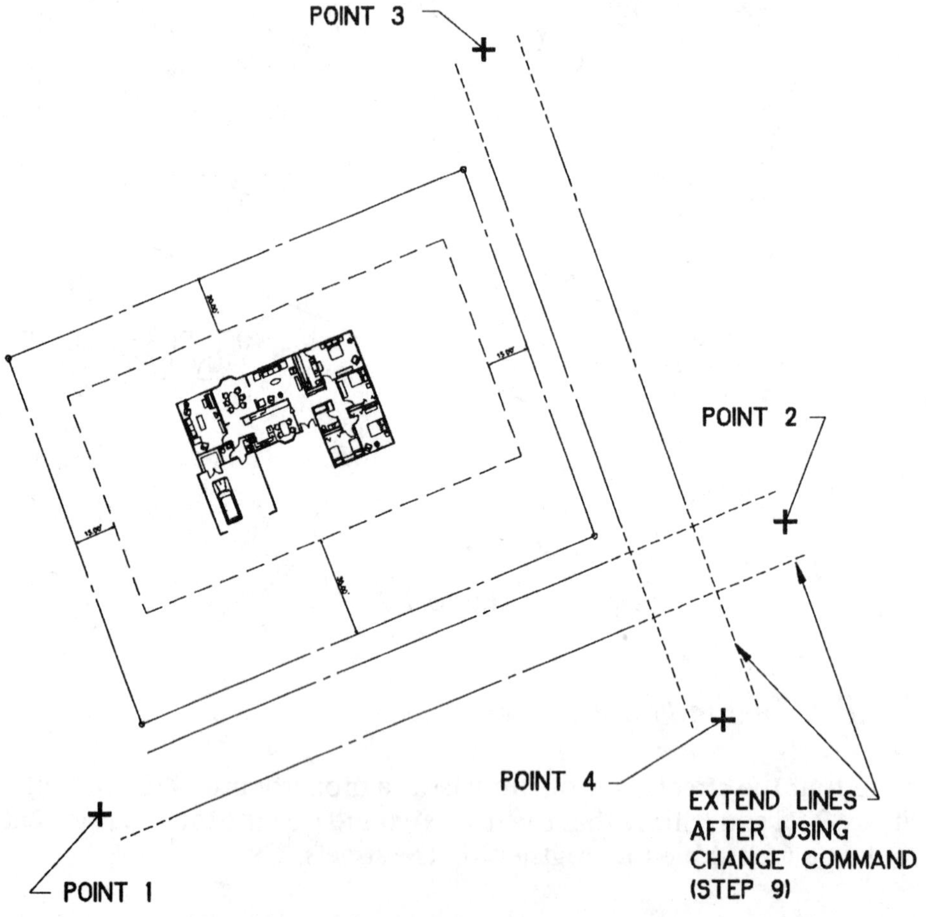

Figure 9-10

YOUR NOTES

STEP 10 *Trimming the Intersection*

Next, use the Trim command to trim the intersection. Use the same technique you used to trim your wall intersections when you were drawing the floor plan.

STEP 11 *Drawing the Driveway*

Now draw two lines from the garage door to the street, using object snap perpendicular to snap to the street line. Refer to Figure 9–11 as necessary. Use the Trim command to trim the street line from between the driveway edges.

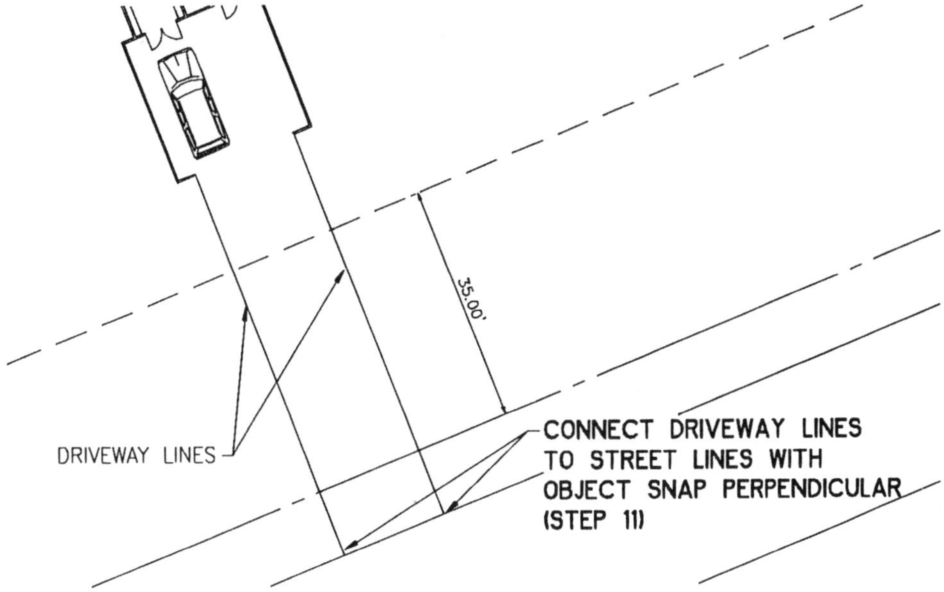

Figure 9-11

STEP 12 *Filleting the Street Corners*

Now use the Fillet command to create the corners. The driveway corners are filleted at a 10-foot radius; the street corners are filleted at a 15-foot radius.

YOUR NOTES

STEP 13 *Placing the Property Corner Circles*

Finally, use the Circle command and object snap intersection to place a circle at each property line corner. Use a circle radius of 1 foot. Your drawing should now look like the one in Figure 9–1.

YOUR NOTES

YOUR NOTES

SUMMARY

- Site plans are used to show the layout of driveways, sidewalks, buildings, and other items on the property.

- Architects use different types of lines on site plans to describe parts of the property. They use different linetypes to describe property lines, setback lines, for example.

- Property lines are described by a direction (heading) and a distance.

- You can use AutoCAD's surveyor's units to construct the property lines from the headings and distances.

- Customized linetypes are easy to create in AutoCAD. You can use the Linetype command to construct different linetypes for your site plans.

- Street intersections can be trimmed in the same manner as wall intersections. Use the Fillet command with an appropriate radius to create the corners.

QUESTIONS

YOUR NOTES

1. What is the purpose of a site plan drawing?

2. What is the line that describes the perimeter of the property called?

3. What are setback lines?

4. What do contour lines describe?

YOUR NOTES

5. What type of dimension units are set in AutoCAD to draw property lines?

PROBLEMS

YOUR NOTES

1. Construct a property line drawing. You may obtain a legal description of an existing property or use one provided by your instructor.

2. Place setback line on the property. Use 35′ for the front, 30′ for the rear and 15′ for the side setbacks.

Getting the Details Right

When Alan Johnson got the job of his dreams, he knew he needed help. Johnson's architectural firm is a three-person operation, and he had never designed a $5 million school before. Using AutoCAD with Softdesk's AdCADD Auto-Architect software, he could easily handle the plan and elevation drawings. Unfortunately, there would also be an enormous number of construction details to draw.

On previous projects, Johnson had found that AutoCAD was not much help in drawing details. Drawing them one line at a time with CAD wasn't much better than using a pencil and paper. Most of the time, he just sketched a detail and had his assistant draft it by hand. Now he would need to hire a detailer.

Another local architect was using an AutoCAD add-on program called The Vertex Detailer, from Vertex Design Systems. He recommended it, and Johnson bought a copy. Johnson was pleased to find that the program helped him put together details by assembling drawings of building materials. All he had to do was select a material (called a "component") from a menu, specify the size, and drag the component into place.

The Vertex Detailer provides a tremendous number of materials in a range of shapes and sizes by using a technique called parametric drawing. Instead of storing individual drawings of each component, it draws them "on the fly" according to the dimensions (or "parameters") that the designer specifies. The program also writes drawing notes automatically: a designer picks a component, picks a location for the note, and The Vertex Detailer draws an arrow and writes a note identifying the component.

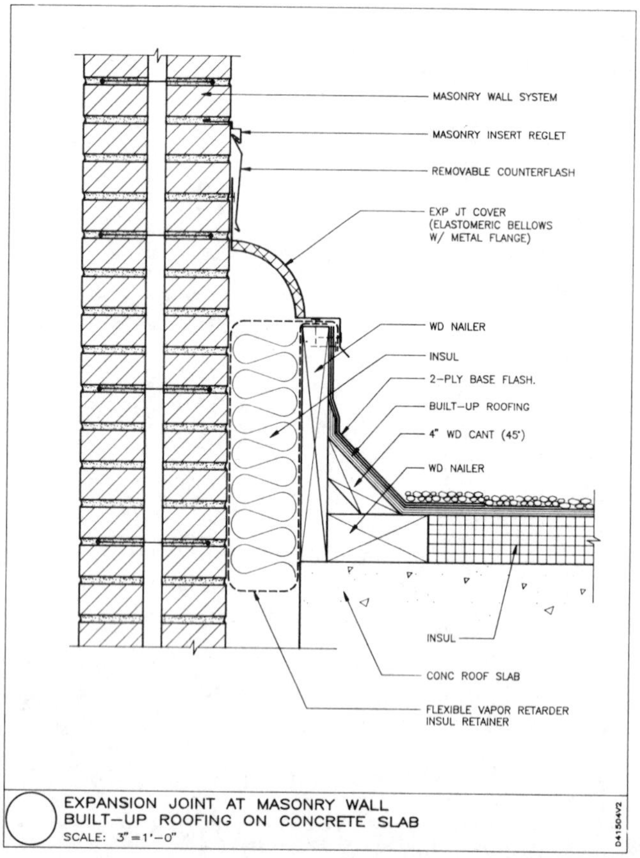

Roof detail produced with The Vertex Detailer and The Built-Up Roofs Dynamic Detail Group

Johnson found that The Vertex Detailer made it practical to use AutoCAD for detailing for the first time. He also discovered that it was now easier to draw a detail on the computer himself than it was to draw a sketch, then have someone else copy it. He didn't have to hire a full-time detailer, and he was able to give his drafting assistant more challenging work.

Said Johnson, "With The Vertex Detailer, I can try out different details as quickly as I get an idea. The result is a ready-to-use detail, not a pile of scribbled tracing paper." The school design was finished promptly, and it was the first time the firm had used CAD for all the drawings on a job.

SESSION

10 Embellishment of the Site Plan

OBJECTIVE

YOUR NOTES

Use this space for notes about your individual plan

In this session, we will complete the site plan that we started in Session Nine. We will add text and dimensions, and we will construct a hatched patio and sidewalk. We will also place the landscaping on the site. The finished drawing from this session is shown in Figure 10–1.

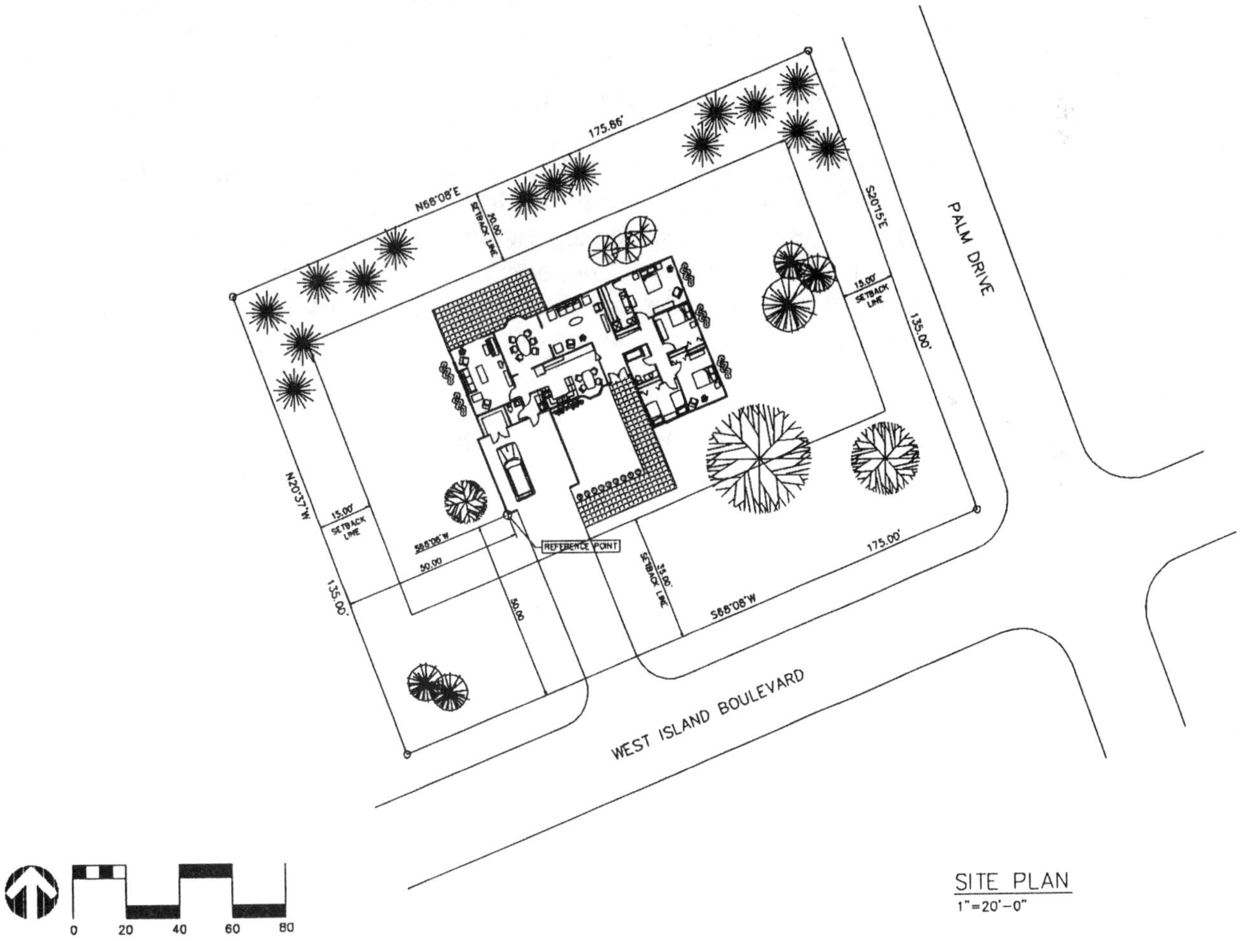

Figure 10-1

YOUR NOTES

Commands used in this session:

circle	insert	pline
dim	layer	snap
extend	line	style
hatch	offset	text

PLANNING THE SITE PLAN

Good designers know that the walls of a house are not the limits of its design. The setting in which a structure resides strongly influences its character and its psychological effect on those who occupy its spaces, both interior and exterior. Setting can also influence the value of the property.

Site planning is an important aspect of sound residential design. The site plan, as a tool of both design and construction, serves many purposes. From a basic level, the site plan shows the location of the structure on the property. Beyond that level, we can show the contour of the ground, the surface textures of sidewalks, patios, and drives; special features such as gardenways, pools, and terraced areas; and the location of landscaping elements.

The site plan is the only plan on which we can relate many of our design ideas. As a design drawing, the site plan is not restricted to relating construction information. It can also convey the character of the setting to people who cannot visualize it from a mere description.

In its construction drawing form, the site plan conveys much necessary information that floor plans, sections, and even building elevations cannot communicate. Our site plan will be sheet number one in our set of plans, because no construction work can begin until the builder consults the site plan.

Our site plan will serve a dual purpose. It will include both the basic information for a construction drawing and the visual information for a design drawing. The dimensions, building location, and text information are necessary construction details, and the landscaping and surface hatching are design descriptions.

PLACING WALKS AND PATIOS

Let's get started by adding a sidewalk and a patio to our site plan. Edit the drawing named SITE, which you began in Session Nine.

YOUR NOTES

STEP 1 *Drawing the Sidewalk*

Zoom into the area of the front door and garage. Select the Line command. Use object snap intersection to start the line at the intersection of the front bedroom (point 1 on Figure 10–2). Use the following command sequence.

Command: **line**
From point: **int**
to *Select point 1.*
to point: **@18<270**
to point: **per**
to *Select point 2.*

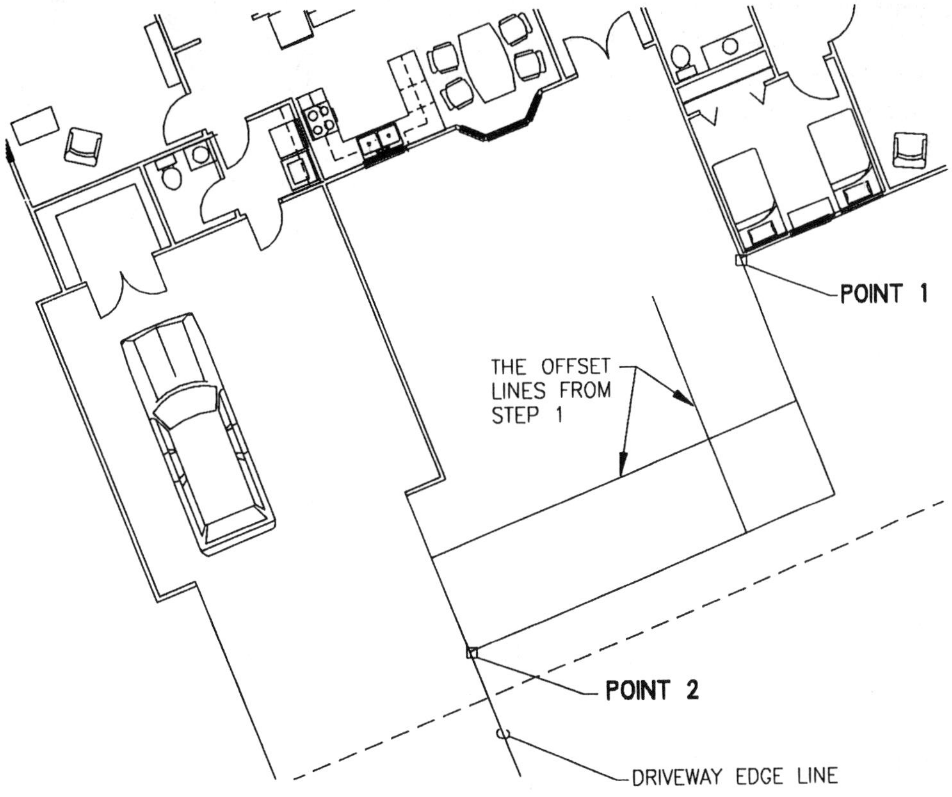

Figure 10-2

YOUR NOTES

Let's now use the Offset command to create the other edge of the sidewalk. Select Offset and set the offset distance to 6 feet. Select each of the sidewalk edges you just constructed and offset them as shown in Figure 10–2.

Now use the Extend command to extend the sidewalk edge to the left of the front door, as shown in Figure 10–3. Fillet the lines to finish constructing the sidewalk.

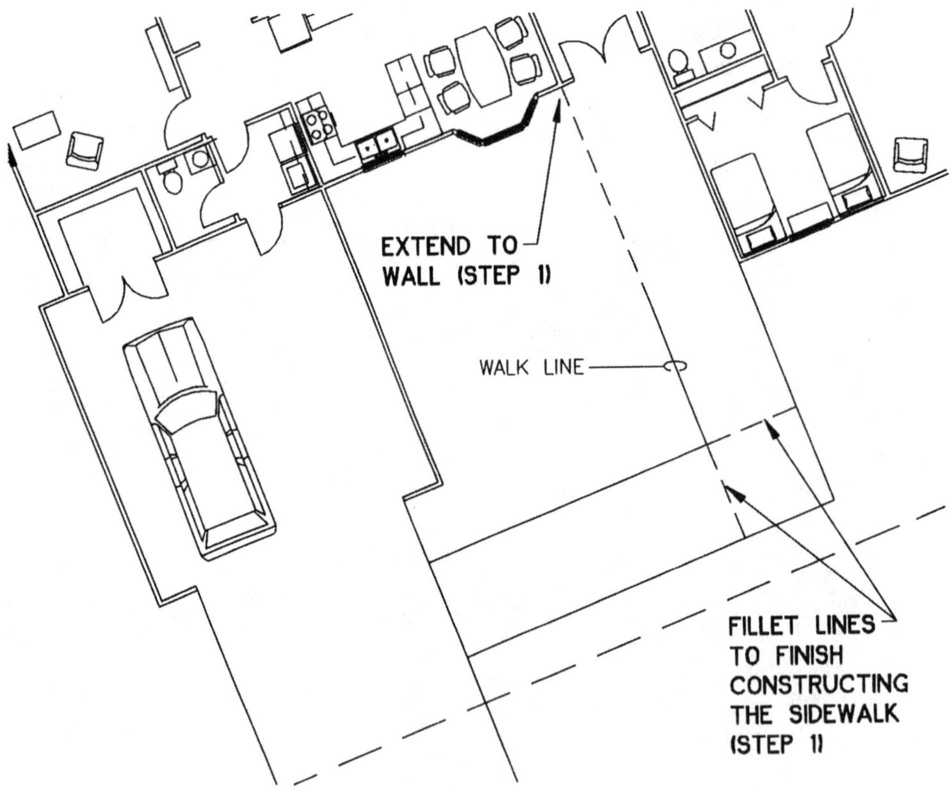

Figure 10-3

STEP 2 *Drawing the Patio*

Use the Snap command to rotate the crosshairs to the same angle as the street. Use the same method we used in Session Nine.

YOUR NOTES

Next, use the following command sequence and refer to Figure 10–4 to draw the patio.

Command: **line**
from point: **int**
of *Select point 1.*
to point: **@12<90**
to point: **@30<0**
to point: **per**
of *Select point 2.*

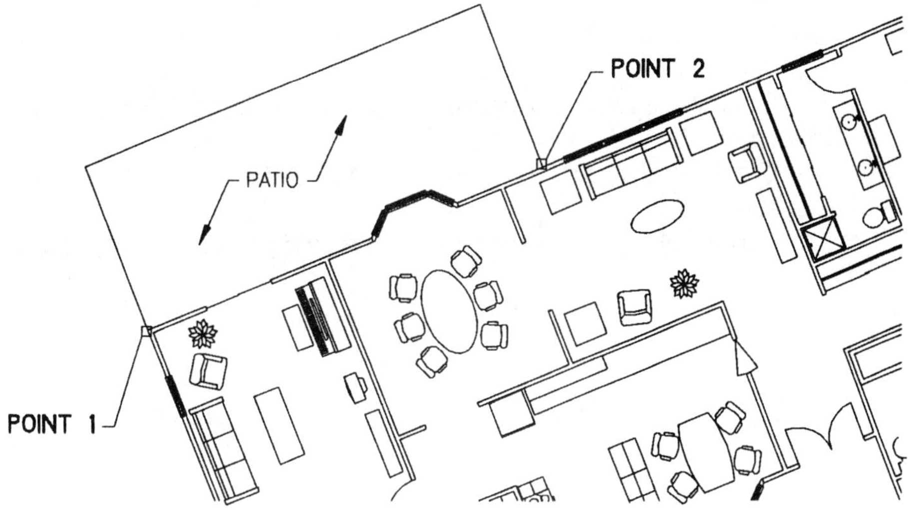

Figure 10-4

HATCHING THE SIDEWALK AND PATIO

Now let's place a hatch pattern on the sidewalk and patio. To do this, we will use the same polyline frame method we used in Session Eight to contain the hatch.

STEP 3 *Constructing the Hatch Boundary*

Start by using the Osnap command to set object snap intersection in continuous mode.

Command: **osnap**
Object snap modes: **int**

YOUR NOTES

Now use the Pline command to place a polyline around the sidewalk. Use the following command sequence and refer to Figure 10–5.

Command: **pline**
From point: *Select point 1.*
Current line width is 0
Arc/Close/Halfwidth/Length/Undo/Width/<Endpoint of line>:
Select point 2.
Arc/Close/Halfwidth/Length/Undo/Width/<Endpoint of line>:
Select point 3.
Arc/Close/Halfwidth/Length/Undo/Width/<Endpoint of line>:
Select point 4.
Arc/Close/Halfwidth/Length/Undo/Width/<Endpoint of line>:
Select point 5.
Arc/Close/Halfwidth/Length/Undo/Width/<Endpoint of line>:
Select point 6.
Arc/Close/Halfwidth/Length/Undo/Width/<Endpoint of line>: **c**

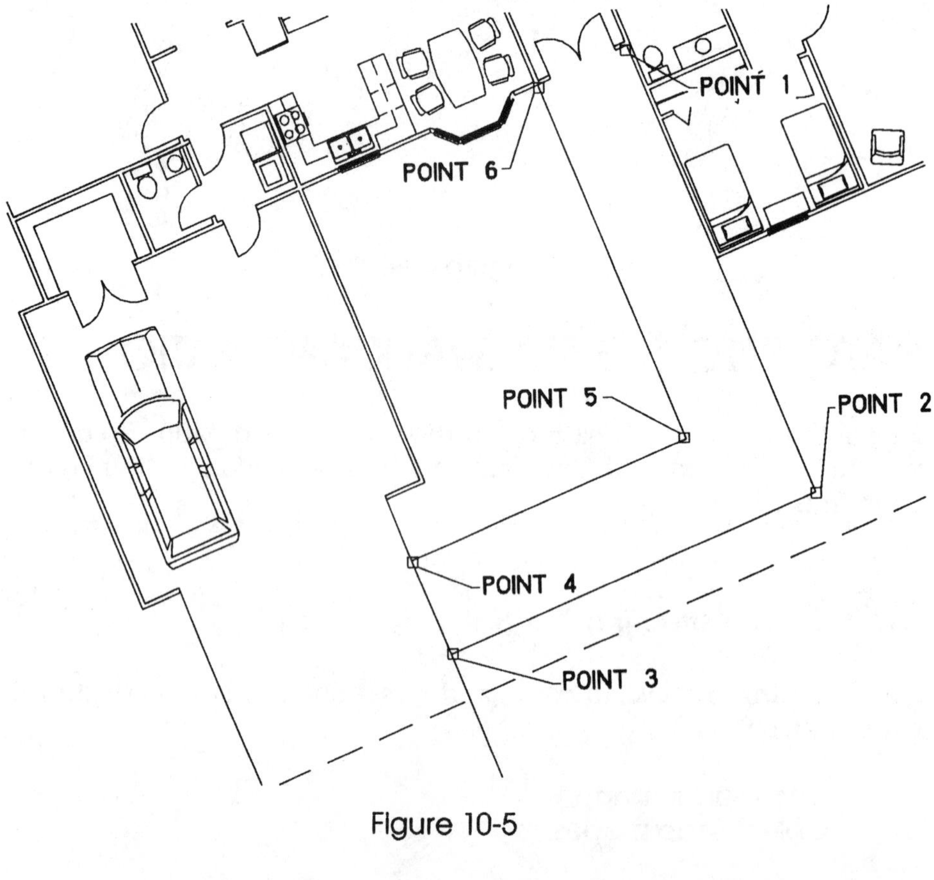

Figure 10-5

YOUR NOTES

STEP 4 *Placing the Hatch*

Now use the Hatch command to place the hatch inside the closed polyline boundary you just created.

Command: **hatch**
Pattern (? or name/U,style): **angle**
Scale for pattern <1.0000>: **5**
Angle for pattern <E>: **S68d08'W**
Select objects: **l**
Select objects: ↵

STEP 5 *Deleting the Hatch Boundary*

Use the following command sequence to erase the polyline boundary. Be sure to use the Erase command immediately after the Hatch command so the polyline boundary will be the "previous" object selected.

Command: **erase**
Select objects: **p**
1 found
Select objects: ↵

Your drawing should now look like the one in Figure 10–6.

STEP 6 *Hatching the Patio*

Repeat the same procedure to place the hatch for the patio. Next, use the Osnap command again to reset the continuous object snap mode to none.

Command: **osnap**
Object snap modes: **none**

YOUR NOTES

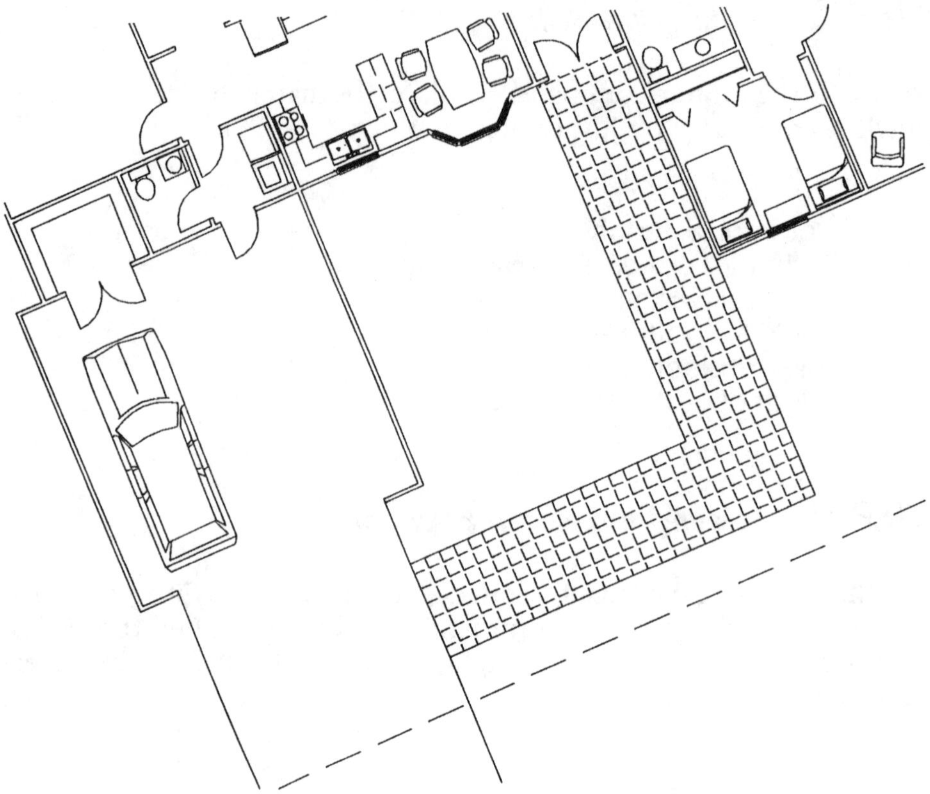

Figure 10-6

PLACING THE PROPERTY LINE TEXT

The property line text gives the distance and direction of the property line. The text for each line is placed at the same angle as the property line to which it refers.

STEP 7 *Building the Text Style*

First let's build a style for the text.

Command: **style**
Text style name (or ?) <default>: **proptxt**
Font file <default>: **simplex**

YOUR NOTES

Height <default>: **1.5**
Width factor <1.00>: ↵

Obliquing angle <0d0'>: ↵
Backwards? <N>: ↵
Upside-down? <N>: ↵
Vertical? <N>: ↵
NOTE is now the current text style.

STEP 8 *Placing the Text*

Now let's place the property line text for the south property line. Refer to Figure 10–7.

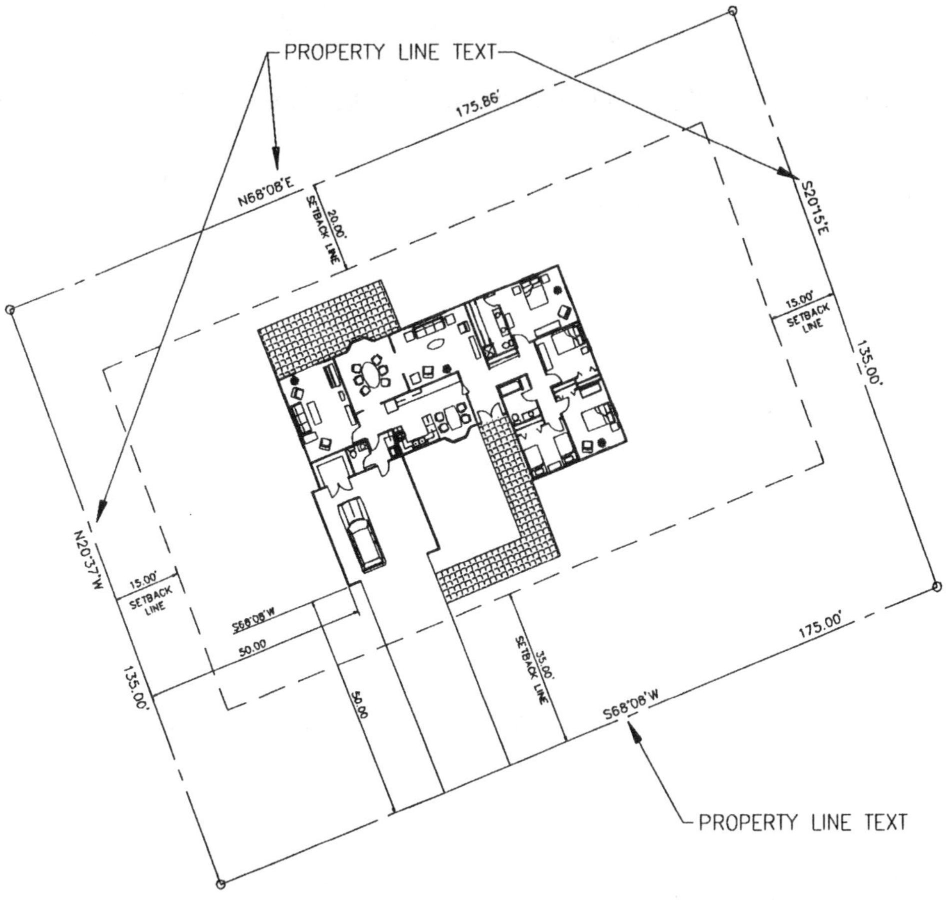

Figure 10-7

YOUR NOTES

Command: **text**
Start point or Align/Center/Fit/Middle/Right/Style: *Place a point above the south dimension line.*
Rotation angle <E>: **S68d08'W**

Text: **S68%%d08'W 175.00'**

Continue to place each of the property line text descriptions. Use the actual property line headings for the text angles, and refer to Figure 10–7.

PLACING THE DIMENSION LINES

Now let's place the dimension lines.

STEP 9 *Setting the Dimension Variables*

Use the Dim/Dimvars command to verify and, if necessary, set the following dimensioning variables.

Dimscale:	6
Dimtxt:	0.12
Dimsoxd:	ON
Dimtad:	ON
Dimtih:	OFF
Dimtix:	OFF
Dimtoh:	OFF

Refer to Figure 10–8 to place the site dimensions.

SPECIFYING THE REFERENCE POINT

Now let's place the reference point specification. This is the point you used to place the floor plan onto the site. The builder will use the same point to place the structure onto the actual building site.

YOUR NOTES

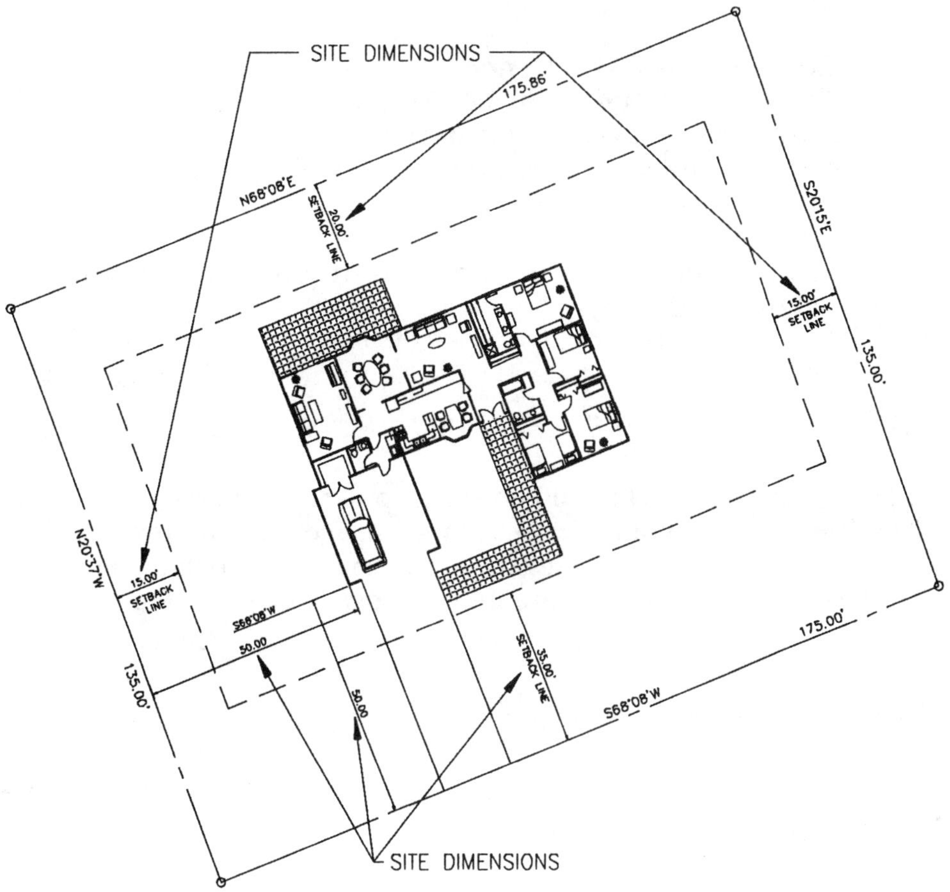

Figure 10-8

STEP 10 *Setting the Crosshairs Angle*

Zoom into the area of the reference point. Use the Circle command and object snap intersection to place a circle with a radius of 1.25 around the reference point.

Now use the Snap command to set the crosshairs at the same angle as the front property line. Remember that we placed the house at the same angle as the front (south) property line. This time, let's use a different method to readjust the crosshairs.

First, zoom to a magnification that displays both the reference point and a part of the front property line. Then use the following command sequence to set the angle of the crosshairs.

Command: **snap**
Snap spacing or ON/OFF/Aspect/Rotate/Style <default>: **r**

YOUR NOTES

Base point <0.00,0.00>: **nea**
to *Select a point on the front property line.*
Rotation angle <default>: **nea**
to *Select a point on the front property line to the right of the previously selected point.*

Your crosshairs should now be rotated to the same angle as the front property line and the floor plan.

STEP 11 *Labeling the Reference Point*

Select the Line command and object snap near. Capture a point on the circle for the From point prompt of the Line command. If you need to, turn off the snap mode by pressing F9. Press the F8 function key to turn on the ortho mode, and draw a line as shown in Figure 10–9.

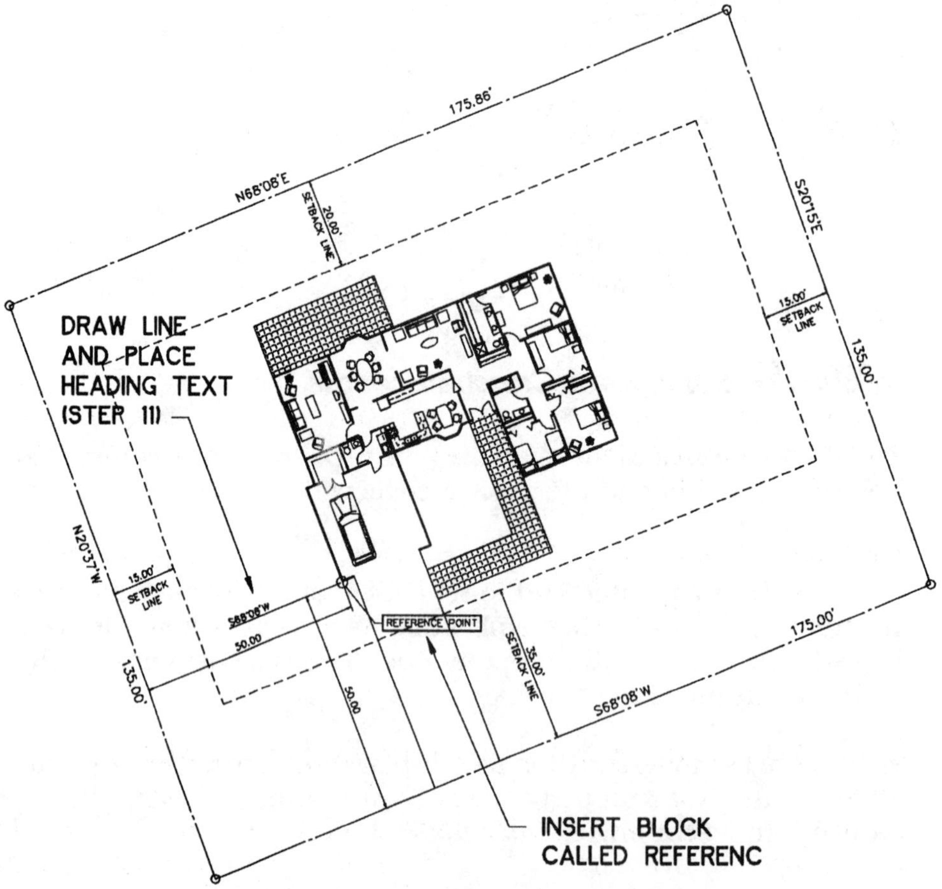

Figure 10-9

YOUR NOTES

Next, use the Text command to place the heading above the line. Insert the block named REFERENC, as shown in Figure 10–9.

STEP 12 *Placing the Street Names Text*

Now build a text style named STREETS. The text font is Simplex and the text height is 3.00. Label the streets as shown in Figure 10–1.

PLACING THE LANDSCAPING

It is time to place the landscaping into your site plan. Create a layer called LANDSCAP. This will allow you to freeze the landscaping later if you want to use the site plan strictly for construction purposes. Make LANSCAP the current layer.

STEP 13 *Inserting Trees and Bushes*

Use the trees and bushes included on the work disk to insert the landscaping. You are the designer here, so please yourself. If you prefer, you may follow the sample landscape design that is shown in Figure 10–1.

You may want to block portions of your landscaping and use the block in several places. Appendix L shows the landscape drawing items along with their insertion points. These items are resident blocks on the prototype drawing.

The trees and bushes are 1′–0" in diameter. You may set the diameter of each tree or bush by using the scale factor. For example, if you want a 20′ diameter tree, use 20 as the scale factor when you insert the tree symbol.

STEP 14 *Inserting the Scale and the North Arrow*

Finally, insert the drawing scale symbol and the north arrow into the site plan, as shown in Figure 10–1. These symbols are named SCALE and NA1, respectively. They resident blocks in the prototype drawing.

YOUR NOTES

PLOTTING INSTRUCTIONS

Now that you have finished, you may want to plot your work. If you have a pen plotter capable of plotting a C-size (24"x18") drawing, you can plot the drawing at a scale of 1"=20'. If you have a dot matrix printer configured to AutoCAD, you can printer plot the drawing. The following is an explanation for each type of plotting.

Pen Plot

From the AutoCAD Main menu, select option 3 (Plot a drawing). Respond to Enter NAME of drawing: with \ACADARCH\SITE and ↵. Next, you are prompted for the part of the drawing to be plotted. Enter L for limits.

AutoCAD will now display the plot parameters. The last line on the screen asks if you want to change anything. Enter Y for yes. Then use the following settings.

Plot NOT written to a file
All entity colors plotted with pen 1
Size in inches
Plot origin at 0.00,0.00
Plotting size: C
Plot NOT rotated
Pen width 0.010
Area fill boundaries NOT adjusted for pen width
Hidden lines NOT removed
Scale: 1=20

Before you proceed, make sure the plotter is ready to plot. A pen of 0.25mm will yield acceptable results. When you are ready, press ↵ and watch your drawing being plotted!

Printer Plot

YOUR NOTES

To printer plot, select option 4 (Printer Plot a drawing) from the AutoCAD Main menu. When asked for the drawing name, enter \ACADARCH\SITE and press ↵. You will be prompted for the part of the drawing to plot. Enter L for limits and ↵. A listing of the plot parameters will be displayed. The last line on the screen asks if you want to change anything. Respond with Y for yes and use the following settings.

Plot NOT written to a file
Size in inches
Plot origin at 0.00,0.00
Plotting size: A
Plot rotated: YES
Hidden lines NOT removed
Scale: F (for fit)

Now prepare the printer and press ↵ to printer plot your drawing. Note that the printer plot will not be plotted to a particular scale.

YOUR NOTES

SUMMARY

- Site plans can convey design information and lend character to the site.
- A construction drawing site plan yields information that cannot be found in other drawings.
- The site plan is usually found at the front of the plan set, because it contains information the builder needs to know before construction begins.
- Hatches can be used to show texture information in a site plan.
- The building should be located relative to a reference point. Don't forget to place a heading to describe the rotation of the building on the site.
- You can use AutoCAD's Snap command to rotate the crosshairs. This is convenient when you are working on site plans that are not oriented along true horizontal and vertical axes.
- Tree symbols can be drawn with a diameter of 1′. When you insert the tree, the insertion scale will describe the diameter of the final tree.

QUESTIONS

YOUR NOTES

1. What are some things you should consider when you are designing the site layout for a building?

___

___

___

2. What are some of the elements shown in a site plan drawing?

___

___

___

3. What command is used in AutoCAD to rotate the crosshair to a specific angle?

___

___

___

4. What is the reference point in a site plan? Why is it important to show a reference point?

___

___

___

YOUR NOTES

PROBLEMS

1. Start a new drawing, using the PSITE prototype drawing. Create a site plan and place a "boxed" building on the site. Use the site items provided as resident blocks in the prototype drawing to create your own site plan.

2. Use AutoCAD's edit commands to create alternate site layouts of your design. Plot each drawing and/or use the Save command to write each layout to disk under a different name.

YOUR NOTES

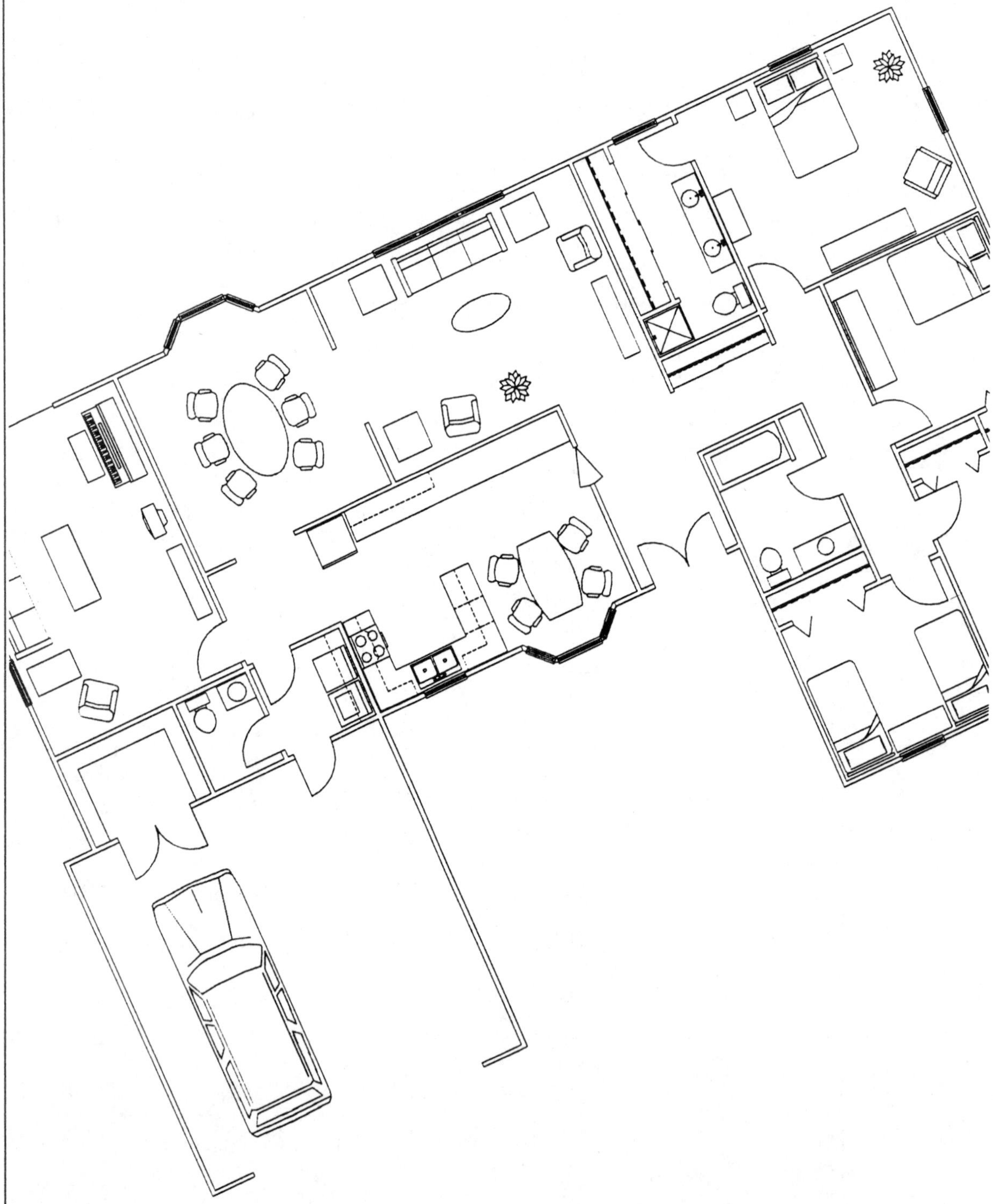

ARCHITECTURAL – FINAL PLOT SCALE	SHEET SIZE A 11 X 8.5	B 17 X 11	C 24 X 18	D 36 X 24	E 48 X 36
1/16	176',136'	272',176'	384',288'	576',384'	768',576'
3/32	132',102'	204',132'	288',216'	432',288'	576',432'
1/8	88',68'	136',88'	192',144'	288',192'	384',288'
3/16	58'–8",45'–4"	90'–8",58'–8"	128',96'	192',128'	256',192'
1/4	44',34'	68',44'	96',72'	144',96'	192',144'
3/8	29'–4",22'–8"	45'–4",29'–4"	64',48'	96',64'	128',96'
1/2	22',17'	34',22'	48',36'	72',48'	96',72'
3/4	14'–8",11'–4"	22'–8",14'–8"	32',24'	48',32'	64',48'
1	11',8'–6"	17',11'	24',18'	36',24'	48',36'
1–1/2	7'–4",5'–8"	11'–4",7'–4"	16',12'	24',16'	32',24'
3	3'–8",2'–10"	5'–8",3'–8"	8',6'	12',8'	16',12'

ENGINEERING – FINAL PLOT SCALE	SHEET SIZE A 11 X 8.5	B 17 X 11	C 24 X 18	D 36 X 24	E 48 X 36
10	110,85	170,110	240,180	360,240	480,360
20	220,170	340,220	480,360	720,480	960,720
30	330,255	510,330	720,540	1080,720	1440,1080
40	440,340	680,440	960,720	1440,960	1920,1440
50	550,425	850,550	1200,900	1800,1200	2400,1800
60	660,510	1020,660	1440,1080	2160,1440	2880,2160
100	1100,850	1700,1100	2400,1800	3600,2400	4800,3600
FULL SIZE	11,8.5	17,11	24,18	36,24	48,36

SCALE CONVERSION CHART

Rows: PLOT SCALE. Columns: FINAL PLOTTED SCALE OF DETAIL. Values: FACTOR TO INSERT OR SCALE.

PLOT SCALE	1/16	1/8	1/4	3/8	1/2	3/4	1	1–1/2	3
1/16	1.00	2.00	4.00	6.00	8.00	12.00	16.00	24.00	48.00
1/8	0.50	1.00	2.00	3.00	4.00	6.00	8.00	12.00	24.00
1/4	0.25	0.50	1.00	1.50	2.00	3.00	4.00	6.00	12.00
3/8	$0.1\overline{66}$	$0.\overline{33}$	$0.\overline{66}$	1.00	$1.\overline{33}$	2.00	$2.\overline{66}$	4.00	8.00
1/2	0.125	0.25	0.50	0.75	1.00	1.50	2.00	3.00	6.00
3/4	0.083	$0.1\overline{66}$	$0.\overline{33}$	0.50	$0.\overline{66}$	1.00	$1.\overline{33}$	2.00	4.00
1	0.0625	0.125	0.25	0.375	0.50	0.75	1.00	1.50	3.00
1–1/2	$0.041\overline{6}$	$0.08\overline{33}$	$0.1\overline{66}$	0.25	$0.\overline{33}$	0.50	$0.\overline{66}$	1.00	2.00
3	$0.0208\overline{3}$	$0.041\overline{6}$	$0.08\overline{33}$	0.125	$0.1\overline{66}$	0.25	$0.\overline{33}$	0.50	1.00

FACTOR TO INSERT OR SCALE

TEXT HEIGHT CHART

PLOTTED DRAWING SCALE		ACTUAL PLOTTED TEXT HEIGHT						
		3/32	1/8	3/16	1/4	3/8	1/2	1
ARCHITECTURAL SCALES	1/16	1'-6"	2'-0"	3'-0"	4'-0"	6'-0"	8'-0"	16'-0"
	3/32	1'-0"	1'-4"	2'-0"	2'-8"	4'-0"	5'-4"	10'-8"
	1/8	9"	1'-0"	1'-6"	2'-0"	3'-0"	4'-0"	8'-0"
	3/16	6"	9"	1'-0"	1'-4"	2'-0"	2'-8"	5'-4"
	1/4	4-1/2"	6"	9"	1'-0"	1'-6"	2'-0"	4'-0"
	3/8	3"	4"	6"	8"	1'-0"	1'-4"	2'-8"
	1/2	2-14"	3"	4-1/2"	6"	9"	1'-0"	2'-0"
	3/4	1-1/2"	2"	3"	4"	6"	8"	1'-4"
	1	1-1/8"	1-1/2"	2-1/4"	3"	4-1/2"	6"	1'-0"
	1-1/2	3/4"	1"	1-1/2"	2"	3"	4"	8"
	3	3/8"	1/2"	3/4"	1"	1-1/2"	2"	4"
ENGINEERING SCALES	10	.9375	1.25	1.875	2.5	3.75	5.0	10.0
	20	1.875	2.5	3.75	5.0	7.5	10.0	20.0
	30	2.812	3.75	5.625	7.5	11.25	15.0	30.0
	40	3.75	5.0	7.5	10.0	15.0	20.0	40.0
	50	4.687	6.25	9.375	12.5	18.75	25.0	50.0
	60	5.625	7.5	11.25	15.0	22.5	30.0	60.0
	100	9.375	12.5	18.75	25.0	37.5	50.0	100.0
	1:1	.0937	.125	.1875	.25	.375	.50	1

DRAWING SHEET LAYERS CHART

DRAWING	SESSIONS	LAYER NAME	LAYER COLOR	ITEMS
Floor Plan	1/2/4	FLPLAN	Cyan	Walls
		DOORS	Blue	Doors
		WINDOWS	Yellow	Windows
		0	White	Dimensions
		ROOM_NAME	Red	Room Labels
Furniture Plan	3	0	White	Misc.
		FURNITURE	White	Furniture
		FURNDET	White	Furniture Details
		OUTLINE	White	Furniture Outlines
Section	5/6	0	White	Dimensions & Notes
		SECTIONS	Cyan	Section Structure
		HATCH	White	Hatching
		DOORS	White	Door Frames
		CABINETS	White	Millwork
Elevations	7/8	0	White	Misc.
		ELEV	White	Windows
		OUTLINE	White	Block Outlines
		DOORS	White	Doors
		DETAIL	White	Block Details
		SHRUBS	Green	Shrubbery Blocks
		TREES	Green	Tree Blocks
		HUMANS	Yellow	Human Blocks
		VEHICLES	Blue	Vehicle Blocks
		MISC_SYMB	White	Misc. Symbol Blocks
Site	9/10	0	White	Text/Misc.
		LINES	White	Property Lines
		LANDSC	Green	Landscaping Blocks

PROTOTYPE DRAWINGS SETTINGS CHART

PPLAN1.DWG *(Session One/Floor Plan)*

Units: Architectural (to 1/16")
Limits: 0,0 (lower left) and 96',72' (upper right)
Grid: 5'-0" and ON
Snap: 1/2" and ON
Current layer: FLPLAN (color: CYAN)
Ortho: ON
Zoom: ALL
Timer: ON

PSECTION.DWG *(Session Five/Building Section)*

Units: Architectural (to 1/16")
Limits: 0,0 (lower left) and 96',72' (upper right)
Snap: 1/2" and ON
Current layer: SECTIONS (color: CYAN)
Ltscale: 12
Timer: ON

PELEVS.DWG *(Session Seven/Exterior Elevations)*

Units: Architectural (to 1/16")
Limits: 0,0 (lower left) and 128',96' (upper right)
Snap: 1" and ON
Grid: 5'-0" and ON
Current layer: ELEV (color: WHITE)
Ortho: ON
Zoom: ALL
Timer: ON

PSITE.DWG *(Session Nine/Site Plan)*

Units: Decimal
- 2 digits to right of decimal
- Surveyor's units
- 2 fractional places for angle measurement
- Direction for angle E: E
- Angles *not* measured clockwise

Limits: 0,0 (lower left) and 480,360 (upper right)
Current layer: LINES (color: WHITE)
Ltscale: 10
Timer: ON

WORK DISK CONTENTS

PPLAN1.DWG: Prototype for Session One (Floor Plan).

ACAD.LSP: AutoCAD LISP auto-load file.

WDPLAN1.DWG: Session Two exercise drawing.

WDPLAN2.DWG: Session Two exercise drawing.

DOORS.TXT: Template file for Session Two.

PSECTION.DWG: Prototype drawing for Session Five (Building Section)

SCHED2: Door schedule file for Session Six.

PELEVS.DWG: Prototype drawing for Session Seven (exterior eleva tions).

PSITE.DWG: Prototype drawing for Session Nine (site plan).

REF.LSP: Reference LISP file.

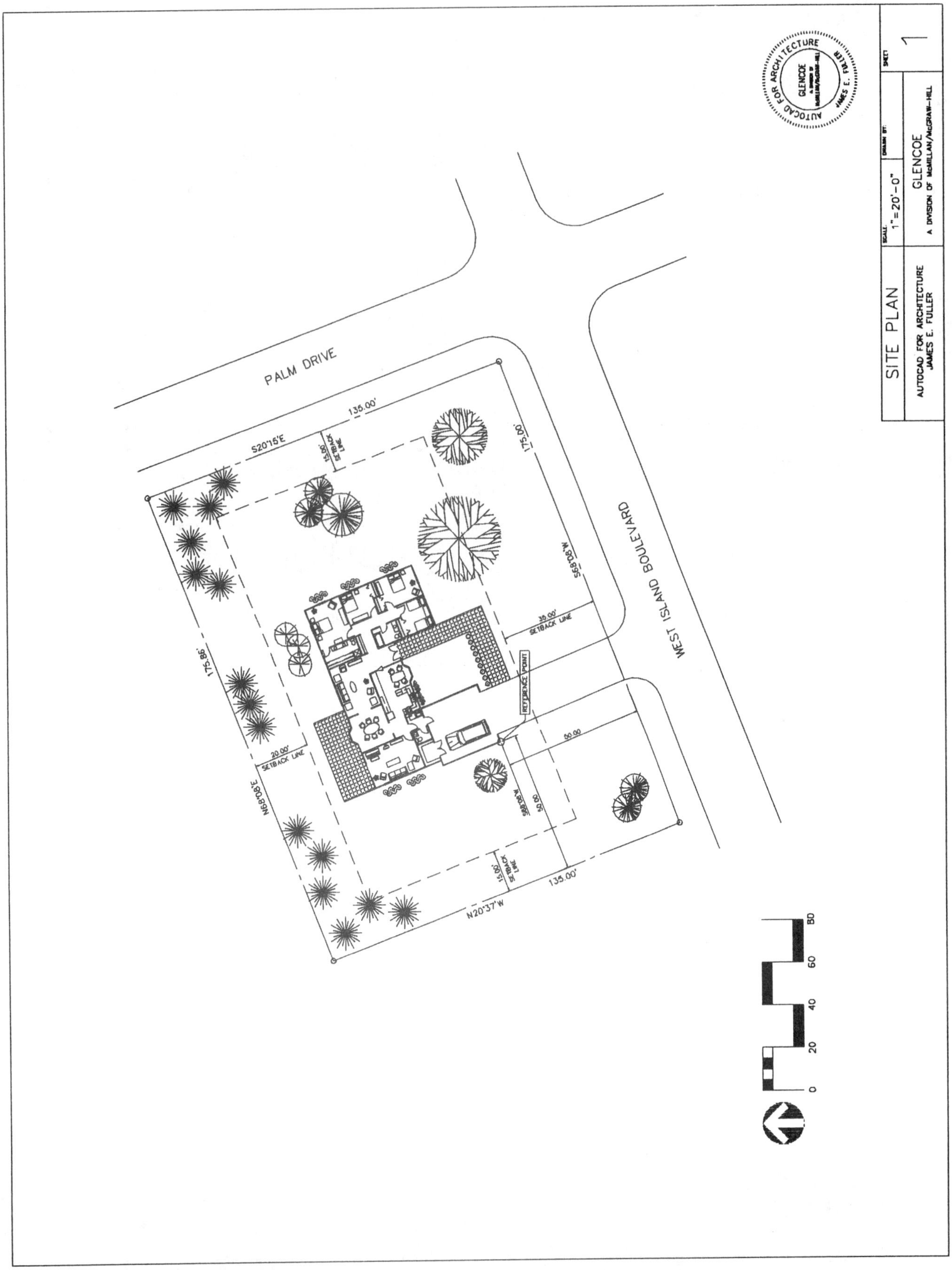
PALM DRIVE
WEST ISLAND BOULEVARD
135.00'
S20°15'E
15.00' SETBACK LINE
175.00'
S68°08'W
35.00' SETBACK LINE
REFERENCE POINT
50.00
175.86'
20.00' SETBACK LINE
N68°08'E
N20°37'W
135.00'
0
20
40
60
80
AUTOCAD FOR ARCHITECTURE
GLENCOE
JAMES E. FULLER
SITE PLAN
AUTOCAD FOR ARCHITECTURE
JAMES E. FULLER
SCALE:
1"=20'-0"
GLENCOE
A DIVISION OF McMILLAN/McGRAW-HILL
SHEET
1

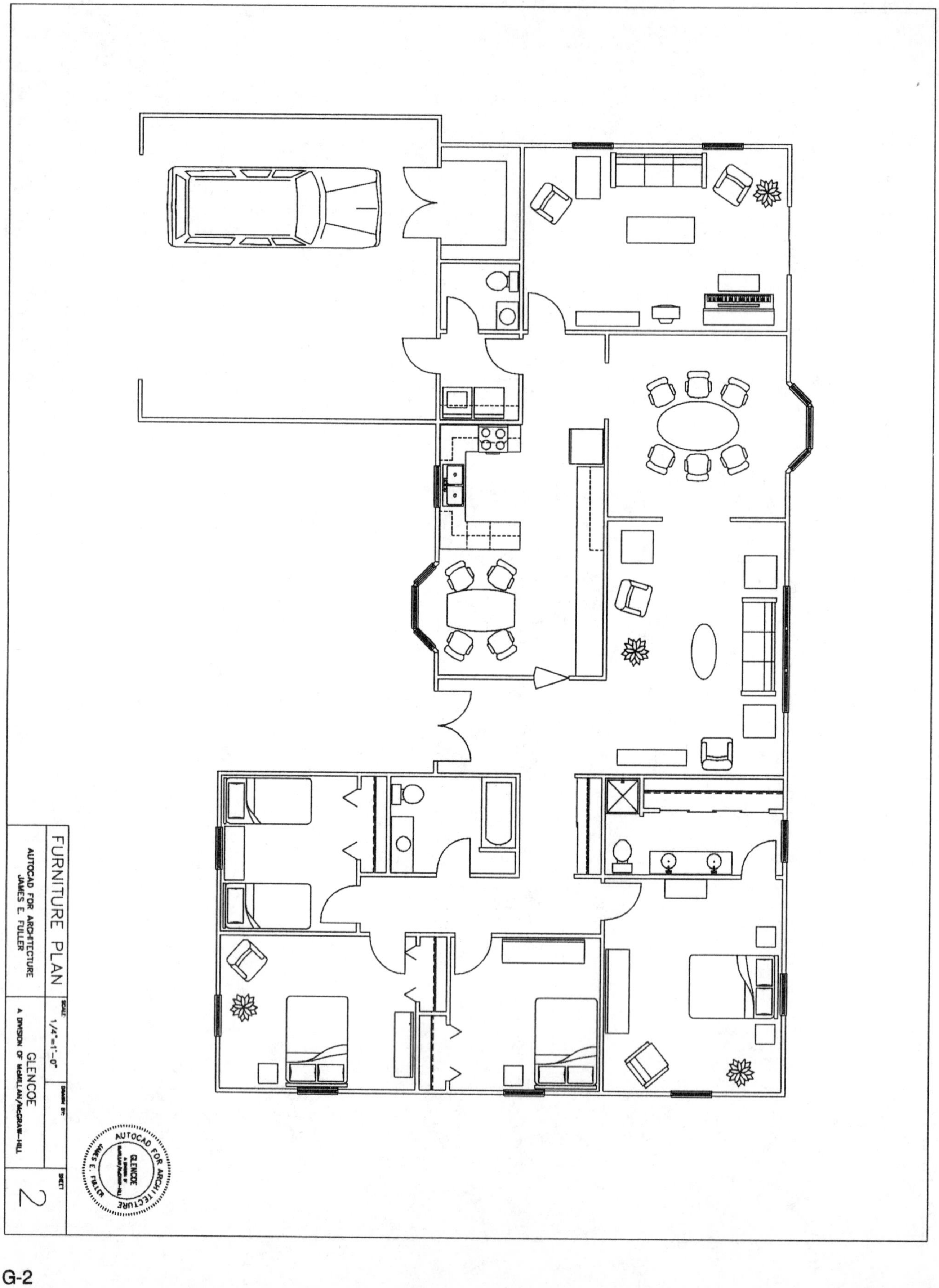
FURNITURE PLAN
AUTOCAD FOR ARCHITECTURE
JAMES E. FULLER
SCALE
1/4"=1'-0"
DRAWN BY:
GLENCOE
A DIVISION OF McMILLAN/McGRAW-HILL
SHEET
2
AUTOCAD FOR ARCHITECTURE
JAMES E. FULLER
GLENCOE

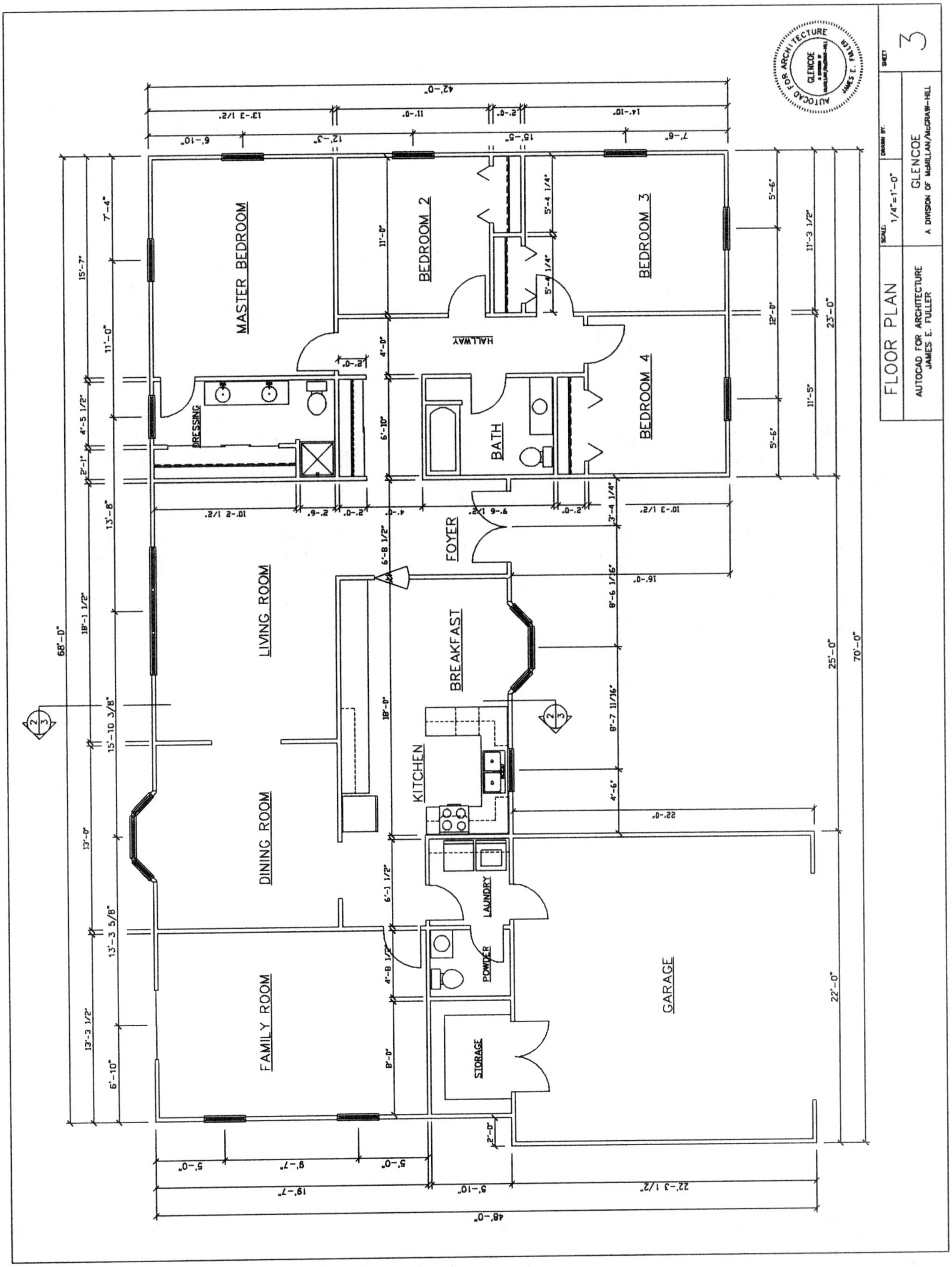
MASTER BEDROOM
BEDROOM 2
BEDROOM 3
BEDROOM 4
HALLWAY
BATH
DRESSING
LIVING ROOM
DINING ROOM
FAMILY ROOM
FOYER
BREAKFAST
KITCHEN
LAUNDRY
POWDER
STORAGE
GARAGE
FLOOR PLAN
AUTOCAD FOR ARCHITECTURE
JAMES E. FULLER
SCALE: 1/4"=1'-0"
GLENCOE
A DIVISION OF McMILLAN/McGRAW-HILL
SHEET 3

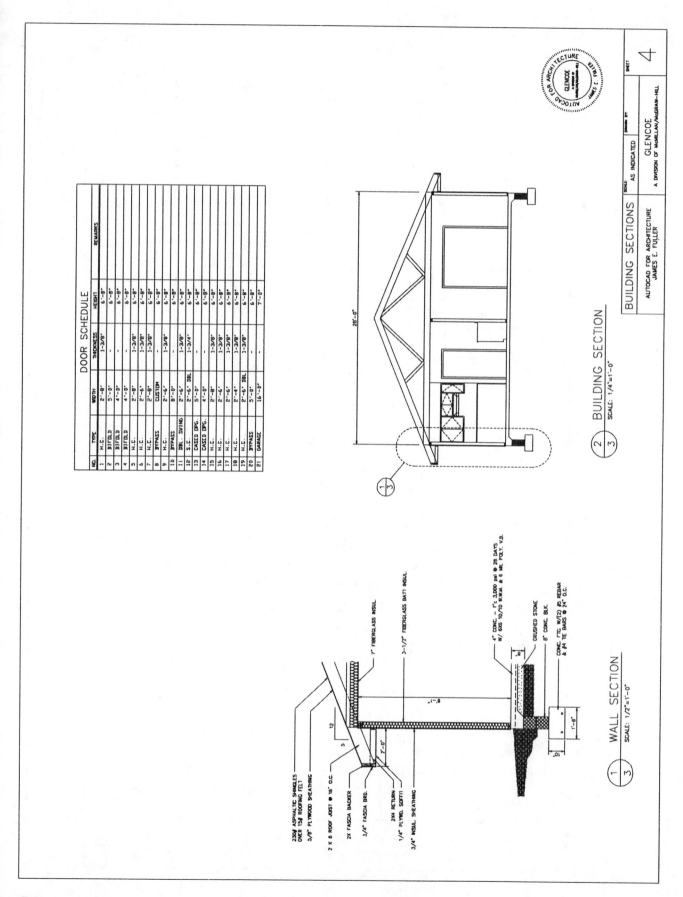

DOOR SCHEDULE					
NO.	TYPE	WIDTH	THICKNESS	HEIGHT	REMARKS
1	H.C.	2'-8"	1-3/8"	6'-8"	
2	BIFOLD	5'-0"	-	6'-8"	
3	BIFOLD	4'-0"	-	6'-8"	
4	BIFOLD	4'-0"	-	6'-8"	
5	H.C.	2'-8"	1-3/8"	6'-8"	
6	H.C.	2'-6"	1-3/8"	6'-8"	
7	H.C.	2'-8"	1-3/8"	6'-8"	
8	BYPASS	CUSTOM	-	6'-8"	
9	H.C.	2'-6"	1-3/8"	6'-8"	
10	BYPASS	8'-0"	-	6'-8"	
11	DBL. SWING	2'-6"	1-3/8"	6'-8"	
12	S.C.	2'-6" DBL	1-3/4"	6'-8"	
13	CASED OPG.	5'-0"	-	6'-8"	
14	CASED OPG.	4'-0"	-	6'-8"	
15	H.C.	2'-8"	1-3/8"	6'-8"	
16	H.C.	2'-6"	1-3/8"	6'-8"	
17	H.C.	2'-6"	1-3/8"	6'-8"	
18	H.C.	2'-4"	1-3/8"	6'-8"	
19	H.C.	2'-6" DBL	1-3/8"	6'-8"	
20	BYPASS	5'-0"	-	6'-8"	
21	GARAGE	16'-0"	-	7'-0"	

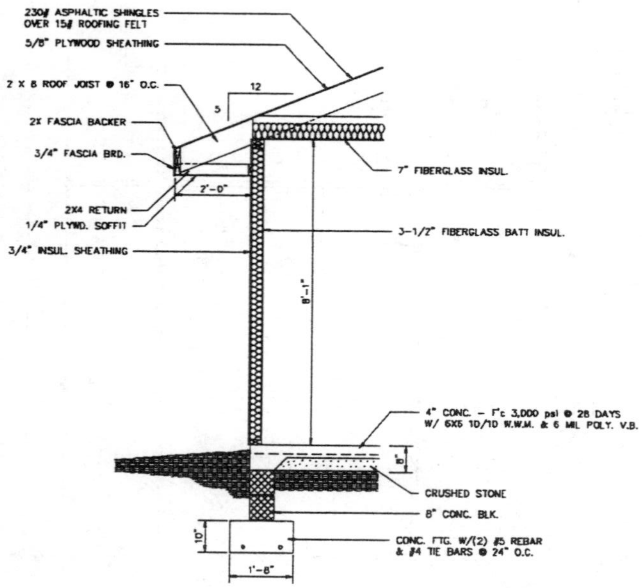

1/3 WALL SECTION
SCALE: 1/2"=1'-0"

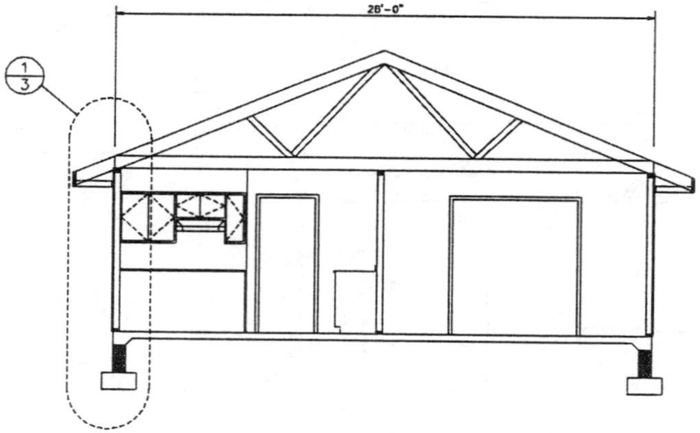

2/3 BUILDING SECTION
SCALE: 1/4"=1'-0"

AUTOCAD FOR ARCHITECTURE — GLENCOE — JAMES E. FULLER

BUILDING SECTIONS	SCALE: AS INDICATED	DRAWN BY:	SHEET
AUTOCAD FOR ARCHITECTURE JAMES E. FULLER	GLENCOE A DIVISION OF McMILLAN/McGRAW-HILL		4

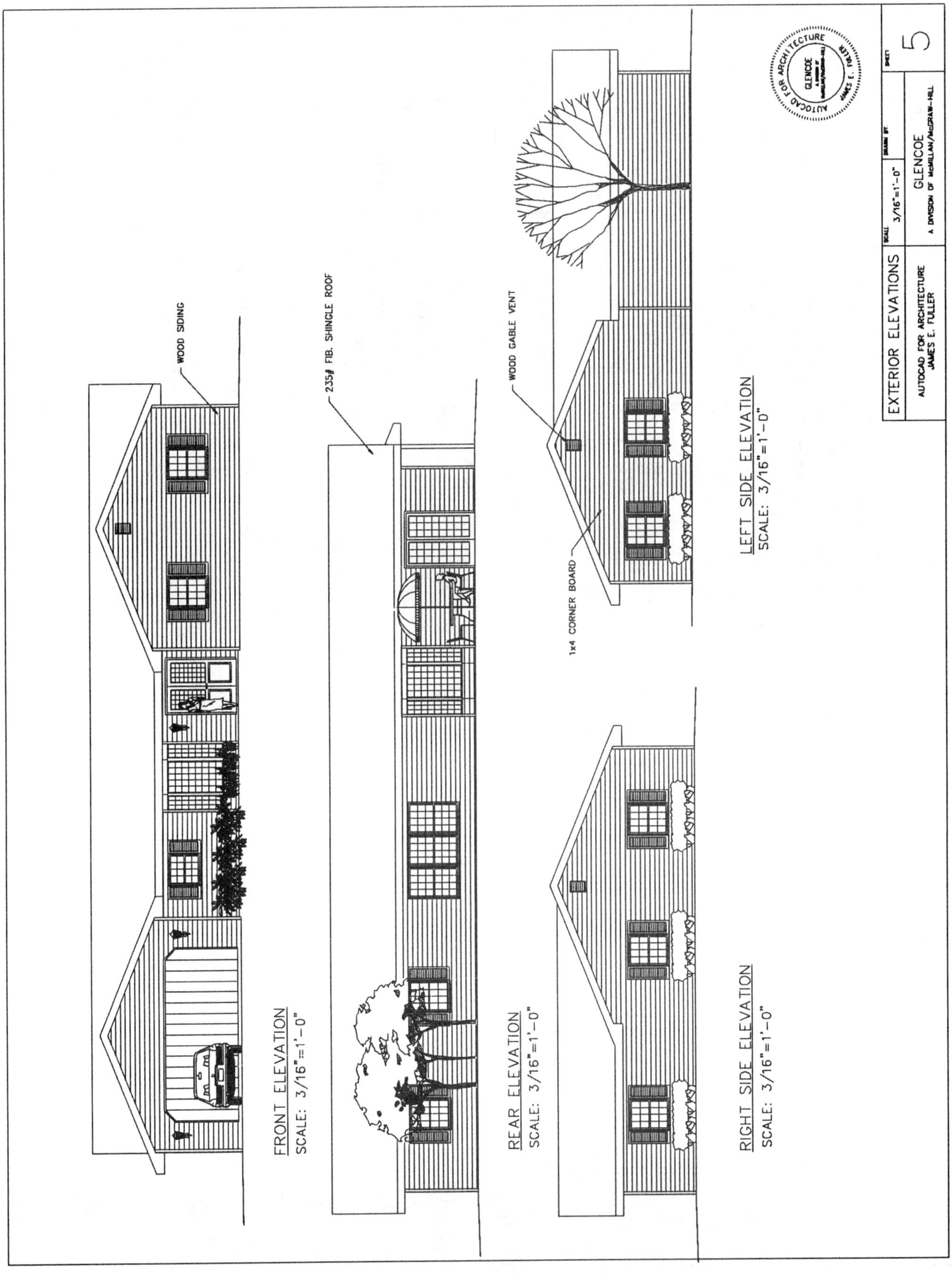
WOOD SIDING
235# FIB. SHINGLE ROOF
WOOD GABLE VENT
1x4 CORNER BOARD
FRONT ELEVATION
SCALE: 3/16"=1'-0"
REAR ELEVATION
SCALE: 3/16"=1'-0"
LEFT SIDE ELEVATION
SCALE: 3/16"=1'-0"
RIGHT SIDE ELEVATION
SCALE: 3/16"=1'-0"
AUTOCAD FOR ARCHITECTURE
GLENCOE
JAMES E. FULLER
EXTERIOR ELEVATIONS
SCALE
3/16"=1'-0"
DRAWN BY
SHEET
5
AUTOCAD FOR ARCHITECTURE
JAMES E. FULLER
GLENCOE
A DIVISION OF McMILLAN/McGRAW-HILL

Appendix H: *Wall Key Plan*

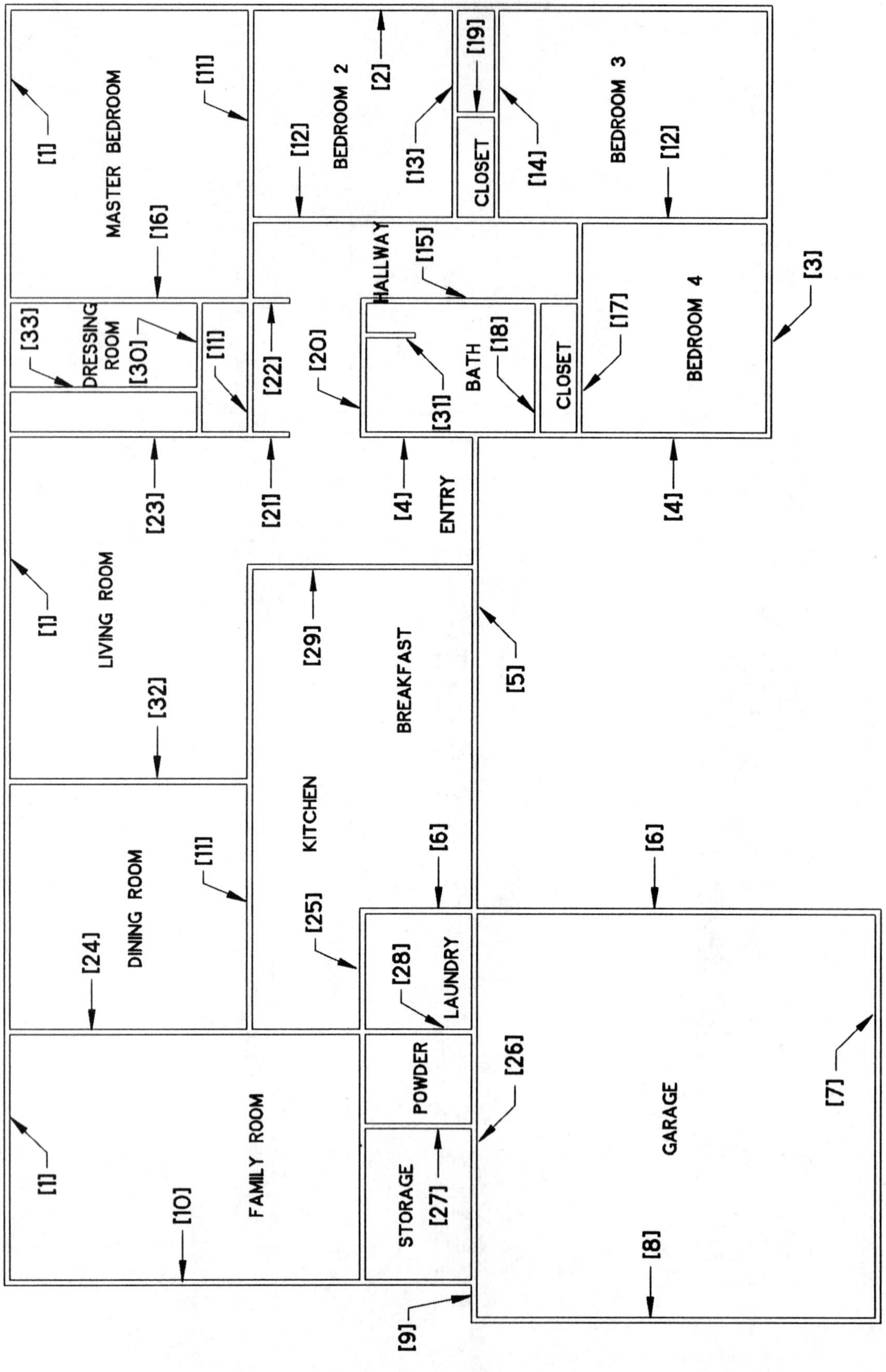

Appendix I: *Door and Window Key Plan*

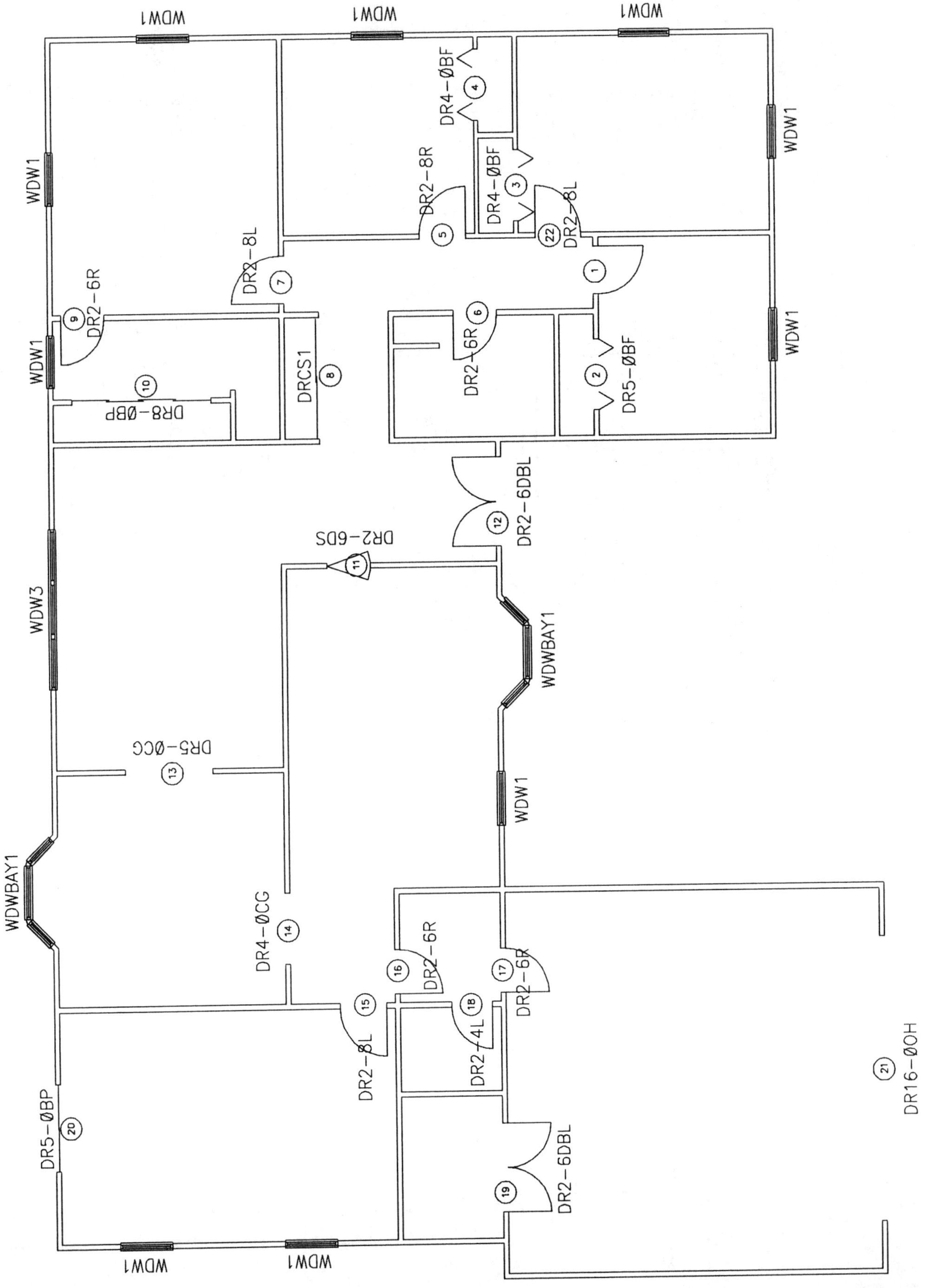

Appendix J: *Furniture Symbols and Layout*

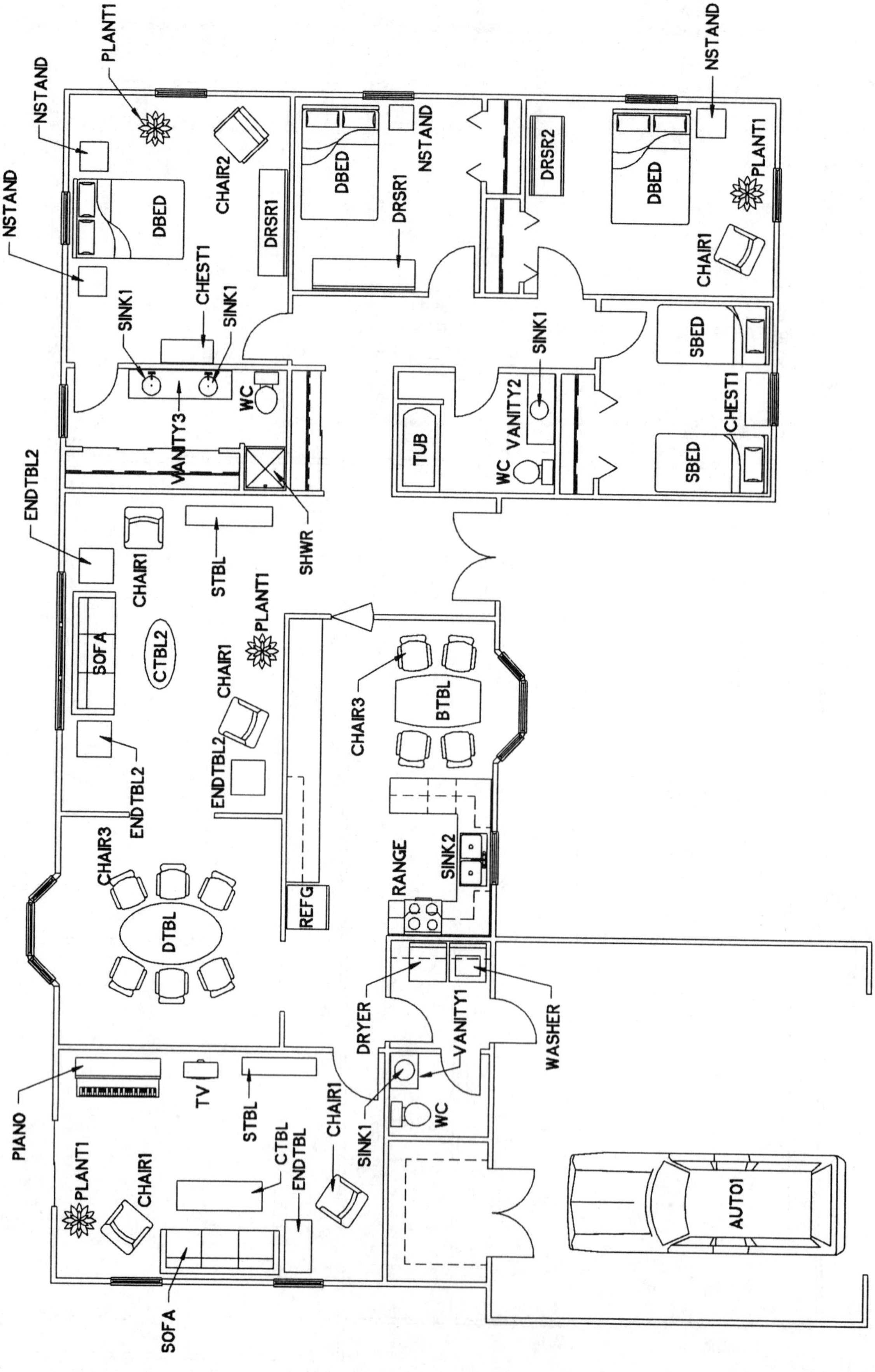

Appendix K: *Dimensioning Key Plan*

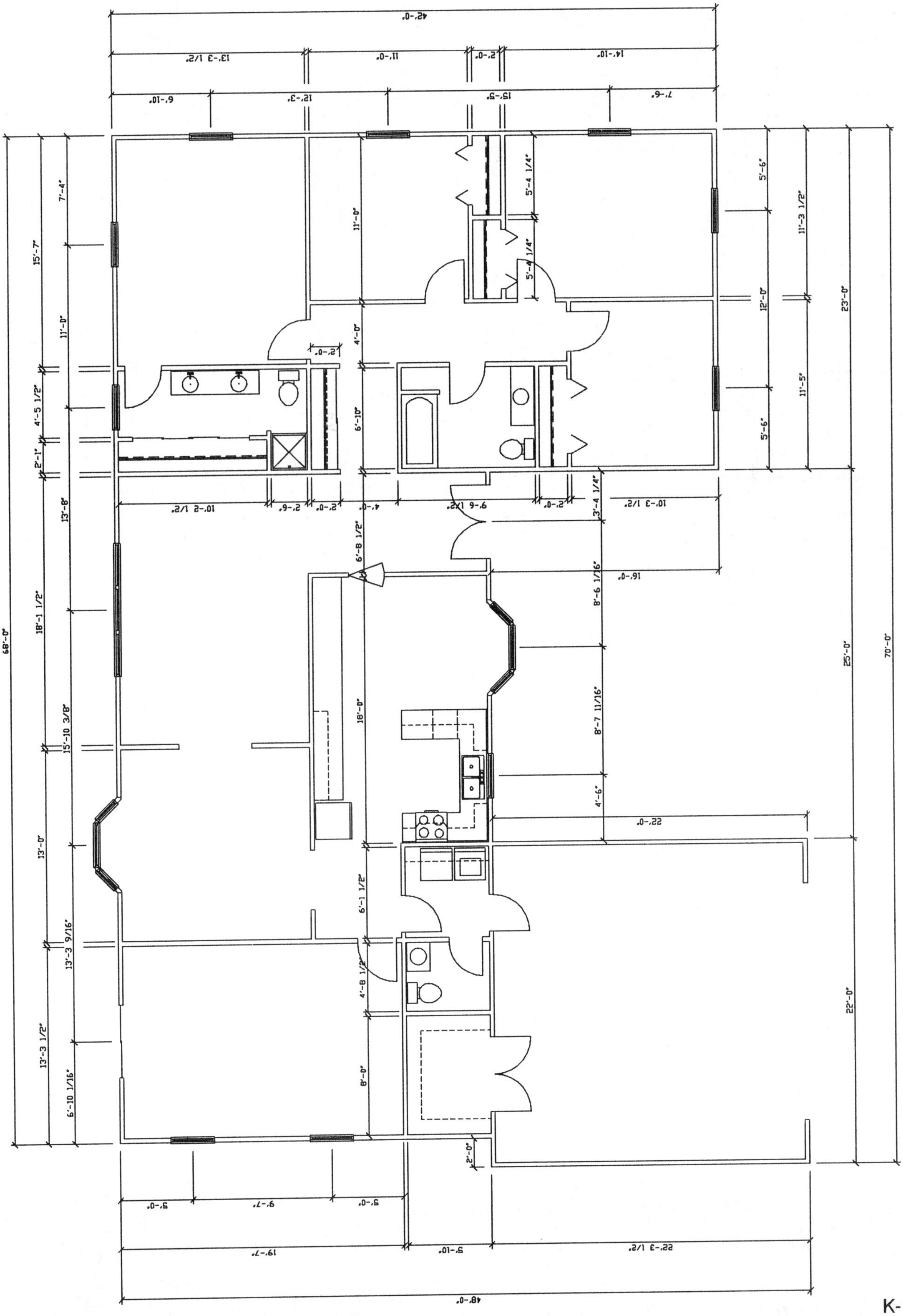

Appendix L: *Work Disk Symbols and Insertion Points*

SESSION TWO

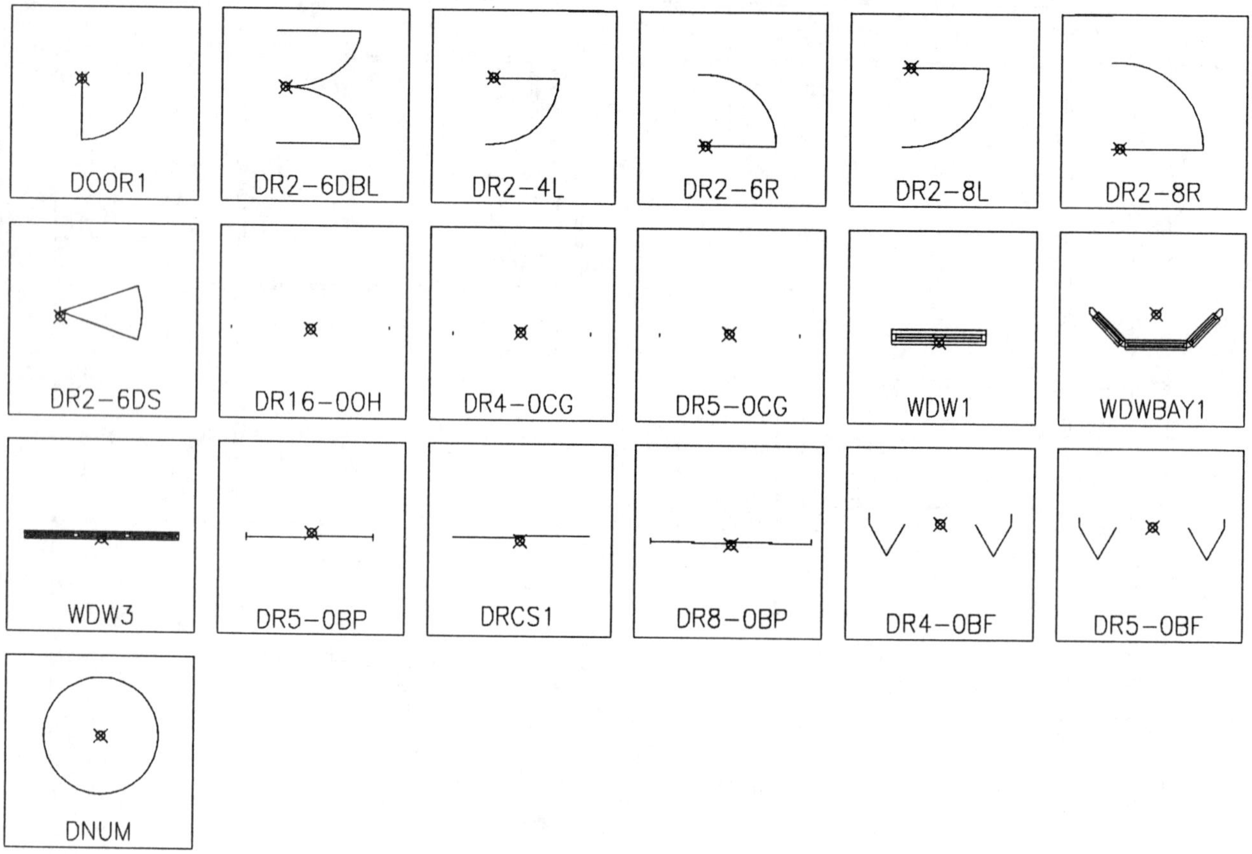

SESSION THREE

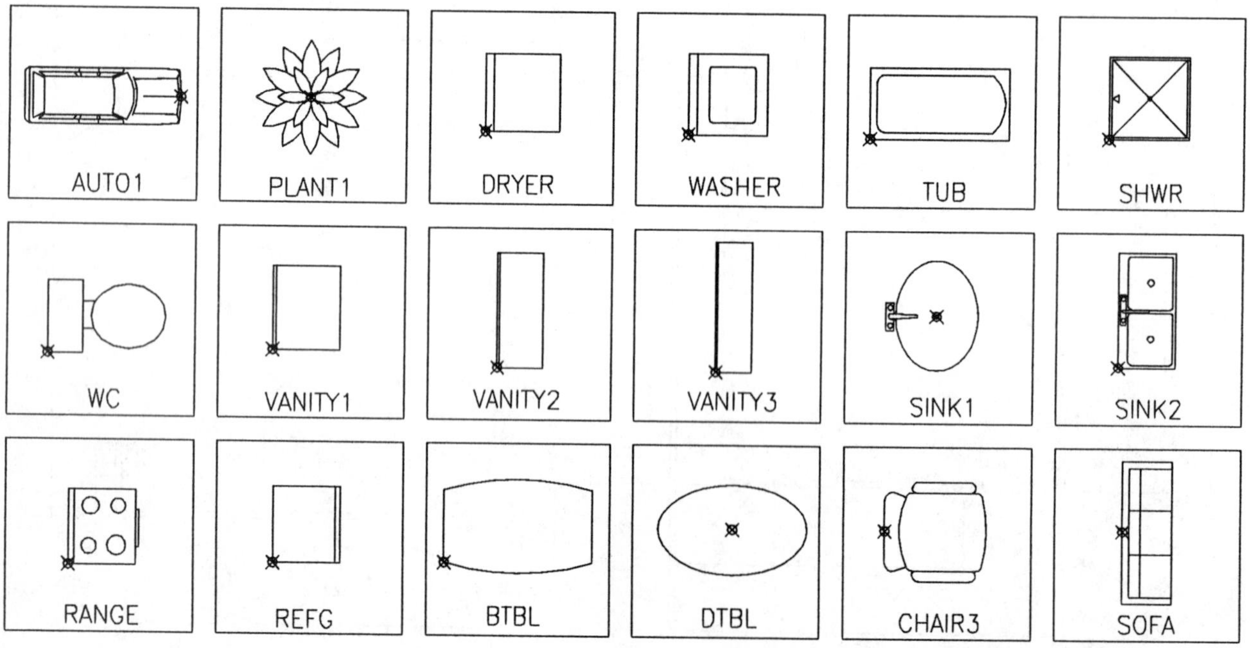

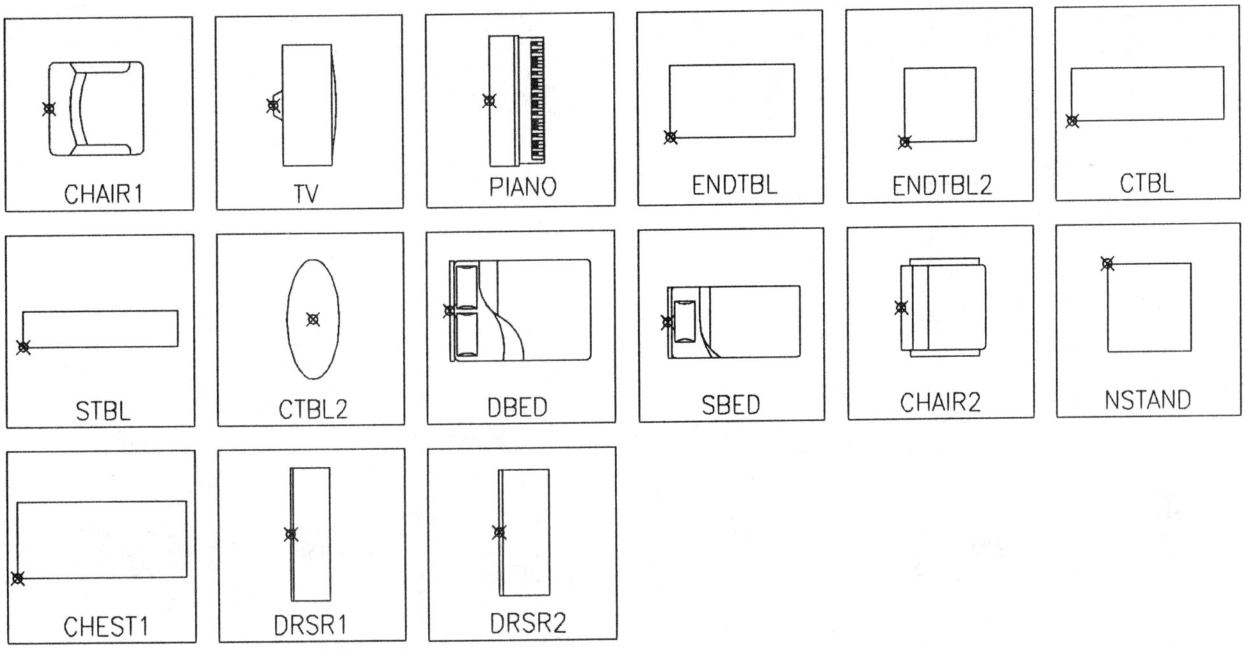

SESSION FIVE

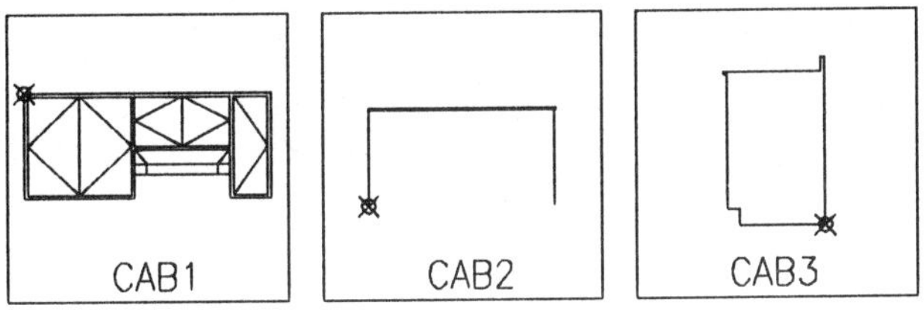

SESSION SIX

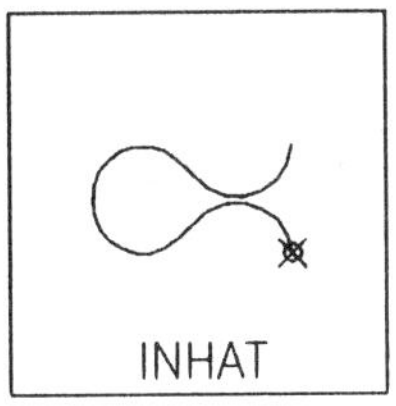

SESSION SEVEN

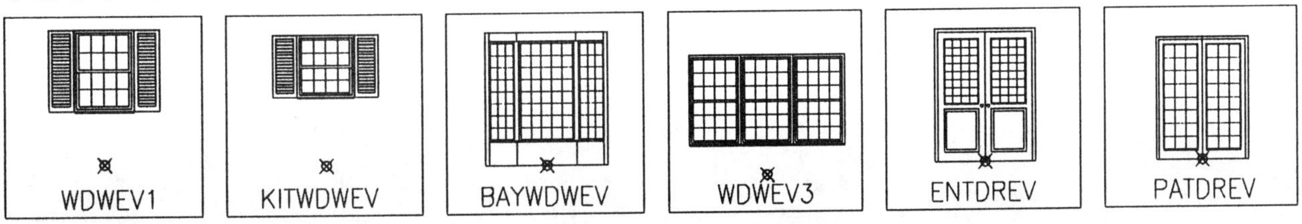

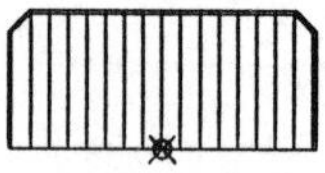
DR16EV

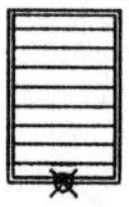
VENT

SESSION EIGHT

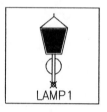

LAMP1

AUTOEV1

HUMAN1

UMBTBL

SHRUB1

SHRUB2

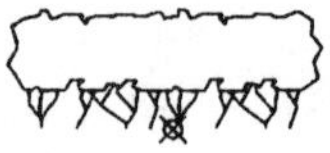
SHRUB3

TREE1

TREE2

TREE3

SESSION TEN

T1

T2

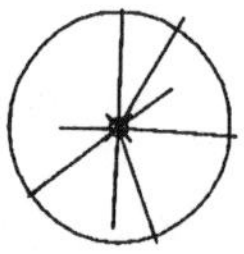
T3

T4

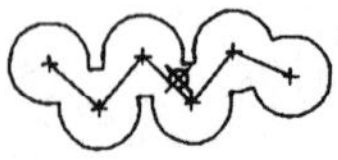
FOLIAGE1

FOLIAGE2

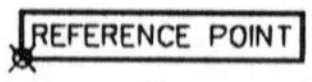

REFERENC

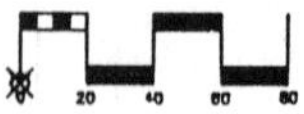
SCALE

NA1

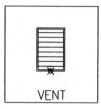

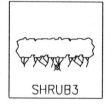

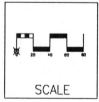

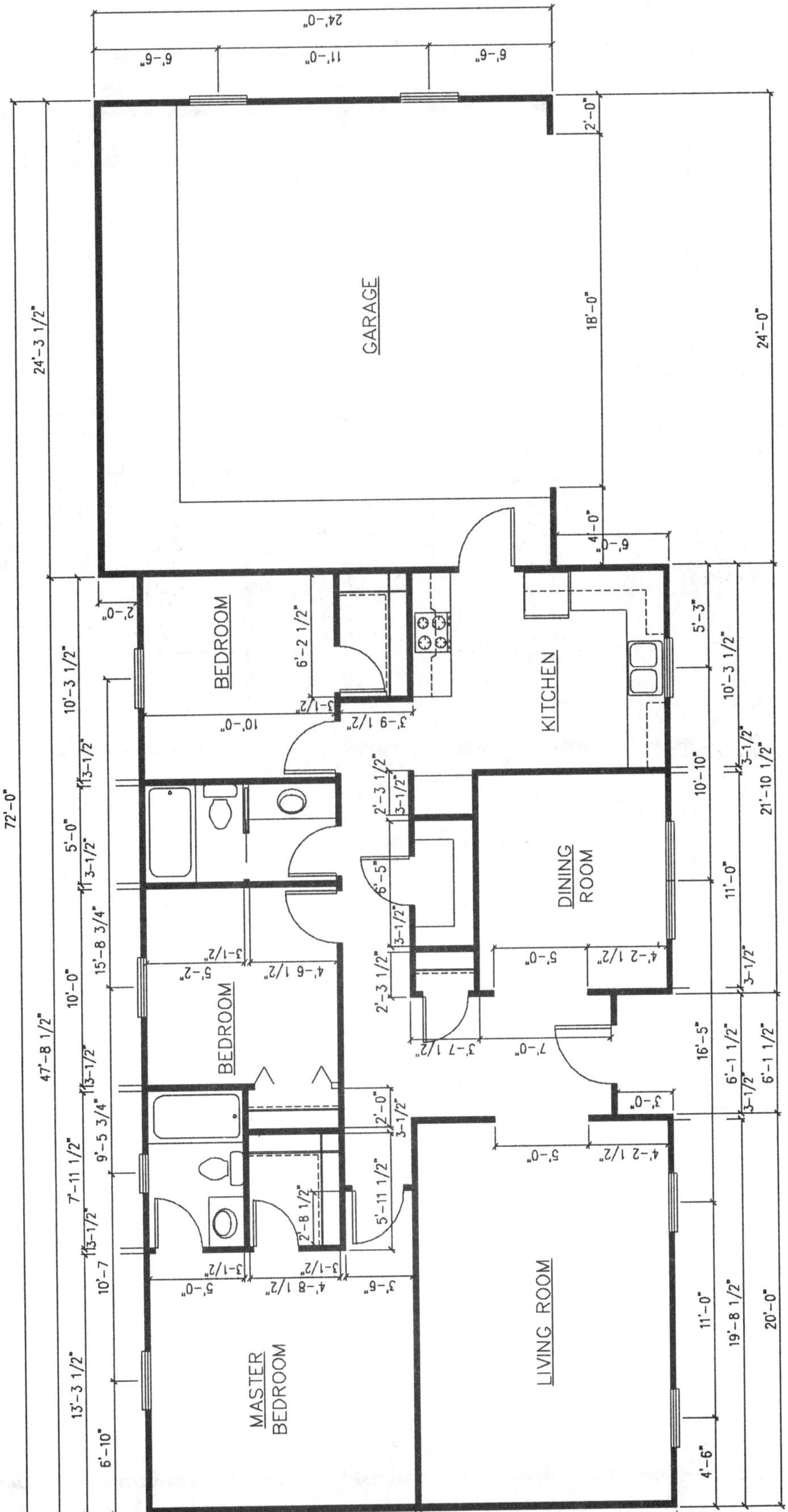
GARAGE
BEDROOM
KITCHEN
DINING ROOM
BEDROOM
MASTER BEDROOM
LIVING ROOM
24'-0"
72'-0"
28'-0"

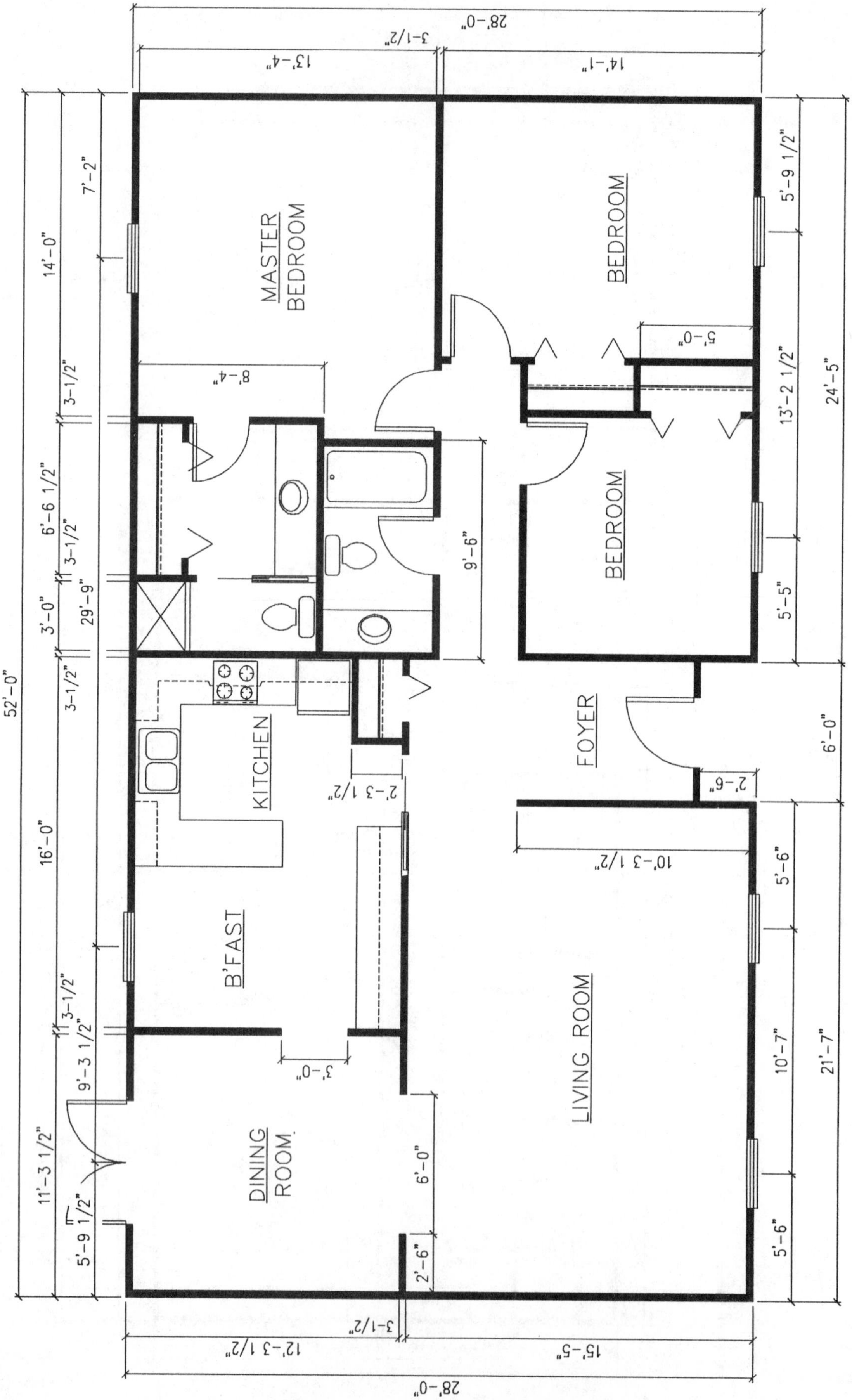
MASTER BEDROOM
BEDROOM
BEDROOM
KITCHEN
B'FAST
DINING ROOM
FOYER
LIVING ROOM
28'-0"
13'-4"
3-1/2"
14'-1"
52'-0"
14'-0"
7'-2"
8'-4"
5'-0"
5'-9 1/2"
13'-2 1/2"
24'-5"
3-1/2"
6'-6 1/2"
3'-0"
29'-9"
9'-6"
5'-5"
6'-0"
2'-6"
2'-3 1/2"
16'-0"
10'-3 1/2"
5'-6"
10'-7"
21'-7"
3'-0"
9'-3 1/2"
11'-3 1/2"
5'-9 1/2"
2'-6"
12'-3 1/2"
15'-5"

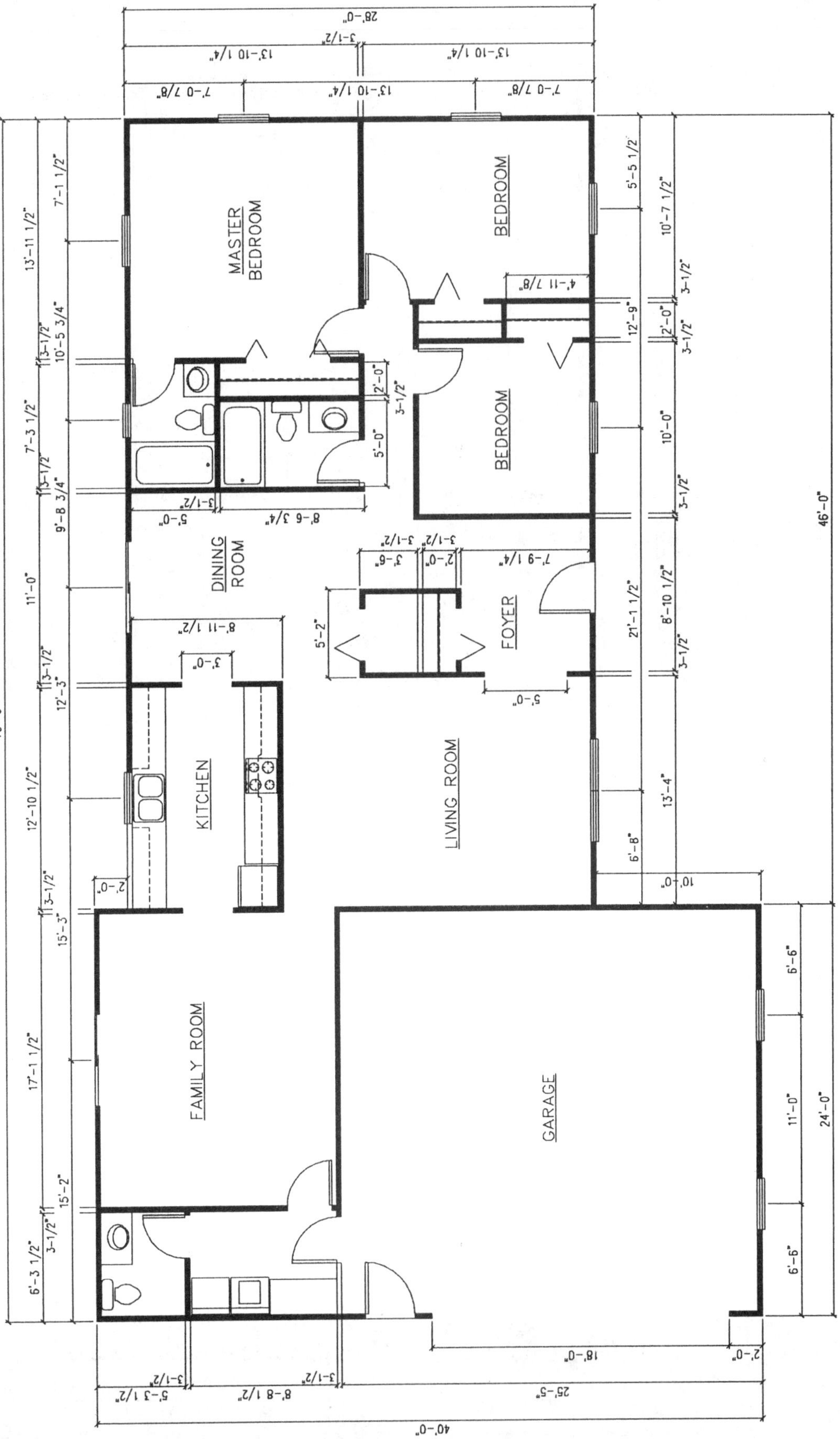
MASTER BEDROOM
BEDROOM
BEDROOM
DINING ROOM
FOYER
KITCHEN
LIVING ROOM
FAMILY ROOM
GARAGE
28'-0"
70'-0"
46'-0"
24'-0"
40'-0"

Appendix M: *Floor Plan Work Exercises*

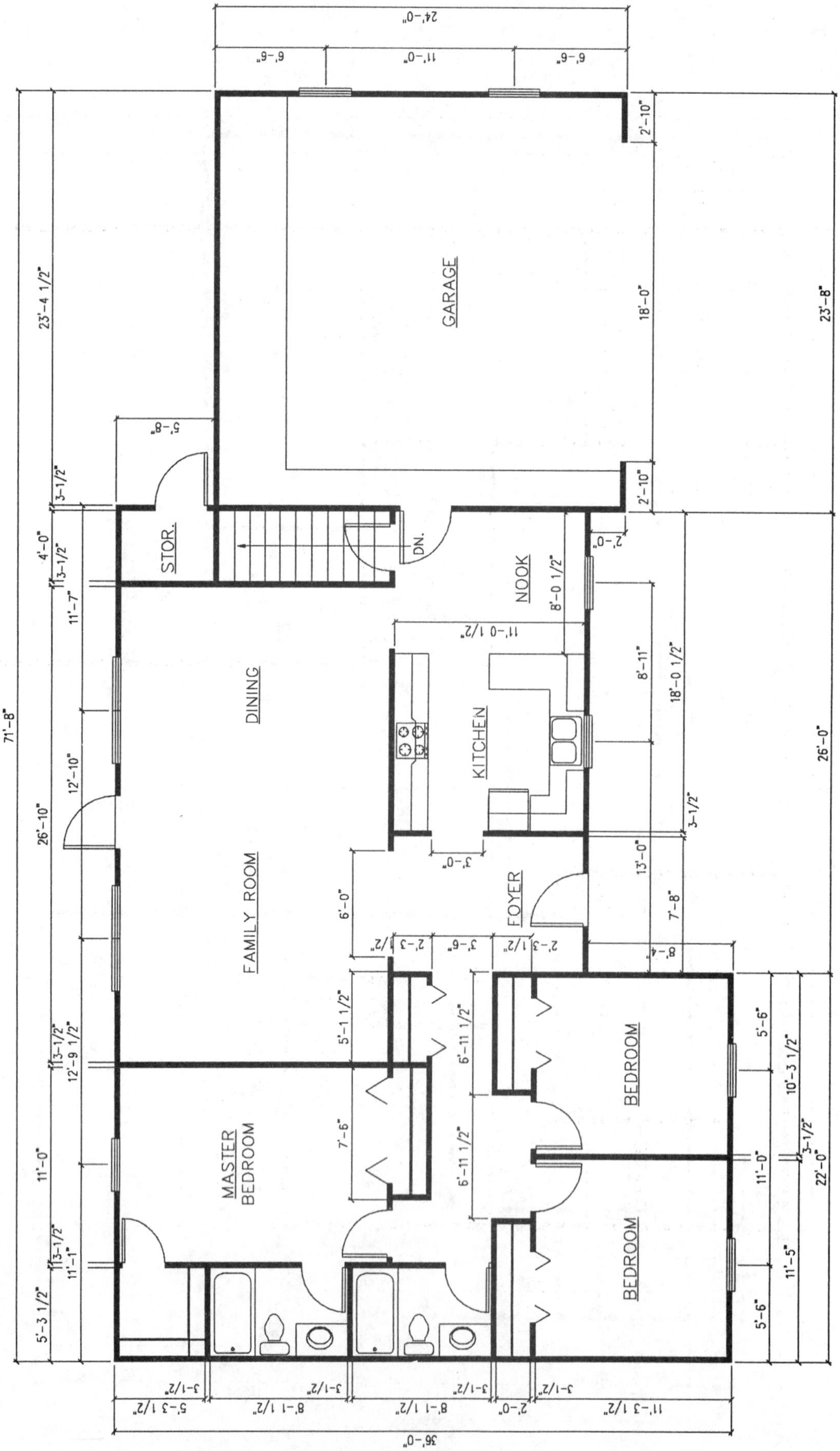

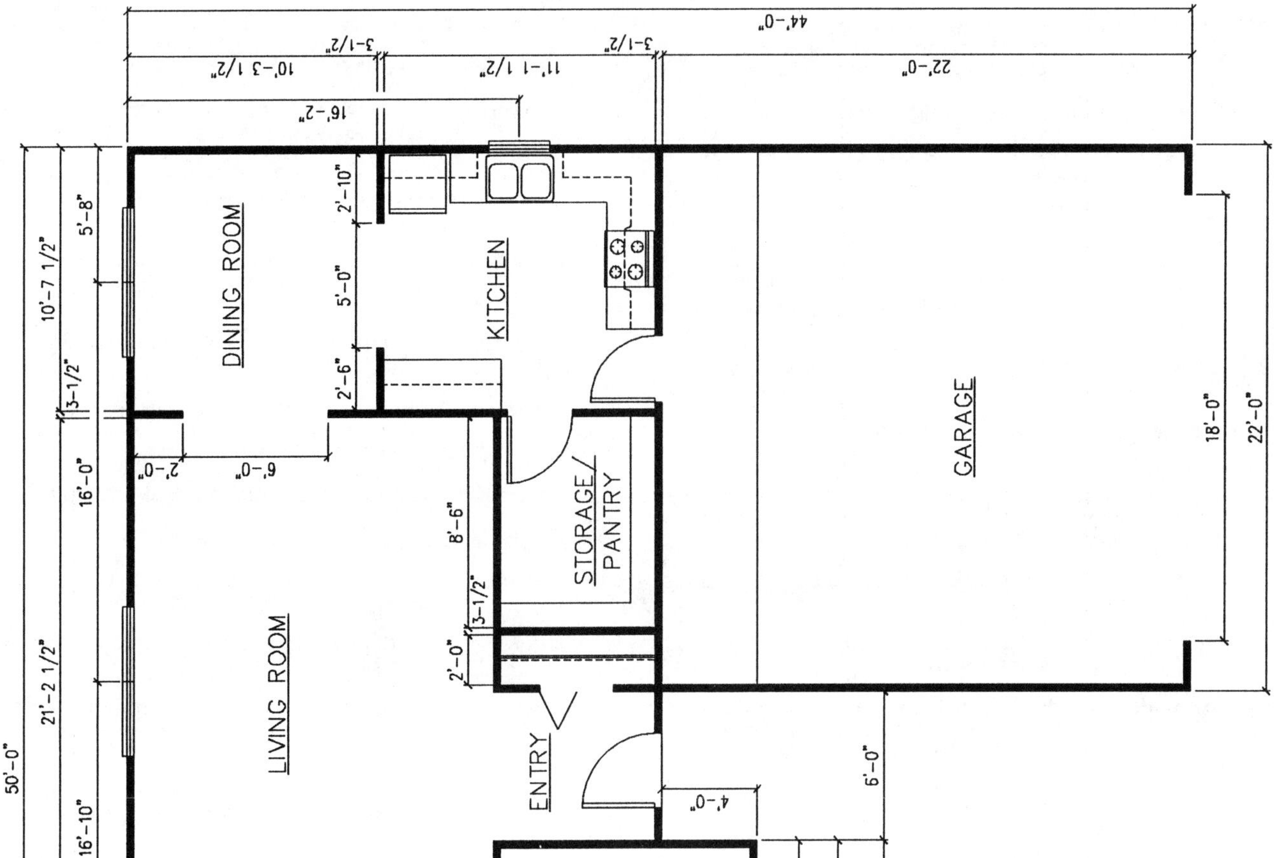
DINING ROOM
KITCHEN
GARAGE
STORAGE/ PANTRY
LIVING ROOM
ENTRY
MASTER BEDROOM
BEDROOM
BEDROOM
44'-0"
22'-0"
50'-0"
26'-0"
18'-0"

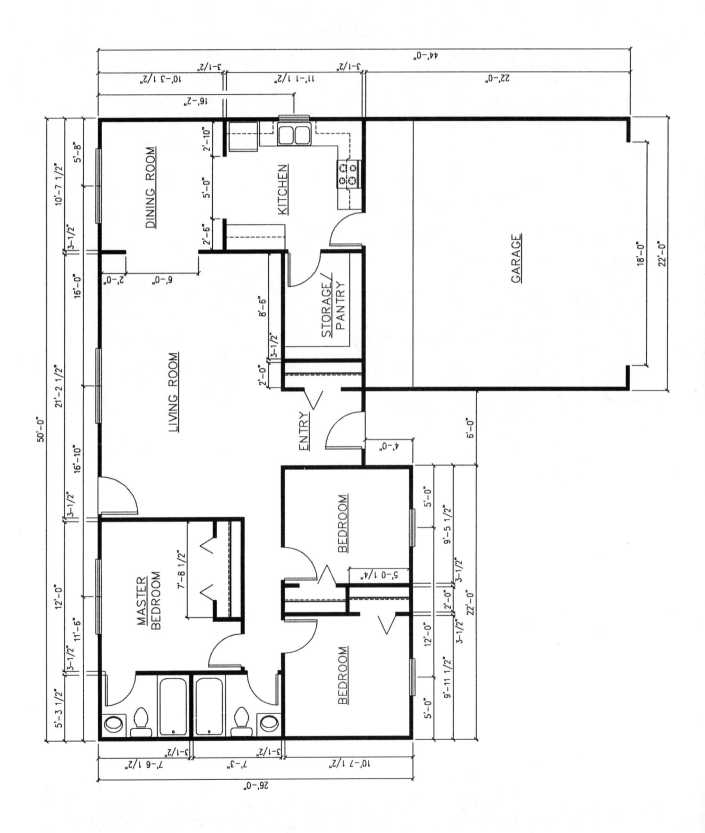

GLOSSARY

Anchor bolt. A bolt or threaded rod anchored into the foundation or basement wall that is used to attach the sill plate to the foundation.

Architect. A professional who designs structures.

Attic. The area enclosed by the ceiling joists and the roof rafters.

Backfill. Earth or stone used to fill the void outside the foundation or basement wall.

Base. The finish trim at the intersection of the wall and floor, sometimes referred to as the base board.

Baseboard. The trim at the intersection of the wall and floor.

Base course. The first course of masonry.

Base line. A reference line used in construction.

Batt. An insulation blanket, usually placed between framing members.

Beam. A horizontal structural member used to carry a load.

Bearing plate. A structural member used to place another structural onto.

Bench mark. A fixed point to measure vertical dimensions. The mark is usually placed on a nonmovable object at the job site.

Blueprint. A copy of an architectural drawing with white lines on a blue background. Modern copies are bluelines; blue lines on a white background.

Bridging. Bracing placed between floor joists to prevent twisting of the joists and to add stiffness to the floor system.

Building codes. Laws designating the requirements for buildings being constructed.

Cantilever. A beam or structure that projects beyond it's supports, with the overhanging end unsupported.

Caulking. A material used to seal construction joints, sealing out water and wind.

Concrete. A mixture of sand, cement, gravel, and water. Concrete cures to a hard, stone-like material.

Contractor. Business and construction manager of a construction project.

Cornice. The part of the roof that overhangs the wall.

Course. A single horizontal row of masonry.

Crosshatching. A series of crossed lines used to delineate a material shown in section on a drawing.

Designer. A person who designs buildings and is not an architect.

Detail. Drawn information of a particular part of building.

Dimension line. A line with either arrows or ticks at each end that designates the distance between the points referred to by the line.

Downspout. A pipe that carries rainwater from the gutter to the ground.

Dry-wall. Interior wall panels, usually composed of gypsum sandwiched between paper facings.

Easement. An area of the property that is reserved as a right of way to place utilities, roadways, etc..

Eave. The part of the roof that projects beyond the wall face.

Elevation. A flat plane drawing of a face of a building. Also a point of vertical dimension, usually referenced to a bench mark.

Facade. The exterior face of a building or structure.

Fascia. A board placed at the rafter end.

Felt underlayment. A tar empregnated paper used under shingles for moisture resistance.

Fixture. A piece of plumbing equipment that is attached to the building.

Flashing. A flat plane material, such as metal sheeting, that is placed around or between materials to resist water penetration.

Floor plan. A horizontal section cut through a building that shows walls, doors, and other features of a building.

Footing. An enlarged part of the lower wall that spreads the load on the wall out to a sufficient area so the earth can support the weight without significant settlement.

Framing. The skeletal construction of structural members of a building.

Frieze. The continuous board placed at the intersection of the soffit and wall face.

Gable. The triangular upper wall area at the end of a roof.

Gable roof. A roof that slopes in two directions.

Grade. The ground level around a building.

Gutter. A horizontal trough used to collect water that runs from a roof to a downspout.

Gypsum board. Interior wall panels made from gypsum sandwiched between two paper facings.

Insulation. A material used to retard the passage of temperature or sound.

Interior trim. Finish materials such as mouldings, base boards, etc.

Jamb. The vertical side parts of a door or window.

Joints. The meeting point of two construction members.

Joist. A horizontal structural member that is the primary part of a floor or ceiling system.

Lavatory. A fixture such as a sink.

Lookout. A horizontal part of the overhang that extends from the building wall to the end of the rafter.

Lot line. The legal boundary of one side of a lot.

Member. Any single piece of structural material used in construction.

Millwork. Any of various types of finished woodwork in a building.

Mortar. A cement, sand, and water mixture used to bond masonry products.

Mullion. A bar separating multiple window sections.

Muntin. A small bar separating different panes of glass within a single window unit.

Orientation. The position of a building on a lot.

Partition. A section of an interior wall.

Plan. A horizontal section through a building that shows the location of walls, doors, etc..

Plate. The top or bottom horizontal members of a wall section.

Plot. The property on which a building is built.

Plywood. A wood sheet made from layer (or plies) of thin wood.

Property line. The boundary line around a lot.

Rafter. The sloping member used to construct a roof.

Restrictions. Requirements, such as minimum square footage, amount of brick, etc. for building on a lot.

Roughing in. The process of building the framework for a building.

Rough opening. The frame opening for a door or window.

Sash. The framework that window glass is placed into.

Schedule. A table of sizes, types, etc. for doors or windows that is a part of the building plans.

Section. A drawing that shows a part of a building cut into so the viewer can see inside.

Setback. The distance from a property line that a building can not built within.

Shingles. Thin material that is placed on a sloping roof to resist water.

Siding. Material placed on the exterior side of a building wall.

Sill. A horizontal piece of wood placed on top of the foundation wall to which a floor joist is attached. Also a horizontal strip at the bottom of a door or window.

Soffit. The flat panel underneath an overhang.

Spacing. The distance that framing materials are placed from each other, usually designated as center to center of the members.

Span. The distance between supports of a framing member.

Specifications. Written document listing constructions directions, quality of materials, and project management techniques for a building. The specifications are a companion to the drawings.

Stud. A vertical framing member in a wall.

Subfloor. The first layer of sheet material placed on the floor joists.

Threshold. The material attached to the floor underneath an exterior door.

Thru-wall flashing. Flashing that is placed within the cavity between the wall framing and brick that turns water out through a weep hole.

Truss. A prefabricated structural member composed of several individual members. Trusses are used for roof and floor construction.

Valley. The interior intersection between two intersecting roof planes.

Vent. An opening for ventilation.

Ventilation. The exchange of air from enclosed spaces of a building.

Wallboard. Sheet material (usually referring to gypsum board) for interior wall faces.

Waterproof. Any material or construction that is used to prevent the passage of water.

Weep hole. A small hole in a brick joint or a wall to allow water or moisture to escape (see thru-wall flashing).

Zoning. Local laws restricting the use of properties.

INDEX